Beasts that Teach, Birds that Tell:
Animal Language in Rabbinic and Classical Literatures

Beasts that Teach, Birds that Tell: Animal Language in Rabbinic and Classical Literatures

Eliezer Segal

Alberta Judaic Studies
2019

ISBN: 978-1-9990438-0-3

First Printing: 2019

Alberta Judaic Studies
16 – 310 Brookmere Rd SW
Calgary, Alberta, Canada T2W 2T7

people.ucalgary.ca/~elsegal

וְאוּלָם שְׁאַל־נָא בְהֵמוֹת וְתֹרֶךָּ וְעוֹף הַשָּׁמַיִם וְיַגֶּד־לָֽךְ׃

אוֹ שִׂיחַ לָאָרֶץ וְתֹרֶךָּ וִיסַפְּרוּ לְךָ דְּגֵי הַיָּם׃

מִי לֹא־יָדַע בְּכָל־אֵלֶּה כִּי יַד־ה' עָשְׂתָה זֹּאת׃

איוב י"ב ז-ט

BUT ASK NOW THE BEASTS, AND THEY SHALL
TEACH THEE; AND THE BIRDS OF THE HEAV-
ENS, AND THEY SHALL TELL THEE:

OR SPEAK TO THE EARTH, AND IT SHALL
TEACH THEE: AND THE FISHES OF THE SEA
SHALL DECLARE UNTO THEE.

WHO KNOWETH NOT IN ALL THESE THAT THE
HAND OF THE LORD HATH WROUGHT THIS?

Job 12:7-9

Contents

Introduction

"YES, BUT HUMANS ARE MORE IMPORTANT THAN ANI-
MALS," SAID BRUTHA.
"THIS IS A POINT OF VIEW OFTEN EXPRESSED BY HU-
MANS," SAID OM.[1]

Tales, legends, fables and myths about animals who converse among
themselves and with humans are staples of traditions that span cultures
and ages. It is not always clear how literally those stories are to be taken.
When hares and tortoises in a fable challenge one another to a race, one
presumes that the Aesopian fabulist did not believe that such exchanges
were actually possible, nor did he expect his audience to accept them at
face value following the momentary suspension of disbelief. The same,
however, cannot necessarily be said about "primitive" cultures that live in
more intimate relationships with nature and non-human creatures.[2] Since
so many cultures possess ancient legends about talking animals, it would
not be surprising if they entertained the possibility that, whatever the current situation might be, at some stage in the distant past animals did speak
and participate in verbal exchanges with people. If that was the case, then
how and why had the situation changed since those primordial times? Furthermore, the precise definitions of "speech" or "conversation" are not
necessarily limited to grammatical spoken languages. To what degree may
we claim that gestures, sounds and other forms of non-verbal body lan-

---

1   Terry Pratchett, *Small Gods: A Novel of Discworld*, 1st U.S. ed. (New York: Harper-
     Collins, 1992), 121.

2   For a fascinating overview of the immense variation that exists on the "speaking ani-
     mal" motif in folk-literature, see Stith Thompson, *Motif-Index of Folk-Literature*,
     Revised and enlarged edition. (Bloomington, IN: Indiana University Press, 1955),
     1:396-399 [items B210-B212].

guage deserve to be classified as legitimate forms of communication and vehicles for the exchange of ideas and the sharing of emotions?

As will become evident in the coming pages, questions of this sort were a topic of lively debate among the philosophical schools of ancient Greece and Rome, and echoes of those speculations are perceptible in Jewish writings from the late Second Commonwealth. In addition to the influences of the Hellenistic intellectual environment, the Jewish treatments of animal languages were of course closely tied to passages in the Bible, notably the serpent's devious eloquence in the garden of Eden,[3] and the episode of Balaam's talking donkey.[4]

For purposes of this study I will generally exclude instances of animal fables of the Aesopian genre.[5] These were an established cross-cultural feature of ancient life in the orient and occident; but it was probably clear to their authors, transmitters and audiences that the talking foxes or eagles

---

3   Karen Randolph Joines, *Serpent Symbolism in the Old Testament: A Linguistic, Archaeological, and Literary Study* (Haddonfield, NJ: Haddonfield House, 1974); James H Charlesworth, "Serpent Symbolism in the Hebrew Bible (Old Testament)," in *Good and Evil Serpent* (New Haven: Yale University Press, 2000), 269–351.

4   The standard taxonomy of the source-documents that constitute the Torah assigns both the garden of Eden story and the tale of Balaam and his ass to the Yahwistic ("J") document, giving rise to the general observation that the authors of J—unlike those of the Priestly Code—were more amenable to the notion of talking animals. See e.g., E. A. Speiser, *Genesis: Introduction, Translation, and Notes*, 1st ed., The Anchor Bible (Doubleday, 1964), 25–26; Theodore Hiebert, *The Yahwist's Landscape: Nature and Religion in Early Israel* (New York: Oxford University Press, 1996), 63 and n. 96, 157; Peter F. Ellis, *The Yahwist: The Bible's First Theologian* (London: G. Chapman, 1969), 128; Claus Westermann, *Genesis 1-11: A Continental Commentary*, trans. John J. Scullion, 1st Fortress Press edition. (Minneapolis: Fortress Press, 1994), 237–238.

5   B. E. Perry, ed., *Aesopica: A Series of Texts Relating to Aesop or Ascribed to Him or Closely Connected with the Literary Tradition That Bears His Name*, New edition. (Urbana: University of Illinois Press, 2007); Jeremy B. Lefkowitz, "Aesop and Animal Fable," in *The Oxford Handbook of Animals in Classical Thought and Life*, ed. Gordon Lindsay Campbell, First Edition. (Oxford: Oxford University Press, 2014), 1–23; P. E. Easterling, "The Literature of the Empire: Between Philosophy and Rhetoric: The Fable," in *The Cambridge History of Classical Literature*, ed. P. E. Easterling and Bernard Knox, vol. 1. Greek Literature (Cambridge: Cambridge University Press, 1982), 699–703.

were to be understood figuratively[6] and need not be justified to any scientific theory.[7] This would also be true for tales about intelligent or virtuous beasts who partake of the virtues of their pious owners, but whose admirable qualities stop short of actual speech; such as: Abraham's camels who refused to enter a dwelling that housed idols[8]; the dogs[9] and donkeys that assisted the Israelites at the Egyptian exodus;[10] the donkeys of Hanina ben Dosa and Rabbi Phineas ben Jair[11] that refused to partake of untithed

---

6   On the other hand, Babrius, one of the primary adaptors of Aesop's fables, insisted in his Prologue that

> in the Golden age not only men but all the other living creatures had the power of speech... Assemblies were held by these creatures in the midst of the forests. Even the pine tree talked, and the leaves of the laurel. The fish swimming about in the sea chatted with the friendly sailor, and quite intelligibly, too, the sparrows conversed with the farmer. Everything grew from the earth, which made no demands on men, and good fellowship prevailed between gods and mortals.

[B. E. Perry, *Babrius and Phaedrus*, The Loeb Classical Library 436 (Cambridge, MA and London, UK: Harvard University Press and W. Heineman, 1984), 2–3]; see Deborah Levine Gera, *Ancient Greek Ideas on Speech, Language, and Civilization* (Oxford and New York: Oxford University Press, 2003), 19–22.

7   David Stern, *Parables in Midrash: Narrative and Exegesis in Rabbinic Literature* (Cambridge, MA: Harvard University Press, 1991), 4–5; See Elimelech Epstein-Halevi, *'Olamah shel ha-Agadah* (Tel-Aviv, Israel: Dvir, 1972), 237–245; *Agadot Ha-Amora'im* (Tel-Aviv: Dvir, 1977), 32–33; Jonah Fraenkel, *The Aggadic Narrative: Harmony of Form and Content*, ed. Me'ir Ayali, Sifriyat "Helal Ben-Ḥayim" (Tel Aviv: Hakibbutz Hameuchad, 2001), 80–97; Shamma Friedman, "The Talmudic Proverb in Its Cultural Setting," *Jewish Studies: An Internet Journal* 2 (2003): 25–82; Lorena Miralles Maciá, "The Fable of 'the Middle-Aged Man with Two Wives': From the Aesopian Motif to the Babylonian Talmud Version in b. B. Qam 60b," *Journal for the Study of Judaism in the Persian, Hellenistic and Roman Period* 39, no. 2 (2008): 267–281; Eli Yassif, "Jewish Folk Literature in Late Antiquity," in *The Cambridge History of Judaism*, ed. Steven Katz, vol. 4. The Late Roman-Rabbinic Period (Cambridge: Cambridge University Press, 2006), 739–240; *The Hebrew Folktale: History, Genre, Meaning*, Folklore Studies in Translation (Bloomington, IN: Indiana University Press, 1999), 205–206; Jacob Neusner, *Praxis and Parable: The Divergent Discourses of Rabbinic Judaism: How Halakhic and Aggadic Documents Treat the Bestiary Common to Them Both*, Studies in Judaism (Lanham, MD: University Press of America, 2006), 135–136, 146–147, 210; Haim Schwarzbaum, "Talmudic-Midrashic Affinities of Some Aesopic Fables," in *Proceedings of the Fourth*

produce[12]; the ox that lowed to announce the destruction of the Temple[13]; or the cow that did not plow on the sabbath.[14]

The studies in the following chapters will be aimed at rabbinic traditions that state, suppose or imply that non-human animals are speaking, or at least understanding, by means of verbal communication in the conventional human sense. The examples include expansions of biblical narratives (notably, the story of the snake in the garden of Eden) as well as tales involving the rabbis themselves.

International Congress for Folk-Narrative Research, ed. G. Megas (Athens, 1965), 466–483. Cf. Eric Lawee, "The Sins of the Fauna in Midrash, Rashi, and Their Medieval Interlocutors," *Jewish Studies Quarterly* 17, no. 1 (2010): 68–69: "Had such expositions imputed speech or interior monologue to the beasts, then they could more easily be assigned to the sphere of didactic animal fables, which did find a place in rabbinic literature." For an instructive observation on the difficulties inherent in drawing sharp borderlines between the talking animals of alleged fact, fables, allegories and folk tales, see Stephen R. L. Clark, "Animals in Classical and Late Antique Philosophy," in *The Oxford Handbook of Animal Ethics*, ed. Tom Beauchamp and R. G. Frey, vol. 1, Oxford Handbooks (Oxford: Oxford University Press, 2011), 51–52; Steven H. Lonsdale, "Attitudes towards Animals in Ancient Greece," *Greece & Rome* 26, no. 2 (1979): 154. Stern (*Parables in Midrash*, 186.) points out the conspicuous scarcity of animal fables in the Bible and in post-biblical Jewish writings, as well as their supplanting in rabbinic discourse by human (royal) parables.

8   [Solomon Schechter, ed., *Aboth De-Rabbi Nathan* (Vienna: Ch. D. Lippe, 1887), 38]; Judah Goldin, ed., *The Fathers According to Rabbi Nathan* (New York: Schocken Books, 1974), 52–53; Géza Vermès, "Ḥanina Ben Dosa (1)," *Journal of Jewish Studies* 23, no. 1 (1972): 45–50; Neusner, *Praxis and Parable*, 202; see also Leib Moscovitz, "'The Holy One Blessed Be He...Does Not Permit the Righteous to Stumble': Reflections on the Development of a Remarkable BT Theologoumenon," in *Creation and Composition: The Contribution of the Bavli Redactors (Stammaim) to the Aggada*, ed. Jeffrey L. Rubenstein, Texts and Studies in Ancient Judaism (Tübingen: Mohr Siebeck, 2005), 125–179.

9   Rabbinic literature does not give the impression that Jews were commonly keeping dogs or cats for companionship or to cultivate affectionate relationships; see Joshua Schwartz, "Cats in Ancient Jewish Society," *Journal of Jewish Studies* 52, no. 2 (2001): 211–234; "Dogs in Jewish Society in the Second Temple Period and in the Time of the Mishnah and Talmud," *Journal of Jewish Studies* 55, no. 2 (2004): 246–277; cf. Francis D. Lazenby, "Greek and Roman Household Pets (1)," *The Classical Journal* 44, no. 4 (1949): 245–252; "Greek and Roman Household Pets (2)," *The*

The body of texts under examination will be limited to works that were produced in late antiquity in Hebrew or Aramaic, but this restriction is inherently problematic in light of the large spans that often separate the original (or attributed) statements of the ancient sages from the dates of the redaction of the works in which those statements are embedded; as the proliferation of spurious medieval compendia that package themselves—and were often accepted—as "midrashic."[15] The relevant rabbinic material will be compared with similar texts from the works of Greek and Latin au-

Classical Journal 44, no. 5 (1949): 299–307.

10   The rabbis read Exodus 22:30 as a reward for the dogs' silence during the exodus as described in Exodus 11:7. See *Mekhilta Kaspa* 20. S. Horovitz and I. A Rabin, eds., *Mechilta D'Rabbi Ismael cum variis lectionibus et adnotationibus* (Jerusalem: Wahrmann, 1970), 321; Jacob Z. Lauterbach, ed., *Mekilta De-Rabbi Ishmael* (Philadelphia: Jewish Publication Society of America, 1933), 3:159; etc.; Viktor Aptowitzer, "The Rewarding and Punishing of Animals and Inanimate Objects: On the Aggadic View of the World," *Hebrew Union College Annual* 3 (1926): 131.

11   *b.Hullin* 7a; Adolf Büchler, *Types of Jewish-Palestinian Piety from 70 B.C.E. to 70 C.E.: The Ancient Pious Men*, Jews' College Publications 8 (London: Jews' College, 1922), 89 and n. 3; Louis Jacobs, "The Story of R Phinehas Ben Yair and His Donkey in B Hullin 7a-B," in *A Tribute to Geza Vermes: Essays on Jewish and Christian Literature and History*, ed. Richard T. White and Philip R. Davies (Sheffield: JSOT Press, 1990), 119; Ofra Meir, "The She-Ass of R. Pinhas ben Yair," *Folklore Research Center Studies* 7 (1983): 132–135 [Hebrew]; see also Moscovitz, "Righteous to Stumble," 137–140; Neusner, *Praxis and Parable*, 202.

12   [Schechter, *Aboth De-Rabbi Nathan*, 38; Goldin, *The Fathers According to Rabbi Nathan*, 53]. *y.Demai* 1:3 [21d-22a]; *y.Shekalim* 5:1 [48d]; *Genesis Rabbah* 60:8 [Julius Theodor and Chanoch Albeck, eds., *Midrash Bereshit Rabba* (Jerusalem, Israel: Wahrman, 1965), 648]. See Jacobs, "Phinehas Ben Yair Donkey"; Meir, "She-Ass" [Hebrew]; Rachel Nissim, "'Demut He-Ḥasid': 'Immut Bein R' Ḥanina Ben-Dosa Le-R' Pinhas ben Ya'ir Le-Or 'Emdat HaZa"L Bi-Va'ayat Ha-Gemul," *'Ale siah / Literary Conversations* 12 (1982): 135–154; Neusner, *Praxis and Parable*, 211; Moscovitz, "Righteous to Stumble," 157–158, 163–172; Eliezer Diamond, "Lions, Snakes and Asses: Palestinian Jewish Holy Men as Masters of the Animal Kingdom," in *Jewish Culture and Society under the Christian Roman Empire*, Interdisciplinary Studies in Ancient Culture and Religion 3 (Leuven: Peeters, 2003), 259–260, 279.

13   *y.Berakhot* 2:4 (5a); *Lamentations Rabbah* 1:16; Jonah Fraenkel, *'Iyyunim Be-'olamo Ha-Ruhani Shel Sippur Ha-Aggadah*, Sifriyat "Helal ben Hayim" (Tel Aviv: Hakibbutz Hameuchad, 2001), 159–163; cf. Neusner, *Praxis and Parable*,

thors, spokesmen for diverse versions of Christianity, as well as with Jewish writings outside the rabbinic corpus (such as the Apocrypha and Pseudepigrapha, Philo of Alexandria, Josephus Flavius, Gnostic teachings); and on occasion (for the sake of contrast) with early medieval Jewish exegetes. Texts that are examined in any detail are set out here in their original languages with accompanying English translations.[16]

As regards their subject matter, the germane texts tend to group themselves around two main types of creatures: snakes (that is, the smooth-tongued tempter of Eden) and birds, particularly ravens and doves; and this situation is reflected in the book's chapter division. These same

193–194.

14 *Pesiḳta Rabbati* 14:2 [Meir Friedmann, *Pesikta Rabbati: Midrasch für den Fest-Cyclus und die ausgezeichneten Sabbathe* (Vienna: [by author], 1880), 56b-57a; William G Braude, trans., *Pesikta Rabbati; Discourses for Feasts, Fasts, and Special Sabbaths*, Yale Judaica Series (New Haven: Yale University Press, 1968), 1:262-264].

15 On the category of "Medieval Midrash" and the methodological considerations for dating and classifying it see Bernard H. Mehlman and Seth M. Limmer, *Medieval Midrash: The House for Inspired Innovation*, Brill Reference Library of Judaism 52 (Brill, 2016); cf. Joseph Dan, *The Hebrew Story in the Middle Ages*, Sifriyyat Keter: ʿAm Yisraʾel ve-Tarbuto (Jerusalem: Keter, 1974), 15–23 [Hebrew]. Out of similar considerations I have excluded *Pereḳ Shirah* from the scope of this study. Its basic premise, that all of creation (including plants and inanimate objects) resound with the praises of the Creator and can be identified with particular scriptural verses, is apparently meant to be understood metaphorically or spiritually. The dating of this work, which is not directly attested until the tenth century, is uncertain. According to Malachi Beit-Arié: "It would appear to be a mystical chapter of Heikhalot literature, dating from late Tannaitic — early Amoraic period, or early Middle Ages." [Malachi Beit-Arié, Jeremy Schonfield, and Emile G. L. Schrijver, *Perek Shirah: An Eighteenth-Century Illuminated Hebrew Book of Praise: Companion Volume to the Facsimile Edition* (London: Facsimile Editions Limited, 1996)]. In his original dissertation he argued more definitively that P*ereḳ Shirah* belongs to an early stratum of the Heikhalot mystical literature [see Malachi Beit-Arié, "Pereḳ Shirah: Mevoʾot u-Mahadurah Biḳortit" (PhD, The Hebrew University, 1966), 72 (Hebrew)].

16 For Greek and Latin works I relied wherever possible for both text and translation on the Loeb Classical Library editions. For Hebrew and Aramaic (and one Arabic instance) I made use of the relevant textual resources in print, facsimile or digital version, as indicated in the notes for each case. For Coptic or Armenian texts, in which languages I pretend to no competence whatsoever, I confined my citations to existing translations.

species were also among the more popular subjects for non-Jewish beliefs and stories about verbal communication among non-human creatures.

Cries of Distress

The Rabbi and the Calf

AND SAM VIMES THOUGHT: WHY IS YOUNG SAM'S NURSERY FULL OF FARMYARD ANIMALS ANYWAY? WHY ARE HIS BOOKS FULL OF MOO-COWS AND BAA-LAMBS? HE IS GROWING UP IN THE CITY. HE WILL ONLY SEE THEM ON A PLATE! THEY GO SIZZLE![1]

By way of an introduction to the to the complexities that are involved in our attempts to learn about Jewish attitudes to animal language from ancient documents, let us take a look at a well-known passage from a classical rabbinic midrashic compendium which relates an episode that it situates in the late second or early third century C.E.

Genesis Rabbah 33:3 (305):[2]

Our Master (*Rabbeinu*) was studying Torah before the synagogue of the Babylonians in Sepphoris.[4]

MS Vatican 30:[3]

רבינו הוה יתיב לעי באורייתא קומי
כנישתא דבבלאי בצפורין.

עבר חד עגל קדמוי אזל למיתנכסא
ושרי געה היך מימור: שיזבי.

---

1   Terry Pratchett, *Thud!: A Novel of Discworld*, 1st ed. (New York: HarperCollins, 2005); see also Terry Pratchett, *Where's My Cow?*, 1st U.S. ed. (New York: Harper-Collins, 2005).

2   Julius Theodor and Chanoch Albeck, eds., *Midrash Bereshit Rabba* (Jerusalem, Israel: Wahrman, 1965), 305 [Hebrew].

3   Michael Sokoloff, ed., *Midrash Bereshit Rabba-Ms. Vat. Ebr. 30* (Jerusalem: Makor, 1982), 33a-33b [Hebrew]. "As if to say" also in MS Vatican 60 [A. P. Sherry, ed., *Midrash Bereshit Rabba Codex Vatican 60 (Ms. Vat. Ebr. 60)* (Jerusalem, Israel: Makor, 1972), 112 [Hebrew].].

Genesis Rabbah 33:3 (305):   *MS Vatican 30:*

A calf passed before him on the way to be slaughtered[5] and began lowing[6] as if to say: Save me!

He said to him: What shall I do for you; for this you were created.

אמר ליה מה אני יכול לעשות לך ולכך נוצרת.

And Rabbi suffered from a toothache for thirteen years.[7]

וחשש את שינו שלש עשרה שנה.

R' Yosé son of R' Avin said: Throughout those thirteen years no woman in the land of Israel miscarried, nor did a woman in

אמ ר׳ יוסי בר׳ אבין כל אותן שלש עשרה שנה שהיה ר׳ חושש את שינו לא הפ[י]לה עברה בארץ יש׳, ולא נצטערה יולדת.

---

4   For a discussion of the historical significance of this reference as regards the relations of the Babylonian and Israel Jewish communities, with possible specific relevance to Rabbi Judah, see Catherine Hezser, *Jewish Travel in Antiquity* (Mohr Siebeck, 2011), 343–344 and n. 134; see also Joshua Schwartz, "Babylonian Commoners in Amoraic Palestine," *Journal of the American Oriental Society* 101, no. 3 (1981): 320; Ze'ev Safrai and Aren M. Maeir, "אתא אגרתא ממערבא ('An Epistle Came from the West'): Historical and Archaeological Evidence for the Ties between the Jewish Communities in the Land of Israel and Babylonia during the Talmudic Period," *The Jewish Quarterly Review* 93, no. 3/4 (2003): 516; Stuart S. Miller, "'Epigraphical' Rabbis, Helios, and Psalm 19: Were the Synagogues of Archaeology and the Synagogues of the Sages One and the Same?," *Jewish Quarterly Review* 94, no. 1 (2004): 320.

5   Michael Sokoloff, *A Dictionary of Jewish Palestinian Aramaic of the Byzantine Period*, Dictionaries of Talmud, Midrash, and Targum (Ramat-Gan, Israel: Bar Ilan University Press, 1990), 351.

6   Ibid., 134.

7   For attempts to identify the exact ailment from which Rabbi Judah was suffering see Ari Shoshan, "The Illness of Rabbi Judah the Patriarch," *Korot: The Israel Journal of the History of Medicine and Science* 7 (1977): 521–524 [Hebrew]; Ofra Meir, *Rabbi Judah the Patriarch: Palestinian and Babylonian Portrait of a Leader*, Sifriyat Helal Ben-Ḥayim (Tel-Aviv: Hakibbutz Hameuchad, 1999), 404 n. 80; Estée Dvorjetski, "The Medical History of Rabbi Judah the Patriarch: A Linguistic Analysis," *Hebrew Studies* 43 (2002): 39–55; cf. Julius Preuss, *Biblical and Talmudic Medicine*, trans. Fred Rosner (Northvale, NJ: J. Aronson, 1993), 285.

Genesis Rabbah 33:3 (305):   *MS Vatican 30:*

childbirth suffer pain.

Some time later, a creeping creature passed before his daughter and she wanted to kill it. He said to her: My daughter, leave it, for it is written (Psalms 145:10) "and his tender mercies are over all his works."[8]

בתר יומין עבר חד שרץ קומי ברתיה ובעת מקטל יתיה. אמ' ברתי שבקיניה דכת' ורחמיו על כל מעשיו.

This story about "Rabbenu"—that is, Rabbi Judah Ha-Nasi[9] known to talmudic tradition as the compiler of the Mishnah[10]—has much to teach us as a hagiographic tale, and as a testimony to rabbinic attitudes about humane-

---

8   See Ofra Meir, *Rabbi Judah the Patriarch: Palestinian and Babylonian Portrait of a Leader*, Sifriyat Helal Ben-Ḥayim (Tel-Aviv: Hakibbutz Hameuchad, 1999), 66; cf. Aaron S. Gross, "Animals, Empathy, and 'Rahamim' in the Study of Religion: A Case Study of Jewish Opposition to Hunting.," *Studies in Religion / Sciences Religieuses* 46, no. 4 (2017): 511–535.

9   See Mordecai Margalioth and Yehudah Aizenberg, eds., *Entsiklopedyah le-Ḥakhme ha-Talmud yeha-Ge'onim*, Revised edition. (Tel-Aviv: Yavneh and Chemed, 1995), 178 [Hebrew]. Ordinarily there would be grounds for some ambivalence as to who is the precise referent to such epithets as "Rabbi," "Rabbenu" or even Rabbi Judah the Prince. In the present instance, however, where the tale (in all the Babylonian and Palestinian sources where it appears) is bundled with numerous other stories involving the same figure, there is no reason to question the identity of the protagonist. For extensive analyses of the rabbinic narrative traditions about Rabbi Judah the Prince see Albert I. Baumgarten, "Rabbi Judah I and His Opponents," *Journal for the Study of Judaism in the Persian, Hellenistic and Roman Period* 12, no. 2 (December 1981): (especially 147); Sacha Stern, "Rabbi and the Origins of the Patriarchate," *Journal of Jewish Studies* 54, no. 2 (2003): 193–215; Ofra Meir, *Rabbi Judah the Patriarch: Palestinian and Babylonian Portrait of a Leader*, Sifriyat Helal Ben-Ḥayim (Tel-Aviv: Hakibbutz Hameuchad, 1999) [Hebrew]. For a survey of his role as a historical and political figure see Aharon Oppenheimer, *Rabbi Judah ha-Nasi* (Jerusalem: Zalman Shazar Center, 2007) [Hebrew]..

10   But cf. Catherine Hezser, *The Social Structure of the Rabbinic Movement in Roman Palestine*, Texte und Studien zum antiken Judentum 66 (Tübingen: Mohr Siebeck, 1997), 414.

ness, suffering and compassion.[11] My immediate concern here is however for a minor detail of the story: namely, the way that the calf communicates with the Jewish sage. With allowances for some very minor orthographic and stylistic variations, all the texts of *Genesis Rabbah* express this communication with words to the effect of "he began lowing *as if to say* [היך מימור]:[12] save me." The implication is that the animal was expressing its distress[13] in a non-verbal manner that was understandable to humans[14] as

---

11 E. Epstein-Halevi *Ha-Agadah Ha-Historit-Biyografit* (Tel Aviv: by author, 1975), 562., compares the attitudes expressed in the story of Rabbi Judah and the calf with some Greek authors (e.g., Aelian, *De Natura Animalium*. 11:6) who speak about temple precincts that served as places of asylum for fleeing animals. For a more thorough discussion of that phenomenon see Attilio Mastrocingue, "Sacred Precinct: Cattle, Hunted Animals, Slaves, Women," in *Antike Mythen, Medien, Transformationen Und Konstruktionen*, ed. Ueli Dill and Christine Walde (Berlin and Boston: De Gruyter, 2009), 339–355. Mastrocingue argues that the institution of asylum for animals preceded that for humans. Meir provides an extensive discussion about the literary crafting of the tale and its moral and psychological perspectives [*Judah the Patriarch*, 311–313].

12 Michael Sokoloff, *A Dictionary of Jewish Palestinian Aramaic of the Byzantine Period*, Dictionaries of Talmud, Midrash, and Targum (Ramat-Gan, Israel: Bar Ilan University Press, 1990), 63, 164.

13 A similar understanding of the distressful lowing of an animal underlies the symbolic explanation offered by Rabbi Jacob of the South for the practice described in *m.Ta'anit* 2:1 of sounding rams' horns on the public fasts that were convened on account of community disasters: "And why do they sound horns? In order to say: Consider us as if we were lowing like a beast before you (כאילו גועים כבהמה לפניך)." [*y.Ta'anit* 2:1 (65a)]

14 A similar textual situation is discernible in the following instance: *Leviticus Rabbah* 11:2 [Mordecai Margulies, ed., *Midrash Vayyikra Rabbah* (New York and Jerusalem: The Jewish Theological Seminary of America, 1993), 291.] regarding the enumeration of the unclean animals in Deuteronomy 14:8: "Moses stated: 'And the swine.' Why was [Rome] represented as a swine? —In order to teach you: Just as this swine kneels down with its hooves outstretched *and says*: 'See that I am clean!', in this way does this evil empire act arrogantly while oppressing and robbing, while giving the impression that it is establishing a tribunal." In the version of the same homily in *Genesis Rabbah* 65:1 [Julius Theodor and Chanoch Albeck, eds., *Midrash Bereshit Rabba* (Jerusalem, Israel: Wahrman, 1965), 713.] the reading in MS London is ... שהוא רובץ מיפשט את טלפיו כלומר שאני טהור—"*as if to say*." The כלומר is found in MS

an anguished cry for help.[15] Some additional factors that enter into our appreciation of the narrative logic include the assumption that the calf was somehow aware of its impending slaughter,[16] and the fact that the sage responds to it by addressing to it an (evidently) audible Hebrew sentence.

The use of Hebrew in a tale (and for that matter, in a collection of several similar tales)[17] that is otherwise formulated in Galilean Aramaic is probably to be explained on the grounds that the expression "for this you were created" is actually a quotation from a well-known tradition ascribed to Rabban Yoḥanan ben Zakkai (*m.Avot* 2:8):[18] "Do not take credit for hav-

---

Vatican 30 [Michael Sokoloff, ed., *Midrash Bereshit Rabba-Ms. Vat. Ebr. 30* (Jerusalem: Makor, 1982).] though it is missing from other witnesses cited in Albeck' critical apparatus; such a reading, however, would appear to have the same implication, namely that the act of showing its hooves is in itself equivalent to making the claim. See Samuel Krauss, *Paras ve-Romi ba-Talmud uva-Midrashim* (Jerusalem: Mossad Harav Kook, 708), 104 [Hebrew]; Jacob Neusner, *Praxis and Parable: The Divergent Discourses of Rabbinic Judaism: How Halakhic and Aggadic Documents Treat the Bestiary Common to Them Both*, Studies in Judaism (Lanham, MD: University Press of America, 2006), 163–165.

15 Cf. J-J Rousseau's theory about the origins of language among primitive man: "The ever-present danger of perishing would not permit of a language restricted to gesture. And the first words among them were not *love me [aimez-moi]* but *help me [aidez-moi]*" [Jean-Jacques Rousseau and Johann Gottfried Herder, *On the Origin of Language*, ed. Alexander Gode and John H. Moran (University of Chicago Press, 1966), 47.]. Questions of animals (especially the snake in the garden of Eden) addressing humans through non-verbal gestures will play a respectable part in the discussions below. See Steven H. Lonsdale, "Attitudes towards Animals in Ancient Greece," *Greece & Rome* 26, no. 2 (1979): 152; Umberto Eco, *The Search for the Perfect Language*, trans. James Fentress, Making of Europe (Oxford, UK and Cambridge, MA: Blackwell, 1995), 111–112; Deborah Levine Gera, *Ancient Greek Ideas on Speech, Language, and Civilization* (Oxford and New York: Oxford University Press, 2003), 42–43, 195–198.

16 See John Heath, *The Talking Greeks: Speech, Animals, and the Other in Homer, Aeschylus, and Plato* (Cambridge: Cambridge University Press, 2005), 45.

17 For a thorough analysis of the evolution of the literary themes in the Palestinian and Babylonian narrative traditions see Shamma Friedman, "La-Aggadah Ha-Hisṭorit Ba-Talmud Ha-Bavli," in *Saul Lieberman Memorial Volume* (New York and Jerusalem: Jewish Theological Seminary of America, 1993), especially 132-135 [Hebrew].

ing practiced[19] much Torah, because it was for this that you were created."
In light of Rabban Yoḥanan's adage, Rabbi Judah's facile quip to the calf
may well be interpreted in the sense of: just as people—or at least, Jewish
men—have the inborn disposition to be students of Torah, so do cattle
have a divinely ordained calling to be slaughtered to provide meat for humans.[20]

The story of Rabbi and the calf is also found in the Palestinian Talmud, a compendium that was produced in circles very close to those that

18   Cf. Jacob Neusner, *A Life of Yohanan Ben Zakkai, ca.1-80 C.E.*, 2nd ed., completely
     revised., Studia post-Biblica 6 (Leiden: Brill, 1970), 99 n. 1; *First Century Judaism
     in Crisis: Yoḥanan Ben Zakkai and the Renaissance of Torah* (Eugene OR: Wipf and
     Stock Publishers, 2006), 97–99.

19   Thus in MS Kaufmann אם עשית תורה הרבה. For a discussion of the readings see
     Charles Taylor, ed., *Sayings of the Jewish Fathers. Sefer Dibre Aboth Ha-Olam.
     Comprising Pirque Aboth in Hebrew and English with Critical Notes and Excur-
     suses*, 2d ed. (Amsterdam: Philo Press, 1970), 47 n. 21; Benzion Dinur, *Pirke Aboth*,
     Dorot (Jerusalem: Bialik Institute, 1972), 66 [Hebrew]; Shimon Sharvit, *Tractate
     Avoth Through the Ages: A Critical Edition, Prolegomena and Appendices*
     (Jerusalem: The Bialik Institute and the Ben-Yehuda Center for the History of He-
     brew, The Hebrew University of Jerusalem, 2004), 93 [Hebrew]; Ze'ev Safrai, *Mish-
     nat Eretz Israel: Tractate Avot (Neziqin 7): With Historical and Sociological Com-
     mentary* (Mishnat Eretz Israel Project, 2013), 143–144 [Hebrew].

20   The Babylonian Talmud (*b.Berakhot* 17a) records in the name of Rabbi Yoḥanan,
     that when Rabbi Meir [as per the readings in MS Munich 95, Paris 671, Cambridge
     T-S NS 216.5 and *'Ein Ya'aḳov*] would conclude the book of Job, he was accustomed
     to remark, "The end of a human is to die, the end of a beast is to be slaughtered, and
     all are destined to die [סוף אדם למות וסוף בהמה לשחיטה והכל למיתה הם עומדים]." See
     Joseph Yahalom, *Poetry and Society in Jewish Galilee of Late Antiquity*, Sifriyat
     "Helal ben Hayim" (Tel-Aviv: Hakibbutz Hameuchad and Yad Izhak Ben-Zvi,
     1999), 26 [Hebrew]. Rabbi Yoḥanan goes on to contrast that dismal projection with
     that of the person who, when arriving at life's end, has accumulated the merits of
     Torah and upright reputation. The thematic connections (or absence thereof) between
     the elements of the passage are discussed by several traditional Jewish commentators
     to the *'Ein Ya'aḳov*, including R' Jacob Ibn Ḥabib, R' Josiah Pinto ["Rif"], R' Jacob
     Reischer, R' Ḥenokh Zundl ["*'Eṣ Yosef*"]. Compare Josephus Flavius' remarkable il-
     lustration about the compassion that is inherent to Hebrew law: "So thorough a les-
     son has he given us in gentleness and humanity that he does not overlook even the
     brute beasts, authorizing their use only in accordance with the Law, and forbidding
     all other employment of them. *Creatures which take refuge in our houses like suppli-*

produced *Genesis Rabbah*. With respect to this detail, however, there is a significant difference in the wording:[21]

y.Kila'im 9:4 (32a); y.Ketubbot 12:5 (34d):

It lowed and said to him: Rabbi, save me![22]

גָּעָה וְאָמ' לֵיהּ ר' שִׁיזְבִי.

According to both passages in the Jerusalem Talmud, and according to all

---

ants we are forbidden to kill [ἃ δ' ὥσπερ ἱκετεύοντα προσφεύγει ταῖς οἰκίαις ἀπεῖπεν ἀνελεῖν.]" (*Contra Apionem* 2:29 (213)) [H. St. John Thackeray, *Josephus: With an English Translation*, vol. 4, Loeb Classical Library (London and New York: William Heinemann Ltd. and G. P. Putnam's Sons, 1926), 378–379.] The passage is cited in connection with the story of Rabbi Judah and the calf in Epstein-Halevi, *Ha-Agadah Ha-Historit-Biyografit*, 561–562 [Hebrew]. Epstein-Halevi also likens this attitude to Plutarch comment about the "Deity, who is not a lover of horses or birds, but a lover of men" (*Numa* 4:3 [Bernadotte Perrin, ed., *Plutarch's Lives*, vol. 1, The Loeb Classical Library [Greek authors] (London and New York: W. Heinemann and Macmillan, 1914), 316–317.]

See also 2 Peter 2:12: "ὡς ἄλογα ζῷα γεγεννημένα φυσικὰ εἰς ἅλωσιν καὶ φθοράν [natural brute beasts, made to be taken and destroyed]"; Jude 10; Charles Bigg, *A Critical and Exegetical Commentary on the Epistles of St. Peter and St. Jude*, International Critical Commentary (Edinburgh: T. & T. Clark, 1987), 280–281, 331.

21 This discrepancy is adduced by Ch. Albeck as evidence for his thesis that the Jerusalem Talmud that was cited by *Genesis Rabbah* was a different recension from the one that has come down to us; see his extensive discussion in: *Mavo U-Maftehot le-Midrash Bereshit Rabba*, Second edition., vol. 1, Veröffentlichungen der Akademie für die Wissenschaft des Judentum (Jerusalem: Shalem Books, 1996), 66–84 [Hebrew]; see also: J. N. Epstein, *Mevo'ot Lesifrut Ha-'Amora'im* (Jerusalem and Tel-Aviv: Magnes and Dvir, 1962), 287–292 [Hebrew]; Epstein-Halevi, *Ha-Agadah Ha-Historit-Biyografit*, 561–562; Margulies, *Midrash Vayyikra Rabbah*, 5:XIX; Günter Stemberger, *Introduction to the Talmud and Midrash*, 2nd ed. (Edinburgh: T. & T. Clark, 1996), 303; Hans-Jürgen Becker, *Die Grossen Rabbinischen Sammelwerke Palästinas: Zur Literarischen Genese von Talmud Yerushalmi Und Midrash Bereshit Rabba*, Texte und Studien zum antiken Judentum 70 (Tübingen: Mohr Siebeck, 1999); Chaim Milikowsky, "On the Formation and Transmission of Bereshit Rabba and the Yerushalmi: Questions of Redaction, Text-Criticism and Literary Relationships," *The Jewish Quarterly Review* 92, no. 3/4 (2002): 521–567.

22 Thus in all the witnesses recorded by Peter Schäfer and Gottfried Reeg, eds., *Synopse zum Talmud Yerushalmi*, Texte und Studien zum Antiken Judentum 67 (Tübin-

the extant textual witnesses to those passages, the calf was able to speak to Rabbi Judah as well as (so we may presume) to hear and understand his response.[23]

A version of the same episode is also found in the Babylonian Talmud.

b.Bava Meṣi'a 85a:[24]	*MS Hamburg 165:*[25]
...as with a certain calf whom they were bringing to slaughter. It went and hanged its head in the lap[26] of Rabbi and wept. He said to it: Go away.[27] For this reason were you created![28]	...כי ההוא עגלא דהוה קא ממטו ליה למשחטיה אזל תלייה לרישיה בכנפיה דר' וקא בכי אמ' ליה זיל לכך נוצרת ...

gen: J.C.B. Mohr (Paul Siebeck), 1992), I/4: 192-193. These include MSS Leiden (used as the basis for the above citation), Vatican, Paris and London; as well as the Venice (editio princeps) and Amsterdam printings and the *'Ein Ya'akov*. So too, in Ketubbot, [ibid., III, 229].according to MS Leiden and the Venice printing. Cf. Jacob Neusner, ed., *Ketubot*, Chicago Studies in the History of Judaism 22 (Chicago: University of Chicago Press, 1985), 347; Sokoloff, *Palestinian*, 546.

23   No variants are recorded in Baer Ratner, *Ahawath Zion we-Jeruscholaim; Varianten und Ergganzungen des Textes des Jerusalemitschen Talmuds*, vol. 6: Kila'im (Vilna: S. P. Garber, 1901), 78.

24   See Raphael Nathan Rabinowitz, *Dikduke Sofrim: Variae Lectiones in Mischnam in Talmud Babylonicum* (Munich, 1883), n. ג; "The Sol and Evelyn Henkind Talmud Text Databank of the Saul Lieberman Institute of Talmud Reseatch of the Jewish Theological Seminary of America," *http://www.lieberman-institute.com.*

25   Lazarus Goldschmidt, ed., *The Babylonian Talmud Seder Nazikin* (Makor, 1969).

26   Michael Sokoloff, *A Dictionary of Jewish Babylonian Aramaic of the Talmudic and Geonic Periods* (Ramat Gan and Baltimore: Bar Ilan University Press and Johns Hopkins University Press, 2003), 264.

27   The word "Go" [זיל] in Rabbi's words is missing from MS Munich 95.

28   As stated, the above reading is supported by most of the witnesses to the passage, including MS Escorial 3-1-G and MS Cremona-Archivio di Stato 58 (which were not used by Rabinowitz's *Dikduke Sofrim*. It may be noted as well that MS Florence II-I-8 omits וקא בכי: "and wept." That expression is not found in the Genizah fragments Cambridge T-S Misc 22 and Oxford Heb. c. 17/6; though it does appear in Cambridge T-S AS 79.11 [as listed by the Friedberg Project for Talmud Bavli Variants].

Indeed, rabbinic literature employs the image of an animal bleating or lowing in distress as an effective metaphor for human helplessness, especially when pleading for divine assistance in a crisis. Thus, when the Mishnah *Ta'anit* (2:1) prescribes the sounding of a horn as part of the procedures in a public fast that was ordained on account of a drought or similar catastrophe, the Jerusalem Talmud (65a) explains the implications of this act: "And why do we sound horns? —As if to say: Consider us as if we were bleating like a beast before you."[29]

This could imply that the calf's communication was achieved only by the hanging of his head, or that it was merely implied by the broader circumstances of the situation. At any rate, the text there shows signs of corruption (presumably in one of its ances- tors). The reading in MS Florence is as follows: אזל תלייה לרישיה בכנפיה דר' זיל לשחיטה כי לכך נוצרתה. See David Rosenthal, *Babylonian Talmud Codex Florence: Florence National Library II 1 7-9* (Jerusalem: Makor Publishing Ltd., 1972), 2:265. Note that fragment Oxford Heb. c. 17/69–78 reads "קבריה לרישיה בכנפיה (לקמיה) אתא": "he came (before him), *buried* his head in his lap."

29 ולמה תוקעין בקרנות לומר חשבינו כאילו גועים כבהמה לפניך. Note the similar usage Ibid., 65b, where R' Ḥuna teaches in the name or R' Simeon ben Ḥalfuta that the repen- tance of the Ninevites in the book of Jonah was insincere. "They placed calves inside and their mothers outside, foals inside and the mares outside, so that these were low- ing [והוון אילין געיי] from one direction and these were lowing from the other direction. Then they said: Unless you have mercy upon us, we will not have mercy on them." On the ideological background to this trope of rabbinic interpretation, Efraim Elim- elech Urbach, "The Repentance of the People of Nineveh and the Jewish-Christian Polemic," *Tarbiz* 20, no. 1 (1950): 118–122 [Hebrew]; Salo Wittmayer Baron, *A So- cial and Religious History of the Jews*, 2d ed., revised and enlarged., vol. Vol. 2: Christian Era. The First Five Centuries (New York: Columbia University Press, 1952), 384 n. 17; Marc G. Hirshman, *A Rivalry of Genius: Jewish and Christian Bib- lical Interpretation in Late Antiquity*, SUNY Series in Judaica (Albany: State Univer- sity of New York Press, 1996), 112, 127; Robert Bonfil, *History and Folklore in a Medieval Jewish Chronicle: The Family Chronicle of Aḥima'az Ben Paltiel*, Studies in Jewish History and Culture 22 (Leiden and Boston: Brill, 2009), 170–171; Rachel Adelman, "Jonah Through the Looking Glass: Pirqe De-Rabbi Eliezer's Portrait of an Apocalyptic Prophet," *ARC* 39 (2011): 85; cf. Michal Bar-Asher Siegal, *Early Christian Monastic Literature and the Babylonian Talmud* (Cambridge UK and New York: Cambridge University Press, 2013), 6–7.

Animals in Distress in Greek and Latin Sources

AND THEN HE'D ARRIVED, AND IT TURNED OUT THAT
RIDCULLY THE BROWN DID SPEAK TO THE BIRDS.

IN FACT HE SHOUTED AT BIRDS, AND WHAT HE NOR-
MALLY SHOUTED WAS, "WINGED YOU, YER BASTARD!"

THE BEASTS OF THE FIELD AND FOWLS OF THE AIR DID
KNOW RIDCULLY THE BROWN. THEY'D GOT SO GOOD AT
PATTERN-RECOGNITION THAT, FOR A RADIUS OF ABOUT
TWENTY MILES AROUND THE RIDCULLY ESTATES,
THEY'D RUN, HIDE OR IN DESPERATE CASES ATTACK VI-
OLENTLY AT THE MERE SIGHT OF A POINTY HAT.[30]

The predicament of the calf expressing its distress is very similar to the situation described by Plutarch, about a century before Rabbi Judah, in his essay *De Esu Carnium* ["On the Eating of Flesh"], a vigorous defence of vegetarianism.[31] In an argument intended to minimize or obliterate the premise that sub-human creatures can be dismissed as essentially lacking

---

30   Terry Pratchett, *Moving Pictures* (London: V. Gollancz, 1990), 23–24.

31   For a survey of relevant texts in Plutarch's corpus see Lynn Thorndike, *A History of Magic and Experimental Science.* (New York: Macmillan, 1929), 1:217-218; Urs Dierauer, *Tier und Mensch im Denken der Antike: Studien zur Tierpsychologie, Anthropologie und Ethik*, Studien zur antiken Philosophie 6 (Amsterdam: Grüner, 1977), 187–193, 285–293; Glen Warren Bowersock, "The Literature of the Empire: Between Philosophy and Rhetoric: Plutarch," in *The Cambridge History of Classical Literature*, ed. E. J. Kenney and W. V. Clausen, vol. 2. Latin Literature (Cambridge: Cambridge University Press, 1982), 665–669; Stephen Thomas Newmyer, *Animals in Greek and Roman Thought: A Sourcebook*, Routledge sourcebooks for the ancient World (London and New York: Routledge, 2011), 15–17; Damianos Tsekourakis, "Pythagoreanism or Platonism and Ancient Medicine: The Reasons for Vegetarianism in Plutarch's 'Moralia,'" in *Aufstieg Und Niedergang Der Römischen Welt / Rise and Decline of the Roman World*, ed. Wolfgang Haase and Hildegard Temporini, vol. Vol. 36.1, Part II: Principate (Berlin and New York: Walter de Gruyter, 1987), 366–393; Stephen Thomas Newmyer, "Plutarch on the Moral Grounds for Vegetarianism," *The Classical Outlook* 72 (1995): 41–43; *Animals, Gods and Humans: Changing Attitudes to Animals in Greek, Roman and Early Christian Ideas* (London: Routledge, 2006), 44–52; "Being the One and Becoming the Other: Animals in Ancient Philosophical Schools," in *The Oxford Handbook of Animals in Classical Thought and Life*, ed. George Lindsay Campbell (Oxford: Oxford University Press, 2014), 527–530.

in intelligence by virtue of their inability to communicate through speech, he describes manifestations of non-verbal utterances that express messages that are very clear to those humans who are receptive to understanding them.[32]

32 Compare this with the observation in his earlier *Symposiacs* 4:4, in which Plutarch relates the discussion that took place at Aidepsos in Euboea, where his brother Lamprias, citing his grandfather's scornful comment about the Jews, mocks the Jewish classification of "lawful" meat by criticizing the unjustifiable consumption of land creatures with whom we share the earth [τὸ δικαιότατον κρέας οὐκ ἐσθίουσιν], "and when they are slaughtered, they make us ashamed of what we are doing, with their hideous cries [καὶ σφάττοντες ἐδυσωποῦντο φωνὴν ἀφιέντα γοερὰν]." William Watson Goodwin, ed., *Plutarch's Miscellanies and Essays*, 6th ed. (Boston: Little, Brown, and Company, 1898), 3:36; see also Howard Williams, "The Ethics of Diet: A Catena of Authorities Deprecatory of the Practice of Flesh-Eating" (Urbana: University of Illinois Press, 2003), 44. For a discussion of the little that is known regarding Plutarch's knowledge of and attitude toward the Jews, their practices and beliefs, see Menahem Stern, *Greek and Latin Authors on Jews and Judaism*, Fontes ad Res Judaicas Spectantes (Jerusalem: Israel Academy of Sciences and Humanities, 1974), 1:545-548.

Plutarch, De Esu Cranium 994E[33]

εἶθ᾽ ἃς φθέγγεται καὶ διέτρισε
φωνὰς ἀνάρθρους εἶναι δοκοῦμεν, οὐ παραιτήσεις καὶ δεήσ-
εις καὶ δικαιολογίας ἑκάστου
λέγοντος 'οὐ παραιτοῦμαί σου
τὴν ἀνάγκην ἀλλὰ τὴν ὕβριν, ἵνα
φάγῃς ἀπόκτεινον, ἵνα δ᾽ ἥδιον
φάγῃς μὴ μ᾽ ἀναίρει᾽

...we go on to assume that when they utter cries and squeaks their speech is inarticulate, that they do not, begging for mercy, entreating, seeking justice, each one of them say, "I do not ask to be spared in case of necessity; only spare me your arrogance! Kill me to eat, but not to please your palate!"

While we must make allowances for the rhetorical flourishes and dramatic irony of Plutarch's phraseology, the passage in its literal sense is attributing to the non-verbal sounds and behaviors of the beasts not just a visceral reflex of distress and imminent danger, but the actual communication of a coherent moral argument targeting the unfairness and stupidity of humans for slaughtering animals as food.[34]

That animals are capable of conveying distress and other feelings to one another in non-verbal ways was acknowledged by Aristotle in the passage in the *Politics* where he outlined the decisive differentiation between

---

33 Plutarch, "On the Eating of Flesh," in *Plutarch's Moralia in Sixteen Volumes*, trans. Harold Cherniss and William Helmbold, vol. 12, The Loeb Classical Library 406 (Cambridge, MA and London: Harvard University Press and William Heinemann Ltd., 1984), 548–551; Stephen Thomas Newmyer, "Speaking of Beasts: The Stoics and Plutarch on Animal Reason and the Modern Case against Animals," *Quaderni Urbinati di Cultura Classica* 63, no. 3, New Series (1999): 64–65; "Plutarch on the Moral Grounds for Vegetarianism," *The Classical Outlook* 72 (1995): 548–551; *Animals in Greek and Roman Thought: A Sourcebook*, Routledge sourcebooks for the ancient World (London and New York: Routledge, 2011), 62–64; Ingvild Sælid Gilhus, *Animals, Gods and Humans: Changing Attitudes to Animals in Greek, Roman and Early Christian Ideas* (London: Routledge, 2006), 64–69.

34 Cf. Umberto Eco, Roberto Lambertini, and Costantino Marmo, "On Animal Language in the Medieval Classification of Signs," in *On the Medieval Theory of Signs*, ed. Umberto Eco and Costantino Marmo, Foundations of Semiotics 21 (Amsterdam and Philadelphia: John Benjamins, 1989), 7–8, 12, 14.

political man and the lower beasts. That important and influential text will be discussed in the next chapter.

Another incident in which beleaguered animals pleaded with humans for help in their distress occurred, according to the reports, in 55 B.C.E. when Pompey organized an impressive crowd-pleasing public entertainment with elephants.[35]

Pliny, Natural History 8:7:21:[36]

Sed Pompeiani amissa fugae spe	But Pompey's elephants when

---

35 On the political and ideological significance of Pompey's displays of elephants in such ceremonies see Gottfried Mader, "Triumphal Elephants and Political Circus at Plutarch, 'Pomp.' 14.6," *The Classical World* 99, no. 4 (2006): 397–403.

36 Pliny the Elder, *Natural History*, ed. H. (Harris) Rackham, Loeb Classical Library (Cambridge, MA: William Heinemann and Harvard University Press, 1972), 3:16-17; cited by Debra L. Nousek, "Turning Points in Roman History: The Case of Caesar's Elephant Denarius," *Phoenix* 62, no. 3/4 (2008): 301 and n. 56; George Jennison, *Animals for Show and Pleasure in Ancient Rome* (Philadelphia: University of Pennsylvania Press, 2005), 51–52; Richard Sorabji, *Animal Minds and Human Morals: The Origins of the Western Debate*, Cornell Studies in Classical Philology; The Townsend Lectures v. 54 (Ithaca, NY: Cornell University Press, 1993), 124–125; Martha Craven Nussbaum, *Upheavals of Thought: The Intelligence of Emotions* (Cambridge and New York: Cambridge University Press, 2001), 89; "Beyond 'Compassion and Humanity,'" in *Animal Rights: Current Debates and New Directions*, ed. Cass R. Sunstein and Martha Craven Nussbaum (Oxford: Oxford University Press, 2004), 299–320; Liliane Bodson, "Attitudes toward Animals in Greco-Roman Antiquity," *International Journal for the Study of Animal Problems* 4, no. 4 (1983): 312–320. In his letter to M. Marius, Cicero recalled of that event that "there was even an impulse of compassion, a feeling that that monsters had something human about them" [esse quandam illi beluae cum genere humano societatem" (*Ad Familiares* 7:1:3; [D. R. Shackleton Bailey, ed., *Cicero: Letters to Friends*, Loeb Classical Library 205 (Cambridge MA and London: Harvard University Press, 2001), 1:174-177].). Pliny's report is embedded into a lengthy discourse on the subject of elephants in which he claims (8.1-8) that the species:

> in intelligence approaches the nearest to man. It understands the language of its country [intellectus illis sermonis patrii], it obeys commands, and it remembers all the duties which it has been taught. It is sensible alike of the pleasures of love and glory, and, to a degree that is rare among men even, possesses notions of honesty, prudence, and equity; it has a religious respect also for the stars, and a veneration for the sun and the moon.

Pliny, Natural History 8:7:21:

misericordiam vulgi inenarrabili habitu quaerentes supplicavere quadam sese lamentatione conplorantes, tanto populi dolore, ut oblitus imperatoris ac munificentiae honori suo exquisitae flens universus consurgeret dirasque Pompeio, quas ille mox luit, inprecaretur.	they had lost all hope of escape tried to gain the compassion of the crowd by indescribable gestures of entreaty, deploring their fate with a kind of wailing, so much to the distress of the public that they forgot the general and his munificence carefully devised for their honor, and bursting into tears rose in a body and invoked curses on the head of Pompey, for which he afterwards paid the penalty.

As regards Rabbi Judah's calf's apparent ability to recognize that he was on the way to be slaughtered, it is intriguing to note Pliny's observation (8.1.5) that this is an instinct common to many animals.[37] In the case of elephants, they can discern (especially by means of their enhanced sense of smell) whether unfamiliar humans have friendly or malicious intentions —and in the latter case, they have ways of notifying their fellows to array

---

Pliny proceeds to describe their reverence for religion and their pious performance of purifications and other rituals, their respect for royal authority, military valor, compassion toward weaker species, sexual modesty, their ability to dance and perform tightrope walking (frontwards and backwards) and other elaborate circus-like tricks. See Thorsten Fögen, "Pliny the Elder's Animals: Some Remarks on the Narrative Structure of Nat. Hist. 8–11," *Hermes* 135, no. 2 (2007): 184–198; "Animal Communication," in *The Oxford Handbook of Animals in Classical Thought and Life*, ed. Gordon Lindsay Campbell, First Edition. (Oxford: Oxford University Press, 2014), 223. Celsus (as reported by Origen, *Contra Celsum* 4:88; Migne *PG* 1163-1164) argued that "no race of animals appears to be more observant of oaths than the elephants are, or to show greater devotion to divine things; and this, I presume, solely because they have some knowledge of God" [Ἐλεφάντων δὲ οὐδὲν εὐορκότερον οὐδὲ πρὸς τὰ θεῖα πιστότερον εἶναι δοκεῖ, πάντως δή που διότι γνῶσιν αὐτοῦ ἔχουσιν]; see Joseph Wilson. Trigg, *Origen*, The Early Church Fathers (London and New York: Routledge, 1998), 54. Origen refutes Celsus's claims in 4:89.

37 For a more general characterization of Pliny's views on animals and their relationships to humans see Dierauer, *Tier und Mensch*, 277–279.

themselves in battle formation to effectively defend themselves against the enemy. Dio Cassius (c. 155–235 C.E.)[38] provides a most elaborate enhancement of the story that illustrates how such events evolve to legendary proportions.

Dio Cassius, *Historiae Romanae 39:38:*[39]

[2] ...ἠλεήθησαν γάρ τινες ὑπὸ τοῦ δήμου παρὰ τὴν τοῦ Πομπηίου γνώμην, ἐπειδὴ τραυματισθέντες.

[3] τῆς μάχης ἐπαύσαντο, καὶ περιιόντες τάς τε προβοσκίδας ἐς τὸν οὐρανὸν ἀνέτεινον καὶ ὠλοφύροντο οὕτως ὥστε καὶ λόγον παρασχεῖν ὅτι οὐκ ἄλλως ἐκ συντυχίας αὐτὸ ἐποίησαν, ἀλλὰ τούς τε ὅρκους οἷς πιστεύσαντες ἐκ τῆς Λιβύης ἐπεπεραίωντο ἐπιβοώμενοι καὶ τὸ δαιμόνιον πρὸς

[4] τιμωρίαν σφῶν ἐπικαλούμενοι. λέγεται γὰρ ὅτι οὐ πρότερον τῶν νεῶν ἐπέβησαν πρὶν πίστιν παρὰ τῶν ἀγόντων σφᾶς ἔνορκον λαβεῖν, ἦ μὴν μηδὲν κακὸν πείσεσθαι. καὶ

[2] ...Some of them, contrary to Pompey's wish, were pitied by the people when, after being wounded

[3] and ceasing to fight, they walked about with their trunks raised toward heaven, lamenting so bitterly as to give rise to the report that they did so not by mere chance, but were crying out against the oaths in which they had trusted when they crossed over from Africa,

[4] and were calling upon Heaven to avenge them. For it is said that they would not set foot upon the ships before they received a pledge under oath from their drivers that they should suf-

---

38 Adam M. Kemezis, *Greek Narratives of the Roman Empire Under the Severans: Cassius Dio, Philostratus and Herodian*, Greek Culture in the Roman World (Cambridge UK and New York: Cambridge University Press, 2014); Fergus Millar, *A Study of Cassius Dio* (Oxford: Clarendon Press, 1964), 36; Glen Warren Bowersock, "The Literature of the Empire: Between Philosophy and Rhetoric: Cassius Dio and Herodian," in *The Cambridge History of Classical Literature*, ed. E. J. Kenney and W. V. Clausen, vol. 2. Latin Literature (Cambridge: Cambridge University Press, 1982), 710–711.

39 Earnest Cary, ed., *Dio's Roman History*, vol. 1, Loeb Classical Library (London and Cambridge, MA: William Heinemann and Harvard University Press, 1961), 3:360–363.

Dio Cassius, *Historiae Romanae 39:38:*

τοῦτο μὲν εἴτ᾿ ὄντως

fer no harm.

[5] οὕτως εἴτε καὶ ἄλλως
πως ἔχει, οὐκ οἶδα: ἤδη γάρ τινες
καὶ ἐκεῖνο εἶπον, ὅτι πρὸς τῷ τῆς
φωνῆς τῆς πατριώτιδος αὐτοὺς
ἐπαΐειν 1 καὶ τῶν ἐν τῷ οὐρανῷ
γιγνομένων συνιᾶσιν, ὥστε καὶ ἐν
ταῖς νουμηνίαις, πρὶν ἐς ὄψιν τοῖς
ἀνθρώποις τὴν σελήνην ἐλθεῖν,
πρός τε ὕδωρ ἀείνων ἀφικνεῖσθαι

[5] Whether this is really so
or not I do not know; for some in
time past have further declared
that in addition to understanding
the language of their native country they also comprehend what is
going on in the sky, so that at the
time of the new moon, before the
luminary comes within the gaze
of men, they reach running water

[6] κἀνταῦθα καθαρμόν τινά
σφων ποιεῖσθαι. ἤκουσα μὲν δὴ
ταῦτα

[6] and there perform a kind
of purification of themselves.
These things I have heard.

Elephants, issuing from remote and mysterious Africa,[40] were understandably a source of imaginative speculation for many Romans, as reflected in
this passage.[41] It is not simply a question of their being able to express
their fears of imminent mortal danger, a reaction which would have been

---

40 It seems likely that the elephants in this case were from Africa rather than Asia.
Plutarch reports [Pompey 12:5] that Pompey made a point of hunting lions and elephants in Libya [Perrin, *Plutarch's Lives*, 1:144–145]. According to Mader, an intended impact of Pompey's elephant demonstration was supposed to evoke memories
of Alexander the Great's employment of the animals from India or Persia; see "Triumphal Elephants," 397 nn. 2; 399; Robin Lane Fox, *Alexander the Great* (London,
England and New York: Penguin Books, 1986), 351–378. Philostratus's *Life of Apollonius of Tyana* (2:11-16) contains a lengthy excursus about the hero's encounters
with elephants in India, from which it became clear that the animals were not only
gifted with a high degree of intelligence, but they were also able to display grief over
their subjection to human masters [Frederick Cornwallis Conybeare, trans.,
*Philostratus. Life of Apollonius of Tyana, Epistles of Apollonius and Treatise of Eu-
sebius.*, Loeb Classical Library (London and New York: William Heinemann and the
MacMillan Co., 1912), 1:141-161]; see also Thorndike, *Magic and Experimental
Science*, 1:256. Philostratus (5:27) also relates that Apollonius refused an invitation
to come to Judea to advise Vespanian about seizing the throne because the natives
there were defiled with bloodshed. See Stern, *Greek and Latin Authors*, 2:339-340.

easy to appreciate in an arena where they were witnessing the ghastly killing of their fellows—but Dio's informant was ascribing to them a very sophisticated understanding of how they had been deceived by their captors.[42] We are evidently meant to imagine some sort of negotiations that took place between the animals and their human neighbors in Africa, a premise that is hard to maintain without assuming that man and beast shared a common language—and likely we are meant to assume that the elephants could understand the words and sentences that were spoken by their human "recruiters." These animals were also able to appreciate the legal or moral significance of the guarantees that they had been promised, and consequently to feel indignation over the violation of those promises, so that they chose to refuse to board the ships—whose purpose and desti-

---

41 For another instance of a misconception about African elephants see William Gowers, "African Elephants and Ancient Authors," *African Affairs* 47, no. 188 (1948): 173–180. Aelian, on the other hand (*De Natura Animalium* 11:14), tells a story about the devoted elephant Nicaea who was able to understand Indian ["παρακατέθετο φωνῇ τῇ Ἰνδῶν, ἧς ἀκούουσιν ἐλέφαντες"]; Alwyn Faber Scholfield, ed., *Aelian: On the Characteristics of Animals*, The Loeb Classical Library (London: W. Heinemann, 1958), 2:367-368; see Howard Hayes Scullard, *The Elephant in the Greek and Roman World*, Aspects of Greek and Roman Life (London: Thames and Hudson, 1974), 222–230; cited by Thorsten Fögen, "Pliny the Elder's Animals: Some Remarks on the Narrative Structure of Nat. Hist. 8–11," *Hermes* 135, no. 2 (2007): 186 n. 6; R. K. French, *Ancient Natural History: Histories of Nature*, Sciences of Antiquity (London and New York: Routledge, 1994), 269; Lucynda Kostuch, "Do Animals Have a Homeland? Ancient Greeks on the Cultural Identity of Animals," *Humanimalia* 9, no. 1 (2017): 76, 79; J. M. Bigwood, "Aristotle and the Elephant Again," *American Journal of Philology* 114, no. 4 (2013): 537–555. Aelian also reports (2:11):

> And I myself have seen one actually with its trunk writing Roman letters on a tablet in a straight line without any deviation. The only thing was that the instructor's hand was laid upon it, directing it to the shape of the letters until the animal had finished writing; and it looked intently down. You would have said that the animals eyes had been taught and knew the letters that he personally witnessed an elephant writing letters with its trunk.

[Scholfield, *Aelian: On the Characteristics of Animals*, 1:108-109]; discussed by Fögen, "Pliny the Elder's Animals," 187.

42 This trait is also mentioned by Pliny (*Ibid.* 8.1): "Maria transituri non ante naves conscendere quam invitati rectoris iureiurando de reditu" [When about to cross the sea, they cannot be prevailed upon to go on board the ship, until their keeper has promised upon oath that they shall return home again].

nation they also must have known.[43] The fact that Dio could include all this as appropriate material for his *Historiae* indicates that such beliefs about animal language and intelligence (at least in Africa) must have been widespread among his target audience.[44]

A more substantial interpretation of the cogency of an animal's cry for help is suggested by Xenophanes' anecdote about Pythagoras and a dog as related by Diogenes Laertius.

---

43 See Jo-Ann Shelton, "Contracts with Animals: Lucretius, De Rerum Natura," *Between the Species* 11 (1995): 115–121. Her clever attempt to extract a theory of contract governing the ethical relationships between humans and domestic animals in Lucretius (and, by extension, in at least one branch or Epicureanism) is not very convincing from a straightforward textual perspective. See also Newmyer, "Being the One," 526.

44 For a more recent investigation into the emotional lives of elephants see Jeffrey Moussaieff Masson and Susan McCarthy, *When Elephants Weep: The Emotional Lives of Animals*, Book Club. (New York: Delta, 1996). T. Fögen notes that the literary genres of Pliny's and Aelian's works on "the nature of animals" should not be classified as primarily scientific—as distinct from those of Aristotle (for whom, e.g., physiological factors play a greater role in the explanation of animal communications)—but as books designed to entertain and edify their readerships, for which purpose they frequently portrayed anthropomorphized animals in order to illustrate moral virtues ("Pliny the Elder's Animals," 190–191). See E. L. Bowie, "The Literature of the Empire: Between Philosophy and Rhetoric: Aelian," in *The Cambridge History of Classical Literature*, ed. E. J. Kenney and W. V. Clausen, vol. 2. Latin Literature (Cambridge: Cambridge University Press, 1982), 680–682.

Diogenes Laertius, Lives of Eminent Philosophers:[45]

They say that, passing a belabored whelp,	καί ποτέ μιν στυφελιζομένου σκύλακος παριόντα φασὶν ἐποικτῖραι καὶ τόδε φάσθαι ἔπος:
He, full of pity, spake these words of dole:	"παῦσαι μηδὲ ῥάπιζ', ἐπεὶ ἦ φίλου ἀνέρος ἐστὶ ψυχή, τὴν
"Stay, smite not! 'Tis a friend, a human soul; knew him straight whenas I heard him yelp!"	ἔγνων φθεγξαμένης ἀΐων.

While it is not clear how literally we are expected to take this ironic quip,[46] it raises the possibility of whether those thinkers who, like Pythagoras,

---

45 Diogenes Laertius, *Lives of Eminent Philosophers*, ed. Robert Drew Hicks, The Loeb Classical Library (London, Cambridge, MA: W. Heinemann and Harvard University Press, 1931), 8:36; Walter Burkert, *Lore and Science in Ancient Pythagoreanism*, trans. Edwin L. Minar Jr. (Cambridge, Mass: Harvard University Press, 1972), 120–121; A. Berriedale Keith, "Pythagoras and the Doctrine of Transmigration," *Journal of the Royal Asiatic Society of Great Britain and Ireland* (1909): 575; Urs Dierauer, *Tier und Mensch im Denken der Antike: Studien zur Tierpsychologie, Anthropologie und Ethik*, Studien zur antiken Philosophie 6 (Amsterdam: Grüner, 1977), 18; Bodson, "Attitudes toward Animals," 313; Stephen R. L. Clark, *Understanding Faith: Religious Belief and Its Place in Society*, St. Andrews Studies in Philosophy and Public Affairs (Exeter, UK and Charlottesville, VA: Imprint Academic, 2009), 110–124; Damianos Tsekourakis, "Pythagoreanism or Platonism and Ancient Medicine: The Reasons for Vegetarianism in Plutarch's 'Moralia,'" in *Aufstieg Und Niedergang Der Römischen Welt / Rise and Decline of the Roman World*, ed. Wolfgang Haase and Hildegard Temporini, vol. Vol. 36.1, Part II: Principate (Berlin and New York: Walter de Gruyter, 1987), 370–371; Stephen R. L. Clark, "Animals in Classical and Late Antique Philosophy," in *The Oxford Handbook of Animal Ethics*, ed. Tom Beauchamp and R. G. Frey, vol. 1, Oxford Handbooks (Oxford: Oxford University Press, 2011), 50–51; Stephen Thomas Newmyer, "Being the One and Becoming the Other: Animals in Ancient Philosophical Schools," in *The Oxford Handbook of Animals in Classical Thought and Life*, ed. George Lindsay Campbell (Oxford: Oxford University Press, 2014), 512; Jan N. Bremmer, *The Rise and Fall of the Afterlife: The 1995 Read-Tuckwell Lectures at the University of Bristol* (London and New York: Routledge, 2002), 13. As Clark put it, "Pythagoras acknowledged the dog's howling as a *complaint*, and so as a communication that placed an obligation (and experienced command) on those who heard it.

subscribed to a belief of inter-species metempsychosis inferred from that doctrine that the souls that inhered in human and animal bodies share some common means of communication, whether verbal or otherwise. In this respect the dilemma of Rabbi Judah's calf could indeed by comparable to that of the "belabored whelp" whose yelp was recognizable to Pythagoras from a previous life.

Augustine of Hippo

We meet with a very close match to the position ascribed to Rabbi Judah in Augustine's *De Civitate Dei* in a passage that comes to refute the suggestion that the biblical precept "Thou shalt not kill" extends to the slaughtering of animals for food. After dismissing as absurd the prospect that such a reading would also prohibit the picking of vegetables, which are also living entities, Augustine proceeds to explain why it is permissible for Christians to kill non-human animals for the convenience of humans.

Augustine of Hippo, The City of God Against the Pagans, 1:20:[47]

cum de frutectis esse, quia nullus eis sensus est, nec de inrationalibus animantibus, volatilibus natatilibus, ambulatilibus reptilibus, quia nulla nobis ratione sociantur, quam non eis datum est nobiscum habere communem (unde iustissima ordinatione creatoris et vita et mors eorum nostris usibus subditur).	...if when we read, "Thou shalt not kill," we do not understand this phrase to apply to bushes, because they have no sensation, nor to the unreasoning animals that fly, swim, walk or crawl, because they are not partners with us in the faculty of reason, the privilege not being given them to share it in common with us—and therefore by the altogether right-

---

46   James Luchte standardly refers to the anecdote as "Xenophanes' jest" [*Pythagoras and the Doctrine of Transmigration: Wandering Souls*, Continuum studies in ancient philosophy (London ; New York: Continuum, 2009), 15]. It is not even stated explicitly that the subject of the sentence is Pythagoras, though this has been universally accepted; Walter Burkert, *Lore and Science in Ancient Pythagoreanism*, trans. Edwin L. Minar Jr. (Cambridge, Mass: Harvard University Press, 1972), 120; Tsekourakis, "Pythagoreanism or Platonism," 370.

47   Augustine, *The City of God*, trans. George E. McCracken, vol. 1, The Loeb Classical Library 411 (Cambridge: Harvard University Press, 1957), 92–93.

Augustine of Hippo, The City of God Against the Pagans, 1:20:

> eous ordinance of the Creator both their life and death are a matter subordinate to our needs.

It is not hard to imagine Augustine responding to the troubled calf, "unde iustissima ordinatione creatoris et vita et mors eorum nostris usibus subditur," for that is the role assigned to all you unreasoning beasts in the divine plan of creation.[48] With Augustine's support this blend of biblical and Stoic[49] teachings would come to dominate the Christian and western thinking about human-animal relationships for the coming centuries.[50]

Concluding Observations

The narratives that were surveyed in this chapter revealed a broad range of assumptions as regards the ability of animals to understand or communicate in human-like language. There appears to be general agreement that the creatures do feel authentic emotions such as fear and distress, and that they are able to convey those feelings in recognizable ways. Beyond that, however, there is nothing approaching a consensus, even within versions of the same tradition. Did the calf beg Rabbi for help in actual words, or only in word-like sounds and expression? Did Dio Cassius expect his readers to accept the possibility that elephants were able to

---

48 Similarly in his On the Ways of Manichaeans: "inasmuch as we can perceive by their cries that animals die in pain, although we make little of this since the beast, lacking a rational soul, is not related to us by a common nature" [Augustine, *The Catholic and Manichaean Ways of Life*, trans. Donald A Gallagher and Idella J. Gallagher, The Fathers of the Church: A New Translation 56 (Catholic University of America Press, 1966), 17:59 (p. 105)]; Gilhus, *Animals, Gods and Humans*, 267–268.

49 As we shall see below.

50 See Richard Sorabji, *Animal Minds and Human Morals: The Origins of the Western Debate*, Cornell Studies in Classical Philology; The Townsend Lectures v. 54 (Ithaca, NY: Cornell University Press, 1993), 201–202; Derek Joseph Wiertel, "Classical Theism and the Problem of Animal Suffering," *Theological Studies* 78, no. 3 (2017): 663–672; Joshua M. Moritz, "Animal Suffering, Evolution, and the Origins of Evil: Toward a 'Free Creatures' Defense," *Zygon* 49, no. 2 (2014): 351.

comprehend the words of human and to negotiate with African natives? It would seem that the cultures in which these stories circulated were not as concerned with their factual or scientific accuracy as they were with their narrative impact and moral effectiveness—not with the neutral amorality of the empirical world, but with one that made sense to human sensibilities. Where necessary, that could require animals to express their feelings in an articulate and grammatical manner.

The Philosophical Debate

VICTOR LOOKED AT THE DOG CAREFULLY.

IT COULDN'T HAVE SPOKEN TO HIM. IT MUST HAVE BEEN HIS IMAGINATION. BUT HE'D SAID THAT LAST TIME, HADN'T HE?

"I WONDER WHAT YOUR NAME IS?" VICTOR SAID, PATTING IT ON THE HEAD.

"GASPODE," SAID GASPODE...

TALKING OF NATURAL, I CAN'T HELP NOTICING THAT—

"BLOODY DESERT, THIS PLACE," SAID GASPODE.

YOU'RE A TALKING DOG.[1]

As regards the rabbinic tale of Rabbi and the calf, the differing assessments of the calf's actions that underlie the textual variations between the Yerushalmi and the other rabbinic texts would seem to reflect divergent attitudes towards the issue of animal language, as it was raised in Aristotle's influential discussion in the *Politics*. In that passage the philosopher claimed to identify the crucial difference between "voice" (φωνή) and meaningful "speech" (λόγος), a distinction that served as a justification for assigning to human beings a unique status in the hierarchy of living creatures.[2] The voice-speech distinction was particularly ingrained in Hellenic

---

1   Terry Pratchett, *Moving Pictures* (London: V. Gollancz, 1990), 109–110.
2   See e.g. Thorsten Fögen, "Animal Communication," in *The Oxford Handbook of Animals in Classical Thought and Life*, ed. Gordon Lindsay Campbell, First Edition. (Oxford: Oxford University Press, 2014), 216–232; Ian Stewart and Jack Cohen, *Darwin's Watch: The Science of Discworld III*, First Anchor Books Edition. (New York: Anchor Books, 2015), 165.

thought by virtue of the fact that the Greek word *logos* encompasses (and some might argue, confuses) the concepts of verbal speech and of rationality.[3]

Speech—A Uniquely Human Gift

The concept of an essential ethical differentiation between humans and the lower animals makes what is perhaps its earliest literary appearance in the writings of Hesiod.

---

3 Stephen Thomas Newmyer, *Animals in Greek and Roman Thought: A Sourcebook*, Routledge sourcebooks for the ancient World (London and New York: Routledge, 2011), 61; Ingvild Sælid Gilhus, *Animals, Gods and Humans: Changing Attitudes to Animals in Greek, Roman and Early Christian Ideas* (London: Routledge, 2006), 38–40; A. A. Long, "Post-Aristotelian Philosophy," in *The Cambridge History of Classical Literature*, ed. P. E. Easterling and Bernard Knox, vol. 1. Greek Literature (Cambridge: Cambridge University Press, 1982), 631; John Heath, *The Talking Greeks: Speech, Animals, and the Other in Homer, Aeschylus, and Plato* (Cambridge: Cambridge University Press, 2005), 7–9. As is evident in the passage that Newmyer cites from the *Parts of Animals*, Aristotle was prepared to acknowledge that some birds are able to communicate with one another.

Hesiod, *Works and Days* (274-281):[4]

ὦ Πέρση, σὺ δὲ ταῦτα μετὰ φρεσὶ
βάλλεο σῇσι, καὶ νυ δίκης ἐπάκ-
ουε, βίης δ᾽ ἐπιλήθεο πάμπαν.

But you, Perses, lay up these things within your heart and listen now to right, ceasing altogether to think of violence.

τόνδε γὰρ ἀνθρώποισι νόμ-
ον διέταξε Κρονίων

For the son of Cronos has ordained this law for men,

---

4   Hugh G. Evelyn-White, *Hesiod the Homeric Hymns and Homerica*, Loeb Classical Library (Cambridge MA and London: Harvard University Press and William Heinemann Ltd., 1977), 22–25; see also Urs Dierauer, *Tier und Mensch im Denken der Antike: Studien zur Tierpsychologie, Anthropologie und Ethik*, Studien zur antiken Philosophie 6 (Amsterdam: Grüner, 1977), 15–18; F. H. Sandbach, "Plato and the Socratic Work of Xenophon," in *The Cambridge History of Classical Literature*, ed. P. E. Easterling and Bernard Knox, vol. 1. Greek Literature (Cambridge: Cambridge University Press, 1982), 97–100; Steven H. Lonsdale, "Attitudes towards Animals in Ancient Greece," *Greece & Rome* 26, no. 2 (1979): 156; Stephen Thomas Newmyer, *Animals in Greek and Roman Thought: A Sourcebook*, Routledge sourcebooks for the ancient World (London and New York: Routledge, 2011); "Being the One and Becoming the Other: Animals in Ancient Philosophical Schools," in *The Oxford Handbook of Animals in Classical Thought and Life*, ed. George Lindsay Campbell (Oxford: Oxford University Press, 2014), 509; Liliane Bodson, "Attitudes Toward Animals in Greco-Roman Antiquity," *Societal Attitudes Toward Animals* 4, no. 4 (1983): 313; Stephen R. L. Clark, "Animals in Classical and Late Antique Philosophy," in *The Oxford Handbook of Animal Ethics*, ed. Tom Beauchamp and R. G. Frey, vol. 1, Oxford Handbooks (Oxford: Oxford University Press, 2011), 47; John Heath, *The Talking Greeks: Speech, Animals, and the Other in Homer, Aeschylus, and Plato* (Cambridge: Cambridge University Press, 2005), 214–215; Shirley Darcus Sullivan, *Psychological and Ethical Ideas: What Early Greeks Say*, Mnemosyne, Bibliotheca Classica Batava 144 (Leiden and New York: E.J. Brill, 1995), 182–185; Jeremy B. Lefkowitz, "Aesop and Animal Fable," in *The Oxford Handbook of Animals in Classical Thought and Life*, ed. Gordon Lindsay Campbell, First Edition. (Oxford: Oxford University Press, 2014), 9–11; Lucynda Kostuch, "Do Animals Have a Homeland? Ancient Greeks on the Cultural Identity of Animals," *Humanimalia* 9, no. 1 (2017): 73.

Hesiod, *Works and Days* (274-281):

ἰχθύσι μὲν καὶ θηρσὶ καὶ
οἰωνοῖς πετεηνοῖς ἐσθέμεν ἀλλήλους, ἐπεὶ οὐ δίκη ἐστὶ μετ᾽
αὐτοῖς:

that fishes and beasts and
winged fowls should devour one
another, for right is not in them;

ἀνθρώποισι δ᾽ ἔδωκε δίκην,
ἣ πολλὸν ἀρίστη γίγνεται:

but to mankind he gave right
which proves far the best.

εἰ γάρ τίς κ᾽ ἐθέλῃ τὰ δίκαι᾽
ἀγορεῦσαι γιγνώσκων, τῷ μέν τ᾽
ὄλβον διδοῖ εὐρύοπα Ζεύς:

For whoever knows the
right and is ready to speak it, far-
seeing Zeus gives him prosperity;

According to this statement in Hesiod, the distinguishing feature that entitles humans to their superior status in the hierarchy of being is their propensity for justice, a virtue that manifests itself in the readiness to *speak out* in public (ἀγορεύω) on its behalf.[5] This was imbued in them

---

5   Commentators have called attention to the fact that the affirmation of justice here stands in contrast to the message voiced previously (207-211) by the hawk to its prey —a lesson intended for kings, though ascribed (ironically?) by Hesiod to a non-human!—in "the fable of the hawk and the nightingale," asserting that—justly or not— the weak are inevitably susceptible to the wills of the more powerful: "You fool, why do you scream? Someone much your better has you.\ You go wherever I conduct you, songstress though you may be.\ I shall make you my dinner, if I wish, or let you go.\ Senseless is he who wishes to set himself against his betters:\ he lacks victory and suffers grief upon grief." For diverse approaches as to how to reconcile the sources or identify Hesiod's real position, See Hugh G. Evelyn-White, ed., *Hesiod. The Homeric hymns. And Homerica*, The Loeb Classical Library 57 (Cambridge MA and London: Harvard University Press and Heinemann, 1982), xviii; Henry Theodore Wade-Gery, "Hesiod," *Phoenix* 3, no. 3 (1949): 88–91; [=Henry Theodore Wade-Gery, *Essays in Greek History* (Oxford: Basil Blackwell, 1958), 10–16]; Lloyd W. Daly, "Hesiod's Fable," *Transactions and Proceedings of the American Philological Association* 92 (1961): 45–51; Robert Lamberton, *Hesiod*, Hermes Books (New Haven: Yale University Press, 1988), 105, 121–124; Stephanie Nelson, "The Justice of Zeus in Hesiod's Fable of the Hawk and the Nightingale," *The Classical Journal* 92, no. 3 (1997): 235–247; V. A. Rodgers, "Some Thoughts on ΔΙΚΗ," *The Classical Quarterly* 21, no. 2 (1971): 289–301; Svein Østerud, "The Individuality of Hesiod," *Hermes* 104, no. 1 (1976): 13–29; M. L. West, *Hesiod: Theogony and Works and Days*, Oxford's World's Classics (Oxford and New York: Oxford University Press, 2008), 50; Tom Hawkins, "Eloquent Alogia: Animal Narrators in Ancient

uniquely by Zeus, and entitles them to protection against violence. The wild and amoral domain of animals enjoys no such privilege.[6]

Plato

In the fable about Prometheus's and Epimetheus's creation of living beings as it is related in Plato's *Protagoras*, each of the species was endowed with some special quality that would ensure its survival in the face of natural dangers or predators. When they came to the physically feeble and vulnerable humans, they compensated them by conferring upon them a number of intellectual, technical or social skills that provided them with protection against the brawnier denizens of the animal kingdom. These traits are presented in the fable as features that are unique to humans— though at this stage, not necessarily as criteria of our species' absolute su-

---

Greek Literature," *Humanites* 6, no. 37 (2017): 7.

6   Hesiod's wording is similar to the sentiment underlying *m.Avot* 3:2: "Rabbi Ḥananiah the deputy of the priests says: Pray for the welfare of the government, for were it not for fear of it we would swallow each other alive." (On the precise reading see Hanoch Yalon, *Introduction to the Vocalization of the Mishnah* (Jerusalem: Bialik Institute, 1964), 94–95 [Hebrew]; Charles Taylor, ed., *Sayings of the Jewish Fathers. Sefer Dibre Aboth Ha-Olam. Comprising Pirque Aboth in Hebrew and English with Critical Notes and Excursuses*, 2d ed. (Amsterdam: Philo Press, 1970), 8, 57; Efraim Elimelech Urbach, *The Sages: Their Concepts and Beliefs* (Cambridge, MA: Harvard University Press, 1987), 596; 959 n. 32. See b.*'Avodah Zarah* 4a: "Just as with the fish of the sea, the larger always swallows up the others, so too with regard to humans, were it not for their fear of the government the greater would swallow up the others." See Deborah Levine Gera, *Ancient Greek Ideas on Speech, Language, and Civilization* (Oxford and New York: Oxford University Press, 2003), 10, 46–49. As far as I can tell, her treatment of Hesiod does not mention this passage which seems to be crucial to the topic.

The traditional understanding was that Hesiod composed this poem in protest of the ill-treatment he suffered at the hand of his brother Perses who usurped and squandered his inheritance with the cooperation of a corrupt judiciary. The historicity of Perses has been called into question by several scholars; see P. B. R. Forbes, "Hesiod versus Perses," *The Classical Review* 64, no. 3/4 (1950): 82–87; John Francis Latimer, "Perses versus Hesiod," *Transactions and Proceedings of the American Philological Association* 61 (1930): 70–79; Zoe Stamatopoulou, "The Quarrel with Perses and Hesiod's Biographical Tradition," *Greek, Roman, and Byzantine Studies* 56, no. 1 (2015): 1–17.

periority, as expressed in the following passage:[7]

Plato, *Protagoras* 322a:[8]

ἐπειδὴ δὲ ὁ ἄνθρωπος θείας μετέσχε μοίρας, πρῶτον μὲν διὰ τὴν τοῦ θεοῦ συγγένειαν ζῴων μόνον θεοὺς ἐνόμισεν, καὶ ἐπεχείρει βωμούς τε ἱδρύεσθαι καὶ ἀγάλματα θεῶν: ἔπειτα φωνὴν καὶ ὀνόματα ταχὺ διηρθρώσατο τῇ τέχνῃ	...he, in the first place, by his nearness of kin to deity, was the only creature that worshipped gods, and set himself to establish altars and holy images; and secondly, he soon was enabled by his skill to articulate speech and words...

In Plato's *Statesman* dialogue, Socrates' interlocutor presents a myth of human history that goes back to the Age of Cronos. This provokes questions as to how they spent their time during this idyllic age when they lacked nothing and therefore had no urgent needs to ask of one another. The stranger imagines a scenario,

---

7　Rabbinic thought did not appear to doubt that animals had methods, presumably non-verbal, of communicating among one another. Thus, *m.Bava Meṣia'* 3:7 records a dispute between the Rabbis and Rabbi Yoḥanan ben Nuri on the question of whether depreciation of produce in the care of a finder or bailee should be estimated according to a percentage or a fixed amount. Rabbi Yoḥanan justifies the latter position by means of the argument "What do the mice care? They consume all the same, whether more or less!"; i.e., there is a maximum quantity that can be consumed by the fixed number of mice on the premises. The Palestinian Talmud (9b) presents a refutation of that reasoning in the name of the sages "there" [תמן אמרין, presumably in Babylonia]: "אלין עכבבריה רשעייה כד אינין חמיין פירייה סגין אינין קריין לחבריהון דיתון ויאכלון עמהון" [Those mice are wicked. When they spot produce they call to their fellows and they join them in eating].See E. S Rosenthal, ed., *Yerushalmi Neziqin* (Jerusalem: Publications of the Israel Academy of Sciences and Humanities. Seciton of Humanities, 1983), 53, 143 [Hebrew].

8　Walter Rangeley Maitland Lamb, trans., *Plato*, vol. 2, Loeb Classical Library 165 (London and Cambridge MA: Harvard University Press, 1924), 132–133; see Dierauer, *Tier und Mensch*, 37–38, 48–49, 66; Deborah Levine Gera, *Ancient Greek Ideas on Speech, Language, and Civilization* (Oxford and New York: Oxford University Press, 2003), 140–142; Liliane Bodson, "Attitudes toward Animals in Greco-Roman Antiquity," *International Journal for the Study of Animal Problems* 4, no. 4 (1983): 313–314; Newmyer, "Being the One," 513–514.

Plato, Statesman 272b:[9]

Εἰ μὲν τοίνυν οἱ τρόφιμοι τοῦ Κρόνου, παρούσης αὐτοῖς οὕτω πολλῆς σχολῆς καὶ δυνάμεως πρὸς τὸ μὴ μόνον ἀνθρώποις ἀλλὰ καὶ θηρίοις διὰ Cλόγων δύνασθαι ξυγγίγνεσθαι...	if the foster children of Cronos, having all this leisure and the ability to converse not only with human beings but also with beasts...

The participants are uncertain how to evaluate that situation, since it depends on whether that gift of universal communication was used to philosophical advantage or wasted on idle chatter.[10]

Isocrates

The noted rhetorician Isocrates (436–338 B.C.E.) asserted unambiguously that it is humanity's ability to speak that sets the species above the other creatures. In the course of his refutation of those who would criticize the pursuit of eloquence as a virtue because it is so often abused and put to nefarious uses, Isocrates reminds his interlocutors that the power of speech is in reality a most precious quality.

---

9   Jeffrey Henderson, ed., *Plato: Statesman, Philebus, Ion*, trans. Harold North Fowler, vol. 8, The Loeb Classical Library 164 (London and New York: William Heinemann ; G.P. Putnam's Sons, 1917), 60-61 (272b-c).

10   Gera, *Greek Ideas on Speech*, 22–23.

Isocrates, Nicocles or the Cyprians 3:5-6:[11]

...καὶ τοσοῦτον διημαρτήκασιν
ὥστ᾽ οὐκ αἰσθονται τοιούτῳ
πράγματι δυσμενῶς ἔχοντες, ὃ
πάντων τῶν ἐνόντων ἐν τῇ τῶν
ἀνθρώπων φύσει πλείστων ἀγαθ-
ῶν αἴτιόν ἐστι.

...they have gone so far astray as
not to perceive that they are hostile to that power which of all the
faculties that belong to the nature
of man is the source of most of
our blessings.

τοῖς μὲν γὰρ ἄλλοις οἷς ἔχομεν
οὐδὲν τῶν ἄλλων ζῴων
διαφέρομεν,

For in the other powers which we
possess we are in no respect superior to other living creatures;

ἀλλὰ πολλῶν καὶ τῷ τάχει καὶ τῇ
ῥώμῃ καὶ ταῖς ἄλλαις εὐπορίαις
καταδεέστεροι τυγχάνομεν ὄντες:

nay, we are inferior to many in
swiftness and in strength and in
other resources;

ἐγγενομένου δ᾽ ἡμῖν τοῦ πείθειν
ἀλλήλους καὶ δηλοῦν πρὸς ἡμᾶς
αὐτοὺς περὶ ὧν ἂν βουληθῶμεν,
οὐ μόνον τοῦ θηριωδῶς ζῆν
ἀπηλλάγημεν, ἀλλὰ καὶ
συνελθόντες πόλεις ᾠκίσαμεν καὶ
νόμους ἐθέμεθα καὶ τέχνας
εὕρομεν,

but, because there has been im-
planted in us the power to persuade each other and to make
clear to each other whatever we
desire, not only have we escaped
the life of wild beasts, but we
have come together and founded
cities and made laws and invented
arts;

---

11 George Norlin, trans., *Isocrates*, The Loeb Classical Library (London and New York: W. Heinemann ltd. and G. P. Putnam's sons, 1928), 1:78-81 [similarly in his Antidosis 153; and Panegyricus 47-50]; see Dierauer, *Tier und Mensch*, 32–33; Ekaterina V. Haskins, *Logos and Power in Isocrates and Aristotle* (University of South Carolina Press, 2004), 87–88; *The Patterns of the Present: Interpreting the Authority of Form* (Albany: SUNY Press, 2001), 164; Gera, *Greek Ideas on Speech*, 142–144; Samuel IJsseling, *Rhetoric and Philosophy in Conflict: An Historical Survey* (The Hague: M. Nijhoff, 1976), 18–19; William Benoit, "Isocrates and Aristotle on Rhetoric," *Rhetoric Society Quarterly* 20, no. 3 (1990): 253–254; "Isocrates and Plato on Rhetoric and Rhetorical Education," *Rhetoric Society Quarterly* 21, no. 1 (1991): 253–254; George A. Kennedy, "Oratory," in *The Cambridge History of Classical Literature*, ed. P. E. Easterling and Bernard Knox, vol. 1. Greek Literature (Cambridge: Cambridge University Press, 1982), 505–514.

Isocrates, Nicocles or the Cyprians 3:5-6:

καὶ σχεδὸν ἅπαντα τὰ δι' ἡμῶν μεμηχανημένα λόγος ἡμῖν ἐστιν ὁ συγκατασκευάσας.

and, generally speaking, there is no institution devised by man which the power of speech has not helped us to establish.

In significant respects, Isocrates is drawing out the conclusions that were implicit in Hesiod's mythological tale: it is only by virtue of our ability to argue persuasively the correctness of our positions (even if this ability lends itself to occasional misuse) that humans can be expected to rise above a social reality in which might makes right.[12] In other respects, perhaps, the human race is at a clear physical disadvantage when compared with other creatures, but our capacity for verbal expression elevates us above them in a qualitative sense that is not confined to a social utilitarianism, though it is a necessary precondition for the kind of political organization that the Athenians equated with civilization.

Aristotle

Hesiod and Plato expressed their perceptions of human distinctiveness in mythic language. A very similar understanding of the special quality was given a more rationalistic formulation by Aristotle.

---

12 A similar idea is expressed by Andromache in Euripides, *Trojan Women, Iphigenia Among the Taurians, Ion*, trans. David Kovacs, Loeb Classical Library 10 (Cambridge, MA: Harvard University Press, 1999), 80–81; cited by Urs Dierauer, *Tier und Mensch im Denken der Antike: Studien zur Tierpsychologie, Anthropologie und Ethik*, Studien zur antiken Philosophie 6 (Amsterdam: Grüner, 1977), 45 n. 25.

Aristotle, Politics1.2 1253a 9-18:[13]

διότι δὲ πολιτικὸν ὁ ἄνθρωπος ζῷον πάσης μελίττης καὶ παντὸς ἀγελαίου ζῴου μᾶλλον, δῆλον.

And why man is a political animal in a greater measure than any bee or any gregarious animal is clear.

οὐθὲν γάρ, ὡς φαμέν, μάτην ἡ φύσις ποιεῖ: λόγον δὲ μόνον ἄνθρωπος ἔχει τῶν ζῴων:

For nature, as we declare, does nothing without purpose; and man alone of the animals possesses speech.

ἡ μὲν οὖν φωνὴ τοῦ λυπηροῦ καὶ ἡδέος ἐστὶ σημεῖον, διὸ καὶ τοῖς ἄλλοις ὑπάρχει ζῴοις (μέχρι γὰρ τούτου ἡ φύσις αὐτῶν ἐλήλυθε, τοῦ ἔχειν αἴσθησιν λυπηροῦ καὶ ἡδέος καὶ ταῦτα σημαίνειν ἀλλήλοις),

The mere voice, it is true, can indicate pain and pleasure, and therefore is possessed by the other animals as well for their nature has been developed so far as to have sensations of what is painful and pleasant and to indicate those sensations to one another,

ὁ δὲ λόγος ἐπὶ τῷ δηλοῦν ἐστι τὸ συμφέρον καὶ τὸ βλαβερόν, ὥστε καὶ τὸ δίκαιον καὶ τὸ ἄδικον:

but speech is designed to indicate the advantageous and the harmful, and therefore also the right and the wrong;

---

13   H. Rackham, ed., *Politics*, Loeb Classical Library 264 (Cambridge MA and London: William Heinemann and Harvard University Press, 1940); cited by Richard Sorabji, *Animal Minds and Human Morals: The Origins of the Western Debate*, Cornell Studies in Classical Philology; The Townsend Lectures v. 54 (Ithaca, NY: Cornell University Press, 1993), 81; Clark, "Animals in Philosophy," 45; *Aristotle's Man: Speculations Upon Aristotelian Anthropology* (Oxford: Clarendon Press, 1983), 23; Dierauer, *Tier und Mensch*, 100–16i, (especially 125); see also: Eric Lawee, "The Sins of the Fauna in Midrash, Rashi, and Their Medieval Interlocutors," *Jewish Studies Quarterly* 17, no. 1 (2010): 69–70; Tom Hawkins, "Eloquent Alogia: Animal Narrators in Ancient Greek Literature," *Humanites* 6, no. 37 (2017): 1; Newmyer, "Being the One," 519.

Aristotle, Politics1.2 1253a 9-18:

τοῦτο γὰρ πρὸς τὰ ἄλλα ζῷα
τοῖς ἀνθρώποις ἴδιον, τὸ μόνον
ἀγαθοῦ καὶ κακοῦ καὶ δικαίου
καὶ ἀδίκου καὶ τῶν ἄλλων
αἴσθησιν ἔχειν:

for it is the special property of man in distinction from the other animals that he alone has perception of good and bad and right and wrong and the other moral qualities,

ἡ δὲ τούτων κοινωνία ποιεῖ οἰκί-
αν καὶ πόλιν.

and it is partnership in these things that makes a household and a city-state.[14]

Indeed it is implicit in Aristotle's famous definitions of the human being as a rational animal and a political animal that no other creatures share in the distinctive qualities of rationality or polis-society.[15] If other species, such as bees, do live in frameworks that appear to operate socially, or to take actions that conform to reason, then the definitions must be refined so

---

14 See also Aristotle, *Posterior Analytics*, ed. Hugh Tredennick, Loeb Classical Library 391 (Cambridge MA and London: Harvard University Press and William Heinemann Ltd., 1966), 1.10 76b; pp. 72–73.

15 See Gera, *Greek Ideas on Speech*, 36–37. Virtually all the writers who deal with this phenomenon are concerned with the language of animals as one key indicator of their possible intelligence. The present discussion will confine itself as strictly as possible to the issue of language and not deal with other aspects of their behavior. For a more general survey of ancient philosophical views on the rationality of animals, see Stephen Thomas Newmyer, "Speaking of Beasts: The Stoics and Plutarch on Animal Reason and the Modern Case against Animals," *Quaderni Urbinati di Cultura Classica* 63, no. 3, New Series (1999): 3–26, etc.; *Animals Sourcebook*, 59–60.

as not to equate phenomena that are not truly identical.[16] He[17] describes the anatomical features that a creature must possess in order to be able to produce sounds; but even these never go beyond the status of ψόφος (incoherent noise) and are not to be regarded as meaningful sound—φωνή. Essentially, Aristotle is here acknowledging that even though non-human creatures can, like Rabbi Judah's calf, communicate certain feelings or even facts by means of sounds, this is a far cry from the sort of coherent speech that equips humans uniquely to conduct rational discourse and thereby to make the moral judgements that are a precondition for political existence.[18] Nevertheless, recent scholarship has raised serious doubts

---

16 For an impressively erudite survey of the Greek concept of man as a "rational animal, [ζῷον λόγον ἔχον, etc.] see Robert Renehan, "The Greek Anthropocentric View of Man," *Harvard Studies in Classical Philology* 85 (1981): 239–259. Rehenan stresses how this definition is at once both distinctly Greek and a persistent fixture of subsequent Christian and Western thinking. Note especially p. 248 where he cites texts from Isocrates and Xenophon to illustrate how "An appreciation of rational speech, λόγος its external manifestation, was particularly characteristic of Greek thought." In n. 27 he astutely compares the Greek approach with that of Genesis. See also Laurence Berns, "Rational Animal-Political Animal: Nature and Convention in Human Speech and Politics," *The Review of Politics* 38, no. 2 (1976): 177–189; Miriam T. Larkin, *Language in the Philosophy of Aristotle* (The Hague and Paris: Mouton, 1971), 18–28; Wen Qiu, "Aristotle"s Definition of Language," *International Journal of English Literature and Culture* 2, no. 8 (2014): 194–202; Fögen, "Animal Communication," 220–221; Thorsten Fögen, "Pliny the Elder's Animals: Some Remarks on the Narrative Structure of Nat. Hist. 8–11," *Hermes* 135, no. 2 (2007): 189–190; Wolfram Ax, "Ψόφος, Φωνή Und Διάλεκτος Als Grundbegriffe Aristotelischer Sprachreflexion," *Glotta* 56, no. 3/4 (1978): 245–271; Jean-Louis Labarrière, "Aristote et la question du langage animal," *Mètis. Anthropologie des mondes grecs anciens* 8, no. 1 (1993): 247–260.

17 *History of Animals* 4:9:535a-536b: A. L. Peck, trans., *Aristotle: History of Animals, Books IV-VI*, Loeb Classical Library (London; Cambridge (Mass.): Harvard University Press, 1993), 72–77; see Fögen, "Animal Communication," 219.

18 The argument that human speech, unlike the sounds emitted by other species, is bound to an internal process of rational thought is found in Plato. See, e.g., *Theatetus* 189E-190A, *Sophist* 263E [Harold North Fowler, ed., *Plato with and English Translation*, vol. 2: Theaetetus, Sophist, Loeb Classical Library (London and Cambridge, MA: William Heinemann and Harvard University Press, 1952), 178–179, 440–443]. The text is cited by Richard Sorabji, *Animal Minds and Human Morals: The Origins of the Western Debate*, Cornell Studies in Classical Philology; The Townsend Lec-

about whether this particular passage in Aristotle, which appears in the context of a preliminary premise and is not repeated or otherwise stressed in his oeuvre, can fairly be accepted as his definitive position on the question.[19]

The Stoic Tradition

In ancient discourse about the ethical status of animals, it was usually the Stoics who were identified as the most consistent deniers of animal intelligence, speech or comprehension.[20] Their sharp distinction between animal sounds and human speech is central to justifying their position.[21]

Diogenes Laertius, Lives of Eminent Philosophers 7.55[22]

Τῆς δὲ διαλεκτικῆς θεωρίας συμφώνως δοκεῖ τοῖς πλείστοις ἀπὸ τοῦ περὶ φωνῆς ἐνάρχεσθαι τόπου. ἔστι δὲ φωνὴ ἀὴρ	In their theory of dialectic most of them [the Stoics] see fit to take as their starting-point the topic of voice. Now voice is a percussion

tures v. 54 (Ithaca, NY: Cornell University Press, 1993), 80 n. 17; Newmyer, "Speaking of Beasts," 103; Liliane Bodson, "Attitudes Toward Animals in Greco-Roman Antiquity," *Societal Attitudes Toward Animals* 1, no. 4 (1983): 314.

19 See Martha Craven Nussbaum, *Aristotle's De Motu Animalium: Text with Translation, Commentary, and Interpretive Essays* (Princeton: Princeton University Press, 1978), 95–97; Gary Steiner, *Anthropocentrism and Its Discontents: The Moral Status of Animals in the History of Western Philosophy* (Pittsburgh: University of Pittsburgh Press, 2005), 57–76.

20 See the discussion in Dierauer, *Tier und Mensch*, 234–38, etc.

21 Sorabji, *Animal Minds*, 20–28, 51–55, 58–61, 81–82, etc.; Newmyer, "Speaking of Beasts"; Gilhus, *Animals, Gods and Humans*, 39–41; Bodson, "Attitudes Toward Animals in Greco-Roman Antiquity," 314; Stephen R. L. Clark, "Animals in Classical and Late Antique Philosophy," in *The Oxford Handbook of Animal Ethics*, ed. Tom Beauchamp and R. G. Frey, vol. 1, Oxford Handbooks (Oxford: Oxford University Press, 2011), 46–47; Fögen, "Animal Communication," 221–223; Gera, *Greek Ideas on Speech*, 210; Gilhus, *Animals, Gods and Humans*, 3–4, 39–41.

22 Diogenes Laertius, *Lives of Eminent Philosophers*, ed. Robert Drew Hicks, The Loeb Classical Library (London, Cambridge, MA: W. Heinemann and Harvard University Press, 1931), 164–165; Stephen Thomas Newmyer, *Animals in Greek and Roman Thought: A Sourcebook*, Routledge sourcebooks for the ancient World (London and New York: Routledge, 2011), 60.

Diogenes Laertius, Lives of Eminent Philosophers 7.55

πεπληγμένος ἢ τὸ ἴδιον αἰσθητὸν ἀκοῆς, ὥς φησι Διογένης ὁ Βαβυλώνιος ἐν τῇ Περὶ φωνῆς τέχνῃ. ζῴου μέν ἐστι φωνὴ ἀὴρ ὑπὸ ὁρμῆς πεπληγμένος, ἀνθρώπου δ᾽ ἔστιν ἔναρθρος καὶ ἀπὸ διανοίας ἐκπεμπομένη, ὡς ὁ Διογένης φησίν, ἥτις ἀπὸ δεκατεσσάρων ἐτῶν τελειοῦται.

of the air or the proper object of the sense of hearing, as Diogenes the Babylonian[23] says in his handbook *On Voice*. While the voice or cry of an animal is just a percussion of air brought about by natural impulse, man's voice is articulate and, as Diogenes puts it, an utterance of reason,[24] having the quality of coming to maturity at the age of fourteen.[25]

The work "On Animals" (*De Animalibus*) attributed to Philo Judaeus of Alexandria, which has survived only in an early medieval Armenian version, has been universally accepted as authentic to him.[26] It is a sort of dia-

23 About him see Dirk Obbink and Paul A. Vander Waerdt, "Diogenes of Babylon: The Stoic Sage in the City of Fools," *Greek, Roman and Byzantine Studies* 32, no. 4 (1991): 355–396; D. M. Schenkeveld, "Studies in the History of Ancient Linguistics: III. The Stoic Texnh ΠΕΡΙ ΦΩΝΗΣ," *Mnemosyne* 43, no. 1/2 (1990): 86–108.

24 Plutarch *De Sollertia Animalium*, mocks the prominent Stoic Chrysippus for equating rationality with syntax: "because pigs do not have syntax, we may eat them." Richard Sorabji, *Animal Minds and Human Morals: The Origins of the Western Debate*, Cornell Studies in Classical Philology; The Townsend Lectures v. 54 (Ithaca, NY: Cornell University Press, 1993), 81; Henry Dyson, *Prolepsis and Ennoia in the Early Stoa* (Berlin: Walter de Gruyter, 2009), 105–106; Newmyer, *Animals Sourcebook*, 13; Ingvild Sælid Gilhus, *Animals, Gods and Humans: Changing Attitudes to Animals in Greek, Roman and Early Christian Ideas* (London: Routledge, 2006), 41–42; Liliane Bodson, "Attitudes Toward Animals in Greco-Roman Antiquity," *Societal Attitudes Toward Animals* 4, no. 4 (1983): 314.

25 Fourteen is designated as the age of full human vocal maturity by Pliny, *Natural History*, ed. H. (Harris) Rackham, Loeb Classical Library (Cambridge, MA: William Heinemann and Harvard University Press, 1972), 3:602-603; Thorsten Fögen, "Animal Communication," in *The Oxford Handbook of Animals in Classical Thought and Life*, ed. Gordon Lindsay Campbell, First Edition. (Oxford: Oxford University Press, 2014), 223..

26 Abraham Terian, ed., *Philonis Alexandrini De Animalibus*, Studies in Hellenistic Judaism no. 1 (Chico, Calif: Scholars Press, 1981); "A Critical Introduction to Philo's Dialogues," *Aufstieg und Niedergang des römischen Welt* 2, no. 21.1 (1984):

logue containing a lecture delivered by Philo's nephew Alexander, and followed by the response or rebuttal of Philo himself. Alexander, basing himself largely on anecdotal examples of clever beasts and birds, argued in favor of the fundamental rationality of animals, whereas Philo countered with fairly standard Stoic arguments against that thesis.[27] Like a good Stoic,[28] Philo built his case upon the distinction between "internal reason" (λόγος ἐνδιάτος) and "uttered reason" (λόγος προσὁρικος), claiming that though animals may possess the latter, they do not have the former,

289–291; Emil Schurer, *The History of the Jewish People in the Age of Jesus Christ (175 B.C.-A.D. 135)*, ed. Géza Vermès and Fergus Millar (Edinburgh: T. & T. Clark, 1973), 865–866; Newmyer, *Animals Sourcebook*, 10–14, 61–62; Ralph Marcus, "The Armenian Translation of Philo's 'Quaestiones in Genesim et Exodum,'" *Journal of Biblical Literature* 49, no. 1 (1930): 61–64; Lia Formigari, *A History of Language Philosophies*, trans. Gabriel Poole, Amsterdam Studies in the Theory and History of Linguistic science 105 (Amsterdam and Philadelphia: John Benjamins Pub, 2004), 48–50; James R. Royse, "The Original Structure of Philo's Quaestiones," in *Studia Philonica 1976-1977*, vol. 4 (Chicago: Philo Institute, 1978), 41–78; "The Works of Philo," in *The Cambridge Companion to Philo*, ed. Adam Kamesar (Cambridge: Cambridge University Press, 2009), 34–38; Katarzyna Jażdżewska, "Dialogic Format of Philo of Alexandria's De Animalibus," *Eos* 102 (2015): 45–56.

27 See Peder Borgen, "Man's Sovereignty Over Animals and Nature According to Philo of Alexandria," in *Texts and Contexts: Biblical Texts in Their Textual and Situational Contexts: Essays in Honor of Lars Hartman*, ed. Tord Fornberg and David Hellholm (Oslo: Scandinavian University Press, 1995), 369–389; R. K. French, *Ancient Natural History: Histories of Nature*, Sciences of Antiquity (London and New York: Routledge, 1994), 182–184; Isaak Heinemann, *Darkhe Ha-Agadah* (Jerusalem: Magnes Press, 1970), 157 and 249 n. 105.

28 See the survey above; and Robert M. Grant, "Theophilus of Antioch to Autolycus," *Harvard Theological Review* 40, no. 4 (1947): 245–249; see Brad Inwood, *Ethics and Human Action in Early Stoicism* (Oxford: Clarendon Press, 1985), 41, 268 n. 5; Tad Brennan, "Stoic Moral Psychology," in *The Cambridge Companion to the Stoics*, ed. Brad Inwood (Cambridge, UK: Cambridge University Press, 2003), 261; Formigari, *A History of Language Philosophies*, 28–29; Dierauer, *Tier und Mensch*, 253–259; Martin Achard, "Philosophie Antique. Logos Endiathetos et Théorie Des Lekta Chez Les Stoïciens," *Laval théologique et philosophique* 57, no. 2 (2001): 225–233; David Winston, "Aspects of Philo's Linguistic Theory," *The Studia Philonica Annual* 3 (1991): 109–125; Long, "Post-Aristotelian Philosophy," 639; Maren R. Niehoff, "Philo and Plutarch as Biographers: Parallel Responses to Roman Stoicism," *Greek, Roman, and Byzantine Studies* 52, no. 3 (2012): 361–392.

namely "articulated vocalization" which is the indispensable hallmark of true rationality.[29]

> However there are two kinds of reason: the one located in the mind is like a spring which issues from the sovereign part of the soul, whereas uttered reason is like a stream which, in the natural usage, courses over the lips and tongue and on to the sense of hearing. But although both kinds of reason appear to be imperfect in animals, they are none the less fundamental.[30]

Accordingly, any mere sounds that are produced by animals can prove nothing meaningful about their intelligence in that they are equivalent to the sounds that issue from musical instruments.[31] Only humans are endowed with the "λόγος προσόρικος"—uttered reason—that is made possible by the mind's governing principle (ἡγεμονικόν).

And though we might well interpret Rabbi Judah's erudite response to the calf as part of an internal conversation that he was conducting with his conscience, or as words that he spoke aloud for the benefit of listeners who might have been present (such as whoever it was whose recollection of the episode allowed it to be preserved in the talmudic corpus), it should be noted that several ancient Greek authorities acknowledged that the in-

---

29 See Thomas M. Conley, "Philo's Rhetoric: Studies in Style, Composition, and Exegesis," Monograph of the Center for Hermeneutical Studies in Hellenistic and Modern Culture 1 (Berkeley: Center for Hermeneutical Studies in Hellenistic and Modern Culture, 1987), 65; Manuel Alexandre Júnior, *Rhetorical Argumentation in Philo of Alexandria*, Brown Judaic Studies Studia Philonica Monographs 322. 2 (Atlanta: Scholars Press, 1999), 249; Adam Kamesar, "The Logos Endiathetos and the Logos Prophorikos in Allegorical Interpretation: Philo and the D-Scholia to the Iliad," *Greek, Roman and Byzantine Studies* 44, no. 2 (2004): 163 and n. 1; James I. Porter, "Philo's Confusion of Tongues: Some Methodological Observations," *Quaderni Urbinati di Cultura Classica* 24, no. 3, New Series (1986): 60 n. 6; Stephen Thomas Newmyer, "Being the One and Becoming the Other: Animals in Ancient Philosophical Schools," in *The Oxford Handbook of Animals in Classical Thought and Life*, ed. George Lindsay Campbell (Oxford: Oxford University Press, 2014), 522.

30 Terian, *Philonis Alexandrini De Animalibus*, 11–12; Newmyer, *Animals Sourcebook*, 13; Gilhus, *Animals, Gods and Humans*, 42–44. See also *De migratione Abrahami* 13.71; Porter, "Philo's Confusion of Tongues: Some Methodological Observations," 59.

31 Newmyer, *Animals Sourcebook*, 61–62.

telligence of animals extended to an ability to understand human speech (though presumably not to catch an allusion to the Mishnah).

Neoplatonists and Skeptics

In the preceding chapter we had occasion to read Diogenes Laertius' account of Pythagoras' intercession on behalf of a distressed pup on the grounds that the canine body was currently inhabited by a transmigrated human soul.[32] This argument was also made by Empedocles,[33] Plutarch and others.[34] The idea was usually expressed in a general sense, to prove

32 This idea was widely associated with Pythagoras by ancient writers. In the speech that Ovid placed in Pythagoras' mouth in Metamorphoses 15:166-175, it says, "The spirit wanders, comes now here, now there, and occupies whatever frame it pleases. From beasts it passes into human bodies, and from our bodies into beasts, but never perishes... so do I teach that the soul is ever the same, though it passes into ever-changing bodies. Therefore, lest your piety be overcome by appetite... do not drive out by impious slaughter what may be kindred souls" [G. P. Goold, ed., *Ovid: Metamorphosis*, trans. Frank Justus Miller, vol. 3, Loeb Classical Library 43 (Cambridge, MA and London: Harvard University Press and W. Heinemann, 1977), 3:376-377]. In his diatribe against Marcion, the church father Epiphanius also inferred a connection between belief in reincarnation and refraining from meat in the doctrines of several Christian groups that he stigmatized as heresies: "For Valentinus and Colorbasus, and all Gnostics and Manichaeans, claim that there is a reincarnation of souls as well as transmigrations of the souls of ignorant persons"; [Frank Williams, trans., *Panarion of Epiphanius of Salamis. Book I (Sections 1-46)*, 2nd ed., revised and expanded., Nag Hammadi and Manichaean Studies 63 (Leiden and Boston: Brill, 2009), Elenchus 24 (p. 322)]; see Gilhus, *Animals, Gods and Humans*, 268–269; John Davidson, *The Gospel of Jesus: In Search of His Original Teachings* (Rockport, MA: Element, 1995), 424–436. On the thesis that Plato's doctrine of reincarnation implies that humans and animals share a common soul see Heath, *The Talking Greeks*, 7 and works listed in n. 22; 313 n. 137.

33 Cited by Plutarch, *De Esu Carnium* 1:7 (p. 559); see Damianos Tsekourakis, "Pythagoreanism or Platonism and Ancient Medicine: The Reasons for Vegetarianism in Plutarch's 'Moralia,'" in *Aufstieg Und Niedergang Der Römischen Welt / Rise and Decline of the Roman World*, ed. Wolfgang Haase and Hildegard Temporini, vol. Vol. 36.1, Part II: Principate (Berlin and New York: Walter de Gruyter, 1987), 367–375. Plutarch directs his arguments explicitly against the Stoics.

34 Historians have long argued over the question of whether the belief in metempsychosis or reincarnation entered Greek thought from foreign sources (Indian or Egyptian) or evolved locally; Walter Burkert, *Lore and Science in Ancient Pythagorean-*

that the animals share a kinship with humans, but few authors went so far as to analyze the full implications of the premise.[35] We do not see the beasts (with the possible exception of parrot-like birds) uttering words or sentences. Is this (as claimed by Aristotle) an anatomical limitation of their vocal system? If so, then we would probably have to accept that animals are capable of rationally understanding the syntactical speech that that they hear from humans around them. On the other hand, since the belief extends to human spirits transmigrating into plants and perhaps even inanimate objects, does this require us to conclude that the spirits somehow forfeit their linguistic rationality as they move to lower planes of existence?[36]

---

ism, trans. Edwin L. Minar Jr. (Cambridge, Mass: Harvard University Press, 1972), 133; see, e.g., A. Berriedale Keith, "Pythagoras and the Doctrine of Transmigration," *Journal of the Royal Asiatic Society of Great Britain and Ireland* (1909): 569–606; Felix M. Cleve, *The Giants of Pre-Sophistic Greek Philosophy: An Attempt to Reconstruct Their Thoughts*, 3d ed. (The Hague: Martinus Nijhoff, 1973), 2:496-503, 519–520; Christoph Riedweg, *Pythagoras: His Life, Teaching, and Influence*, trans. Steven Rendall (Ithaca: Cornell University Press, 2005), 26, 55–56. For readable surveys that explain Pythagoras' role in the evolution of afterlife ideas among the Greeks, and the diverse interpretations, customs and problematic features of those beliefs among subsequent Hellenic thinkers, see Jan N. Bremmer, *The Rise and Fall of the Afterlife: The 1995 Read-Tuckwell Lectures at the University of Bristol* (London and New York: Routledge, 2002), 11–15; Carl Huffman, "The Pythagorean Conception of the Soul from Pythagoras to Philolaus," in *Body and Soul in Ancient Philosophy*, ed. Dorothea Frede and Burkhard Reis (Berlin and Boston: De Gruyter, 2009), 21–44; Riedweg, *Pythagoras*, 62–63; Leonid Zhmud, *Pythagoras and the Early Pythagoreans*, trans. Kevin Windle and Rosh Ireland (Oxford: Oxford University Press, 2012), 221–236.

35 For an instructive survey of several scholars who did pose such questions see Burkert, *Lore and Science*, 133–135. Porphyry wrote that "since they are kin, if it appeared that they have also, as Pythagoras said, been allocated the same soul, someone who did not refrain from injustice towards relatives would justly be judged impious" [G. Clarke, trans., *Porphyry: On Abstinence from Killing Animals*, Ancient Commentaries on Aristotle (London, New Delhi, New York and Sydney: Bloomsbury, 2014), 3:26:1 (p. 97)].

36 In Plutarch's dialogue "Gryllus" or "Beasts are Rational," it is a uniquely articulate pig who argues for the superiority of animals over humans (transl. Cherniss and Helmmhold 12;492-531); see Clark, "Animals in Philosophy," 38, 49; Fögen, "Animal Communication," 222–223; cf. Gera, *Greek Ideas on Speech*, 12; Hawkins,

The Neoplatonist Porphyry pointed out that those animals that are taught to obey human calls,[37] or even to imitate human sounds on command, must possess a degree of comprehension;[38] and he assembles a considerable body of anecdotal evidence about animals—and especially birds—who, while perhaps not able to speak grammatical sentences in the language of humans (usually identified as Greek), provided serious reason to believe that they were processing information in ways that attest to real intelligence.[39] Indeed, he proposes that we relate to animal communications as we would to strange and foreign human languages, in which case we

---

"Eloquent Alogia," 7–10. It is hard to decide how seriously we are intended to take the arguments raised in a whimsical work that, after all, takes the form of a debate between Odysseus and a companion whom Circe has transformed into a swine. At any rate, the crux of Gryllus' case, as found in #9 (pp. 525–530) is that, notwithstanding their ability to obey spoken human instructions, it is the self-taught (= instinctive?) capabilities demonstrated by animals that reveal their superior degree of intelligence. Porphyry [*On Abstinence* 3:27] claimed that the Pythagorean ethic did indeed urge refraining from causing avoidable harm to plants; see Tsekourakis, "Pythagoreanism or Platonism," 372.

37 See Newmyer, "Being the One," 512–515, 530–531. Note also Xenophon's advice with regards to the best names to apply to dogs, in his *Cynegeticus* ("On Hunting") 7:5 [E. C. Marchant, *Xenophon: Scripta Minora*, The Loeb Classical Library (London and New York: W. Heinemann and G.P. Putnam's Sons, 1918), 414–415]; cited by Steven H. Lonsdale, "Attitudes towards Animals in Ancient Greece," *Greece & Rome* 26, no. 2 (1979): 149.

38 "One central argument for animal rationality in Book 3 is that animals have language (see e.g. 3.3-4). Porphyry takes this to be an obvious truth" [Miira Tuominen, *The Ancient Commentators on Plato and Aristotle*, Ancient Philosophies 6 (Berkeley: University of California Press, 2009), 276].

39 *De Abstinentia* 3.3-6 [Thomas Taylor, trans., *Porphyry: Selected Works*, Great Works of Philosophy Series 6 (Lawrence, KN: Selene Books, 1988), 94–101; Clarke, *Porphyry on Abstinence*, 81–85, 166–167]; cited by Sorabji, *Animal Minds*, 82; Newmyer, "Speaking of Beasts," 106; Formigari, *A History of Language Philosophies*, 50; Clark, "Animals in Philosophy," 37–38, 46; Lonsdale, "Attitudes towards Animals in Ancient Greece," 152; Dierauer, *Tier und Mensch*, 80–89, 170–172; Benjamin Acosta-Hughes, *Polyeideia: The Iambi of Callimachus and the Archaic Iambic Tradition*, Hellenistic Culture and Society 35 (Berkeley: University of California Press, 2002), 188–189; Fögen, "Animal Communication," 217, 219, 222; Gilhus, *Animals, Gods and Humans*, 26.

acknowledge that the foreigners are conversing in real languages even though we might not happen to know how to decipher them.[40]

A similar position was advocated by the Skeptic philosopher and physician Sextus Empiricus:[41]

Sextus Empiricus, Outlines of Pyrrhonism I, 74-76:

μάλιστα μὲν ὁρῶμεν τὰ ζῷα, περὶ ὧν ὁ λόγος, καὶ ἀνθρωπίνας προφερόμενα φωνάς, ὡς κίττας καὶ ἄλλα τινά. ἵνα δὲ καὶ τοῦτο ἐάσωμεν, εἰ καὶ μὴ συνίεμεν τὰς φωνὰς τῶν ἀλόγων καλουμένων ζῴων, ὅλως οὐκ ἔστιν ἀπεικὸς διαλέγεσθαι μὲν ταῦτα ἡμᾶς δὲ μὴ συνιέναι· καὶ γὰρ τῆς τῶν βαρβάρων φωνῆς ἀκούοντες οὐ συνίεμεν ἀλλὰ μονοειδῆ ταύτην εἶναι δοκοῦμεν.

...we certainly see animals—the subject of our argument—uttering quite human cries,—jays, for instance, and others. And, leaving this point also aside, even if we do not understand the utterances of the so-called irrational animals, still it is not improbable that they converse although we fail to understand them; for in fact when we listen to the talk of barbarians we do not understand it, and it seems to us a kind of uniform chat-

---

40   In support for this claim he brings ancient literary and recent anecdotal accounts of individuals who were able to understand the speech of various creatures. See Newmyer, *Animals Sourcebook*, 67. Porphyry includes some brief thoughts about why the Jews, along with the Phoenecians, abstain from eating pig, based on this theory that societies refrain from consuming animals that perform useful functions, whereas pigs are not found at all in the lands of the Jews, Phoenecians or Ethopians. He remarks that Hebrews would face death rather than violate the sacred prohibition, even in the face of a royal decree; a virtue that he contrasts with his own people's readiness to submit to human opinion. See *De Abstinentia* 1:14; 2:61 (transl. T. Taylor, 12, 32]; Menahem Stern, *Greek and Latin Authors on Jews and Judaism*, Fontes ad Res Judaicas Spectantes (Jerusalem: Israel Academy of Sciences and Humanities, 1974), 2:424, 433–435.

41   For a rigorous analysis of the very little that can be known with certainty about this philosopher's time, place and life, see D. K. House, "The Life of Sextus Empiricus," *The Classical Quarterly* 30, no. 1 (1980): 227–238; see also Mary Mills Patrick, *Sextus Empiricus and Greek Scepticism* (Cambridge: Deighton Bell & Co., 1899); Dierauer, *Tier und Mensch*, 256; Fögen, "Animal Communication," 222; see also Long, "Post-Aristotelian Philosophy," 636.

Sextus Empiricus, Outlines of Pyrrhonism I, 74-76:

ter..[42]

Concluding Observations

One way or another, it is clear that questions related to the status of animal languages were a serious and on-going topic of inquiry among philosophers in the Greco-Roman world, a topic that was understood to have major implications with regard to defining humanity's place in the hierarchy of the universe,[43] as well as for determining correct ethical policies for the obtaining of food and the humane treatment of animals.[44] The central current of philosophical thinking extending from pre-Socratics through Aristotle, Plato and especially the Stoics, seemed determined to deny the linguistic competence of non-humans.

---

42 [Robert Gregg Bury, ed., *Sextus Empiricus*, vol. 1, The Loeb classical Library (London and Cambridge, MA: William Heinemann and Harvard University Press, 1961), 44–45]. See Lia Formigari, *A History of Language Philosophies*, trans. Gabriel Poole, Amsterdam Studies in the Theory and History of Linguistic science 105 (Amsterdam and Philadelphia: John Benjamins Pub, 2004), 47; Newmyer, *Animals Sourcebook*, 65; Lucynda Kostuch, "Do Animals Have a Homeland? Ancient Greeks on the Cultural Identity of Animals," *Humanimalia* 9, no. 1 (2017): 73. Hesiod's description of the fearsome monster Typhon includes mention of its numerous heads some of which "uttered every kind of sound unspeakable, for at one time they made sounds such that gods understood" [φθέγγονθ᾽ ὥστε θεοῖσι συνιέμεν] (Theogeny 830); cited by Steven H. Lonsdale, "Attitudes towards Animals in Ancient Greece," *Greece & Rome* 26, no. 2 (1979): 157–158; see also Jenny Strauss Clay, "The Generation of Monsters in Hesiod," *Classical Philology* 88, no. 2 (1993): 110. On the equating of barbarians with wild beasts see Gilhus, *Animals, Gods and Humans*, 228, 264.

43 A low opinion of the spiritual or intellectual ability of animals was also relevant to the Greeks' general aversion to the Egyptian depictions of their gods in the form of animals; Clark, "Animals in Philosophy," 43; Gilhus, *Animals, Gods and Humans*, 229.

44 In addition to the works cited in the previous section, see Heath, *The Talking Greeks*, especially 213-314; Robert M. Grant, *Early Christians and Animals* (London and New York: Routledge, 1999), 10–11.

There were nevertheless dissenters to the dominant position, among Neoplatonists and Skeptics, who were prepared to consider that animals (especially parrots and similar birds) are imbued with modes of communication that demonstrate rational thinking and might function in ways that are comparable to human speech.

To a significant extent all the sides were taking into account the empirical evidence of animal behavior, and their arguments are backed by impressively detailed naturalistic observation. For the majority school, the social communication conducted by animals, as long as it is not governed by the truly rational λόγος προσόρικος that can only be expressed in grammatical speech (preferably in Greek), was a mere instinctive trait that was not enough to elevate the beasts to the status of what the Judeo-Christian traditions would regard as a holy or divinely imbued soul. The dissenters, particularly when advocating vegetarianism, could effectively invoke the same evidence to assert the fundamental intelligence—and hence the ethical "sanctity"—that is common to all zoological species.

Sharpened Tongues like a Serpent

The Talking Snake in Non-Rabbinic Jewish Texts

THE THING ABOUT WORDS IS THAT MEANINGS CAN
TWIST JUST LIKE A SNAKE, AND IF YOU WANT TO FIND
SNAKES LOOK FOR THEM BEHIND WORDS THAT HAVE
CHANGED THEIR MEANING.[1]

It is very understandable that questions regarding animal languages would arise among Jewish readers, particularly in connection with the character of the snake in Genesis Chapter 3[2]. It is assumed there as a perfectly natu-

---

1   Terry Pratchett, *Lords And Ladies* (Random House, 2008), 179.

2   Note that the same cannot be said for the Bible's other famous talking beast, Balaam's ass. In that case, the text makes it clear that the angel of the Lord was invisibly manipulating the animal's uncooperative behavior (Numbers 22:22), and in the end (verse 28) "the Lord opened the mouth of the ass" to argue with Balaam. Rabbinic tradition classified this as a rare miracle; see *m*.Avot 5:6: "Ten things were created at twilight [of the first Friday]: the mouth of the earth [that swallowed up Korach and his congregation], the mouth of the well [that accompanied the Israelites in the wilderness] and the mouth of the ass..."; see Shimon Sharvit, *Tractate Avoth Through the Ages: A Critical Edition, Prolegomena and Appendices* (Jerusalem: The Bialik Institute and the Ben-Yehuda Center for the History of Hebrew, The Hebrew University of Jerusalem, 2004), 186 [Hebrew]; Ze'ev Safrai, *Mishnat Eretz Israel: Tractate Avot (Neziqin 7): With Historical and Sociological Commentary* (Mishnat Eretz Israel Project, 2013), 311 [Hebrew]; Louis Ginzberg, *The Legends of the Jews*, trans. Henrietta Szold (Philadelphia, PA: The Jewish Publication Society of America, 1909), 5:109, n. 99. Isaak Heinemann suggested that Philo omitted mention of Balaam's ass in his writings because it contradicted his rationalistic approach to the consistency of the laws of nature; *Darkhe Ha-Agadah* (Jerusalem: Magnes Press, 1970), 80, 156. Nevertheless, as will be noted below, medieval Jewish commentators would direct their attention to this episode, whether to elucidate the precise mechanism by

---

ral state of affairs that the snake was able to take part in conversations with Eve and with God. Though he is initially introduced as being "more subtle (ערום) than any beast of the field" (Genesis 3:1), there is no specific indication in the text that it is his ability to speak or understand a human-like language that constitutes the defining feature of his extraordinary subtlety or intelligence,[3] nor is this mentioned in verse 14 in connection with the changes that God imposes on the snake (and his species) as punish-

means of which the ass was made to speak, or in order to compare it with the speaking of the snake in the garden of Eden. See Ingvild Sælid Gilhus, *Animals, Gods and Humans: Changing Attitudes to Animals in Greek, Roman and Early Christian Ideas* (London: Routledge, 2006), 162–163. An instance from Greek literature that might be comparable is Homer's *Iliad* 19:403-408 in which "from beneath the yoke spake to [Achilles] the horse Xanthus, of the swift-glancing feet;... and the goddess, white-armed Hera, gave him speech [αὐδήεντα δ᾽ ἔθηκε θεὰ λευκώλενος Ἥρη]: "Aye verily, yet for this time will we save thee, mighty Achilles, etc." [Homer, *Iliad*, ed. William F. Wyatt, trans. A. T. Murray, 2nd ed., Loeb Classical Library 170–171 (Cambridge, Mass: Harvard University Press, 1999), 2:364-365]. Although it seems quite obvious that this was a case of special divine interference and not a general attributing of speech to Xanthus or other horses, the passage generated some discussion among ancient and modern commentators. Chrysippus stressed that the Greek terms employed by Homer demonstrate that the horse was not being enabled to make any normal equine sounds, but was being endowed with the human capability of speech [Hans Friedrich August von Arnim, *Stoicorum Veterum Fragmenta*, Editio stereotypa editionis primae., Sammlung wissenschaftlicher Commentare (München: K.G. Saur, 2004), 2:144 p. 2:44; John Heath, *The Talking Greeks: Speech, Animals, and the Other in Homer, Aeschylus, and Plato* (Cambridge: Cambridge University Press, 2005), 39-40 and n. 3; 54; Jenny Strauss Clay, "Demas and Aude: The Nature of Divine Transformation in Homer," *Hermes* 102 (1974): 132]. Similarly, S. I. Johnston argues that a careful reading indicates that Hera was not merely placing a particular text in the horse's mouth for the occasion, but was giving him the ability to be a speaking creature, thereby evoking an older epic tradition of wondrous horses); see "Xanthus, Hera and the Erinyes (Iliad 19.400-418)," *Transactions of the American Philological Association (1974-)* 122 (1992): 87 and n. 6; 95–98; Caroline Alexander, *The War That Killed Achilles: The True Story of the Iliad* (London: Faber & Faber, 2010), 262 n. 27. As Heath put it: "The horse does not have the power to speak what it chooses—Xanthus is no Mr. Ed." Similar questions could be posed with respect to Balaam's ass: Was the angel performing an act of ventriloquism on a completely passive beast; or was it bestowing on her the ability to express her own thoughts? At any rate, neither option, it would seem, indicates that the animal in its

ment for his misdeed.[4]

This topic was of concern to several Jewish authors who were writing during the Second Temple era, and their combined testimonies indicate the development of relatively detailed exegetical traditions regarding the linguistic competence of animals in the earliest stage of creation.

The Book of Jubilees

The Pseudepigraphic *Book of Jubilees*,[5] an expanded version of parts of Genesis, inserts (3:28) the following short addition after its account of the snake's being cursed by God for his role in enticing Eve and Adam to sin in the garden of Eden:[6]

> normal state possesses the power of verbal communication (though it might have implications with respect to her ability to understand human speech). See George W. Savran, "Beastly Speech: Intertextuality, Balaam's Ass and the Garden of Eden," *Journal for the Study of the Old Testament* 64 (December 1994): 33–55 especially 39-40; Robert Alter, *The Art of Biblical Narrative*, Rev. & updated ed. (New York: Basic Books, 2011), 133; Jonathan D. Safren, "Balaam and Abraham," *Vetus Testamentum* 38, no. 1 (1988): 107–108.

3　Cf. H. W. Basser, "Josephus as Exegete," *Journal of the American Oriental Society* 107, no. 1 (1987): 27.

4　On the special religious status of snakes in Greco-Roman culture, which might have had some influence on Jewish attitudes towards the species, see Gilhus, *Animals, Gods and Humans*, 108–111. On tame and domesticated snakes see Francis D. Lazenby, "Greek and Roman Household Pets (1)," *The Classical Journal* 44, no. 4 (1949): 248–249.

5　For a comprehensive study of Jubilees, its method, ideology and religious views, see Cana Werman, *The Book of Jubilees: Introduction, Translation, and Interpretation*, Between Bible and Mishnah: The David and Jemima Jeselsohn Library (Jerusalem: Yad Izhak Ben-Zvi, 2015), 1–77 [Hebrew]; Michael Segal, *The Book of Jubilees: Rewritten Bible, Redaction, Ideology, and Theology*, Supplements to the Journal for the Study of Judaism 117 (Atlanta: Society of Biblical Literature, 2007). This passage is not discussed there.

6　R. H. Charles, ed., "The Book of Jubilees," in *The Apocrypha and Pseudepigrapha of the Old Testament*, vol. 2: Pseudepigrapha (Oxford: Clarendon Press, 1913, 1913), 17; George H. Schodde, trans., *The Book of Jubilees* (Oberlin, OH: E. J. Goodrich, 1888), (2:24) 13; Werman, *Jubilees*, 189. Charles provides an extensive listing of ancient works that have versions of this "common Jewish belief"; including: Josephus *Antiquities* [see below], "Conflict of Adam and Eve," and Philo, *Quaestiones in Gen.*

On that day [of Adam's expulsion from Eden] was closed the mouth[7] of all beasts... so that they could no longer speak; for they had spoken one with another with one lip and with one tongue.

The author of this addition was evidently trying to reconcile the inconsistency between the early chapters of Genesis, in which snakes (and perhaps other creatures as well) were able to speak, with the subsequent narrative —as well as the empirical reality of our world in which this is no longer the case.[8] The text in Jubilees implies that in nature's primordial state all creatures shared a common language—presumably Hebrew, the language

1:32. On the primordial language as Hebrew: Targum Yerushalmi to Genesis 11:1; J. VanderKam, *The Book of Jubilees*, Guides to Apocrypha and Pseudepigrapha (Sheffield: Sheffield Academic Press, 2001), 32.] stresses that the wording in Jubilees implies that not only the snake but *all* creatures had been capable of speech prior to the sin in the garden of Eden. See also James L. Kugel, *A Walk Through Jubilees: Studies in the Book of Jubilees and the World of Its Creation*, Supplements to the Journal for the Study of Judaism v. 156 (Leiden and Boston: Brill, 2012), 42; John C. Poirier, *The Tongues of Angels: The Concept of Angelic Languages in Classical Jewish and Christian Texts* (Tübingen: Mohr Siebeck, 2010), 13; Michael E. Stone and Esther Eshel, "4QExposition on the Patriarchs," in *Qumran Cave 4*, ed. Magen Broshi, vol. 14: Parabiblical Texts, Discoveries in the Judean Desert 19 (Oxford: Clarendon Press, 1995), 219–221; Zvi Ron, "The Book of Jubilees and the Midrash on the Early Chapters of Genesis," *Jewish Bible Quarterly* 41, no. 3 (2013): 146–147; Umberto Eco, *The Search for the Perfect Language*, trans. James Fentress, Making of Europe (Oxford, UK and Cambridge, MA: Blackwell, 1995), 41–45, 112, 115.

7   Perhaps this explanation was inspired by the wording of the Hebrew text (Genesis 3:14): "dust shalt thou eat all the days of thy life."

8   We find out further on in the story (12:25-27) that the original language of creation, Hebrew, had to be re-learned by Abraham from the instruction of the angel narrator, "for from the day of the collapse it had disappeared from the mouths of all mankind." It was only then that Abraham was able to read and copy "his father's books." Most scholars seem to identify the "day of the collapse" with the tower of Babel episode; but it is conceivable that it refers to the expulsion from Eden and somehow ties into the current passage—implying that humans were also deprived of their knowledge of the sacred language, perhaps to prevent its great power from being abused. This narrative as regards the primacy of Hebrew became influential in Christian tradition largely through Augustine's *City of God* 16:11. Milka Rubin, "The Language of Creation or the Primordial Language: A Case of Cultural Polemics in Antiquity," *Journal of Jewish Studies* 49, no. 2 (1998): 306–333; Yonatan Moss, "The Language of Paradise: Hebrew or Syriac? Linguistic Speculations and Linguistic Realities in Late Antiquities," in *Paradise in Antiquity: Jewish and Christian*

of creation and revelation[9]; but as a result of the snake's abuse of that ability, God now removed it not only from him and his species, but from all creatures other than humans.[10]

The same premise was stated by Josephus Flavius in his paraphrase of Genesis in *the Jewish Antiquities*.[11]

Views, ed. Markus N. A. Bockmuehl and Guy G. Stroumsa (Cambridge and New York: Cambridge University Press, 2010), 120–137; Deborah Levine Gera, *Ancient Greek Ideas on Speech, Language, and Civilization* (Oxford and New York: Oxford University Press, 2003), 21; Steven D. Fraade, "Moses and Adam as Polyglots," in *Envisioning Judaism: Studies in Honor of Peter Schäfer on the Occasion of His Seventieth Birthday*, ed. Raanan Shaul Boustan et al., vol. 1, 2 vols. (Tübingen: Mohr Siebeck, 2013), 186–194; J. T. A. G. M. van. Ruiten, *Primaeval History Interpreted: The Rewriting of Genesis 1-11 in the Book of Jubilees* (Boston: Brill, 2000), 119–120, 348–360; Seth Schwartz, "Language, Power and Identity in Ancient Palestine," *Past & Present*, no. 148 (1995): 29–31; Phillip Michael Sherman, *Babel's Tower Translated: Genesis 11 and Ancient Jewish Interpretation*, Biblical Interpretation Series 117 (Leiden: Brill, 2013), 113–120; Tom Hawkins, "Eloquent Alogia: Animal Narrators in Ancient Greek Literature," *Humanites* 6, no. 37 (2017): 3. For our current purposes it is convenient to separate the question of the primordial language of creation (the one spoken by Eve, Adam and the snake) from that of the universal language spoken before the division of tongues at the tower of Babel. A very precise formulation of the issue may be found in Rubin 312.

9　See Menahem M. Kasher, *Torah Shelemah (The Complete Torah)* (Jerusalem, Israel: The Torah Shelemah Institute, 1992), 1:251-252 [Hebrew]; Elimelech Epstein-Halevi, *Parashiyot Ba-Agadah Le-or Meḵorot Yevaniyyim* (Haifa: Haifa University Press, 1973), 44 [Hebrew].

10　When we bear in mind the treatment of this topic in Greek philosophic literature, we might find good reasons to expect our author to demonstrate some awareness of the relationship between general rationality and the specific ability to express things in spoken language. In the present instance, ambiguity exists as to whether the "closing of their mouths" left the animal species rational but merely unable to express their thoughts coherently. But the authors of these texts were after all not philosophers and were unlikely to have been concerned with such theoretical matters.

11　For a readable and eminently knowledgeable survey of the exegetical character of the *Antiquities*, including its relationships to other works and traditions of the time, see Louis H. Feldman, "Josephus as Rewriter of the Bible," in *Josephus's Interpreta-*

Josephus Flavius and the Universal Language

Flavius Josephus, Jewish Antiquities 1:4:[12]

[41] ὁμοφωνούντων δὲ κατ᾽ ἐκεῖνο καιροῦ τῶν ζῴων ἁπάντων ὄφις συνδιαιτώμενος τῷ τε Ἀδάμῳ καὶ τῇ γυναικὶ φθονερῶς μὲν εἶχεν ἐφ᾽ οἷς αὐτοὺς εὐδαιμονήσειν ᾤετο πεπεισμένους τοῖς τοῦ θεοῦ παραγγέλμασιν;

[41] But while all the living creatures had one language, at that time the serpent, which then lived together with Adam and his wife, shewed an envious disposition, at his supposal of their living happily, and in obedience to the commands of God;

[42] οἰόμενος δὲ συμφορᾷ περιπεσεῖσθαι παρακούσαντας ἀναπείθει κακοήθως τὴν γυναῖκα γεύσασθαι τοῦ φυτοῦ τῆς φρονήσεως ἐν αὐτῷ λέγων εἶναι τήν τε τἀγαθοῦ καὶ τοῦ κακοῦ διάγνωσιν, ἧς γενομένης αὐτοῖς μακάριον καὶ μηδὲν ἀπολείποντα τοῦ θείου διάξειν βίον.

[42] and imagining, that when they disobeyed them, they would fall into calamities, he persuaded the woman, out of a malicious intention, to taste of the tree of knowledge, telling them, that in that tree was the knowledge of good and evil; which knowledge, when they should obtain, they would lead a happy life; nay, a life not inferior to that of a god

It appears more probable that Josephus's introduction of the "common language" theme[13] was stimulated by exegetical considerations arising

---

tion of the Bible, Hellenistic Culture and Society 27 (Berkeley, Los Angeles, London: University of California Press, 1998), 14–73.

12   H. St. John Thackeray, *Josephus: With an English Translation*, vol. 4, Loeb Classical Library (London and New York: William Heinemann Ltd. and G. P. Putnam's Sons, 1926), 20–21; Flavius Josephus, *Flavius Josephus, Translation and Commentary*, ed. Louis H. Feldman, vol. 3: Judean Antiquities I–IV (Leiden, Boston, Koln: Brill, 2000), 16–18, nn. 90, 104.

13   Note Whiston's note [*The Complete Works of Josephus Flavius* (Nashville: T. Nelson Publishers, 1998).] containing an extensive excursus about his own "conjecture" regarding the primordial universal language. See also Basser, "Josephus as Exegete"; Ann Cline Kelly, "Talking Animals in the Bible: Paratexts as Symptoms of Cultural Anxiety in Restoration and Early Eighteenth-Century England," *Journal for Eighteenth-Century Studies* 33, no. 4 (2010): 446–447; Harry Austryn Wolfson, "The Veracity of Scripture in Philo, Halevi, Maimonides, and Spinoza," in *Alexander*

from the specific biblical text than that he was transmitting a received tradition.[14] Josephus's anticipation of reactions from skeptical readers would likely have impelled him to come up with an explanation for how a snake could be conversing with human beings.[15] Because he ascribes speaking ability equally to all species in the primordial state of creation, there was no need for him to come up with a profound metaphysical or scientific reason why it was the snake who was assigned the role of instigating the disobedience of the first human couple; its psychological motivation was nothing deeper than petty envy at Adam and Eve's domestic contentment which gave rise to a desire to sabotage their relationship with God.[16] Conceivably, Josephus felt that any other species could have served that narrative purpose just as well.

Unlike Jubilees' author, Josephus does not provide an explanation for when or how the initial situation came to an end.

Philo Judaeus of Alexandria

In Philo of Alexandria's allegorical homily on the creation of the world,[17]

Marx; Jubilee Volume on the Occasion of His Seventieth Birthday, ed. Saul Lieberman, vol. English Section (New York: The Jewish Theological Seminary of America, 1950), 612–613.

14 I am here following the methodological approach to the study of the exegetical literature of the Second Temple period as outlined by Israel Knohl:

> Even though much of this literature does not explicitly present itself as exegesis, scholars have shown that numerous details in these texts, and particularly in those narratives that expand upon the biblical narrative, can best be appreciated when viewed as interpretations. Indeed, the interpretative element in these texts seems to be onf their most important defining characteristics" ["Cain: Son of God or Son of Satan?," in *Jewish Biblical Interpretation and Cultural Exchange*, ed. Natalie B. Dohrmann and David Stern, Jewish Culture and Contexts (Philadelphia: University of Pennsylvania Press, 2008), 37].

15 Compare with the very systematic discussion of the pertinent exegetical possibilities and pitfalls in William Adler and Paul Tuffin, trans., *The Chronography of George Synkellos: A Byzantine Chronicle of Universal History from the Creation* (New York and Oxford: Oxford University Press, 2002), 11.

16 See Basser, "Josephus as Exegete," 27–28.

17 The prevalent scholarly classification places *De Opificio Mundi* among Philo's "Expositions of the Law" works rather than his "Allegorical Commentary." For discus-

which contains interpretations of the first three chapters of Genesis, the Jewish philosopher insists [56 (157)][18] that the episode of the serpent ("It is said that in olden time the venomous earth-born crawling thing could send forth a man's voice, and that one day it approached the wife of the first man and upbraided her for her slowness and her excessive prudence"[19]) should not be treated as a frivolous literary fantasy of the sort produced by conventional poets:[20]

Philo, De Opificio Mundi, 56 (157):

Ἔστι δὲ ταῦτα οὐ μύθου πλάσματα, οἷς τὸ ποιητικὸν καὶ σοφιστικὸν χαίρει γένος, ἀλλὰ δείγματα τύπων ἐπ᾽ ἀλληγορίαν παρακαλοῦντα κατὰ δι᾽ ὑπονοιῶν ἀποδόσεις. ἑπόμενος δέ τις εἰκότι στοχασμῷ φήσει προσηκόντως τὸν εἰρημένον ὄφιν ἡδονῆς εἶναι σύμβολον.

Now these are no mythical fictions, such as poets and sophists delight in, but modes of making ideas visible, bidding us resort to allegorical interpretation guided in our renderings by what lies beneath the surface. Following a probable conjecture one would say that the serpent spoken of is a

sions of the classification, and the place of this work within it, see Emil Schurer, *The History of the Jewish People in the Age of Jesus Christ (175 B.C.-A.D. 135)*, ed. Géza Vermès and Fergus Millar (Edinburgh: T. & T. Clark, 1973), 832, 840–846; Samuel Sandmel, *Philo of Alexandria: An Introduction*. (New York: Oxford University Press, 1979), 47–76; David T. Runia, "Exegesis and Philosophy: Studies on Philo of Alexandria," Collected Studies CS332 (Aldershot: Variorum, 1990), 5–6.

18 F. H. Colson and G. H Whitaker, eds., *Philo*, Loeb Classical Library (London and Cambridge, MA: William Heinemann and Harvard University Press, 1949), 124–127.

19 λέγεται τὸ παλαιὸν τὸ ἰοβόλον καὶ γηγενὲς ἑρπετὸν [ὄφις] ἀνθρώπου φωνὴν προίεσθαι καί ποτε προσελθὸν τῇ τοῦ πρώτου φύντος ἀνδρὸς γυναικὶ τῆς βραδυτῆτος καὶ τῆς ἄγαν εὐλαβείας ὀνειδίσαι

20 On the extent to which Philo resorts to allegorical interpretation because of difficulties that warrant rejection of the literal meaning, see Harry Austryn Wolfson, *Philo: Foundations of Religious Philosophy in Judaism, Christianity, and Islam* (Cambridge MA: Harvard University Press, 1948), 1:116-127. He adduces the instance of the talking snake on pp. 1:120-121. See David T. Runia, *Philo of Alexandria: On the Creation of the Cosmos According to Moses*, Philo of Alexandria Commentary Series 1 (Atlanta: Society of Biblical Literature, 2005), 374–376; Heinemann, *Darkhe Ha-Agadah*, 80.

Philo, De Opificio Mundi, 56 (157):

fit symbol for pleasure...[21]

Philo proceeds to enumerate several distinctive characteristics of the snake that qualify it to serve as a most fitting symbol for the sensual pleasure (ἡδονή) that seduces men away from their proper contemplative vocation. The combination of serpentine traits—its absence of limbs, its creeping on its belly with head held downward, its swallowing earth and its emitting venom—lend themselves to being applied allegorically to insidious pleasure, even as Philo treats the man and woman in the story as allegorical representations.[22] The depiction of the snake as capable of communicating

21 See Dorothy Sly, *Philo's Perception of Women*, Brown Judaic Studies 209 (Atlanta: Scholars Press, 1990), 90; Daniel Boyarin, *Carnal Israel: Reading Sex in Talmudic Culture*, The New Historicism 25 (Berkeley: University of California Press, 1993), 81; Serge Ruzer, "The Seat of Sin in Early Jewish and Christian Sources," in *Transformations of the Inner Self in Ancient Religions*, ed. Jan Assmann and Guy G. Stroumsa, Studies in the History of Religions (Supplements to Numen) 83 (Leiden, Boston, Köln: Brill, 1999), 375–376; Menahem M. Kasher, *Torah Shelemah (The Complete Torah)* (Jerusalem, Israel: The Torah Shelemah Institute, 1992), 1:252.

22 For an extensive discussion on how Philo employs the image of the snake to convey his ideas about sexual desire, see *Runia Creation*, 369, 374–379; William Loader, *Philo, Josephus, and the Testaments on Sexuality: Attitudes Towards Sexuality in the Writings of Philo and Josephus and in the Testaments of the Twelve Patriachs* (Grand Rapids, MI: Eerdmans, 2011), 66–75; See also A. Peter Booth, "The Voice of the Serpent: Philo's Epicureanism," in *Hellenization Revisited: Shaping a Christian Response Within the Greco-Roman World*, ed. W. Helleman (Lanham, MD: University Press of America, 1994), 159–172; Cline Kelly, "Talking Animals in the Bible," 439. A similar excursus is found in Philo's *On Husbandry* 22:96-97 [Colson and Whitaker, *Philo*, 3:156-157]. The text is incorporated into a comparison of the symbolisms of the respective snakes in the garden of Eden, Moses' brazen serpent and the one to which Jacob likens Dan in his final blessing blessing (Genesis 49:17):

> Told in this way, these things are like prodigies and marvels, one serpent emitting a human voice and using quibbling arguments to an utterly guileless character, and cheating a woman with seductive plausibilities; and another proving the author of complete deliverance to those who beheld it. But when we interpret words by the meanings that lie beneath the surface, all that is mythical is removed out of our way, and the real sense becomes as clear as daylight. Well then, we say that the woman is Life depending on the senses and material substance of our bodies; that her serpent is pleasure, a crawling thing with many a twist, powerless to raise

in human language dovetails with the imagery of its ubiquitous and nigh-irresistible seductiveness:

Philo, De Opificio Mundi, 57 (160)

φωνὴν δ' ἀνθρώπειον ὄφις λέγεται προίεσθαι, διότι μυρίοις ὑπερμάχοις καὶ προαγωνισταῖς ἡδονὴ χρῆται τὴν ἐπιμέλειαν καὶ προστασίαν αὐτῆς ἀνειληφόσιν, οἳ τολμῶσιν ἀναδιδάσκειν ὅτι πάντων τὸ κράτος ἀνῆπται μικρῶν τε καὶ μεγάλων οὐδενὸς ὑπεξῃρημένου τὸ παράπαν...

And the serpent is said to have uttered a human voice, because pleasure employs innumerable champions and defenders who take care to advocate its interests, and who dare to assert that the power over everything, both small and great, does of right belong to it without any exception whatever...

LVIII (163): ἀπόχρη δὲ δείγματος ἕνεκα καὶ τὰ νῦν εἰρημένα, ὧν χάριν ἀνθρωπίνην φωνὴν ἔδοξεν ὁ ὄφις προίεσθαι.

But what has been already said is sufficient to show what the reasons were on account of which the serpent appears to have uttered a human voice.

The considerations that impelled Philo to interpret the snake as an allegorical image are also raised briefly in his *Quaestiones* [Ζητήματα καὶ λύσεις][23] to Genesis.[24] In response to a question about why the Bible sin-

itself upright, always prone, creep ing after the good things of earth alone, making for the hiding-places afforded to it by the body, making its lair in each of the senses as in cavities or dug-outs, giving advice to a human being, athirst for the blood of anything better than itself, delighting to cause death by poisonous and painless bites....

23   On this work see Schurer, *History of the Jewish People*, 826–830.

24   Philo, *Questions and Answers on Genesis*, trans. Ralph Marcus, vol. Supplement I, Loeb Classical Library (London and Cambridge, MA: William Heinemann and Harvard University Press, 1953), *31; 1:18-19. See: Samuel Belkin, *The Midrash of Philo*, ed. Elazar Hurvitz (New York: Yeshiva University Press, 1989), 52–53. Belkin compares this interpretation with rabbinic traditions that speak of the snake being preordained (מתוקן) for evil. In this connection [Avigdor Shinan, ed., *Midrash Shemot Rabbah, Chapters I-XIV* (Jerusalem: Dvir, 1984), 107–108 [Hebrew]]. See also *t.Soṭah* 4:17 (ed. Lieberman, 176); and Hai Gaon. Cf. Eliezer Segal, "'The Same from Beginning to End': On the Development of a Midrashic Homily," *Journal of Jewish Studies* 32, no. 2 (1981): 158–165.

gles out the snake for being "most cunning"—φρονιμώτατος[25]—Philo says that "to me, however, it seems that this was said because of the serpent's inclination toward passion, of which it is the symbol. And by passion is meant sensual pleasure, for lovers of pleasure are very clever and skilled in arts and means."[26] At any rate, he concludes (maybe because of the difficulties he felt regarding the notion of literally ascribing wisdom to the snake) that the characterization was being applied to this particular serpent alone, and not to an entire genus.[27]

25　The usual meaning of the Greek word is closer to "sane" or "sensible."

26　*Runia Creation*, 369. The equating of snakes with erotic or sensual pleasures reminds us of the tale told by Aelian, *De Natura Animalium* 6:17, from "the country of those known as Judaeans or Edomites the natives of the time of Herod the King" [ἐν τῇ τῶν καλουμένων Ἰουδαίων γῇ ἢ Ἰδουμαίων ἦδον οἱ ἐπιχώριοι καθ᾽ Ἡρῴδην τὸν βασιλέα ἐρασθῆναι], about a passionate love affair between a beautiful girl and an obsessively possessive snake. See Aelian, *On the Characteristics of Animals*, trans. Alwyn Faber Scholfield, The Loeb Classical Library 446 (Cambridge MA: Harvard University Press, 1958), 2:30-31; Menahem Stern, *Greek and Latin Authors on Jews and Judaism*, Fontes ad Res Judaicas Spectantes (Jerusalem: Israel Academy of Sciences and Humanities, 1974), 2:408-409.

27　When coupled with the identification of the primordial serpent as Satan (or the arch-demon Samma'el), as attested widely in Apocryphal and rabbinic traditions, it could ostensibly have been inferred that an attempt at allegorization underlies the dictum ascribed to Rabbi Simeon ben Lakish (*b.Bava Batera* 16a): "the same one is Satan, the evil inclination and the angel of death." If anything, however, the proof-texts (mostly from Job)　and the treatments of the respective images in the literature achieve the opposite objective—rather than making the snake a symbol for erotic urges (in a manner comparable to Philo), they result in portrayals of Satan in very vivid mythic colors. Nehama Leibowitz reflects the widespread view (apparently under the influence of medieval moralistic and kabbalistic interpretations) that the rabbis were equating the snake with the evil inclination = Satan, but cites in evidence only R' Simeon ben Lakish's dictum ["The Serpent—the Evil Impulse—(2, 15-17; 3, 1-9) Anatomy of Temptation," in *Studies in the Book of Genesis in the Context of Ancient and Modern Jewish Bible Commentary*, trans. Aryeh Newman (Jerusalem: World Zionist Organization, Dept. for Torah Education and Culture, 1972), 29]. At any rate, Rabbi Simeon ben Lakish's statement contain no reference to the snake, and accordingly, unlike Philo, the question of its speaking ability was not a pertinent factor in his exegesis. In *Pirkei deRabbi Eliezer* 13, it is clear that the serpent is not equated with Satan, but was possessed ("parasitic" to use the language of R. Adelman) by Samma'el as the most suitable instrument for his nefarious plot; see Gerald

Philo devotes a separate discussion in his *Quaestiones* 1:32 to explaining how it was that the snake was able to express itself like a human:[28]

> Did the serpent speak in the manner of men?
>
> First, it is likely that not even in the beginning of the world's creation were the other animals without a share in speech, but that man excelled in voice (or utterance), being more clear and distinct. Second, when some miraculous deed is prepared, God changes the inner nature. Third, because our souls are filled with many sins and dear to all utterances except one or another tongue to which they are accustomed; but the souls of the first creatures, as being pure from evil and untainted, were particularly keen in becoming familiar with every sound. And since they were not provided only with defective

Friedlander, ed., *Pirke de Rabbi Eliezer (The Chapters of Rabbi Eliezer the Great)*, 2d American ed. (New York: Hermon Press, 1965), 92–93; Rachel Adelman, "The Return of the Repressed: Pirqe De-Rabbi Eliezer and the Pseudepigrapha," Supplements to the Journal for the study of Judaism ; v. 140 (Leiden: Brill, 2009), 52, 61–62, 78–83; Ryan Scott Dulkin, "The Devil Within: A Rabbinic Traditions-History of the Samael Story in Pirkei De-Rabbi Eliezer," *Jewish Studies Quarterly* 21, no. 2 (2014): 153–175. For a survey of the equation of the serpent with Satan in rabbinic and other Jewish sources see Efraim Elimelech Urbach, *The Sages, Their Concepts and Beliefs*, trans. Israel Abrahams (Cambridge, MA: Harvard University Press, 1987), 167–170; Leo Jung, "Fallen Angels in Jewish, Christian and Mohammedan Literature. A Study in Comparative Folk-Lore," *The Jewish Quarterly Review* 15, no. 4 (1925): 489–490; cf. Ishay Rosen-Zvi, "Two Rabbinic Inclinations?: Rethinking a Scholarly Dogma," *Journal for the Study of Judaism in the Persian, Hellenistic and Roman Period* 39, no. 4–5 (2008): 513–539. In Christian literature, the book of Revelation contains two mentions (12:9, 20:2) of "that serpent of old, called the Devil and Satan." Evidently, the second-century Irenaeus was the first of the Church Fathers to make that identification; see Donald E. Gowan, *From Eden to Babel: A Commentary on the Book of Genesis 1-11*, International Theological Commentary (Grand Rapids: W.B. Eerdmans Pub. Co, 1988), 157. In the "Acts of Philip" 11:3-6 a demonic dragon traces a serpentine "autobiography" that extends from the garden of Eden through the "watchers," the serpents of Pharaoh's magicians that were bested by Moses' and Aaron's staffs and the creatures that served Solomon in the construction of the Jerusalem Temple. See François Bovon and Christopher R. Matthews, eds., *The Acts of Philip: A New Translation* (Waco, Tex: Baylor University Press, 2012), 82; Christopher R. Matthews, *Philip, Apostle and Evangelist: Configurations of a Tradition*, Supplements to Novum Testamentum 105 (Leiden and Boston: Brill, 2002), 211–212.

28 Philo, *Questions and Answers on Genesis*, Supplement I:19.

senses, such as belong to a miserable bodily frame, but were provided with a very great body and the magnitude of a giant, it was necessary that they should also have more accurate senses, and what is more, philosophical sight and hearing. For not inaptly do some conjecture that they were provided with eyes with which they could see those natures and beings and actions which were in heaven, and with ears to perceive sounds of every kind.

This detailed speculation about the quality of animal perception in the pristine early days of creation is a truly extraordinary text. In Philo's reconstruction of that era, all living creatures shared a spiritual or intellectual purity that manifested itself both in their astute understanding and in their ability to communicate. Accordingly, if humans held a privileged position *vis à vis* other living creatures, it was only to a relative degree, apparently by virtue of the superior physiological make-up that allows them to make themselves heard with greater clarity. Although sinfulness has blurred it all throughout their subsequent evolution as flawed organisms, those ideal creatures of yore—including the mythologically conceived first humans,[29] who were endowed with perfect, titanic bodies and phenomenal

29 Ginzberg, *Legends*, 5:79 n. 22; Efraim Elimelech Urbach, *The Sages: Their Concepts and Beliefs* (Cambridge, MA: Harvard University Press, 1987), 229–232; Alexander Altmann, "The Gnostic Background of the Rabbinic Adam Legends," in *Essays in Jewish Intellectual History* (Hanover, NH: University Press of New England for Brandeis University Press, 1981), 10; Gershom G. Scholem, *Origins of the Kabbalah*, trans. R. J. Zwi Werblowsky, 1st English ed. (Philadelphia and Princeton: Jewish Publication Society and Princeton University Press, 1987), 73; Saul Lieberman, "How Much Greek in Jewish Palestine?," in *Studies and Texts*, ed. Alexander Altmann, vol. 1. Biblical and Other Studies (Cambridge MA: Harvard University Press, 1963), 135–141; Gershom G. Scholem, *Jewish Gnosticism, Merkabah Mysticism, and Talmudic Tradition* (New York: Jewish Theological Seminary of America, 1960); Fritz Isaac Baer, "On the Problem of Eschatological Doctrine during the Period of the Second Temple," *Zion* 23–24, no. 1–2 (1959 1958): 21–25 [Hebrew]; Alan F. Segal, *Two Powers in Heaven: Early Rabbinic Reports About Christianity and Gnosticism* (Waco, Tex: Baylor University Press, 2012), 11–115; Howard Schwartz, *Tree of Souls: The Mythology of Judaism: The Mythology of Judaism* (St. Louis MO: Oxford University Press USA, 2004), 128; Susan Niditch, "The Cosmic Adam: Man as Mediator in Rabbinic Literature," *Journal of Jewish Studies* [34], no. 2 (1983): 137–146; Adelman, "The Return of the Repressed," 97 and n. 67. Urbach, whose understanding of Philo's opinion is based on the passage in *Legum Allegoria* 2.4 (13) [Loeb 1:232-23] about separate creations of the first Adam, who was a "genus" and of the subsequent specific mortal human, stresses the differences—or

sense and intellectual perception—were then able to communicate with one another.[30]

Several threads of Philo's thought and method about the absence of speech in animals come together in an intriguing discussion in his commentary on the biblical tale of the Tower of Babel: *On the Confusion of Tongues*. As background and justification for his preference of an allegorical interpretation of the story, he refers to unidentified contemporaries, "persons who cherish a dislike of the institutions of our fathers and make

even conscious opposition—in the rabbinic legends that tell of a single earthly Adam whose stature was afterwards reduced from his original gigantic proportions and superhuman perfection. Altmann, Urbach, Segal (to some extent) and others note that these legends were probably reacting to Gnostic conceptions of the "complete man," "first man" and similar images of a primordial quasi-divine (or divine) being. Niditch on the other hand argues that the actual sources cited as evidence of the Gnostic imagery have little or nothing to do with the rabbinic depictions; and that the rabbinic texts are to be understood on their own terms as reflecting Jewish religious values and homiletical conventions. Even scholars like Lieberman and Scholem, who claim to find Gnostic references in rabbinic texts, do not cite these examples. Cf. Itamar Gruenwald, "The Problem of the Anti-Gnostic Polemic in Rabbinic Literature," in *Studies in Gnosticism and Hellenistic Religions: Presented to Gilles Quispel on the Occasion of His 65th Birthday*, ed. Roelof van den Van den Broek and Maarten Jozef Vermaseren, Etudes preliminaires aux religions orientales dans l'Empire romain ; t. 91 (Leiden: EJBrill, 1981), 186. Other scholars have sought to find a source for the midrashic depiction of the primordial Adam in Aristophanes' speech at Plato's Symposium; not so much in the conspicuous androgynous theme, but in such premises as that the original human nature was different from the present one, or that the primordial man threatened to make war on the gods. (See Urbach, *Sages*, 228–229, 788–789.) For a good survey of scholarship about Philo's relationship to Gnosticism see Robert McLachlan Wilson, "Philo and Gnosticism," *The Studia Philonica Annual* 5 (1993): 84–92.

30   Jewish legends about Adam as a giant abound in talmudic and midrashic literature, as noted by Belkin, *Midreshe Filon*, 74.. See for example *Leviticus Rabbah* 14:1 [Mordecai Margulies, ed., *Midrash Vayyikra Rabbah* (New York and Jerusalem: The Jewish Theological Seminary of America, 1993), 296–297]: R. Berakhiah and R. Halabo in the name of R' Ishmael bar Nahman said: At the time that the holy one created the first man, he created him without form and he extended from one end of the earth until the other... R' Judah bar R' Simon in the name of R' Joshua ben Levi said: At the time that the holy one created the first man, he created him so as to fill the entire world, from the east to the west.. from the north to the south...

it their constant study to denounce and decry the Laws,"[31] who had made the accusation that stories in the Law of Moses are no less mythological than legends that are circulated among the pagans, thereby demonstrating the inconsistency and unfairness of the superior Jewish attitude toward myths.[32] "For see your so-called holy books contain also myths, which you regularly deride when you hear them related by others."

As an example, they cite the following myth:[33]

As for the Adam's infinite vision (by virtue of the primordial light) see, e.g., *b.Ḥagigah* 12a:

> ...Rabbi Eleazar says: The light that the Holy One created on the first day, with it Adam could gaze from one end of the world to the other. When the Holy One observed the generation of the flood and the generation of the division [i.e., of the tower of Babel] and saw that their deeds were perverse, he stood and hid it away...

See additional sources listed in the critical apparatus and by Daniel Chanan Matt, *Zohar: Annotated & Explained*, SkyLight illuminations (Woodstock, VT: SkyLight Paths Publishing, 2002), 1:192. Some of these relate to the traditions about Adam being adored by angels and mistaken for God.

31 See Wolfson, *Philo: Foundations of Religious Philosophy in Judaism, Christianity, and Islam*, 1:55-71; David M. Hay, "Philo's References to Other Allegorists," *Studia Philonica Annual* 6 (1980): 41–75; See Maren R. Niehoff, *Jewish Exegesis and Homeric Scholarship in Alexandria* (Cambridge and New York: Cambridge University Press, 2011), 77–94.

32 See Richard Layton, "Didymus the Blind and the Philistores: A Contest over Historia in Early Christian Exegetical Argument," in *Studies on the Texts of the Desert of Judah: New Approaches to the Study of Biblical Interpretation in Judaism of the Second Temple Period and in Early Christianity : Proceedings of the Eleventh International Symposium of the Orion Center for the Study of the Dead Sea Scrolls and Associated Literature, Jointly Sponsored by the Hebrew University Center for the Study of Christianity, 9–11 January, 2007*, ed. Gary A. Anderson, Ruth A. Clements, and David Satran, 106 (Leiden and Boston: Brill, 2013), 246–248.

33 B. E. Perry traces the myth to a lost collection of Aesopian fables by the orator Demetrius of Phalerum (c. 350 – c. 280) which can be substantially reconstructed from a poem by the Alexandrian poet Callimachus ["Demetrius of Phalerum and the Aesopic Fables," *Transactions and Proceedings of the American Philological Association* 93 (1962): 312–314]. M. Niehoff is doubtful whether such a version ever existed. She notes that on several specific details, Philo's version agrees with that of Callimachus rather than Demetrius [*Jewish and Homeric*, 87; see also *Polyeideia: The Iambi of Callimachus and the Archaic Iambic Tradition*, Hellenistic Culture and

Philo, The Confusion of Tongues 3:(6-8):[34]

ἕτερος δέ τις συγγενὴς τούτῳ περὶ τῆς τῶν ζῴων ὁμοφωνίας πρὸς μυθοπλαστῶν ἀναγράφεται· λέγεται γάρ, ὡς ἄρα πάνθ᾽ ὅσα ζῷα χερσαῖα καὶ ἔνυδρα καὶ πτηνὰ τὸ παλαιὸν ὁμόφωνα ἦν, καὶ ὅνπερ τρόπον ἀνθρώπων Ἕλληνες μὲν Ἕλλησι, βαρβάροις δὲ βάρβαροι νῦν οἱ ὁμόγλωττοι διαλέγονται, τοῦτον τὸν τρόπον καὶ πάντα πᾶσι περὶ ὧν ἢ δρᾶν ἢ πάσχειν τι συνέβαινεν ὡμίλει, ὡς καὶ ἐπὶ ταῖς κακοπραγίαις συνάχθεσθαι κἄν, εἴ πού τι λυσιτελὲς ἀπαντῴη, συνευφραίνεσθαι.

Another similar story is to be found in the writings of the mythologists, telling of the days when all animals had a common language. The tale is that in old days all animals, whether on land or in water or winged, had the same language, and just as among men to-day Greeks talk with Greeks and barbarians with barbarians if they have the same tongue, so too every creature conversed with every other, about all that happened to be done to them or by them, and in this way they mourned together at misfortunes, and rejoiced together when anything of advantage came their way.

Buoyed by their successes in consolidating themselves into a cohesive society capable of true social harmony, the animals approached the gods demanding from them the additional gift of eternal youth. As a precedent they cited the case of the serpent that (as they understood it) was able to achieve that objective by replacing not only its aged skin, but also its very

Society 35 (Berkeley: University of California Press, 2002), 178–182]. Issues on which the traditions disagree include: whether the animal "language" was indeed a human language or merely a form of (possibly non-verbal) communication; unlike Philo's version where the impudent animals are punished, like the builders of the tower of Babel, by being divided into numerous languages, Callimachus tells of the capacity for speech being transferred from the animals to humans, resulting in a situation in which different people come to speak in voices resembling different animals (a detail that Callimachus might have inserted in order to poke fun at particular individuals or literary types in his own time); whether the protest is the work of all the animals collectively or represented by the fox or swan [ibid., 180–182]; Gera, *Greek Ideas on Speech*, 31–32; Hawkins, "Eloquent Alogia," 4–5.

34 F. H. Colson and G. H Whitaker, eds., *Philo*, Loeb Classical Library (London and Cambridge, MA: William Heinemann and Harvard University Press, 1949), 4:12-15.

flesh. They were, however, punished for the insolence of their demand and for accusing the gods of injustice—the punishment consisted of their being deprived of the common language that had enabled them to progress to such an advanced and civilized state. Philo's interlocutors were claiming that, other than the fact that the characters in this tale were animals rather than humans, there was no significant difference between this legend and the Torah's myth in which God confuses the languages of the nations in response to their ambitious quest to "build ourselves a city, and a tower whose top is in the heavens; let us make a name for ourselves" (Genesis 11:3).

Philo does not appear to refute his opponents specifically by denying the possibility that animals could ever have known how to converse or think in the nuanced manner described in the quoted myth (an argument that would have been perfectly consistent with the Stoic position he advocated in *De Animalibus*). Nevertheless, some such notion probably lies at the bottom of his response, as we have seen elsewhere in his writings. Ultimately, however, it is not merely the depiction of a sophisticated animal society that is impossible to accept; but the literal sense of the Tower of Babel story is also so fraught with logical flaws (and here too, it seems that Philo is acknowledging the difficulties raised by his opponents)[35] that the only acceptable way out of them is by completely abandoning literal or historical readings in favor of an allegorical interpretation, as a lesson about the importance of internal unity of the soul and *logos* in the face of all the divisive internal and external forces that threaten to divert us from our proper spiritual goals.[36]

Gnostics: Ophites and Naasenes

An influential religious outlook that is difficult to situate for purposes of the present inquiry is the diverse assortment of esoteric movements that

---

35 The most powerful of these arguments include: the absurdity of presuming that unilingualism is morally preferable to multilingualism; the falseness of the implication dividing nations and tongues actually solved the problem by eliminating or decreasing the evil in the world.

36 See Gera, *Greek Ideas on Speech*, 31–32.

are conventionally grouped together under the rubric "Gnostic."[37] The name itself alludes to their conviction that the path to salvation and immortality demands mastery ("knowing"; γνῶσις) of a secret doctrine that is revealed to a select group of the enlightened. Our information about gnostic beliefs derives principally from the writings of Christian heresiographers, notably Irenaeus,[38] who were concerned with indicting gnosticism as an unacceptable, heretical variant of authentic Christian doctrine. These hostile, second-hand accounts have recently been supplemented by the discovery of a library of gnostic documents at Nag Hammadi in Egypt. Although, as noted, most of the evidence that we possess about gnosticism indicates that they were a movement (or perhaps several of them) that arose and achieved self-definition within early Christianity,[39] scholars have argued that the doctrine drew, at least in part, from pagan spirituality (especially the Isis mystery cult) or from mystical currents of Judaism.[40]

37 For some influential examples of discussions that call into question the accuracy or usefulness of employing this as a category, see Karen L. King, *What Is Gnosticism?* (Cambridge, MA: Belknap Press of Harvard University Press, 2003); Michael A. Williams, *Rethinking "Gnosticism": An Argument for Dismantling a Dubious Category* (Princeton, NJ: Princeton University Press, 1996). This weighty issue is not directly pertinent to this study.

38 For useful introductions to Irenaeus and his writings about gnosticism see Bentley Layton, ed., *The Gnostic Scriptures: A New Translation with Annotations and Introductions*, 1st British ed. (London: SCM Press, 1987), 170–172; Stephen O. Presley, *The Intertextual Reception of Genesis 1-3 in Irenaeus of Lyons*, The Bible in Ancient Christianity 8 (Leiden and Boston: Brill, 2015), 1–44.

39 E.g., authors cited by Daniel Boyarin, *Border Lines: The Partition of Judaeo-Christianity*, Divinations (Philadelphia: University of Pennsylvania Press, 2004), 56–57; 94 and notes.

40 Although many scholars have treated any interpretations of biblical passages and Apocryphal or Pseudepigraphic works as "Jewish" influences, Gershom Scholem made what strikes me as a more challenging argument for the thesis that gnostic themes were central to the streams of rabbinic Heikhalot or Merkavah mysticism that were prevalent at least as early as the early second century C.E.; see his *Jewish Gnosticism*, 257–76; Joseph Dan, "Samael and the Problem of Jewish Gnosticism," in *Perspectives on Jewish Thought and Mysticism*, ed. Alexander Altmann et al. (Amsterdam: Harwood Academic Publishers, 1998), 257–276. The likelihood that a gnostic text derives (even indirectly) from Jewish interpretations is increased by the presence of word-plays that only make full sense in Aramaic or Hebrew; such as the

For our purposes, there are particular types of Christian gnosticism that are relevant to the study of ideas about animal speech. These include the movements that Irenaeus designates as the "Ophites ['Οφιανοί]" from the Greek word for snake, ὄφις;[41] or perhaps the "Naaseni," from the Hebrew word for snake: נחש.[42] Significant features of the Naasene veneration of snakes likely derive from pagan mystery cults. Insofar as they draw upon biblical sources, the significant texts for them were Numbers 21:8-9 in which Moses averts a plague by fashioning a bronze serpent; and John

numerous variations on the root חיה and חוה in the senses "life," "snake," "instruct," "beast," "midwife" and "Eve" that appear to underlie the garden of Eden story in *Hypostasis of the Archons* 90; see Bentley Layton, "The Hypostasis of the Archons, or 'The Reality of the Rulers,'" *Harvard Theological Review* 67, no. 4 (1974): 55–56; Birger A. Pearson, "Jewish Haggadic Traditions in The Testimony of Truth from Nag Hammadi (CG Ix.3)," in *Ex Orbe Religionum: Studia Geo Widengren*, ed. J. Bergman, K. Drynjeff, and H. Ringgren, Studies in the History of Religions; Supplements to Numen 21–22 (Leiden: Brill, 1972), 463–465; ="Jewish Haggadic Traditions in the Testimony of Truth from Nag Hammadi (CG Ix, 3)," in *Religious Syncretism in Antiquity: Essays in Conversation with Geo Widengren*, by Birger A. Pearson (Missoula: Scholars Press, 1975), 205–222; "'She Became a Tree': A Note to GC II 4:89, 25-26," *Harvard Theological Review* 69, no. 3–4 (1976): 413–415; Jean-Daniel Kaestli, "L'interpretation du serpent de Genese 3 dans quelques textes gnostiques et la question de la gnose 'ophite,'" in *Gnosticisme et monde hellenistique: actes du colloque de Louvain-la-Neuve, 11-14 mars 1980 ils* (Louvain-La-Neuve: Universite Catholique de Louvain, 1982), 122 n. 37.

41 As noted by Tuomas Rasimus, the term "Ophite" was probably not used by the actual followers of the sect and was likely applied pejoratively by their opponents; see his "Ophite Gnosticism, Sethianism and the Nag Hammadi Library," *Vigiliae Christianae* 59, no. 3 (2005): 236. Its earliest appearance is in Pseudo-Tertullian or Clement of Alexandria, around 220 C.E.. Rasimus (238-240) argues convincingly that with regard to the interpretations of the serpent's role in Genesis 3, subsequent authors of heresiological catalogues (including several linked to Hippolytus' *Syntagma*) are all directly or independently derivative of Irenaeus.

42 Hans Jonas, *The Gnostic Religion: The Message of the Alien God & the Beginnings of Christianity*, 3rd edition. (Boston: Beacon Press, 2001), 92–94; Maria Grazia Lancellotti, *The Naassenes: A Gnostic Identity Among Judaism, Christianity, Classical and Ancient Near Eastern Traditions*, Forschungen zur Anthropologie und Religionsgeschichte 35 (Münster: Ugarit-Verlag, 2000). The only early source of information about the Naasenes is Hippolytus, *Refutatio* 5. It states there (Ch. 2) that the Naasenes reduced the whole story about Eden to an elaborate allegory about cosmol-

3:14-15 where Moses's serpent is interpreted as a symbol for the Son of Man as the means for achieving eternal life.[43] The Naasenes, possibly under the influence of Philo, identified the biblical serpent with Christ *qua* the divine Logos, and built around this conception an elaborate mythic cosmology.[44] These themes in themselves are of no direct relevance to the present question.[45] On the other hand, the Ophite writings expound the character and role of the talking serpent in the garden of Eden, and for this reason they may have an understandable bearing on the general topic of animal speech. According to T. Rasimus, "Even though the portrayal of the snake in Irenaeus' Ophite account consists of several motifs, the main source of the snake imagery is Gen 3 and those Judeo-Christian traditions that identified the serpent of paradise with the devil. The purpose of the positive evaluation of the serpent's advice is undoubtedly the criticism of the creator's commandment."[46] That is to say, once the God of the Hebrew

ogy, mind, spirit and similar themes. All that he says about the snake is that "the serpent is a moist substance," functioning as one of the primal elements of creation. Mira Beth Wasserman proposes a thematic association between snakes and heretics [*min*] in the talmudic tale of Ben Dama in *b.ʿAvoda Zarah* 27b in which Rabbi Ishmael invokes Ecclesiastes 10:8: "One who breaks through a fence shall be bitten by a snake" [*Jews, Gentiles, and Other Animals: The Talmud After the Humanities*, Divinations: Rereading Late Ancient Religion (Philadelphia: University of Pennsylvania Press, 2017), 130–134, 270–272]. Though she prefers (following D. Boyarin and others) to identify this *min* as a Jewish Christian, the centrality of snakes to Gnostic myth might have given rise to the currency of such a metaphoric association in rabbinic parlance. See also Gerrit Bos, "Jewish Traditions on Divination with Birds (Ornithomancy)," 2015, 2 n. 10, https://www.researchgate.net/ publication/ 280976904_ Jewish_Traditions_ on_ Divination_ with_ Birds_ Ornithomancy.

43 Kaestli, "Serpent de Genese 3," 131.

44 On the fundamental differences between Ophites and Naasenes see Rasimus, "Ophite Gnosticism," 245–246; Kaestli, "Serpent de Genese 3," 116–118; cf. R. P. Casey, "Naassenes and Ophites," *The Journal of Theological Studies* 27, no. 108 (1926): 374–387.

45 The same can be said regarding the category of "Sethian" gnosticism whose character and relationship to Ophitism has been the topic of much scholarly discussion, but which evidently does not concern itself with the serpent in paradise; see Rasimus, "Ophite Gnosticism," 247–249..

46 Tuomas Rasimus, "The Serpent in Gnostic and Related Texts," in *Colloque International "L'évangile Selon Thomas et Les Textes de Nag Hammadi": (Québec, 29-31*

Bible has been demoted to the status of the inferior Demiurge who created the physical non-spiritual world, the serpent's urging the first humans to attain spiritual enlightenment takes on heroic dimensions.[47] Viewed from this perspective, it is germane to look at how the gnostics understood its power of speech and the mechanism of its conversations with Eve and Adam in paradise.

In the spirit of Philo, the second-century gnostic teacher Apelles, a disciple of Marcion, challenged the coherence of any literal reading of the biblical account of the temptation of Adam and Eve. Assuming that that ancient snake was of essentially the same species as the snakes of later times, then "how can the serpent, created voiceless and mindless in nature by God, speak reasonably and vocally?"[48]

Indeed, accounts of Ophite traditions portray the serpent in a positive light (while not necessarily denying some of its conventionally evil associations),[49] as subversively undermining the role of the demiurge Ialdabaoth over the earthly creation by bringing wisdom to the first mortals. Whatever foreign elements might have played a role in inspiring this imaginative exegesis, it is reasonable to suppose that it was founded in significant part on reflections of the biblical story, probably in comparison with other passages that refer to serpents in more favorable contexts, especially, as was noted previously, Numbers 21:8-9 (the brass serpent that cures the people from the venom of the snakes) and the angelic *seraphim* that figure among the divine retinue before the throne of the Lord in Isaiah 1:6, 8.

Mai 2003) (Québec: Presses de l'Université Laval and Peeters, 2007), 424. Rasumus states that the accounts of Celsus / Origen and Irenaeus share "an extensive use of Jewish materials." The examples he cites consist basically of standard terms from the Hebrew Bible or Apocrypha; see "Ophite Gnosticism," 243 and n. 22 (see also 245 and n. 27; cf. 249 and n. 41).

47 Compare the depiction of the snake in the "Apocryphon of John" 22:9-20; Layton, *The Gnostic Scriptures*, 45–46; James M. Robinson and Richard Smith, eds., *The Nag Hammadi Library in English*, 4th rev. ed., Coptic Gnostic Library Project (Leiden and New York: E.J. Brill, 1996), 2:126-129.

48 Robert M. Grant, *Early Christians and Animals* (London and New York: Routledge, 1999), 5–6.

49 See, e.g., Kaestli, "Serpent de Genese 3," 118–119.

This kind of exegetical speculation might well have evolved in Jewish circles.

Irenaeus' detailed account of the Ophite version of the serpent's seduction of Eve and Adam (30:7)[50] does not provide much detail as regards the precise mechanism of the serpent's communication, but it does relate their belief that it was used by the female divinity of wisdom (Sophia) as the instrument for undermining the hegemony of the creator god:

> But their mother (Sophia) cunningly devised a scheme to seduce Eve and Adam, by means of the serpent, to transgress the command of Ialdabaoth. Eve *listened to this* as if it had proceeded from a son of God, and yielded an easy belief.[51]

Irenaeus also writes about unidentified gnostics who held a somewhat different position about the relationship of Sophia to the snake:

> [1:30:7] Some assert that it was wisdom (Sophia) herself who became the snake; accordingly she remained hostile to the creator of Adam, and introduced acquaintance [that is to say, *gnosis*] into humankind. For this reason the snake was said to be prudent than all (others).[52]

Documents from the Nag Hammadi library provide us some more explicit detail. For example, as characterized by E. Pagels, the author of the "Testimony of Truth"[53] "dared to tell the story of Paradise from the serpent's point of view, and depicted the serpent as a teacher of divine wisdom who desperately tried to get Adam and Eve to open their eyes to their creator's true—and despicable —nature."[54] This is not literally accurate, in that the fragmentary text is not a first-person account narrated by the serpent; and

---

50 See Rasimus, "Serpent," 423.

51 Layton, *The Gnostic Scriptures*, 176; Rasimus, "Ophite Gnosticism," 238. Not more informative is Epiphanius' account of the "Gospel of Eve" in which the first woman "got the food of knowledge by a revelation from the serpent"; [2:6; *Panarion of Epiphanius of Salamis. Book I (Sections 1-46)*, 2nd ed., revised and expanded., Nag Hammadi and Manichaean Studies 63 (Leiden and Boston: Brill, 2009), 92; Layton, *The Gnostic Scriptures*, 205].

52 Layton, *The Gnostic Scriptures*, 181; Presley, *The Intertextual Reception of Genesis 1-3 in Irenaeus of Lyons*, 67.

53 *Testimony of Truth* 45,30-47,10; 47,15-48,4, in: Richard Smith, ed., *The Nag Hammadi Library in English*, 4th rev. ed. (Leiden and New York: E.J. Brill, 1996), 406–416.

yet it does correctly indicate that the serpent's cogent and complex theological argumentation is of a quality that must have been communicated by means of language.

> But the serpent was wiser than all the animals that were in Paradise, and he persuaded Eve, saying, "On the day when you eat from the tree which is in the midst of Paradise, the eyes of your mind will be opened." And Eve obeyed...[55]

The narration here sticks very close to the language in Genesis, depicting the serpent as acting of his own volition and by virtue of his extraordinary (whether individual or species-defined) intelligence. Consequently the text has little that is novel to contribute to this investigation into the phenomenon of animal language.

The Nag Hammadi text known as *The Origin of the World* contains a similar account of the garden of Eden story in which a "beast"[56] is generated by Sophia in order to bring enlightenment to humanity:

> An androgynous human being was produced, whom the Greeks call Hermaphrodites; and whose mother the Hebrews call Eve of Life (*Zoë*), namely, the female instructor of life. Her offspring is the creature that is lord. Afterwards, the authorities called it "Beast," so that it might lead astray their modeled creatures. The interpretation of "the beast" is "the instructor." For it was found to be the wisest of all beings...
>
> Then came the wisest of all creatures, who was called Beast. And when he saw the likeness of their mother Eve he said to her, "What did God say to you? Was it 'Do not eat from the tree of knowledge'?" She said, "He said not only, 'Do not eat from it,' but, 'Do not touch it, lest you die.'" He said to her, "Do not be afraid. In death you shall not die. For he knows that when you eat from it, your intellect will become sober and you will come to be like gods, recognizing the difference that obtains between evil men and good ones. Indeed, it was in jealousy that he said this to you, so that you would not eat from it."

54 Elaine H. Pagels, *Adam, Eve, and the Serpent*, 1st Vintage Books ed. (New York: Vintage Books, 1989), 87.

55 Robinson and Smith, *The Nag Hammadi Library in English*, (p. 411); Elaine H. Pagels, *The Gnostic Gospels*, 1st Vintage Books ed. (New York: Vintage Books, 1981), 35.

56 Kaestli, "Serpent de Genese 3," 120.

Now Eve had confidence in the words of the instructor... When they saw that the ones who had modeled them had the form of beasts, they loathed them: they were very aware.

Then when the rulers knew that they had broken their commandments, they entered Paradise... Then they said to [the woman], "What is this that you have done?" She answered and said, "It is the instructor who urged me on, and I ate."

Then the rulers came up to the instructor. Their eyes became misty because of him, and they could not do anything to him. They cursed him, since they were powerless.

Most explicit, from this perspective, is the Nag Hammadi text known as *The Hypostasis of the Archons* or *The Reality of the Rulers*. The primordial female spiritual principle enters temporarily into the body of the serpent with the specific purpose of enticing the earthly Eve to disobey the deity's prohibition and partake of the enlightenment contained in the forbidden fruit.

Then the Female Spiritual Principle came [in] the Snake, the Instructor; and it taught [them], saying, "What did he [say to] you [pl.]? Was it, 'From every tree in the Garden shall you [sing.] eat; yet—from[the tree] of recognizing evil and good do not eat?'"

The carnal Woman said, "Not only did he say 'Do not eat,' but even 'Do not touch it;[57] for the day you [pl.] eat from it, with death you [pl.] are going to die'"

And the Snake, the Instructor, said, "With death you [pl.] shall not die; for it was out of jealousy that he said this to you [pl.]. Rather your [pl.] eyes shall open and you [pl.] shall come to be like gods, recognizing evil and good."

And the Female Instructing Principle was taken away from the Snake, and she left it behind merely a thing of the earth.[58]

57 The discrepancy between God's actual command (Genesis 2:17), "thou shalt not eat of it: for in the day that thou eatest thereof...) and the snake's expansion of that into (3:3) "neither shall ye touch it" was a favorite motif of rabbinic expositions about the destructive potential of excessive stringency and other ways of tampering with the truth. Ginzberg, *Legends*, 1:72; 5:95 n. 61; Kasher, *Torah Shelemah*, 2:223-224.

58 Layton, "Hypostasis," 391; text: [8-9]; "The Hypostasis of the Archons (Conclusion)," *The Harvard Theological Review* 69, no. 1/2 (1976): 39–40; Layton, *The Gnostic Scriptures*, 71; Smith, *The Nag Hammadi Library in English*, 152–160; Mar-

This last statement, that the serpent's ability to speak was a temporary phenomenon that was removed after it had achieved its objective, is evidently responding to the difficulty that is stimulated by the Genesis story, of how to bring the talking animal in the garden of Eden into harmony with the reality of the snakes in our own world who lack any such ability. We have already met up with similar solutions to the conundrum in ancient Jewish sources, and will have further occasions to see them discussed in subsequent exegesis.[59]

The Rabbis and the Snake

Compared to the ample discussions that we encountered among non-rabbinic authors with regard to the snake's ability to speak—and the broader ramifications of that premise *vis à vis* the relationships of animals to humans, or of the pre-Eden and post-Eden realities—the teachings of the ancient rabbinic sages, as preserved in the literature of the Midrash and Talmuds, contains very little to indicate that they were concerned about such questions.[60] For whatever reasons, the story of Adam and Eve did not at-

---

viii W. Meyer et al., eds., *The Nag Hammadi Scriptures*, International ed., 1st ed. (New York: HarperOne, 2007), 192–193; David Brakke, *The Gnostics: Myth, Ritual, and Diversity in Early Christianity* (Cambridge, MA: Harvard University Press, 2010), 66–67.

59 An admirably succinct (yet thorough) summary of the portrayals of the snake and its relationship to Sophia (including absences) in gnostic documents may be found in Rasimus, "Ophite Gnosticism," 259. A more detailed comparison is conducted by Kaestli, "Serpent de Genese 3," 118–125.

60 In rabbinic thought, the sin of Adam and Eve did not generally occupy anything approaching its centrality in Pauline Christianity; see the discussion (which compares rabbinic, Apocryphal and Christian sources) in Urbach, *Sages*, 420–430. It should be noted as well that the preferred literary formats of midrash tended to exclude Genesis 3 from their purview. The extant compendia of Tanna'itic midrash focused on passages in the Torah that lend themselves to halakhic exegesis, and accordingly there is no Tanna'itic midrash at all (from either of the two chief schools of Rabbi Akiva or Rabbi Ishmael) to the book of Genesis; see, e.g., Günter Stemberger, *Introduction to the Talmud and Midrash*, 2nd ed. (Edinburgh: T. & T. Clark, 1996), 269–270.. As well, the most prominent format for aggadic midrash consisted of "*petiḥta*" proem homilies designed to culminate in the first verse of the day's scriptural lection; and the story of the Garden of Eden did not occur within an appropriate unit, with the

tract a great deal of exegetical or homiletical attention; and for the most part, the midrashic interpreters appear quite content to accept the story at its literal face value.

An apparent exception to the above rule is the following passage, which demonstrates some awareness that the existence of a talking snake is a notable phenomenon that should not be taken for granted:

Deuteronomy Rabbah 5:10:[61]

Says Rabbi Joshua of Sikhnin[62] in the name of Rabbi Levi:[63] The primordial snake could converse	א"ר יהושע דסכנין בשם ר' לוי, הנחש הראשון היה מסיח כבני אדם, כיון שלא היו אדם וחוה מבקשים לאכול מאותו

second division of Genesis beginning (in the ancient Palestinian triennial cycle) at the episode's conclusion at 3:24; see Adolf Büchler, "The Reading of the Law and Prophets in a Triennial Cycle," *The Jewish Quarterly Review* 5–6, no. 3, 1, Old Series (1893): 5:442; Jacob Mann, *The Bible as Read and Preached in the Old Synagogue: A Study in the Cycles of the Readings from Torah and Prophets, as Well as from Psalms, and in the Structure of the Midrashic Homilies*, Library of Biblical Studies (New York: KTAV, 1971); Joseph Heinemann, "The Triennial Lectionary Cycle.," *Journal of Jewish Studies*, no. 19 (1968): 41–48; "The Proem in Aggadic Midrashim—A Form-Critical Study," in *Studies in Aggadah and Folk-Literature*, ed. Dov Noy and Joseph Heinemann, Scripta Hierosolymitana 22 (Jerusalem: Magnes Press, 1971), 100–122; Stemberger, *Introduction to the Talmud and Midrash*, 265–268; Schurer, *History of the Jewish People*, 2:450-451 and nn. 119, 120.

61   Saul Lieberman, *Midrash Debarim Rabbah* (Jerusalem: Wahrmann Books, 1974), 100 [Hebrew]; see Marc Bregman, *Tanhuma-Yelammedenu Literature: Studies in the Evolution of the Versions* (Piscataway, NJ: Gorgias Press, 2003), 180–184 [Hebrew].

62   See Wilhelm Bacher, *Die Agada der palästinensischen Amoräer* (Strassburg i. E: K. J. Trübner, 1892), 2:302-303; = *Agadat Amora'e Erets-Yiśra'el*, trans. Alexander Siskind Rabinovitz (Tel-Aviv: Dvir, 1928), 2:2:10; Ch. Albeck, *Introduction to the Talmud. Babli and Yerushalmi* (Tel-Aviv: Dvir, 1969), 331; Mordecai Margalioth and Yehudah Aizenberg, eds., *Entsiklopedyah le-Ḥakhme ha-Talmud yeha-Ge'onim*, Revised edition. (Tel-Aviv: Yavneh and Chemed, 1995), 2:190. Bacher in fact notes that Joshua of Sikhnin, who brings more than a hundred of Levi's dicta, has no other apparent function in rabbinic literature. I was unable to find a mention of this midrash in the relevant sections of Bacher's chapter on Rabbi Levi. According to Zahava Neuberger (Keller), Rabbi Levi is the most frequently cited sage in *Deuteronomy Rabbah* ("The Printed Edition of Midrash Devarim Rabba: Its Character and Place in the Tanhuma-Yelamdenu Literature" [PhD, The Hebrew University of Jerusalem, 1999], 185 n. 4 [Hebrew]).

Deuteronomy Rabbah 5:10:

like humans.[64] When Adam and
Eve did not want to eat from that
tree, he began to speak slander-
ously about his creator. He said to
them: From this very tree did the
creator eat, and then he created his
world and commanded you not to
eat from it and build a new world.

What did the holy one do to
him? He chopped off his legs and
cut off his tongue to prevent him
from speaking.[65]

אילן, התחיל לומ' לשון הרע על בוראו,
אמ' להן מן האילן הזה אכל הבורא וברא
עולמו, וצוה אתכם שלא תאכלו ממנו
ותבראו עולם אחר.

מה עשה לו הקב"ה, קצץ רגליו
וכרת את לשונו, שלא היה מסיח.

Note that this version of the tradition, though cited in the name of a third-
century authority, is preserved only in a relatively late "midrash" of dubious provenance.[66] S. Lieberman situates both versions of *Deuteronomy
Rabbah* (the standard printings and his own edition) within the extensive
"middle stratum" of the genre, which he dates at the transitional period be-

63   Rabbi Levi was a specialist in aggadic preaching in the academy of Rabbi Yoḥanan.
     Wilhelm Bacher, *Die Agada der palästinensischen Amoräer* (Strassburg i. E: K. J.
     Trübner, 1892), 2:296-300; = *Agadat Amora'e Erets-Yiśra'el*, trans. Alexander Sis-
     kind Rabinovitz (Tel-Aviv: Dvir, 1928), 2:2:5-8 [Hebrew]; Ch. Albeck, *Introduction
     to the Talmud. Babli and Yerushalmi* (Tel-Aviv: Dvir, 1969), 256–257 [Hebrew];
     Mordecai Margalioth and Yehudah Aizenberg, eds., *Entsiḵlopedyah le-Ḥakhme ha-
     Talmud yeha-Ge'onim*, Revised edition. (Tel-Aviv: Yavneh and Chemed, 1995),
     2:247-248.
64   In L. Feldman's notes to Josephus *Antiquities* discussed above, he refers to this text
     as reflecting a similar tradition about primordial languages [*Flavius Josephus, Trans-
     lation and Commentary*, ed. Louis H. Feldman, vol. 3: Judean Antiquities I-IV
     (Leiden, Boston, Koln: Brill, 2000), 18 n. 104].
65   Cf. Leo Jung, "Fallen Angels in Jewish, Christian and Mohammedan Literature. A
     Study in Comparative Folk-Lore," *The Jewish Quarterly Review* 16, no. 1 (1925):
     77–79.
66   Evidently, *Deuteronomy Rabbah* (particularly the material included in Lieberman's
     manuscript) is an authentic Palestinian compendium. For a survey of the scholarly
     opinions on its dating and provenance, see Stemberger, *Introduction to the Talmud
     and Midrash*, 306–308.

tween the Byzantine, Persian and Arab eras; i.e., from the end of the fifth until the beginning of the eighth centuries.[67]

In characteristic rabbinic style, the earlier, more "classical" midrashic compendium to Genesis, *Genesis Rabbah* 20:5,[68] in its passage related to the snake's punishment (to Genesis 4:14-15), stresses such themes as the appropriateness of the punishment,[69] divine mercy, and some eschatological patterns and verbal similarities with other places in the Bible.[70] Most significantly, it expounds how each component in the curse corresponds to a particular crime of the snake, whether it is one that is explicitly recorded in the scriptural account or one that was introduced by the rabbinical tradition:

Genesis Rabbah 20:5:

"Upon thy belly shalt thou go"— At the moment when the Holy One said to him "upon thy belly shalt thou go," the ministering angels descended and chopped off his arms and his legs, and his	על גחונך תלך - בשעה שאמר לו הקב"ה על גחונך תלך, ירדו מלאכי השרת וקצצו ידיו ורגליו והיה קולו הולך מסוף העולם ועד סופו... ר' איסי ורבי הושעיא בשם ר'

---

67 I was unable to find a mention of this passage in expected places (e.g., in the listing of "Sources without Parallel Passages" on p. 89) in Zahava Neuberger (Keller), "The Printed Edition of Midrash Devarim Rabba: Its Character and Place in the Tanhuma-Yelamdenu Literature" (PhD, The Hebrew University of Jerusalem, 1999).

68 Julius Theodor and Chanoch Albeck, eds., *Midrash Bereshit Rabba* (Jerusalem, Israel: Wahrman, 1965), 186.

69 On the rabbinic portrayals of "measure for measure" [מידה כנגד מידה or במידה שאדם מודד בה מודדים אותו] in the meting out of divine justice see Heinemann, *Darkhe Ha-Agadah*, 70–74 [Hebrew]; Saul Lieberman, "On Sins and Their Punishment," in *Texts and Studies* (Ktav, 1974), 29–56; Urbach, *Sages*, 436–439; Ishay Rosen-Zvi, "Measure for Measure as a Hermeneutical Tool in Early Rabbinic Literature: The Case of Tosefta Sotah," *Journal of Jewish Studies* 57, no. 2 (2006): 269–286.

70 See Jacob Neusner, *Praxis and Parable: The Divergent Discourses of Rabbinic Judaism: How Halakhic and Aggadic Documents Treat the Bestiary Common to Them Both*, Studies in Judaism (Lanham, MD: University Press of America, 2006), 136–137: "The key is the metaphorization of the snake: he is like a human being of a certain sort. He is compared, specifically, to named figures; the story of each derives from Scripture's facts. Hence the way lies open for imputing to the snake other human qualities."

Genesis Rabbah 20:5:

voice went from one end of he world to the other...[71]

אחא:

Rabbi Isi and Rabbi Hosha'yah in the name of Rabbi Ḥiyya the great[72] [said four things]:[73]

[1] The Holy One said to him: I appointed you king over the cattle and over the wild beasts, though you did not ask.

אמר לו הקב"ה אני עשיתיך מלך
על הבהמה ועל החיה ואתה לא בקשת.

[2] I made you to walk upright like a human though you did not ask. "Upon thy belly shalt thou go."

אני עשיתיך שתהא מהלך קוממיות
כאדם ואתה לא בקשת, על גחונך תלך.

[3] I made you to eat food like a human, though you did not ask—"And dust shalt thou eat all

אני עשיתיך שתהא אוכל מאכלות
כאדם ואתה לא בקשת —ועפר תאכל כל
ימי חייך.

71　See Menahem M. Kasher, *Torah Shelemah (The Complete Torah)* (Jerusalem, Israel: The Torah Shelemah Institute, 1992), 1:268 [#89]; Leo Jung, "Fallen Angels in Jewish, Christian and Mohammedan Literature: A Study in Comparative Folk-Lore," *The Jewish Quarterly Review* 16, no. 2 (1925): 79; Jacob Neusner, *Praxis and Parable: The Divergent Discourses of Rabbinic Judaism: How Halakhic and Aggadic Documents Treat the Bestiary Common to Them Both*, Studies in Judaism (Lanham, MD: University Press of America, 2006), 137. On the "ministering angels" see Alexander Kohut, *Ueber die jüdische Angelologie und Daemonologie in ihrer Abhängigkeit vom Parsismus* (Leipzig: Kraus Reprint, 1866), 18–19. Kohut argued that the concept was a Jewish adaptation of a Persian belief.

72　Günter Stemberger, *Introduction to the Talmud and Midrash*, 2nd ed. (Edinburgh: T. & T. Clark, 1996), 90; Wilhelm Bacher, *Die Agada der Tannaiten.* (Strassburg: K.J. Truebner, 1890), 2:520-530; = *Agadot Ha-Tanna'im*, trans. Alexander Siskind Rabinovitz (Jerusalem, Israel: Dvir, 1922), 2:2:177-184; Mordecai Margalioth and Yehudah Aizenberg, eds., *Entsiḳlopedyah le-Ḥakhme ha-Talmud yeha-Ge'onim*, Revised edition. (Tel-Aviv: Yavneh and Chemed, 1995), 117–119.

73　That is to say: the following four ways in which the snake's punishment corresponded to his transgression.

Genesis Rabbah 20:5:

the days of thy life."

[4] You wanted to kill Adam and to marry Eve—"And I will put enmity between thee and the woman."[74]	אתה בקשת להרוג את האדם ולישא את חוה —ואיבה אשית בינך ובין האשה.
Indeed, what he wanted was not given to him, and what was given to him he did not want!	הוי מה שבקש לא ניתן לו, ומה שבידו ניטל ממנו.

Variations on this exposition are found in other early rabbinic collections: *t.Soṭah* 4:17 (MS Vienna),[75] *Avot deRabbi Natan* A 1[76] and in a *baraita* in the Babylonian Talmud (*Soṭah* 9b). In spite of the surface similarities that stem from their reliance on the same biblical text and their acceptance of a common theological framework, all these other versions differ crucially

---

74   The notion that there was a sexual relationship between the snake and Eve is found in ancient traditions. This is implied in the boast of the martyred mother in 4 Maccabees that "nor did the destroyer, the deceitful serpent, defile the purity of my virginity." See additional sources cited in Efraim Elimelech Urbach, *The Sages: Their Concepts and Beliefs* (Cambridge, MA: Harvard University Press, 1987), 169, 760–761; Israel Knohl, "Cain: Son of God or Son of Satan?," in *Jewish Biblical Interpretation and Cultural Exchange*, ed. Natalie B. Dohrmann and David Stern, Jewish Culture and Contexts (Philadelphia: University of Pennsylvania Press, 2008), 46–47; Louis Ginzberg, *The Legends of the Jews*, trans. Henrietta Szold (Philadelphia, PA: The Jewish Publication Society of America, 1909), 1:58, 5:59; Mira Wasserman, *Jews, Gentiles, and Other Animals: The Talmud After the Humanities*, Divinations: Rereading Late Ancient Religion (Philadelphia: University of Pennsylvania Press, 2017), 87–8, 261 nn. 27–28.

75   Saul Lieberman, ed., *The Tosefta* (New York: The Jewish Theological Seminary of America, 1995), 3:176 [Hebrew]; *Tosefta Ki-Feshutah* (New York and Jerusalem: Jewish Theological Seminary of America, 1995), 8:653 [Hebrew]; see Neusner, *Praxis and Parable*, 50.

76   Solomon Schechter, ed., *Aboth De-Rabbi Nathan* (Vienna: Ch. D. Lippe, 1887), 3a [Hebrew]; Hans-Jürgen Becker, ed., *Avot De-Rabbi Natan: Synoptische Edition Beider Versionen*, Texts and Studies in Ancient Judaism 116 (Tubingen: Mohr Siebeck, 2006), 18–19; Judah Goldin, ed., *The Fathers According to Rabbi Nathan* (New York: Schocken Books, 1974), 10; Kasher, *Torah Shelemah*, 1:254.

from the *Deuteronomy Rabbah* passage as regards the issue that concerns us in the present study. Significantly, there is nothing in those texts that would suggest that the snake was punished by being deprived of his tongue or his power of speech—an idea that received attention in other ancient (and medieval) commentaries. Because those expositions adhere so closely to the wording in the scriptural curse, the allusion to the serpent's "mouth" comes to be associated with eating, which was the act of disobedience that Eve and Adam were persuaded to perform in disobedience to God's command. The curse of having to eat dust is portrayed as the suitable punishment for abetting the crime of eating the forbidden fruit. Nothing in the curse or punishment relates to the snake's ability to speak, which is treated as a simple, unproblematic detail of the narrative.[77]

Following is another rabbinic tradition that may contain some indirect assumptions about snakes' competence in understanding human speech.

Avot deRabbi Natan B[78]

Rabbi says: If the serpent had not been cursed, he would have been of great utility to the world, because man would have introduced him into use instead of the horse, mule and donkey and he would have carried out manure for man to the gardens and orchards.

רבי אומר אילו לא נתקלל הנחש תיקון גדול היה בו לעולם שהיה אדם מכניסו תחת הסוס תחת הפרד תחת החמור ומוציא בו (אבנים) [זבלים] לגנים ולפרדסאות.

        Rabbi Simeon ben Eleazar[79] says: If the serpent had not been

ר' שמעון בן אלעזר אומר אילו לא נתקלל הנחש תיקון גדול היה לו לעולם

---

77 *PRE Friedlander*, 99–100. inserts a very elaborate and grisly list of punishments that were inflicted on the snake, and the absence of anything related to speaking is quite conspicuous.

78 Solomon Schechter, ed., *Aboth De-Rabbi Nathan* (Vienna: Ch. D. Lippe, 1887), 5; Hans-Jürgen Becker, ed., *Geniza-Fragmente zu Avot de-Rabbi Natan*, Texte und Studien zum antiken Judentum 103 (Tübingen: Mohr Siebeck, 2004), 6; Anthony J. Saldarini, ed., *The Fathers According to Rabbi Nathan (Abot De Rabbi Nathan) Version B: A Translation and Commentary*, Studies in Judaism in Late Antiquity v. 11 (Leiden: Brill, 1975), 32–33.

79 Stemberger, *Introduction to the Talmud and Midrash*, 88; Bacher, *Die Agada der Tannaiten.*, 2:422-436; = *Agadot Ha-Tanna'im*, 2:2:106-115.

Avot deRabbi Natan B

cursed, he would have been of
great utility to the world because
a man would have brought two
serpents for himself and would
have sent one to the to the north
and one to the south, and in thirty
days they would have brought
him silver and gold and precious
stones and pearls.

שהיה אדם קונה לו ב' נחשים (ודורך)
[ומדריכן] אחד לצפון ואחד לדרום עד ל'
יום היו מביאין לו כסף וזהב ואבנים
טובות ומרגליות

This whimsical musing about what the lives of serpents would have been
like if they had not been cursed assumes that they originally had legs and,
presumably, that they walked erect and had arms. By the same token, their
ability to carry out human commands probably implies that they understood speech.[80] Admittedly, we might argue against this thesis by pointing
out how common experience attests that dogs and other beasts can be
trained to carry out simple verbal instructions; however, Rabbi Simeon
ben Eleazar's scenario of the snake retrieving valuables from different
places implies a higher degree of linguistic comprehension. Thus, by indirect inference we may suppose that, at least according to Rabbi Simeon
ben Eleazar, the power of speech was one of the abilities of which the
snake was deprived when he was cursed.[81]

---

80   To be sure, there are passages in rabbinic literature that speak of snakes and other
     predatory beasts as carrying out missions on behalf of God or the rabbis. For exam-
     ple, a fascinating passage in *Genesis Rabbah* 10:7 [Theodor and Albeck, *Bereshit
     Rabba*, 79–83]. *Leviticus Rabbah* 22:4 [Margulies, *Midrash Vayyikra Rabbah*, 503–
     511.] and elsewhere (see parallels cited in Albeck's and Margulies' notes) collects
     numerous instances to illustrate the premise that "the Holy One uses all creatures to
     serve as his agents, even by means of a snake, a scorpion, a mosquito or a frog." So
     too, in *b.Shabbat* 110a (as perceived by the sages in the Talmud) a man is executed
     by means of a snake's bite for having violated a rabbinic edict limiting the permissi-
     ble festivities at weddings, in the spirit of Ecclesiastes 10:8: "whoso breaketh
     through a fence, a serpent shall bite him." See Neusner, *Praxis and Parable*, 111,
     131–132, 152–154.
81   Saldarini, n. 40, stresses that according to other passages in rabbinic literature Rabbi
     Simeon ben Eleazar envisaged the primordial snake as camel-like, and that was the

Concluding Observations

The combined testimonies of Jubilees, Josephus and Philo demonstrate that Jews during the late Second Commonwealth era were involved in systematic exegetical study of the Hebrew scriptures—an enterprise that included thoughtful attempts to account for the lacunae, contradictions and general difficulties that they encountered in their reading. Understandably, their interpretations extended beyond narrow philological concerns, and included defenses of the sacred text's ethical integrity and scientific rationality. Nevertheless, it would appear that their chief objective was to explicate the text, and not just to make use of convenient quotations for homiletical purposes.

In this context, the interpreters were confronted with a formidable challenge in the Bible's unexplained description of the snake in Eden as a being capable of intelligent conversation. The exegetical challenge was at once a logical one (insofar as snakes do not speak) and a narrative one (in that the text does not furnish any explanation for the phenomenon or for its eventual termination). It is remarkable that all those Jewish authors[82] arrived at a solution that was roughly identical: namely, that in the initial stage of the world's history, all living creatures were able to speak, and that they shared a common language. The uniformity of the testimonies from these otherwise diverse authors argues strongly for the likelihood that they were drawing from an interpretative tradition that was well entrenched in the Jewish community at that time. Nevertheless, we should not easily dismiss the possibility that they were influenced by historical assumptions about a primordial Golden Age that were widespread in the dominant Greek culture. Even the Gnostic traditions, however we might choose to define their relationship to the Jewish factions of the time, were clearly responding to a significant degree to the exegetical questions of how the snake could be talking to Eve and Adam. Of course by depicting the serpent as a metaphysical being, or at least as having been possessed

feature that made him suitable for long journeys in search of treasure.

82 Philo's position is not entirely consistent on these points. In his philosophical commentary he seems determined to dismiss the depiction of the snake as purely (but felicitously) allegorical, whereas in the *Quaestiones* he subscribes to the thesis that all living species once shared a common tongue.

by the supernatural power of divine Sophia, the Gnostics were in effect exempting the episode from the criteria of narrative credibility that would otherwise be applied to a historical narrative.

The corpus of talmudic and midrashic literature scarcely yielded a single discussion that went beyond a literal acceptance of the scriptural story about the talking reptile. To put it another way, the rabbis were pleased to discuss *what* he said and *why* he said it; but they evinced no curiosity as to *how* that was possible or what changes might have occurred between Eden and the later ages when neither snakes nor any other non-human creatures were able to converse with or understand the speech issuing from the mouths of human beings.

Appendix: Medieval Jewish Commentators on the Snake in Eden

The dearth of ancient rabbinic discussions about the problem of the talking snake appears more startling when we compare it with the situation that prevailed among Jewish exegetes in the early medieval era. As we emerge from the "late antiquity" that produced the Talmuds and classic midrashic compendia, and venture into the Middle Ages, we are faced with a renewed and urgent-looking interest in the question of animal languages. As was the case among the non-rabbinic texts that we examined from the Second Commonwealth era, most of the medieval rabbinic discussions of this question tended to concentrate on the biblical story of the snake in the garden of Eden; and in doing so the commentators grappled with several very similar theological and philosophical issues. For purposes of the present illustrative survey, I shall confine myself principally to a number of post-talmudic works of "midrash" and particularly to commentators who were cited by Abraham Ibn Ezra in his (uncharacteristically) protracted analysis of the opening verses of Genesis Chapter 3.

Saadiah Gaon:

A lengthy and thoughtful discussion about various aspects of the snake's role in the garden of Eden story may be found in the Arabic commentary of Saadiah (ben Joseph al-Fayyumi) Gaon[83] to Genesis as published by M. Zucker.[84]

Although the opening lines of the pertinent discussion are missing, it is clear that the author was responding to commentators who were claiming that the snake was actually some sort of angelic being basing themselves on the semantic overlapping of the Hebrew word *saraph* to designate both a snake and a kind of angel.[85] He retorts that nothing can be proven from this fact because the usage is merely

83 On Saadia's scriptural exegesis see Henry Malter, *Saadia Gaon: His Life and Works* (New York: Hermon Press, 1969), 145–146; Michael Friedländer, "Life and Works of Saadia," *Jewish Quarterly Review* 5, no. 2, Old Series (1893): 187–190; Robert Brody, "The Geonim of Babylonia as Biblical Exegetes," in *Hebrew Bible / Old Testament. I: From the Beginnings to the Middle Ages (Until 1300)*, ed. Magne Saebo, vol. Part 2: The Middle Ages (Vandenhoeck & Ruprecht, 2000), 74–88; Robert Brody, *Sa'adyah Gaon*, trans. Betsy Rosenberg (Oxford and Portland, OR: The Littman Library of Jewish Civilization, 2013), 58–78; Howard Theodore Kreisel, "Philosophical Interpretations of the Bible," in *The Cambridge History of Jewish Philosophy*, ed. Steven Nadler and T. M. Rudavsky, vol. 1. From Antiquity to the Seventeenth Century (Cambridge: Cambridge University Press, 2009), 92–94.

84 Moshe Zucker, ed., *Saadya's Commentary on Genesis* (New York: The Jewish Theological Seminary of America, 1984), 68-69 [Arabic]; 282-283 [Hebrew]. The relevant passage is preserved in the Genizah fragment Cambridge 27.53. As we will be noting below, there is good reason to cast doubts on Zucker's assumption that this text is indeed by Saadiah.

85 It appears very likely that the missing sections also included responses to other objections and proposed interpretations. As we have already had occasion to observe, the identification of the serpent in Eden with the seraphim in Isaiah's mystical vision is found in the Nag Hammadi Gnostic text "On the Origin of the World" ("The Untitled Text") Bentley Layton, ed., *Nag Hammadi codex II, 2-7: together with XIII, 2*, Brit. Lib. Or. 4926(1), and P. OXY. 1, 654, 655: with contributions by many scholars*, Nag Hammadi Studies 20–21 (Leiden ; New York: E.J. Brill, 1989).] It would eventually be suggested by Simon Patrick, Lord Bishop of Ely in his 1694 commentary to Genesis; see Cline Kelly, "Talking Animals in the Bible," 444; Joseph Blenkinsopp, *Creation, Un-Creation, Re-Creation: A Discursive Commentary on Genesis 1-11* (London and New York: T & T Clark, 2011), 65. In Numbers 21:6-8 the *saraph* and *naḥash* appear to function interchangeably; John 3:14 equates that serpent with the "son of man," an analogy that inspired some gnostics to identify the serpent in Eden as Christ; Rasimus, "Serpent," 427–428.

homonymous; and it is inconceivable that an angel would be subject to petty human emotions or capable of deception.[86]

Whether the snake was acting in the capacity of a beast, an angel or a prophet, it is hard to justify the fact that in the end God held him to be culpable and punished him for his misdeeds. Thus, Saadiah observes that according to the existing interpretations, the only possible way out of the severe exegetical conundrum would be by interpreting all the punishments that were meted out—including those of Eve and Adam—as allegories; and for the sake of maintaining consistency, this premise would have to be extended to the whole of the garden of Eden story. This, he assumes, is a solution that is too radical to be acceptable.

At this point Saadiah steps back to consider why the commentators allowed themselves to get embroiled in such a broad range of diverse and unconvincing explanations. Ultimately it all boils down to the fact that the description of the biblical snake is completely at odds with what we know about the familiar zoological species.[87] After all, ordinary snakes do not talk, nor do they appear to have the intelligence or moral discernment that would render them subject to reward or punishment.[88] If that were not the case and snakes indeed were created as moral beings subject to rules and prohibitions, then the same criteria of moral responsibility should apply to all other non-human creatures, "since reason demands that there is no distinction to be made in this respect between a snake, a camel or a frog." Saadiah is in no doubt that such a conclusion is inadmissible and that the human species is unique in its moral faculty, its intellect and in its ability to communicate through coherent speech.[89]

---

86   For this reason he also claims in his commentary to Job 1:6 that the Satan in Job cannot have been an angel, but was actually a human being like the other members of the "sons of God" (i.e., "distinguished men"). Yosef Kafaḥ, ed., *Iyov 'im Targum u-Feirush Rabbenu Sa'adiyah ben Yosef al-Fayumi* (Jerusalem: American Academy for Jewish Research, 1973), 26–32 [Hebrew].

87   In the *Book of Beliefs and Opinions* 2:3 he listed as one of the acceptable grounds for rejecting literal interpretation when it "differs from what true speculation requires"; see Raphael Jospe, *Jewish Philosophy in the Middle Ages*, EMUNOT: Jewish philosophy and Kabbalah (Boston: Academic Studies Press, 2009), 69.

88   Zucker notes that this was a central controversy in Muslim Kalam and that Saadiah's position corresponds (as usual) with that of the Mu'tazila. See *Saadya's Commentary on Genesis*, 284, n. 404.

89   Mubashir records Saadiah's retort to certain rationalist commentators who wanted to see the snake as occupying (until he was punished) a position midway between humans and beasts: "this view is wrong for several reasons. (1) because reason cannot conceive of a state midway between speaking and non-speaking creatures." [Moshe

In view of all the objections that might be leveled against the previously pro-posed interpretations, Saadiah proposes his own original solution:

> I hereby submit an explanation that is impervious to any possible objections: God... created numerous snakes, just as he created numerous individuals be-longing to every other living species. And when he wished to subject Man to a test, he altered the nature of one particular snake, endowing him with a human form. He then charged him with positive and negative commands and made him subject to reward and punishment; and admonished him that if he should behave disobediently then he would restore him to his original form, even as he had said [to Adam], "for dust thou art, and unto dust shalt thou return" (Genesis 3:19).[90]

Saadiah's claim that the lone snake was given fully human form is, as far as I am aware, unique in the exegetical literature; but if nothing else, it makes it easier to explain how the snake was equipped with the anatomical mechanisms that enabled it to produce the range of sounds that qualify as speech.[91] To be sure, this radically

Zucker, ed., *A Critique against the Writings of R. Saadya Gaon by R. Mubashshir Halevi* (New York: Feldheim, 1955), 97.]. This is of course an established doctrine of Greek philosophical schools (see above); however Saadiah prefers to adduce proof-texts from the Bible, most of them chosen and interpreted with his characteristic in-genuity. Saadiah was notorious for his insistence that humans, by virtue of their ra-tional intelligence and as the last beings to be created by God, are the pinnacle of creation, and that all other creatures, not excluding the astronomical bodies and an-gels, are subordinate to them. See Sa'adia ben Joseph, *The Book of Beliefs and Opin-ions*, trans. Samuel Rosenblatt, Yale Judaica series v. 1 (New Haven: Yale Univ. Press, 1948), 180–183; Malter, *Saadia*, 212-214 (especially 212, n. 485); Howard Theodore Kreisel, *Prophecy: The History of an Idea in Medieval Jewish Philosophy*, Amsterdam Studies in Jewish Thought 8 (Kluwer Academic Publishers, 2001), 89–90, and n. 164. For a brilliantly erudite survey of Jewish and Patristic authors who discuss Man's occupying a mid-point between angels and animals, see Ginzberg, *Le-gends*, 5:65-66, n. 6. On humans as the ultimate purpose of creation see ibid., 5:67-68 n. 8.

90 In Saadiah's Arabic translation of Genesis 3:1 (according to accurate texts) he uses an expression that translates as "became" / "was made intelligent"; Zucker, *Saadya's Commentary on Genesis*, 69, 283–284; Yosef Kafaḥ, ed., *Peirushei Rabbeinu Sa'adiah Ga'on 'al ha-Torah*, new revised. (Jerusalem: Mossad Harav Kook, 1984), 20, n. 1; Y. Ratzaby, *Mi-Perushe Rav Se'adyah La-Mikra* (Jerusalem: Mossad Harav Kook, 2004), 23. In his commentary, he explains that this was a very deliberate choice intended to allude to this interpretation.

91 For similar arguments among eighteenth-century Christian English thinkers see Cline Kelly, "Talking Animals in the Bible," 446.

novel interpretation invites a number of new objections and difficulties, but Saadiah believed that they could be dealt with relative ease.[92]

In his commentary to Genesis, Rabbi Abraham Ibn Ezra (see below) records a different discussion by Saadiah about how the snake was able to speak. Following is the relevant passage as it appears in the two editions of Ibn Ezra's commentary:[93]

Version A:[94]   *Version B:*[95]

And R' Saadiah said: Now that it   The Gaon said that the serpent

---

92 For example: the thesis posits that an ostensibly beneficent God transformed the snake with the specific purpose of testing the humans and entrapping them to sin. This becomes subsumed under the general theology governing free will and retribution. Saadiah's response here is consistent with his position (in line with that of the Mu'tazila) that the issuing of commandments—and the free will that allows us to disobey them—are a necessary precondition for making people deserving of divine rewards; and even though some people may end up being punished for transgressions, the overall result is beneficial to humanity (see the *Book of Beliefs and Opinions* 4:3-6 [Sa'adia ben Joseph, *The Book of Beliefs and Opinions*, 183–204.] See Malter, *Saadia*, 211, 215–217; Brody, *Sa'adyah Gaon*, 54, 71.

To take another possible objection—why was Eve not suspicious when a strange creature or third human being showed up and began speaking to her, when she and Adam were suppose to be the only beings with that ability? To this Saadiah replies that she might well have expressed initial surprise and puzzlement, but that the Torah does not record every trivial conversational detail. Similar questions were raised by seventeenth-century English skeptics; see Cline Kelly, "Talking Animals in the Bible," 443–446.

93 On Ibn Ezra's attitude toward Saadiah see Ezra Zion Melammed, *Bible Commentators*, Publications of the Perry Foundation for Biblical Research in the Hebrew University of Jerusalem (Jerusalem: Magnes Press, 1975), 2:654-664 [Hebrew]. Our current passage is listed on p. 663 among "disputes between Saadiah and other scholars." See also Asher Weiser, ed., *Perushe Ha-Torah Le-Rabbenu Avraham Ibn Ezra* (Jerusalem: Mosad Harav Kook, 1976), 1:67-68 [Hebrew].

94 Based on the Naples 1488 printing. For a more complete list of available texts see Menachem Cohen, ed., *Mikra'ot Gedolot "Haketer,"* vol. 1: Genesis Part 1 (Ramat-Gan, Israel: Bar-Ilan University Press, 1997), Introduction: 13.

95 Originally published from MS British Library Add., 27,038 (Margoliouth 1073/7) in the Hebrew section of Michael Friedländer, *Essays on the Writings of Abraham Ibn Ezra*, Jewish Philosophy in the Middle Ages (London: Trübner and Co. for the Society of Hebrew Literature, 1877). For additional bibliographical details see Asher Weiser, ed., *Perushe Ha-Torah Le-Rabbenu Avraham Ibn Ezra* (Jerusalem: Mosad

Version A:

has been established for us that speech and intelligence are qualities exclusive to humanity, we are compelled to conclude that the serpent, as well as the ass, did not speak, but rather an angel was speaking on their behalf.

Version B:

did not speak, only an angel was speaking on its behalf.

And the Gaon's proof is that it is impossible for a serpent to speak in human language, because it is principally a matter of convention;[96] and it does not possess the appropriate limbs for speech.[97]

Ibn Ezra's summary of Saadiah's position is clearly different from what we read previously in the Arabic commentary published under his name by M. Zucker.[98] There he was apparently arguing against the claims of others that the snake itself was an angel. Here, on the other hand, Saadiah is cited as saying that an angel separate from the snake was speaking through its mouth—performing a kind of ventriloquism with the snake,[99] analogous to what happened with Balaam's ass.[100]

Harav Kook, 1976), 1:137, n. *; Cohen, *Haketer*, 1: Genesis Part 1:13.

96   Translation according to ed. Weiser: כי עקרו הסכמה. The meaning is unclear, but seems to express the dominant view among medieval Jewish rationalists that (contrary to the belief that Hebrew was the primordial divine language of creation) all language evolved naturally as a matter of social convention. For an excellent survey of the major Jewish discussions of this topic see Josef Stern, "Meaning and Language," in *The Cambridge History of Jewish Philosophy*, ed. Steven Nadler and T. M. Rudavsky (Cambridge UK and New York NY: Cambridge University Press, 2009), 230–266. See also Elimelech Epstein-Halevi, *Parashiyot Ba-Agadah Le-or Meḳorot Yevaniyyim* (Haifa: Haifa University Press, 1973), 43–44., who cites the main Greek philosophers and schools who took positions on this controversy about the origins of language. The *Haketer* edition (ed. M. Cohen) reads: ההכרה (recognition); which should perhaps be read as ההברה (in the sense of "the ability to pronounce or enunciate"); see Eliezer Ben-Yehuda, *A Complete Dictionary of Ancient and Modern Hebrew*, vol. 2 (New York: T. Yoseloff, 1960), 2:1030 [meaning ב] [Hebrew].

97   See Basil Herring, "Speaking of Man and Beast," *Judaism* 28, no. 2 (1979): 171 and n. 9.

98   Questions have been raised regarding several passages in M. Zucker's edition of Saadiah's commentary to Genesis as to whether they are really be Saadiah; and this is one of the texts that is considered problematic; see Kreisel, *Prophecy*, 34, n. 17.

Rabbi Samuel ben Hophni Gaon

Ibn Ezra also reports a response by a later Gaon of the Sura talmudic academy, Rabbi Samuel ben Hophni:[101]

Version A:	*Version B:*
And R' Samuel ben Hophni responded to them.	And R' Samuel ben Hophni said that the serpent did speak.[102]

99 A. Greenbaum, *The Biblical Commentary of Rav Samuel ben Hofni Gaon* (Jerusalem: Mossad Harav Kook, 1978), 41, n. 17.] cites an unpublished passage from Judah Ibn Balaam's *Kitab al-Tarjih* to Numbers in which the author takes Saadiah to task for unnecessarily disregarding the explicit wording of the text (Numbers 22:28): "And the Lord opened the mouth of the ass." [Salomon Fuchs, *Studien über Abu Zakaria Jachja (R. Jehuda) Ibn Bal'âm* (Berlin: . Itzkowski, 1893), ix–x.] Rabbi Mubashir Ha-Levi in his critical gloss on Saadiah cites the Gaon's position as "the speech which he created next to the ass and Balaam heard it as if it were issuing through its tongue." M. Zucker comments: "that the words of Ibn Ezra to Genesis there, that according to R' Saadiah the snake did not speak, are not accurate, because in the manuscript versions of Saadiah's commentary it states in various copies that the power of speech was given to the snake." Zucker, *Mubashir*, 95, n. 158.] See also Ratzaby, *Mi-Perushe Rav Se'adyah*, 88.

100 Rabbi David Ḳimhi objected to any interpretation that equated the speech of the snake to that of Balaam's ass: "if it was a miraculous occurrence like the ass's speaking to Balaam, why does it not say here 'And the Lord opened the mouth of the serpent' as it said 'and the Lord opened the mouth of the ass?; Moshe Kamelhar, ed., *Peirushei Rabbi David Ḳimhi 'al ha-Torah* (Jerusalem: Mossad Harav Kook, 1970), 33 [Hebrew].' In a similar vein, Leo Jung, ["Fallen Angels in Jewish, Christian and Mohammedan Literature. A Study in Comparative Folk-Lore," *The Jewish Quarterly Review* 16, no. 1 (1925): 85.] notes that only the mouth of Balaam's ass, and not that of the snake, was included among the prominent miracles that were created on twilight of the first Friday; see below.

101 Died in 1013, as demonstrated by Jacob Mann ["The Last Geonim of Sura," *The Jewish Quarterly Review* 11, no. 4 (1921): 409–422.] based on Genizah documents, and accepted by David Sklare and others; and contrary to the older assumption (still in circulation) that placed it in 1034 [see *Samuel Ben Ḥofni Gaon and His Cultural World: Texts and Studies*, Etudes sur le judaïsme médiéval t. 18 (Leiden and New York: E.J. Brill, 1996), 2, 10].

102 Aaron Greenbaum, ed., *The Biblical Commentary of Rav Samuel ben Hofni Gaon* (Jerusalem: Mossad Harav Kook, 1978), 40–41, n. 17; David Berger, "Judaism and

Ibn Ezra's terse report about Rabbi Samuel ben Hophni's position in Version A[103] does not contain the arguments for that position (as stated in Version B) that the snake did speak;[104] though one may assume that he felt simply that there was no compelling reason here to reject the straightforward sense of the biblical account.[105] It is not clear whether he envisaged this as a general characteristic that originally pertained to all snakes (or to all animal species), or as a phenomenon unique to this snake, in the spirit of Saadia's hypothesis about a uniquely human-like snake being fashioned in order to test Adam and Eve.

General Culture in Medieval and Early Modern Times," in *Judaism's Encounter with Other Cultures: Rejection or Integration?*, ed. Gerald J. Blidstein and Jacob J. Schacter (Northvale, NJ: Jason Aronson, 1997), 70–71, n. 16.

103 On his commentary and biblical exegesis see Greenbaum, *Ben Hofni Commentary*, 11–26; Sklare, *Samuel Ben Ḥofni*, 12–16, 42; Weiser, *Perushe Ha-Torah*, 1:68-69; Robert Brody, *The Geonim of Babylonia and the Shaping of Medieval Jewish Culture* (New Haven: Yale University Press, 1998), 296–297. Brody notes how Samuel ben Hophni came to be regarded as quite a radical rationalist who strove to minimize the number of miracles.

104   A similar discussion appears in Ibn Ezra's Commentary to Numbers 22:28; Weiser, *Perushe Ha-Torah*, 3:180-181:The sages stated (*m.Avot* 5:6) that ten things were created at the twilight of the first sabbath [including the mouth of Balaam's ass]. In my opinion, the reason why the Lord decreed to create these signs is because they lie outside the causal sequence of nature.

> And the Gaon said that the ass did not speak.
> And Rav Samuel ben Hophni refuted him on this.
> And Rabbi Solomon the Spaniard, the poet, thought to rescue him from the refutation.
> You should know that rationalists were compelled to reject the literal interpretation, because they claimed that the Lord would introduce an exception to alter the normal course of nature that he had created, unless it is to confirm one of his prophets.
> But what they said is not true. For take the case of Hananiah Mishael and Azariah —a sign was performed on their behalf even though they were not prophets...
> And the correct view is that the ass did speak.
> And if you understand the mystery of Abraham's angels, and Jacob, then you will have grasped the truth.

(This last last remark has generally been understood to mean that God is able to make people think that they are seeing angels. See Weiser n. 70.) The notion that miracles are introduced principally or exclusively to confirm the missions of prophets is maintained by the Kalam; see Harry Austryn Wolfson, *The Philosophy of the Kalam*, Structure and Growth of Philosophic Systems from Plato to Spinoza 4

Rav Hai Gaon

Responsum of Rav Hai Gaon, *Ḳohelet Shelomoh #3:*[106]

And you inquired regarding our opinion in the matter of the serpent and his speaking to Eve; and the words of the Lord and the arguments that apply to this. And that we should subsequently relate to the matter of Balaam's ass and how it happened that she spoke....

Indeed, these matters are susceptible to several approaches, but we shall deal with them briefly here. Know that the matter of the serpent is an extremely difficult one; and the truth of the matter as it was in the root and branch[107] at the time of the creation and the sin, neither we nor anyone else can fathom. However, we shall cite the views that were expressed about it and present them logically; and we shall discuss whatever lends itself to logical explanation in conformity with the text—and even if it allows for two or more interpretations that are not contradictory, indeed the more likely one is more plausible.

What is credible according to the written text is that this serpent said what the Torah ascribed to it, because they said so, and it follows from this that it was able to speak. We do not know whether it spoke in the style of a human or in some other manner; only that when God chastised him about it and punished him, we know that he sinned because a punishment can only come to one who deserves it, and it is not appropriate to punish someone unless he has transgressed a divine commandment.

However, when the Torah says "and the serpent was more cunning than all the beasts of the field," it is possible that the serpent alone was cunning; but it is also possible that the entire species of serpents was like that at the time of the creation.

(Cambridge MA: Harvard University Press, 1976), 571.

105 Greenbaum, *Ben Hofni Commentary*, 40–41, n. 17. Greenbaum shows that the relevant quotes were reported incorrectly by earlier scholars. At any rate, he points to Ben Hophni's comments to Genesis 48:19 (pp. 332-335) where he upholds a literal reading of the episode of the sun standing still in Joshua 10:13 against those who would insist that it was scientifically impossible.

106 Solomon Aaron Wertheimer, *Ḳohelet Shelomoh* (Jerusalem: A. M. Luntz, 1899), 13–14. In the translation I have omitted the customary pious blessings attached to the divine and to biblical saints.

107 The expression is taken from Malachi 3:19 where it apparently has the meaning of "completely." The usage here is not entirely clear.

In this responsum ascribed to R' Hai[108] Gaon (939-1038),[109] the author surveys several possible interpretations of the snake's speaking. He allows for the likelihood that in such sublime and primordial matters we might not be able to arrive at absolute certainty regarding the true details of the story. At any rate, he takes the very commendable methodological approach of identifying those explanations that are plausible and consistent with the wording of the text—even if that leaves us with more than one such option. Preference is to be given to the interpretation that best satisfies those criteria.

In view of the various doubts and difficulties that pertain to the proposed explanations,[110] Hai favors accepting a straightforward literal reading of the biblical passage rather than interpreting it as an allegory or imposing a farfetched philosophical explanation. Accordingly, the snake must have been an intelligent and morally competent creature who was able to converse with Eve, and did so with malicious intent; otherwise it would not have been deemed culpable. Hai resigns himself cautiously to his inability to solve some of basic theoretical questions to which bolder commentators did claim to provide answers; such as: exactly how did the human and the reptile

---

108 I have chosen to use the conventional and familiar form "Hai" rather than what is likely the more authentic "Hayya"; see Sh. Morag, "On the Form and Etymology of Hai Gaon's Name," *Tarbiz* 31, no. 1 (1961): 188–190 [Hebrew]; Simha Assaf, *Tekufat Ha-Ge'onim Ve-Sifrutah* (Jerusalem: Mossad Harav Kook, 1955), 198; Brody, *Geonim of Babylonia*, 11, n. 35.

109 According to Wertheimer (Introduction, 6-7), the responsum belongs to a collection of inquiries submitted from the Jewish community of Qabis, Tunisia. The questioners' tone suggests to me that they were being provoked by Karaites. According to Sklare, *Samuel ben Hofni*, 76-77, Hai does not figure among the *Ge'onim* who polemicized explicitly with the Karaites. However, D. Sperber makes a persuasive argument for at least one instance in which he conducts a sophistiated implicit debate with them in response to a challenge conveyed to him by the Rabbinite community of Kairouan; see "Divrei Rav Hai Ga'on 'al Teki'at Shofar veha-Pulmus ha-Kara'i," in *Bi-Hyoto Karov: Asuppat Ma'amarim la-Yamim ha-Nora'im le-Zikhro shel Yehi'el Shai Finfter*, ed. Elchanan Ganzel (Merkaz Shapira: Yeshivat Or Etzion, 2000), 246–254 [Hebrew]; *Minhage Yisra'el: Mekorot Ve-Toladot*, vol. 1 (Jerusalem: Mosad Harav Kook, 1989), 219–238 [Hebrew]; see also Brody, *Geonim of Babylonia*, 99 and n. 68.

110 The responsum here does not provide details, though based on comparison with Saadiah, Ibn Ezra and others we can reconstruct several of the interpretations that he had in mind.

converse? Was the snake unique in its ability to speak, or was this capability common to other creatures as well? Neither science nor logic nor textual analysis can provide answers to these questions, and presumably we do not need to know those peripheral details in order to elicit the important religious lessons from the story.[111]

As we shall be observing below, Abraham Ibn Ezra adopted very similar strategies in dealing with the issues raised by the passage.

Rabbi Solomon Ibn Gabirol:

Notwithstanding the outstanding contributions of Solomon Ibn Gabirol (Andalusia, c. 1021-c.1058)[112] to Hebrew poetry, philosophy and liturgy, our knowledge of his activity as a Bible exegete is based entirely on brief quotations such as this one in Ibn Ezra's commentary:[113]

Version A:

And now Rabbi Solomon the Spaniard, author of the metered poems,who was a learned man, responded to R' Samuel.

Version B:

And R' Solomon Ibn Gabirol said: If the serpent spoke, then why do its progeny not still speak today? Note that there is no reference in the text to its lips being silenced.

---

111 For a brief but knowledgeable assessment of Hai's intellectual life see Assaf, *Tekufat*, 199–200. Assaf notes that Hai was influenced by Saadiah to take an interest in philosophy and philology, but to a far more limited extent.

112 C. Sirat places his birth in 1021/2 an his death "between 1054 and 1058"; see *A History of Jewish Philosophy in the Middle Ages* (Cambridge, UK, New York and Paris: Cambridge University Press and Editions de la Maison des Sciences de l'Homme, 1985), 68–69; see also Raphael Loewe, *Ibn Gabirol*, Jewish Thinkers (London: Peter Halban, 1989), 17–24.

113 Sara Klein-Braslavy, "The Philosophical Exegesis," in *Hebrew Bible / Old Testament. I: From the Beginnings to the Middle Ages (Until 1300)*, ed. Magne Saebo, vol. Part 2: The Middle Ages (Vandenhoeck & Ruprecht, 2000), 304–306. The two pages devoted to Ibn Gabirol do in fact cover virtually all the surviving examples, including the current one about which she concludes: "Ibn Gabirol does not present here a philosophical exegesis, but only attempts to neutralize the supernatural dimension of the story and thereby harmonize between it and logical, and not necessarily philosophical, thought." See also Loewe, *Ibn Gabirol*, 25; Weiser, *Perushe Ha-Torah*, 1:68.

In one manuscript of his Genesis commentary,[114] Ibn Ezra cites approvingly an interpretation by Ibn Gabirol of the garden of Eden story in which all the components are explained allegorically, with the serpent symbolizing physical desire:

> Behold I shall now reveal to you through an esoteric allusion about the garden and the rivers and the garments, for I have not found this secret among any of the great authorities other than Rabbi Solomon ben Gabirol of blessed memory, because he was a very wise man in matters related to the secret of the soul...
>
> Adam represents the Wisdom that assigned names. And Eve, as the word suggests, is the vital spirit. And thesnake represents the faculty of bodily desire, as is implied by the name, which is etymologically related to the word for"divination" [נַחֵשׁ‎ יְנַחֵשׁ‎] (Genesis 44:15).[115]

---

114 Michael Friedländer, *Essays on the Writings of Abraham Ibn Ezra*, Jewish Philosophy in the Middle Ages (London: Trübner and Co. for the Society of Hebrew Literature, 1877), 40 [Hebrew]; cited by Sirat, *Jewish Philosophy in the Middle Ages*, 79.

115 Kamelhar, *Peirushei RaDa"K*, 33, also concludes that it can only be properly appreciated at the esoteric level (offering an elaborate demonological interpretation inspired by *Pirke deRabbi Eliezer*). Whereas Ḳimḥi was evidently impelled to eschew a literal reading on account of exegetical considerations, it would appear that Ibn Gabirol was more actively drawn to an allegorical interpretation that would express his Neoplatonic philosophical beliefs. For synopses of Ibn Gabirol's philosophical views, see Isaac Husik, *A History of Mediaeval Jewish Philosophy* (Mineola, NY: Dover Publications, 2002), 63–79; Julius Guttmann, *The Philosophy of Judaism: The History of Jewish Philosophy from Biblical Times to Franz Rosenzweig* (Northvale, NJ: J. Aronson, 1988), 89–103; Salo Wittmayer Baron, *A Social and Religious History of the Jews*, 2nd Revised edition., vol. Vol. 8: Philosophy and Science: High Middle Ages (New York: Columbia University Press, 1958), 82–87; Jacques Schlanger, *La Philosophie de Salomon Ibn Gabirol. Étude d'un Néoplatonisme*, Études sur le judaîsme médiéval t. 3 (Leiden: E. J. Brill, 1968), 110–316; Fernand Brunner, *Métaphysique d'Ibn Gabirol et de La Tradition Platonicienne*, ed. Daniel Schulthess, Variorum Collected Studies Series CS589 (Aldershot and Brookfield, VT: Ashgate, 1997); Loewe, *Ibn Gabirol*; Sirat, *Jewish Philosophy in the Middle Ages*, 68–81; Sarah Pessin, *Ibn Gabirol's Theology of Desire: Matter and Method in Jewish Medieval Neoplatonism* (Cambridge and New York: Cambridge University Press, 2013); Jospe, *Jewish Philosophy in the Middle Ages*, 107–131.

Rabbi Tobiah ben Eliezer

Rabbi Tobiah ben Eliezer, *Midrash Lekah Tov* to Genesis 3:1:[116] And in which language did the serpent speak to the woman? —In the holy tongue. For regarding him it is written "and the serpent was cunning"; and he walked erect; and he knew the language of man.

> Or you can say: in his own language; for beasts possess languages, a different one for each species. And just as he assigned them names, for he knew how to assign names to each one, so could he converse with the serpent.

In his explanation of the snake's "cunning," the eleventh century Rabbi Tobiah ben Eliezer of Kastoria in the Balkans,[117] deals with various aspects of the Torah's depiction of the snake, its behavior and the curse that was imposed upon it. Presumably from a simple literal reading of the biblical narrative, Rabbi Tobiah had no reason to question that the snake was able to converse in the same language as the humans. The fact that this ability no longer persists in snakes or in any other non-human creatures need not trouble us, since after all, the snake of the garden of Eden also demonstrated additional qualities that are no longer found in other species, such as its ability to walk upright; as could be inferred from the fact that "upon thy belly shalt thou go" (Genesis 3:14) was included in the curse.[118]

---

116 Tobiah ben Eliezer, *Midrash Lekah Tov*, ed. Salomon Buber (Jerusalem, 1959), 24.
117 On the book, its author and provenance, Ibid., Introduction: 6b-13b; Joshua Starr, *The Jews in the Byzantine Empire, 641-1204*, Judaica Series 8 (New York: B. Franklin, 1970), 216; Salo Wittmayer Baron, *A Social and Religious History of the Jews*, 2nd Revised edition., vol. Vol. 6: Laws, Homilies, and the Bible: High Middle Ages (New York: Columbia University Press, 1958), 173–175, 411, n. 27; Stemberger, *Introduction to the Talmud and Midrash*, 389–390; Israel M. Ta-Shma, "Midrash 'Lekah Tov'—Rik'o ve-'Ofyo," in *Studies in Medieval Rabbinic Literature*, vol. 3. Italy & Byzantium, 5 vols. (Jerusalem: Bialik Institute, 2005), 259–294; Jonathan Jacobs, "The Allegorical Exegesis of Song of Songs by R. Tuviah Ben 'Eli'ezer: Lekah Tov, and Its Relation to Rashi's Commentary," *AJS Review* 39, no. 1 (April 2015): 76.
118 This is taught explicitly in midrashic literature; e.g., *Genesis Rabbah* 19:1 (p. 171) Rabbi Tobiah cites the midrash (*Genesis Rabbah* 19:3, p. 172, and parallels listed by Theodor) about the snake pushing Eve against the tree of knowledge of good and evil in order to convince her that touching it would have no perilous consequences. Similarly in *Avot deRabbi Natan* A 1 (ed. Schechter 4): "He arose and touched the tree with his hands and feet..." See also *PRE Friedlander*, 95; Ginzberg, *Legends*, 1:71-72; 5:94-95; Jung, "Fallen Angels 2," 92–95; Adelman, "The Return of the Repressed," 82–83.

What remains for the commentator, therefore, is to determine in what language it was that the snake was conversing with Eve. Rabbi Tobiah presents two possible answers to this question. The first, predictably, is that he spoke Hebrew, the primordial language of creation. There are actually two assumptions that underlie this interpretation: (1) that humans were speaking Hebrew rather than some other language; and: (2) that the snake spoke the same language as the humans. Implied in all this is yet a third factor: was the snake unique ("cunning") in his linguistic gift, or was that ability shared by the other living species at that time?[119]

The second possibility entertained by the *Leḳaḥ Ṭov* is that each animal species had its own individual language, but that Adam was endowed with the special ability to understand those languages, as implied in his ability to bestow upon them appropriate names (Genesis 2:19-20).[120] Given this premise, "Snakish" is just one of the languages that the polyglot first human was able to understand.

Clearly, Rabbi Tobiah devoted considerable reflection on the nature of the snake's communication and on its broader implications as it related to the ability of non-human species to understand or speak languages. According to the first explanation, we are apparently intended to understand that it was only the snake who was cursed by losing his ability to understand Hebrew;[121] whereas other animals never possessed such an ability.

119 Ginzberg, *Legends*, 5:94, n. 58., "The older rabbinic literature does not know of the original language spoken by man and the animals, and even Lekah, Gen. 3. 1, maintains that only the serpent spoke Hebrew (i.e., the original speech of man...)." He is distinguishing this assertion from the midrashic teaching, based on the etymological connection between the Hebrew words for "man" and "woman" (which does not have equivalents in Greek or Aramaic) that "from this you may deduce that the Torah was given in the holy tongue. R' Phineas and Rabbi Hilkiah in the name of R' Simon: Just as it was given in the holy tongue, so was the world created in the holy tongue"; *Genesis Rabbah* 18:4 [pp. 164-165].

120 Cf. ibid., 1:61-62; 5:83-84. A midrashic tradition found in the *Tanḥuma* texts to the beginning of Deuteronomy interpret Genesis 2:20, which literally speaks of Adam assigning [plural] "names" to the animals, as implying that he knew the proverbial "seventy languages" of humanity and was able to name each creature in every one of those languages; Fraade, "Moses and Adam as Polyglots."

121 It is convenient to assume that Hebrew remained the common language of humanity until the division among Noah's sons after the flood, or the tower of Babel, when Hebrew was confined to the line of Abraham. As far as I can see, no such statement is found explicitly in the *Leḳaḥ Ṭov*; see ed. Buber 1:25b-25a; 27a-27b.

Rabbi Abraham Ibn Ezra

In the foregoing pages were found several occasions to cite the twelfth-century biblical commentator, the itinerant Spaniard Abraham ben Meir Ibn Ezra (1092-1167),[122] as a source for our quotations from other theologians and exegetes. [123] It remains to take a look at Ibn Ezra's own views concerning the question of the snake's speaking, as well as some other opinions that he cites but whose authors he does not identify.

Rabbi Abraham Ibn Ezra Commentary to Genesis 3:1:

(Version A):[124]

"And the serpent"— There are some who say that the woman understood and knew the language of the animals. They explain "the serpent said" as: through gestures...

Others, however, said that he was Satan. But how could they fail to see the end of the section, for how can Satan creep on his belly, and how can he eat dirt, and what sense is there to the curse "and he will strike your head"?

And there are many who got themselves entangled by investi-

Version B

"More cunning than all the beasts of the field"—but not more than the man.

And others maintained that it was Satan, who is a demon, that spoke through him.

---

122 For a readable and erudite portrait of Ibn Ezra's exegetical enterprise see Nahum M. Sarna, "Abraham Ibn Ezra as an Exegete," in *Rabbi Abraham Ibn Ezra: Studies in the Writings of a Twelfth-Century Polymath*, ed. Isadore Twersky and Jay Harris (Cambridge MA and London: Harvard University Press, 1993), 1–27; see also Kreisel, "Philosophical Interpretations of the Bible," 88–92, 95–96; Melammed, *Bible Commentators*, 2:519-714 [Hebrew].

123 On Ibn Ezra's attitudes toward rabbinic interpretation and other commentators see Sarna, "Abraham Ibn Ezra as an Exegete," 12–17.

124 Weiser, *Perushe Ha-Torah*, 1:25; H. Norman Strickman and Arthur M Silver, *Ibn Ezra's Commentary on the Pentateuch* (New York, N.Y: Menorah, 1988), 66–67.

(Version A):   *Version B*

gating this: why was the snake
cursed, and whether it had a full
intellect, or whether it had been
commanded not to entice the
woman?[125]

Ibn Ezra's first suggestion (somewhat analogous to the second explanation of the
Lekah Tov) is that rather than the snake knowing how to speak in a human language,
it was Eve who was able to understand the language of the snake. As a rationalist
who was unwilling to allow for suspensions of the familiar course of nature, Ibn Ezra
proposes that this serpentine "language" did not take the form of audible sounds of
the kind that define human speech, since snakes are not anatomically equipped to
produce such sounds—and so, presumably, they never were—but rather, the snake
communicated with Eve through a "body language" of hints, gestures or other signs
that she was capable of understanding.[126]

The terse comment in Version B takes a similar approach, proposing that the
snake, while perhaps more intelligent than other dumb beasts, was nevertheless not

---

125 At this point he cites Saadiah's interpretation, as discussed above.

126 Compare Ķimḥi: "Why does it state 'and the serpent was more cunning' if he did not
really speak?" He goes on to dismiss the prospect of conducting a meaningful conversion in pantomime: "It is very unlikely that a woman could understand such matters from mere hints. Furthermore, even if the woman understood the serpent's hints,
how could he understand the woman's response?"
The fact that Ibn Ezra focuses his hypothesis only on Eve and the snake, but says
nothing here about Adam or other snakes or creatures, I take to be a consequence of
his exegetical context; the snake and Eve are the ones who are directly conversing in
the text that he is trying to elucidate, though presumably Adam would also have
known how to decipher the snake's sign language. On the other hand, though the
snake's ability to express himself might have derived from his distinctive "cunning,"
it is likely that for Ibn Ezra it was a "natural" ability that would have been common
to the other members of his species, but not necessarily to other creatures. Evidently,
Ibn Ezra was avoiding taking questionable stands on any more questions than were
absolutely required for the elucidation of the text. Cf. Basil Herring, "Speaking of
Man and Beast," *Judaism* 28, no. 2 (1979): 171–172.

as smart as a human.[127] Although the author does not reject those explanations out of hand, neither does he endorse them.[128]

Ibn Ezra now proceeds to dismiss the explanations that equate the snake with Satan. He expresses his amazement that anyone could have proposed such an interpretation, since it so patently conflicts with the outcome of the story. After all, the punishment that was imposed on the snake at the end only makes sense with reference to a physical snake.

The claim that the serpent was Satan, though it is attested in ancient Jewish works like the Apocalypse of Baruch,[129] in Gnostic texts and in Christian tradition,[130] is notably absent from classical rabbinic literature until it surfaced in medieval "midrashic" or mystical compendia like *Pirḳei deRabbi Eliezer*.[131]

127 This point appears at the conclusion of the discussion in Version A.

128 I imagine that he was uneasy with the fact that the snake was clever enough to take in Eve—and through her, Adam.

129 Greek Baruch 9:3; James H. Charlesworth, ed., "3 (Greek Apocalypse of) Baruch," in *The Old Testament Pseudepigrapha*, trans. H. E. Gaylord Jr., 1st ed. (Garden City, NY: Doubleday, 1983), 658, 673.

130 Grant, *Early Christians and Animals*, 4–5.

131 For a survey of the evolution of the depictions of Samma'el / Satan, including specific references to his identification with the serpent in the garden of Eden, see Jung, "Fallen Angels 2," 85–88; Dan, "Samael and the Problem of Jewish Gnosticism." A more detailed assessment of the theme's appearance in *Pirḳei deRabbi Eliezer*, which acknowledges that work's paradoxical character as a "late midrash" that nonetheless is the stage for the reemergence of ancient (and likely, suppressed) mythological motifs, may be found in Knohl, "Cain: Son of God or Son of Satan?," 38, 47–50. They stress that the identification of the serpent with Satan or Samma'el is a late development that is absent from classical rabbinic sources. Nevertheless, Knohl (43-46) makes a persuasive case for a reconstruction of the biblical text as a redactional reconciliation between original contradictory traditions, one of which (J) saw humanity as the cursed descendants of an evil Cain, whereas the other (P) did not contain the story of Abel's murder and hence could trace the human race back through a Cain who was Adam's righteous firstborn. Note however Targum Pseudo-Jonathan to Genesis 3:6: "And the woman saw Sammael the angel of death and was afraid." Avigdor Shinan, *The Embroidered Targum: The Aggadah in Targum Pseudo-Jonathan of the Pentateuch*, Publications of the Perry Foundation for Biblical Research in the Hebrew University of Jerusalem (Jerusalem: Magnes Press, the Hebrew University, 1992), 130–134 [Hebrew]; see Michael Maher, "Targum Pseudo-Jonathan, Genesis," The Aramaic Bible 1B (Collegeville, MN: Liturgical Press, 1992), 26 and n. 8. Scholarly consensus dates Targum Ps.-Jonathan no earlier than the seventh or eighth century, after the advent of Islam and the appearance of *Pirḳei deRabbi Eliezer*; see

After presenting this array of reasonable and less-reasonable explanations, Ibn Ezra goes on to offer his own preferred reading of the snake's character and its ability to converse.

Version A:

The most reasonable approach in my eyes is to accept the matters literally: the serpent did speak and used to walk with erect posture; and he who instills intelligence in human beings instilled it in him. Behold, the verse attests that he was more cunning than any of the beasts of the field— just not more than a human.

Version B:

The simple approach is to accept the literal sense; and after the Lord forced it to eat dust, it fell from having the highest status of all created living things, to eating all fruits and herbs.

As grasped in a thoughtful summary by Jean-Louis Ska,[132] Ibn Ezra's decision to opt for a literal reading of the Garden of Eden story and of the snake's role therein followed plausibly from the premises that (a) God is after all able to endow creatures with intelligence, and (b) the principal alternative explanation, that the snake was an angel or was manipulated by an angel, would be inconsistent with the kinds of behavior that can legitimately be ascribed to angels, who are (according to the view prevailing among medieval Jewish philosophers) obedient servants of God and unable to act immorally. It was noted previously that even if the snake was Satan or a proxy for him, then the physical punishments that were meted out to him make no sense.[133] At any rate, Ibn Ezra's explanation seems to imply that the snake's

Shinan, *Embroidered Targum*, 193–198 [Hebrew]; Maher, "Ps.-Jonathan Gen," 11– 12.

132 "The Study of the Book of Genesis: The Beginning of Critical Reading," in *The Book of Genesis: Composition, Reception, and Interpretation*, ed. Craig A. Evans, Joel N. Lohr, and David L. Petersen, Supplements to Vetus Testamentum 152 (Brill, 2012), 6–7. After summarizing Ibn Ezra's method of dealing with the passage, Ska observes, "Ibn Ezra is not only looking for 'meaning' in the account in Genesis. He is looking for logic and inner coherency."

133 This point is argued by Ḳimḥi, ibid.: "If we were to accept R' Saadiah's thesis, that neither the serpent not the ass spoke, but rather an angel spoke on their behalf, then why was the serpent cursed? Furthermore: How would an angel entice the woman to transgress a divine command?... And if we posit that it was in order to test the woman that the angel intended to test whether she would transgress God's word, then where did the serpent sin in all this?"

punishment, in addition to making it creep on its belly and bear the enmity of women, also involved the removal of its cunning and its speech.[134]

Once those possibilities have been eliminated, then we are left with the more plausible understanding,[135] that primordial snake in the narrative was really an intelligent, human-like being who was able (in some manner or other) to converse with Eve and entrap her, and was subject to punishment for his willful subversion of the divine commands.[136]

134 Ķimḥi objects cogently that if that were indeed the case, then depriving of the snake of its intelligence should have been mentioned explicitly in the curse, since that would have constituted its most important component.

135 For some salient observations regarding the rationalist underpinnings of Ibn Ezra's exegetical enterprise see Raphael Jospe, "Biblical Exegesis as a Philosophic Literary Genre: Abraham Ibn Ezra and Moses Mendelssohn," in *Jewish Philosophy and the Academy*, ed. Emil L. Fackenheim and Raphael Jospe (Madison, Teaneck and London: Fairleigh Dickinson University Press and Associated University Presses in association with the Minneapolis Institute of Arts, 1996), 48–92.

136 Regarding Ibn Ezra's claim that the snake was originally erect, full-limbed, intelligent, and superior to the other beasts—but not to man, Ķimḥi comments that "this is the view of our sages." See *Genesis Rabbah* 7:5 [ed. Theodor-Albeck, p. 54]; 19:1 [p. 171]. Nevertheless, he subjects the claim to serious criticism. If God really created a being or species that was comparable to Man (evidently sharing the divine image), then it deserved to be mentioned no less than Man in the scriptural account of the creation in the first chapter of Genesis.

A Bird of the Air will Carry Your Voice

"I'M A RAVEN, AREN'T I?" IT SAID. "ONE OF THE FEW
BIRDS WHO SPEAK. THE FIRST THING PEOPLE SAY IS,
OH, YOU'RE A RAVEN, GO ON, SAY THE N WORD... IF I
HAD A PENNY EVERY TIME THAT'S HAPPENED, I'D—"...

"...LOOK, I DIDN'T ASK TO DO THIS, YOU KNOW. I WAS
ASLEEP ON MY SKULL, NEXT MINUTE HE HAD A GRIP ON
MY SKULL, AS I SAID, I'M NATURALLY AN OCCULT
BIRD."[1]

In surveying the statements of the various philosophers who discussed the issue of animal language, we noted that some of them—including Aristotle, Alexander (the nephew of Philo) and Porphyry—made special reference to birds as a species that comes closest to emulating speech. Although the capability is most popularly associated with members of the parrot family (including parakeets, budgerigars and cockatoos),[2] it has been observed as well among mynahs, starlings, mockingbirds and the corvid family that includes crows and ravens. It was the last-mentioned group (which was perhaps the most ubiquitous in their environment) that

---

1   Terry Pratchett, *Soul Music: A Novel of Discworld* (New York: HarperPrism, 1995), 58.

2   The parrot or parakeet (βιττακος) with its amazing ability to imitate human speech was introduced into Greek discourse by the fifth-century B.C.E. Ctesiasin his *Indica* (as preserved by the ninth-century Patriarch of Constantinople Photius in his *Bibliotheca*); and it subsequently became a staple in the arguments about animal intelligence. J. M. Bigwood, "Ctesias' Parrot," *The Classical Quarterly* 43, no. 1 (1993): 321–327; Deborah Levine Gera, *Ancient Greek Ideas on Speech, Language, and Civilization* (Oxford and New York: Oxford University Press, 2003), 208–209.

figures most prominently in rabbinic traditions about talking animals.[3]

Noah and the Raven

The story of Noah's flood describes the destruction of non-human creatures as well as humans, and this might be taken to imply that those creatures possessed enough intelligence and moral judgment to be culpable for their sins, yet the midrashic expositions do not introduce speaking animals

---

3   W. H. Thorpe, "Talking Birds and the Mode of Action of the Vocal Apparatus of Birds," *Proceedings of the Zoological Society of London* 132, no. 3 (May 1, 1959): 441–455.

in that context.[4] On the other hand, *Genesis Rabbah* 33:5[5] records an extensive dialogue that took place between Noah and the raven:[6]

Genesis Rabbah 33:5:   *MS. Oxford Heb. e. 73/17:*[7]

"[And he sent forth a raven,]   "ויצא יצא ושוב"
which went forth to and fro
[Hebrew: *va-Shov*]"—

---

4   In the declaration of his intention to send the flood (Genesis 6:7), God says "I will destroy man whom I have created from the face of the earth; both man, and beast, and the creeping thing, and the fowls of the air; for it repenteth me that I have made them." On the other hand, the prelude to the flood states (5-6) "And God saw that the wickedness of *man* was great in the earth... And it repented the Lord that he had made *man* on the earth," without mentioning the other creatures. From this it might be understood that the destruction of the other beings was merely a form of collateral damage; i.e., if the chosen form of punishment was a flood, then (at least according to the assumptions of the biblical authors, and as learned from their experiences of natural floods and other disasters) it was impossible to ensure a distinguishing between the different species of victims. Such a reading of the scriptural narrative would in fact imply that animals are easily expendable and their lives or sufferings have no inherent worth in the larger divine plan. *Genesis Rabbah* 28:6 deals with this question and proposes to explain (according to Rabbi Judan) that the animals were destroyed because they were accessories to the people's sins (because the easy availability of meat and animal products promoted their moral decadence); or (according to Rabbi Phineas) because God was merely venting his rage at them out of frustration for having to destroy his beloved children, though their own status was equivalent to that of inanimate objects. For a more thorough discussion of rabbinic and Jewish exegetical understandings of the animals' culpability or their right to be saved on the ark in the flood story–where the primary sins ascribed to them involved interspecies cross-breeding, against which they had somehow been admonished, see Viktor Aptowitzer, "The Rewarding and Punishing of Animals and Inanimate Objects: On the Aggadic View of the World," *Hebrew Union College Annual* 3 (1926): 134–135, etc.; cf. Ian Stewart and Jack Cohen, *Darwin's Watch: The Science of Discworld III*, First Anchor Books Edition. (New York: Anchor Books, 2015), 166. The discussions extend to the animals who evidently perished in the plague of the Egyptian first-born (Exodus 12:12) and the rewarding of dogs for their assistance in the exodus as understood in rabbinic tradition (11:7). In the sources cited by Eric Lawee the animals do not have speaking parts.

Genesis Rabbah 33:5:

R' Judan in the name of
R' Judah be"R Simon:[8] He began to respond with retorts
[*meshivo teshuvot*]. He said to
him: From among all the domestic animals and the fowl

MS. Oxford Heb. e. 73/17:

ר' יודן בש' רבי יודה ביר סימון:
התחיל משיבו תשובות אמר לו מכל
בהמה ועוף שיש כן אן את משליח אילא
לי.

אמר לו מה צורך לעולם לך,
לאכילה לקורבן.

---

5   Julius Theodor and Chanoch Albeck, eds., *Midrash Bereshit Rabba* (Jerusalem, Is-
     rael: Wahrman, 1965), 309–310; Gerrit Bos, "Jewish Traditions on Divination with
     Birds   (Ornithomancy),"   2015,   https://www.researchgate.net/   publication/
     280976904_ Jewish_Traditions_ on_ Divination_ with_ Birds_ Ornithomancy.
     Parallel versions are listed in the critical apparatus to *Genesis Rabbah*. In connection
     with the version in *b.Sanhedrin* 108b, R' Meir Abulafia was impelled to write in his
     Yad Ramah commentary: "This is not to say that this is a miracle tale; but rather,
     even domestic and wild animals and fowl are capable of conversing among them-
     selves; however it is not true speech but mere signs. Some people are able to under-
     stand them."

6   For another passage in rabbinic literature that seems to mention talking ravens, see
     t.Shabbat 6:6 discussed elsewhere. On divinations of this kind see Gideon Bohak,
     Ancient Jewish Magic: A History, 1st pbk. ed. (Cambridge, UK and New York: Cam-
     bridge University Press, 2011); Giuseppe Veltri, *Magie Und Halakha: Ansätze Zu
     Einem Empirischen Wissenschaftsbegriff Im Spätantiken Und Frühmittelalterlichen
     Judentum*, Texte und Studien zum antiken Judentum 62 (Tübingen: Mohr, 1997), 93–
     220. Pliny, *Natural History* 10:60 (121-125) [transl. Rackham, 370-373] invites his
     readers to "Let us also repay due gratitude to the ravens!" He tells us of one well-
     known raven who picked up the habit of talking ("is mature sermoni adsuefactus")
     and began to daily salute the emperor and the populace in the forum. The bird be-
     came so beloved of the people that it merited a grand funeral, and intense hatred of
     its slayer. As noted astutely by T. Fögen, notwithstanding the central place that this
     story occupies in Pliny's treatment of ravens (which amounts, in turn, to almost half
     of his discussion about birds), it provides no real information about the contents of
     the raven's supposed speech or its salutation: "The story is much more concerned
     with the moral qualities of the bird than with its speech faculty, or, in other words,
     with its *officium* towards the royal family as well as with the Roman public rather
     than with its *ingenium*. With its respectful conduct, the raven behaves almost like a
     good Roman citizen." ["Pliny the Elder's Animals: Some Remarks on the Narrative
     Structure of Nat. Hist. 8–11," *Hermes* 135, no. 2 (2007): 191]. Pliny was also person-
     ally acquainted with a black crow who was remarkable "for uttering sentences of

Genesis Rabbah 33:5:

that are found here, I am the only one that you are sending forth.

He said: What need does the world have of you? For food? For sacrifice?

Rabbi Berachiah in the name of Rabbi Abba bar Ka-

MS. Oxford Heb. e. 73/17:

רבי ברכיה בש׳ ר׳ אבא בר כהנא
אמר: א׳ לו הקדוש ברוך הוא: קבלו

---

several words [plura contexta verba exprimens] and frequently learning still more words in addition."

7 Julius Theodor and Chanoch Albeck, eds., *Midrash Bereshit Rabba* (Jerusalem, Israel: Wahrman, 1965), 309–310. For the Hebrew text I combined the readings of the two Genizah manuscripts (#2 and #3) with variants form MS Vatican 30, as transcribed by Michael Sokoloff, ed., *The Geniza Fragments of Bereshit Rabba*, Publications of the Israel Academy of Sciences and Humanities: Section of Humanities (Jerusalem: The Israel Academy of Sciences and Humanities, 1982), 124–125 [Hebrew]. Sokoloff argues persuasively that his MS #2, a palimpsest, is "undoubtedly the most important" of the manuscripts in his study, the oldest surviving exemplar of *Genesis Rabbah* (p. 20). He further argues that it was the actual *vorlage* of MS Vatican 30, considered the finest complete version of the midrash; see Michael Sokoloff, "The Hebrew of 'Běréšit Rabba' According to Ms. Vat. Ebr. 30," *Lěsonénu: A Journal for the Study of the Hebrew Language and Cognate Subjects* 33, no. 1 (1968): 35–42; *Bereshit Rabba Geniza*, 26–50; cf. Lewis M. Barth, *An Analysis of Vatican 30*, Monographs of the Hebrew Union College 1 (Cincinnati: Hebrew Union College-Jewish Institute of Religion, 1973), 66–80. Sokoloff includes a systematic comparison between the readings of MS #2 and Vat. 30 to our present passage in *Bereshit Rabba Geniza*, 51.

8 On these rabbis see Ch. Albeck, *Introduction to the Talmud. Babli and Yerushalmi* (Tel-Aviv: Dvir, 1969), 329–330 [Hebrew]; Günter Stemberger, *Introduction to the Talmud and Midrash*, 2nd ed. (Edinburgh: T. & T. Clark, 1996), 103; Wilhelm Bacher, *Die Agada der palästinensischen Amoräer* (Strassburg i. E: K. J. Trübner, 1892), 3.160-220 [current passage on p. 180]; = *Agadat Amora'e Erets-Yiśra'el*, trans. Alexander Siskind Rabinovitz (Tel-Aviv: Dvir, 1928), 3:1:148-201 [current passage on p. 165] [Hebrew]; Mordecai Margalioth and Yehudah Aizenberg, eds., *Entsiḳlopedyah le-Ḥakhme ha-Talmud yeha-Ge'onim*, Revised edition. (Tel-Aviv: Yavneh and Chemed, 1995), 2:172.

Genesis Rabbah 33:5:	*MS. Oxford Heb. e. 73/17:*
hana said: The holy one said to him: Accept him because the world will eventually have a need for him.	שהעולם עתיד לצרך לו
	א' לו: אמתיי
He said to him: When?	אמר לו: עד "יבשת המים מעל הארץ" עתיד צדיק אחד לעמוד ולייבש את העולם ואני מצריכו להם הדה ה"ד
He said to him: "...until the waters were dried up from off the earth." One righteous man will arise and dry out the world, and I will cause him to need them. This is what is written: "until the waters were dried up from off the earth."	(מ"א יז, ו): "והעורבים מביאים לו לחם וגו'..."
Rabbi Akiva expounded the story of the generation of the flood in Ginzak of Media;[9] and when he mentioned to them the story of the raven they wept,	דרש ר"ע מעשה דור המבול בגונזך שלמדיי ולא בכו וכיון שהזכיר להם מעשה עורב מיד בכו

---

9 For various theories about the exact location of Ginzak see Ben-Zion Eshel, *Jewish Settlements in Babylonia during Talmudic Times: Talmudic Onomasticon* (Jerusalem: The Magnes Press, the Hebrew University, 1979), 87–88. Akiva's presence in Ginzak is mentioned in several places in the Babylonian Talmud, at least in some of the manuscripts: *b. Ta'anit* 11b, *b. 'Avodah Zarah* 34a, 39a. In other witnesses the name appears as that of the Babylonian sage or exilarch "Mar 'Uḳba." G. Alon seems to prefer the reading "Akiva" in all the instances. While noting the diverse theories that try to account for his widespread travels (especially the one that ties it to the Bar Kokhba revolt), he concludes that "It is a much more reasonable assumption that Rabbi Akiba journeyed abroad in the service of a program to re-establish the bonds between the mother country and its Sanhedrin, on the one hand, and the scattered Jewish communities of the Diaspora on the other." See *The Jews in Their Land in the Talmudic Age, 70-640 C.E.*, trans. Gershon Levi (Jerusalem: Magnes Press, 1980), 236–237; cf. Jacob Neusner, *A History of the Jews in Babylonia* (Brill, 1966), 2:98-99.

Genesis Rabbah 33:5:   *MS. Oxford Heb. e. 73/17:*

and he applied to them this scriptural text (Job 24:20): "The womb shall forget him; the worm shall feed sweetly on him; he shall be no more remembered; and wickedness shall be broken as a tree."

"The womb [Hebrew: *reḥem*] shall forget him"— They caused compassion [*raḥamim*] to be forgotten from creatures, and even so did the holy one cause his compassion to be forgotten from them...

וקרא עליהם המקרא הזה (איוב
כד, כ):

"ישכחהו רחם מתקו רמה עוד לא
יזכר ותשבר כעץ עולה"

ישכחהו רחם הן שכחו רחמי מן
הבריות אף הקב"ה שיכח רחמיו מהם ...

According to R' Judah be"R Simon's exposition, the raven refused to accept his mission until Noah reassured him that ravens would eventually be given a privileged role in feeding the prophet Elijah in the wilderness, as related in 1 Kings 17:1-6.[10]

---

10 See Louis Ginzberg, *The Legends of the Jews*, trans. Henrietta Szold (Philadelphia, PA: The Jewish Publication Society of America, 1909), 1:38-39, 1:163-164; 5:55 n. 176, 5:185 n. 46. The version in *b.Sanhedrin* has the raven accusing Noah of sending him away so that Noah could have a liaison with his mate. See David Marcus, "The Mission of the Raven (Gen. 8:7)," *The Journal of the Ancient Near Eastern Society* 29 (2002): 76–77. Dina Stein has argued that a consistent thread running through the biblical story and subsequent folkloric and midrashic expositions focuses on the categorization of the human and animal realms; see "Noah, his Family, and Other Animals: Midrash, Folklore and the Interpretation of a Biblical Story (or: Homage to Structuralism)," ed. Avigdor Shinan and Salomon, *Jerusalem Studies in Hebrew Literature* 25: TEXTURES: Culture, Literature, Folklore, for Galit Hasan-Rokem, Volume 1 (2013): 87–105 [Hebrew]; Mira Wasserman, *Jews, Gentiles, and Other Animals: The Talmud After the Humanities*, Divinations: Rereading Late Ancient Religion (Philadelphia: University of Pennsylvania Press, 2017), 112–113. On the institutional setting of the exposition as a public homily delivered in the synagogue see Moshe David Herr, "Aggadah u-Midrash be-'Olamam shel ḤaZa"L be-Eretz Yis-

This expansion of the biblical story finds a nominal justification in certain features of the text that are being read according to familiar midrashic tropes. The occurrence of a conversation was extrapolated from a farfetched word-play on the word שוב that was clearly meant to denote returning motion, in the sense of "forth and back,"[11] but is read here in the (additional) sense of "response" or "retort." The link to the story of Elijah being fed by ravens is facilitated by the transformation of the clause "until the waters were dried up from off the earth" from part of the narration into the content of God's reply to the (otherwise unstated) argument of the raven.[12] These hermeneutical devices are so contrived and unconvincing as to make it likely that they were tacked on after the fact, and that the dialogue originated in Rabbi Judah's narrative imagining of the raven's predicament.

The juxtaposition of the anecdote about Rabbi Akiva's experience preaching the raven episode indicates that it originated in the setting of a synagogue sermon. However, given that Akiva predated Judah be"R Simon by several generations, we do not really know what was the gist of his discourse.[13]

---

rae'el: Meḳomot Hithavut, Sibbot Tzemiḥah u-Zmanei 'Arikhah," in *Higayon le-Yonah: New Aspects in the Study of Midrash, Aggadah and Piyut in Honor of Professor Yona Fraenkel*, ed. Jacob Elbaum, Galit Hasan-Rokem, and Joshua Levinson (Jerusalem: The Hebrew University Magnes Press, 2006), 135–136 [Hebrew].

11 Wilhelm Gesenius, E. Kautzsch, and A. E. Cowley, *Gesenius' Hebrew Grammar*, 13th English ed. (Oxford: The Clarendon press, 1976), 997.

12 For examples of this aggadic trope of dividing biblical verses into conversations between multiple speakers, see Isaak Heinemann, *Darkhe Ha-Agadah* (Jerusalem: Magnes Press, 1970), 132. Similarly, the link between Noah's raven and the ones that fed Elijah may be viewed as an extension of the tendency described by Heinemann (29-34) to identify minor biblical figures with more prominent ones.

13 In fact, several good witnesses, including MS Vatican 30, have the reading "when he mentioned to them the story of *Job* they wept." While it is somewhat more difficult to explain the juxtaposition of the passage at this particular point in the Noah narrative, it does make good psychological sense on its own as a contrast between the congregation's responses to a global catastrophe (whose proportions were too great to inspire heartfelt empathy) and a visceral identification with the tangible suffering of the individual Job; and it corresponds to the verse from Job that is expounded in relation to this episode. See Michael Sokoloff, ed., *The Geniza Fragments of*

Completely absent from the midrashic story is any hint of a theoretical rationale for the assumption that the raven could converse with Noah.[14] Did Rabbi Judah subscribe to the position that we found in Jubilees and Josephus, that during the earliest stages of creation all animals possessed that ability (perhaps until the tower of Babel), or did he perhaps ascribe a special status to ravens (in keeping with some of the notions that we will be encountering later on in this chapter)? It seems most probable that he had no serious interest in such academic questions—but only with the most effective way to convey a discourse that was emotionally moving and religiously edifying.

A very similar account of a conversation between Noah and the raven is found in the Babylonian Talmud, albeit in the name of a prominent Palestinian sage:[15]

b.Sanhedrin 108b: *MS Jerusalem Yad HaRav Herzog:*

"And he sent forth a raven"   "וישלח את הערב"

Said Rabbi Simeon ben Lakish:[16] the raven's retort to Noah was irrefutable. He said to him: Your master despises me: of the clean beast seven, of the unclean two. And you despise me,

א"ר שמעון בן לקיש: תשובה נצחת השיבו עורב לנח. אמ' לו: רבך שנאני ואתה שנאתני. רבך שנאני מן הטהרה שבעה ומן הטמאה שנים. ואתה שנאתני שאם פוגעין בי חמה או צנה לא

Bereshit Rabba, Publications of the Israel Academy of Sciences and Humanities: Section of Humanities (Jerusalem: The Israel Academy of Sciences and Humanities, 1982), 51. Verses from Job (especially the depiction of the corrupt and uncaring society in Ch. 24) figure prominently in midrashic expositions of the generation of Noah's flood.

14 Deborah Levine Gera argues that, for Homer, the ability to communicate with animals was an indication of a being's inferior, animal-like status, as evidenced by the case of the brutish Cyclops Polyphemus who was barely able to comprehend human language but had the facility to communicate with his flocks [*Greek Ideas on Speech*, 4, 12–17]. .

15 See Raphael Nathan Rabinowitz, *Dikduke Sofrim: Variae Lectiones in Mischnam in Talmud Babylonicum* (Munich, 1883), 9:345, nn. ד, ה.

16 He was a second-generation Palestinian amora; see Bacher, *palästinensischen Amoräer*, 1:340-418; Albeck, *Intro. to Talmuds*, 190–191; Stemberger, *Introduction to the Talmud and Midrash*, 86; Margalioth and Aizenberg, *Encyclopedia*, 2:318-320.

b.Sanhedrin 108b:	*MS Jerusalem Yad HaRav Herzog:*
for if the sun or the cold[17] should assault me, will the world not be lacking one creature!	נמצא עולם חסר בריה אחת.
Or, perhaps it is that you are in need of my wife?	או שמא לאשתי אתה צריך.
He said to him: Wicked one! If I am forbidden to the one who is [normally] permitted to me, is that not true all the more with one who is forbidden to me![18]	אמ' לו: רשע ומה במותר לי נאסר לי בנאסר לי לא כל שכן.

As in the *Genesis Rabbah* passage, neither Rabbi Simeon ben Laķish nor the Talmud's redactors raise any questions about the raven's ability to argue with Noah.[19] The Talmud does not explicitly identify any textual feature in the biblical verse that triggered this interpretation. It might have been the same word-play of "*va-shov*" that inspired R' Judah be"R Simon in the Palestinian midrash. [20] Alternatively, the comment might have been

---

17 MS Munich 95 and printed editions read "the prince of sun or the prince of cold."

18 On the tradition that the passengers of the ark did not have sexual relations during the flood, an idea that has both textual and moral roots, see the sources assembled by Louis Ginzberg, *The Legends of the Jews*, trans. Henrietta Szold (Philadelphia, PA: The Jewish Publication Society of America, 1909), 5:188-189 n. 54, to 1:166.

19 It was however problematic for Ḥanokh Zundel ben Joseph, author of the *'Anaf Yosef* commentary to the *'Ein Ya'aķov*, who wrote:

> It is not outrageous that animals might have possessed intelligence in primordial times. In any case, the retorts could have taken the form of twittering with their tongues, as when they communicate among one another. And Noah would understand them by means of his wisdom... Alternatively, we might say that it did not speak even by means of twittering; rather on seeing its reluctance to accept its mission, Noah was able to infer its intention and its retort.

20 This was apparently the view of Baḥya ben Asher [*Be'ur 'al ha-Torah*, ed. Charles Ber Chavel (Jerusalem: Mosad ha-Rav Kook, 1966), 1:114-115]. It was also argued by Rabbi Elijah Mizraḥi in his supercommentary to Rashi's commentary on Genesis. Rabbi Samuel Edels (Maharsha) objected that there is no hint of this in the Babylo-

sparked by the use of the emphatic form וַיְשַׁלַּח ("*he sent forth*" instead of the more standard וַיִּשְׁלַח), which could indicate a repeated or forceful expulsion in the face of the bird's resistance.[21]

The pericope in its final form is structured so that Noah gets the last word, labeling the raven as a "wicked one." Nonetheless, it seems quite clear that Rabbi Simeon ben Lakish was sympathetic to the bird's "irrefutable" arguments, as were R' Judah be"R Simon and perhaps Rabbi Akiva's audience in the *Genesis Rabbah* text.[22]

The Dove and the Olive Leaf

Genesis Rabbah 33:6:[23]	*MS. Oxford Heb. e. 73/17:[24]*
...R' Birai[25] said: The gates of the garden of Eden opened for her and she brought it.	...ר' ביריי א' נפתחו לה שערי גן עדן והביאה אותו
Said R' Abbahu:[26] If it were	א' ר' אבהוא אילו מגן עדן הביאה

---

nian Talmud passage; and that the same usage is also found elsewhere in the Bible in contexts that do not lend themselves to this kind of interpretation. The absence of the specific quote here is not in itself troubling, since it is common for midrashic interpretations to be based on portions of the verses that lie outside the quotes in the written documents.

21 Francis Brown, *The New Brown, Driver, and Briggs Hebrew and English Lexicon of the Old Testament* (Lafayette, IN: Associated Publishers and Authors, 1981), 1018–1019; Gesenius, Kautzsch, and Cowley, *Gesenius' Hebrew Grammar*, 141–142.

22 The traditional commentators to the Talmud have to cautiously navigate the positive and negative attitudes towards the Raven. Note especially Rabbi Jacob Reischer's *'Iyyun Ya'akov* to the *'Ein Ya'akov*.

23 Theodor and Albeck, *Bereshit Rabba*, 311. The critical apparatus includes references to parallel versions of the passage.

24 Text based on Genizah texts transcribed by Sokoloff, *Bereshit Rabba Geniza*, 25–26.

25 See Ch. Albeck, *Introduction to the Talmud. Babli and Yerushalmi* (Tel-Aviv: Dvir, 1969), 230–231.

26 See Wilhelm Bacher, *Die Agada der palästinensischen Amoräer* (Strassburg i. E: K. J. Trübner, 1892), 2:88-142; Saul Lieberman, *Greek in Jewish Palestine: Studies in the Life and Manners of Jewish Palestine in the II-IV Centuries C. E* (New York: The Jewish Theological Seminary of America, 1942), 21–33; Albeck, *Intro. to Talmuds,*

Genesis Rabbah 33:6:

from the garden of Eden that she brought it, then she should have brought something finer—either cinnamon or balsam.

Rather, she was hinting to him. She was saying to him: Noah, something bitter from this one[27] is preferable to something sweet from under your hand.

MS. Oxford Heb. e. 73/17:

אותו היה לה להביא דבר מעולה או
קינמון או פיפסלמון

אלא רמז רמזה לו אמ' לו נח מוטב
מר מזה ולא מתוק מתחת ידיך

b.Sanhedrin 108b

"And the dove came in to him in the evening; [and, lo, in her mouth was an olive leaf plucked off]"

Said R' Jeremiah ben Eliezer:[28] The dove said before the holy one: Master of the uni-

MS Jerusalem Yad HaRav Herzog:

ותבא אליו היונה לעת ערב וג'

א"ר ירמיה בן אלעזר: אמרה יונה
לפני הק'ב'ה: רב' שלעו' יהיו מזונותי
מרים כזית ויהיו מסורים בידך ואל יהו

217–218; Günter Stemberger, *Introduction to the Talmud and Midrash*, 2nd ed. (Edinburgh: T. & T. Clark, 1996), 89; Lee I. Levine, "R. Abbahu of Caesarea," in *Christianity, Judaism and Other Greco-Roman Cults: Studies for Morton Smith at Sixty*, ed. Jacob Neusner, Studies in Judaism in Late Antiquity 12 (Leiden: Brill, 1975); Mordecai Margalioth and Yehudah Aizenberg, eds., *Entsiklopedyah le-Ḥakhme ha-Talmud yeha-Ge'onim*, Revised edition. (Tel-Aviv: Yavneh and Chemed, 1995), 1:10-12.

27   On the olive's bitterness see Asaph Goor, "The Place of the Olive in the Holy Land and Its History through the Ages," *Economic Botany* 20, no. 3 (1966): 223; see also Jehuda Feliks, *Plant World of the Bible* (Ramat Gan: Masadah, 1968), 51.

28   See Albeck, *Intro. to Talmuds*, 342.

b.Sanhedrin 108b	*MS Jerusalem Yad HaRav Herzog:*
verse, may my nourishment be as bitter as the olive and dependent upon your hand, rather than as sweet as honey and dependent upon the hand of flesh-and-blood!	מתוקים כדבש ויהיו מסורים ביד בשר ודם

This touchingly simple interpretation, ascribed to two different Palestinian Amoras, finds symbolic meaning in the fact that, of all the objects that the dove might have brought back from its flight, it was a leaf from a bitter olive that she chose. The resulting lesson expresses a sublime declaration of faith and trust in God's goodness. Although the setting here is a universal one in a story that occurred before the appearance of Abraham, it is not unlikely (as noted by some traditional Jewish commentators) that the rabbis had in mind the depiction of the Jewish people as a dove, in keeping with common imagery.[29] In *Genesis Rabbah* the leaf is plucked from a tree in the garden of Eden, whereas in the Talmud it is assumed to be from an ordinary earthly tree.

In Rabbi Abbahu's exposition the dove appears to be speaking to Noah, though it is possible to understand that the message was implicit in

---

29 See below in connection with *b.Giṭṭin* 51b; Hermann Leberecht Strack and Paul Billerbeck, *Kommentar zum Neuen Testament aus Talmud und Midrasch* (Munich: Beck, 1922), 1:123-125; Joshua Abelson, *The Immanence of God in Rabbinical Literature* (New York: Hermon Press, 1969), 220; Ingvild Sælid Gilhus, *Animals, Gods and Humans: Changing Attitudes to Animals in Greek, Roman and Early Christian Ideas* (London: Routledge, 2006), 248. A very different perspective on the reality and symbolism of doves is found in Epiphanius:

> Doves are insatiable and incessantly promiscuous, lecherous, given to the pleasure of the moment, and weak and small besides. But because of the harmlessness, patience and forbearance of doves—and even more, because of the Holy Spirit's appearance in the form of a dove — the divine Word would have us imitate the will of the Holy Spirit and the harmlessness of the harmless dove and be wise in good but innocent in evil"

[Frank Williams, trans., *Panarion of Epiphanius of Salamis. Book I (Sections 1-46)*, 2nd ed., revised and expanded., Nag Hammadi and Manichaean Studies 63 (Leiden and Boston: Brill, 2009), 3:8-9 (p. 268)]; see Gilhus, *Animals, Gods and Humans*, 7–8.

the mere fact that she was carrying the olive leaf; whereas in Rabbi Jeremiah's her words or thoughts are addressed to God. In such a symbolic homiletical context, it seems to be of little usefulness to raise questions about whether or not the rabbis imagined the dove to be formulating its idea in an audible language.

Rav Kahana and the Doves

Arguably, the closest thing that the Talmud offers us to an explicit debate over the verbal abilities of any non-human creatures is the following pericope in *b.Ḥullin* 139b. In the context of a discussion about the biblical law of sending away the mother bird from the nest before taking the eggs or fledglings (Deuteronomy 22:6-7),[30] the Mishnah (*Ḥullin* 12:1) singles out "Herodian doves"[31] as a domesticated species that are exempted from that obligation on the grounds that, according to the rabbinic interpretation, it applies only to undomesticated free-range fowl. In this connection, a Babylonian sage relates his personal observations of this species of bird:

b.Ḥullin 139b: *Genizah fragment Oxford Heb. c. 21/2.*[32]

Says Rav Kahana: I personally   אמ' רב כהנא לדידי חזיאן לי וקימן
saw them and they stood sixteen   שיתסר דארי בפתי מילא
rows each a mile wide.[33]

---

30   For a discussion of the rabbinic understandings and applications of this precept see Eliezer Segal, "Justice, Mercy and a Bird's Nest," *Journal of Jewish Studies* 42, no. 2 (1991): 176–195.

31   Herod's proclivity for doves is mentioned by Josephus *Wars* 5:4:4. For a brief survey of the historical sources, including the relevant rabbinic texts, Emil Schurer, *The History of the Jewish People in the Age of Jesus Christ (175 B.C.-A.D. 135)*, ed. Géza Vermès and Fergus Millar (Edinburgh: T. & T. Clark, 1973), 1:310 and n. 77. See also Eliezer David Oren, "The 'Herodian Doves' in the Light of Recent Archaeological Discoveries," *Palestine Exploration Quarterly* 100, no. 1 (1968): 56–61.

32   As recorded by the Friedberg Project for Talmud Bavli Variants.

33   Translation according to Michael Sokoloff, *A Dictionary of Jewish Babylonian Aramaic of the Talmudic and Geonic Periods* (Ramat Gan and Baltimore: Bar Ilan University Press and Johns Hopkins University Press, 2003), 947.

b.Ḥullin 139b:

Genizah fragment Oxford Heb. c. 21/2:

And they said: *Ḳyré, kyré.*

ואמרן קירי כירי

There was one who did not know how to say it. Her companion said to her: Blind fool![34] Say:*Ḳyré, kyré!*

הואי חדא דלא הוה קא ידעא למימר אמרה לה חברתה סומה אימא קירי כירי

She said: Blind fool! Say *Ḳyré, kyré!*[35]

אמרה סומה קירי כירי

They brought her and slaughtered her.

אתיוה שחטוה

Said Rav Ashi: R' Ḥanina said to me: [Merely] words.

אמ' רב אשי אמ' לי ר' חנינה מילין

---

34 Most translators follow the text and explanation of Rashi, according to whom "סומה" or "סומא" has its usual meaning of "blind" and is meant here as an insult. D. Sperber brings the Soncino English translation (by Eli Cashdan) "You blind fool" ["On a Meaning of the Word 'Milah,'" *Revue des Etudes Juives* 125 (1966): 385; =*Magic and Folklore in Rabbinic Literature*, Bar-Ilan Studies in Near Eastern Languages and Culture (Ramat-Gan: Bar-Ilan University Press, 1994)]. Sokoloff (*Babylonian*,812) reads "סלמא'" without identifying his source, and he merely comments "n.m. (unclear)." No such reading is recorded by Raphael Nathan Rabinowitz, *Diḳduḳe Sofrim: Variae Lectiones in Mischnam in Talmud Babylonicum* (Munich, 1883), 6 [Chulin]: 201a–201b n. ק. or in the texts listed at the Friedberg or Lieberman sites.

35 Or: "The blind fool said *Ḳyré, kyré.*" My translation suggests the possibility that the second dove's indiscretion consisted of her stupidly including the insulting epithet "blind fool" as part of her address to her royal master. The standard interpretations assert that she garbled *kyré* into something similar-sounding but inappropriate. Sperber cites the text without the line describing the second dove's action. If this is not just an accidental omission, then he might regard that line as a dittography (though it is found in all the textual witnesses and is central to Rashi's explanation). The implication would then be that the second dove did not respond to the advice or correct herself, and that this was the cause of her being slaughtered. For a quite different perspective on the text see Tal Ilan, *Massekhet Hullin: Text, Translation, and Commentary*, A Feminist Commentary on the Babylonian Talmud V/3 (Tübingen: Mohr Siebeck, 2017), 603–605.

b.Ḥullin 139b:	*Genizah fragment Oxford Heb. c. 21/2:*
"Merely words"?! Is such a thing conceivable?	מילין סל' דע'
—Rather: by means of [magic] spells.[36]	אלא במילין

The precise text and meaning of this supposed exchange between the two doves is difficult to determine with any degree of certainty.[37] The Aramaic words that are used to replicate the crucial bird sounds are virtually indistinguishable from one another in manuscript: קירי (probably from the Greek "κύριε" = "lord, master");[38] כירי (likely an alternative transliteration

---

36   On the use of מילה or מילין to designate magic spells, charms and amulets in numerous Babylonian and Palestinian texts, as well as in other Aramaic magical inscriptions, see Sperber, "Meaning of Milah"; "Varia Midrashica," *Revue des Etudes Juives* 129 (1970): 85.

37   Numerous variations are recorded by Rabinowitz, *Diḳduḳe Sofrim*, 16 [Chulin]: 201a-201b n. ק. I also consulted the listings of the Lieberman Institute and Friedberg Genizah sites. The combinations for the statement of the second dove are as follows (as recorded in the Lieberman Institute site): Bologna - Archivio di Stato Fr. Ebr. 348: כירי; Vatican 122: כירי כירי; Vatican 121: קירי כירי; Oxford - Bodl. heb. c. 21 (2666) 23, Munich 95 and Soncino printing: קירי בירי.

38   Samuel Krauss, *Griechische und lateinische Lehnwörter im Talmud, Midrasch und Targum* (Berlin: S. Calvary, 1898), 287, 539; Michael Sokoloff, *A Dictionary of Jewish Babylonian Aramaic of the Talmudic and Geonic Periods* (Ramat Gan and Baltimore: Bar Ilan University Press and Johns Hopkins University Press, 2003), 578, 1016. Sokoloff adds "mng. of passage uncertain." Elsewhere (p. 1016) Sokoloff renders קירי קירי in our pericope as "interj. (type of cry)." Perhaps he is reading it as a meaningless onomatopoeic representation of cooing or some other kind of non-verbal bird sound. This would presumably require an extensive reinterpretation of the subsequent discussion in the Talmud. Jastrow, 636, also refers to "doves who utter a sound like קירי קירי." E. D. Mortensen adduces ornithological research by Bernd Heinrich and Peter Enggist-Düblin that catalogued the calls uttered by ravens, and recorded that "Some of the more common include … *krapp...kra, kaah, kruk, kwulkulkul, ko-pick*, … quork, percussive sounds, and hollow metallic bell-like sounds" [Eric David Mortensen, "Raven Augury from Tibet to Alaska," in *Communion of Subjects: Animals in Religion, Science, and Ethics*, ed. Paul Waldau and

of the same word, but possibly from "χείριϛ" = "captive, slave");[39] or the dubious בירי (whose meaning remains questionable).

However we might choose to understand the details of the conversation between the two doves, the tale speaks of one bird advising another as to what it should be saying—presumably employing understandable words (in Greek), with the result that the bird gets slaughtered. On the other hand, the matter might revolve merely on how to correctly interpret the natural cooing sounds that issued from the dove's throat. According to Rashi, the problem was that she replaced the word for "master" with one for "slave"; in order thereby to cast insulting aspersions on King Herod, the owner of those "Herodian doves" who, according to the rabbinic tradition, was particularly sensitive when it came to any reminders of his controversial status as an erstwhile slave who had usurped the Judean throne. This display of insolence cost the bird her life.[40]

Kimberley Patton (New York: Columbia Univ Press, 2006), 432–433 n. 6].

39 Krauss, *Lehnwörter*, 287; Marcus Jastrow, *Dictionary of the Targumim, the Talmud Babli and Yerushalmi, and the Midrashic Literature* (Peabody, MA: Hendrickson Publishers, 2005), 636; Sokoloff, *Babylonian*, 578. Rashi refers us to the passage in b. '*Eruvin* 53b where, among a selection of humorous anecdotes about mispronunciations and dialectical variations, there is a story about a Galilean woman who addressed a judge as מרי כירי [or: מארי כיראי, as in the Genizah fragment Cambridge (CUL) Or. 1080.13.5]. Though the context there also makes it clear that her usage was (comically) inappropriate, it does not really explain why. There as well, Rashi comments that she said "slave" instead of the intended "master [קירי]" —for which he refers the reader back to the current pericope in *Ḥullin*. Notwithstanding the great variety of readings in the '*Eruvin* pericope, Rabinowitz concludes plausibly that כירי is to be preferred on the grounds that a ב is most unlikely to get confused for a ק [*Diḳduḳe Sofrim*, 5. 'Eruvin: 203 n. מ].

40 Clearly Rav Kahana did not live during a time when Herod was alive or his influence could have still constituted a threat. Rashi was evidently responding to this difficulty when he ascribed the slaughter to "slaves who remained from the time of Herod." In fact, the story makes sense (albeit with a considerably weaker textual connection to the talmudic context) if we remove the allusions to Herod that Rashi himself introduced. Insolence toward any master by a creature lower in the food-chain would bring about similar consequences. On the talmudic portrayals of and attitudes toward Herod; see Daniel R. Schwartz, "Hordos Ba-Meḳorot Ha-Yehudim: Meḳorot, Sikkumim, Parshiyyot Nivḥarot ve-Ḥomer 'Ezer," in *Ha-Melekh Hordos u-Teḳufato*, ed. Mordechay Naor, Sidrat 'Idan 5 (Jerusalem: Yad Izhak Ben-Zvi, 1984), 38–42

What is of interest for the current study is the response of the later sages[41] to Rav Kahana's anecdote.[42] Rabbi Ḥanina dismissed it as nothing more than so many idle words. The anonymous editors of the pericope considered it inconceivable that a respectable sage would have uttered a patently false report of something that he claimed to have personally witnessed. For this reason they reinterpreted—or slightly emended—Rabbi Ḥanina's comment so that "words" does not have the connotation of a

---

[Hebrew]; Richard Lee Kalmin, *Jewish Babylonia Between Persia and Roman Palestine* (New York, NY: Oxford University Press, 2006), 50–53, 207–208.

41 The chronology and identification of the sages in this pericope are hard to pin down with confidence, especially when we bear in mind that the names Ḥanina and Kahana reappear quite often among the rabbis. Ch. Albeck observed how difficult it often is to identify which of the numerous Rabbis Ḥanina, Ḥananiah or Ḥinena is being mentioned in any particular talmudic passage; [see *Introduction to the Talmud. Babli and Yerushalmi* (Tel-Aviv: Dvir, 1969), 155–156.] The one who standardly is mentioned without a patronymic or other identifier was Rabbi Ḥanina bar Ḥama, a first-generation Palestinian Amora, probably of Babylonian origin. See Mordecai Margalioth and Yehudah Aizenberg, eds., *Entsiḳlopedyah le-Ḥakhme ha-Talmud yeha-Ge'onim*, Revised edition. (Tel-Aviv: Yavneh and Chemed, 1995), 133–135. The Ḥanina in our passage is being cited personally by Rav Ashi, the sixth-generation Babylonian Amora who died in 427 according to the *Epistle of Rav Sherira Gaon*; see Albeck, *Intro. to Talmuds*, 427–430; Margalioth and Aizenberg, *Encyclopedia*, 66–68; Günter Stemberger, *Introduction to the Talmud and Midrash*, 2nd ed. (Edinburgh: T. & T. Clark, 1996), 98]. There is, however, no prominent Ḥanina who is contemporary to Ashi, and the older namesakes whom Rav Ashi might be quoting normally appear with their patronymics: son of Rav Ikka and bar Minyomi (Albeck, *Intro. to Talmuds*, 408–409). As for Kahana, the name [or, to be precise: the Aramaic identification as "priest"] recurs in every Amoraic generation (ibid., 174, 203, 295, 413, 435). I think that the most likely candidate here would be Rav Ashi's own teacher (Albeck, 413; cf. his observation on 435: "among the five Amoraim named Kahana it is difficult to assign the attributions to each of them").

42 A similarly structured pericope is found in *b. 'Avodah Zarah* 38b. There, Rabbah bar bar Ḥanna expounds an amazing herbal preparation that blossoms instantly and has the power to make a person "feel cooled from the hair of the head down to the toenails." Similarly to our *Ḥullin* passage, "Rav Ashi said: R' Ḥanina [in MS Paris 1337: "Ḥinen"' and in R' Ḥananel's commentary "Huna"; see Shraga Abramson, *Masekhet 'Avodah Zarah* (New York: The Jewish Theological Seminary of America, 1957), 186.] told me that this is an empty tale; others say: through magical

mere fiction, but refers rather to a magical incantation that allowed the doves to conduct a conversation.

Prior to the Talmud's harmonizing reinterpretation of the Rabbi Ḥanina's remark, it would appear that Rav Kahana and Rabbi Ḥanina did indeed take opposing positions as regards the possibility of birds carrying on conversations with one another. The conclusion, if it is indeed original to the passage,[43] still makes allowance for the possibility that they can be made to speak by means of magic spells.

These opposing attitudes toward speaking doves are reminiscent of Herodotus' discussion (2:54-57)[44] of various traditions and theories about the migration of oracular cults from Thebes to Greece. In this connection, he cites a number of legends and explanations that he gleaned from respective sources. The most straightforward of these he heard from the priests in Egyptian Thebes[45] who spoke of the abduction of two of their priestesses by Phoenicians and their subsequent relocation to Libya and Dodona in Epirus where they proceeded to establish versions of their na-

---

spells."Note that in that version, the "magic spells" reading is cited simply as an alternative text and not as the solution to an objection, as it is in *Ḥullin*. That likely reflects the earlier tradition in *Ḥullin* as well, though the manuscripts support the current reading. This seems to hold true for all the direct witnesses for *'Avodah Zarah* [see *Diḳduḳe Sofrim*, 10. Abodah Sarah: 87 n. ٦]. It should nevertheless be noted that the reading of R' Ḥananel in *'Avodah Zarah* accords with the dialectical format of *Ḥullin*: "'Merely words'?! Is such a thing conceivable?—Rather: by means of magic spells." See Alexander Kohut and Samuel Krauss, eds., *Aruch Completum ['Arukh Ha-Shalem]* (Jerusalem: Makor, 1969), 5:142 and n. 11. On the editorial tendency to fashion dialectical literary connections between units of talmudic learning Eliezer Segal, *Case Citation in the Babylonian Talmud: The Evidence of Tractate Neziqin*, Brown Judaic Studies 210 (Atlanta: Scholars Press, 1990), 152.

43 Thus according to R' Ḥananel and Rashi, cited by Sperber. None of them offers any suggestions as to why Rav Kahana would have wanted to endow the birds with the ability to speak.

44 *Herodotus, with an English Translation*, Loeb Classical Library 117–120 (London: W. Heinemann, 1921), 1:342-345.

45 "The tale of the Theban priestesses who were carried into Libya and Greece is so obviously of Greek origin, that it is impossible to think of it as Egyptian; it is part and parcel of a rather elaborate theory which clearly did not originate with Herodotus" [William Arthur Heidel, "Hecataeus and the Egyptian Priests in Herodotus, Book II," *Memoirs of the American Academy of Arts and Sciences* 18, no. 2 (1935): 66].

tive cult, devoted to Zeus.[46] The priestesses at Dodona, on the other hand, framed the event in mythic terms:[47]

Herodotus, The Histories, 2:55:

δύο πελειάδας μελαίνας ἐκ Θηβέων τῶν Αἰγυπτιέων ἀναπταμένας τὴν μὲν αὐτέων ἐς Λιβύην τὴν δὲ παρὰ σφέας ἀπικέσθαι,ἱζομένην δέ μιν ἐπὶ φηγὸν αὐδάξασθαι φωνῇ ἀνθρωπηίῃ ὡς χρεὸν εἴη μαντήιον αὐτόθι Διὸς γενέσθαι, καὶ αὐτοὺς ὑπολαβεῖν θεῖον εἶναι τὸ ἐπαγγελλόμενον αὐτοῖσι, καί σφεας ἐκ τούτου ποιῆσαι. [3] τὴν δὲ ἐς τοὺς Λίβυας οἰχομένην πελειάδα λέγουσι Ἄμμωνος χρηστήριον κελεῦσαι τοὺς

Two black doves had come flying from Thebes in Egypt, one to Libya and one to Dodona; the latter settled on an oak tree, and there uttered human speech, declaring that a place of divination from Zeus must be made there; the people of Dodona understood that the message was divine, and therefore established the oracular shrine. The dove which came to Libya told the Libyans (they say) to make an oracle of Ammon; this

---

46 See O. Kimball Armayor, "Did Herodotus Ever Go to Egypt," *Journal of the American Research Center in Egypt* 15 (1978): 60–61; Shawn O'Bryhim, "An Oracular Scene from the Pozo Moro Funerary Monument," *Near Eastern Archaeology* 64, no. 1/2 (2001): 67–70; Lucynda Kostuch, "Do Animals Have a Homeland? Ancient Greeks on the Cultural Identity of Animals," *Humanimalia* 9, no. 1 (2017): 75.

47 See Howard Fremont Stratton, *Dodona* (Philadelphia: Privately printed, 1937), 45, 54–58.

Herodotus, The Histories, 2:55:

Λίβυας ποιέειν· ἔστι δὲ καὶ τοῦτο   also is sacred to Zeus.[48]
Διός.

Herodotus himself prefers to reconstruct a historical kernel for the myths, one that eliminates the most blatant supernatural elements.[49] For this purpose he proposes a theory of how the original tale of the two ladies later came to be told about miraculous birds:

---

48 Mathias Delcor has noted the importance of the dove to the Near-Eastern cult of Astarte ["The Selloi of the Oracle of Dodona and the Oracular Priests of the Semitic Religions," in *Wort, Lied, Und Gottesspruch: Beiträge Zur Septuaginta: Festschrift Für Joseph Ziegler*, ed. Josef Schreiner, Forschung zur Bibel 1–2 (Würzburg: Echter Verlag, 1972), 32–34]; see also Shawn O'Bryhim, "A New Interpretation of Hesiod, 'Theogony' 35," *Hermes* 124, no. 2 (1996): 137-138 and n. 31; Tom Hawkins, "Eloquent Alogia: Animal Narrators in Ancient Greek Literature," *Humanites* 6, no. 37 (2017): 13. The dove also had associations with Aphrodite; see Jessica Piccinini, "Renaissance or Decline? The Shrine of Dodona in the Hellenistic Period," in *Hellenistic Sanctuaries: Between Greece and Rome*, ed. Milena Melfi and Olympia Bobou (Oxford: Oxford University Press, 2016), 160 n. 31. The actual oracular revelations at Dodona seem to have taken the form of rustling of leaves. In the Phaedrus 275b [transl. Fowler pp. 564-565], Plato alludes to those ingenuous folks who once believed "that the words of the oak in the holy place of Zeus at Dodona were the first prophetic utterances" [οἱ δέ γ᾽, ὦ φίλε, ἐν τῷ τοῦ Διὸς τοῦ Δωδωναίου ἱερῷ δρυὸς λόγους ἔφησαν μαντικοὺς πρώτους γενέσθαι]. See James George Frazer, *The Golden Bough: A Study in Magic and Religion*, ed. Robert Fraser, Reissued., Oxford World's Classics (Oxford: Oxford University Press, 2009), 159. An exhaustive listing of authors (including Homer, Hesiod, Aeschylus, Ovid, Strabo and Sophocles) is provided by Sarah Iles Johnston, *Ancient Greek Divination*, Blackwell Ancient Religions (Malden, MA and Oxford: Wiley-Blackwell, 2008), 65. Strabo (Book 7, Fragments) discusses the various traditions about oracles originating in the oak (ἐκ δρυὸς ὑψικόμοιο Διὸς βουλὴν ἐπακοῦσαι), in the flights of the three doves (ἴσως δέ τινα πτῆσιν αἱ τρεῖς περιστεραὶ ἐπέτοντο ἐξαίρετον, ἐξ ὧν αἱ ἱέρειαι παρατηρούμεναι προεθέσπιζον) or old women in the temple (γυναῖκες γραῖαι τρεῖς περὶ τὸ ἱερὸν σχολάζουσαι); and like Herodotus he speculates about various naturalistic theories by which to account for their evolutions [Horace Leonard Jones, ed., *The Geography of Strabo*, vol. 6, Loeb Classical Library (Cambridge MA and London: Harvard University Press and William Heinemann Ltd., 1960), 322–323].

49 Detlev Fehling, *Herodotus and His "Sources": Citation, Invention, and Narrative Art*, ARCA Classical and Medieval Texts, Papers, and Monographs 21 (Leeds: Fran-

57. πελειάδες δέ μοι δοκέουσι κληθῆναι πρὸς Δωδωναίων ἐπὶ τοῦδε αἱ γυναῖκες, διότι βάρβαροι ἦσαν, ἐδόκεον δέ σφι ὁμοίως ὄρνισι φθέγγεσθαι· [2] μετὰ δὲ χρόνον τὴν πελειάδα ἀνθρωπηίῃ φωνῇ αὐδάξασθαι λέγουσι, ἐπείτε συνετά σφι ηὔδα ἡ γυνή· ἕως δὲ ἐβαρβάριζε, ὄρνιθος τρόπον ἐδόκεέ σφι φθέγγεσθαι, ἐπεὶ τέῳ ἂν τρόπῳ πελειάς γε ἀνθρωπηίῃ φωνῇ φθέγξαιτο

57. Moreover, I think that the women were called doves by the people of Dodona for the reason that they were Barbarians and because it seemed to them that they uttered voice like birds; but after a time (they say) the dove spoke with human voice,[50] that is when the woman began to speak so that they could understand; but so long as she spoke a Barbarian tongue she seemed to them to be uttering voice like a bird: for had it been really a dove, how could it speak with human voice?[51]

The divergent approaches taken by Herodotus and his various informants with respect to the doves' abilities to speak, the extent of supernatural contribution to the phenomenon and the credibility of the traditions would appear to be eminently comparable to the disagreement between Rav Kahana and Rabbi Ḥanina in the Talmud passage.

cis Cairns, 1990), 65–68; W. W. How and J. Wells, *A Commentary on Herodotus with Introduction and Appendixes* (Oxford and New York: Oxford University Press, 1991), 195; Maurice Hutton, "The Mind of Herodotus," *Transactions and Proceedings of the American Philological Association* 42 (1911): 38; A. W. Gomme, "The Legend of Cadmus and the Logographi.-II," *The Journal of Hellenic Studies* 33 (1913): 235–236; Heidel, "Hecataeus and Egyptian Priests," 56–67; Donald Lateiner, *The Historical Method of Herodotus*, Phoenix Supplementary Volumes 23 (Toronto and Buffalo: University of Toronto Press, 1991), 84–85; Robin Waterfield, "On 'Fussy Authorial Nudges' in Herodotus," *The Classical World* 102, no. 4 (2009): 490–491; Sarah Iles Johnston, *Ancient Greek Divination*, Blackwell Ancient Religions (Malden, MA and Oxford: Wiley-Blackwell, 2008), 63–65; John Heath, *The Talking Greeks: Speech, Animals, and the Other in Homer, Aeschylus, and Plato* (Cambridge: Cambridge University Press, 2005), 16.

50 Writers like Sextus Empiricus and Philo (cited elsewhere in this study) compared or equated the differing languages of barbarians and Greeks with the communications between animals and humans.

51 See Rosaria Vignolo Munson, *Black Doves Speak: Herodotus and the Languages of Barbarians* (Washington and Cambridge MA: Harvard University Press for the Center for Hellenic Studies, 2005), 3, 96–99.

Rav 'Ilish and the Augur

b.Giṭṭin 45a:[52]	*MS St. Petersburg Yevr. (Firkovich) 1.187:*

The daughters of Rav Naḥman used to stir[53] a cauldron[54] with their hands.[55]

Rav 'Ilish was puzzled about it. It is written : "One man among a thousand have I found, but a woman among all those have I not found" (Ecclesiastes 7:28); and yet there are the daughters of Rav Nahman!

Circumstances brought it about that they were taken captive, and he was also taken captive with them.

בנתיה דרב נחמן בחשן קידרא בידיהו.

וקשיא ליה לרב עיליש. כתיב אדם
אחד מאלף מצאתי ואשה בכל אלה לא
מצאתי, הא איכא בניתיה דרב נחמן.

גרמא להו גרמה להו מילתא
אישתבאן ואישתבאיי איהו נמי בהדיהו.

---

52   Textual variants were consulted from Lieberman Institute and Friedberg sites, and Meyer S. Feldblum, ed., *Diḳduḳe Sopherim Tractate Gittin* (New York: Horeb, Yeshiva University, 1966).

53   J. N. Epstein, *Der Gaonäische Kommentar Zur Ordnung Tohoroth: Eine Kritische Einleitung Zu Dem R. Hai Gaon Zugeschriebenen Kommentar* (Berlin: Mayer & Müller, 1915), 143; Michael Sokoloff, *A Dictionary of Jewish Babylonian Aramaic of the Talmudic and Geonic Periods* (Ramat Gan and Baltimore: Bar Ilan University Press and Johns Hopkins University Press, 2003), 196.

54   See Joshua Brand, *Kele Zekhukhit Be-Sifrut Ha-Talmud* (Jerusalem: Mossad haRav Kook, 1978), 487–488 [Hebrew]. On associations between cauldrons and oracles (especially at Dodona) see Sarah Iles Johnston, *Ancient Greek Divination*, Blackwell Ancient Religions (Malden, MA and Oxford: Wiley-Blackwell, 2008), 66–72.

55   Rashi: "An observer would suppose that their righteousness rendered them invulnerable to the fire."

b.Giṭṭin 45a:

MS St. Petersburg Yevr. (Firkovich) 1.187:

One day a certain man was sitting next to him who understood the language of birds. A raven came and called to him.,

He said to him: What does it say? He said: "Ilish, flee, 'Ilish, flee!"

He said, The raven is a liar, and I do not rely on it.[56]

Meanwhile a dove came and called. He asked, What is it saying? He said: "'Ilish, flee, "Ilish flee!"

He said: The community of Israel[57] is likened to a dove.[58] Infer from this that a miracle occurs.

יומא חד הוה יתיב גביה ההוא
גברא דהוה קא ידע בלישנא דציפורא.
אתא עורבא וקא קרי.

אמר ליה מאי קאמ'. אמ' ליה
עיליש ברח עיליש ברח.

אמ' עורבא שקרא הוא לא סמיכנא
עליה.

אדהכי אתא יונה קא קריא.

אמ' ליה מאי קא אמרה. אמ' ליה
עיליש ברח עיליש ברח.

אמ' כנסת ישראל כיונה מתילא.
שמע מינה מיתרחיש ליה ניסא.

---

56 Rabbi Jacob Reischer in his *'Iyyun Ya'aḳov* commentary to the *'Ein Ya'aḳov* asked why, if Rav 'Ilish had no faith in the raven, he had asked the man about its message.

57 See Efraim Elimelech Urbach, *The Sages: Their Concepts and Beliefs* (Cambridge, MA: Harvard University Press, 1987), 524.

58 In *b.Berakhot* 53b and *b.Shabbat* 49a this association is derived by means of a homiletical exposition of Psalms 65:14. See also *b.Sanhedrin* 108b. In *Song of Songs Rabbah* 1:64 several allegorical comparisons are expounded based on Song of Songs 1:15.

b. Giṭṭin 45a:

MS St. Petersburg Yevr. (Firkovich) 1.187:

He said: I will go and see whether they have remained faithful, and I will take them back. He said: Women relate among themselves[59] all that involves them in the privy.

אמ' אזיל איחזי אי קיימן בהימנותייהי אהדרינהי.

אמ' נשי כל מילי דאית להי סדרן להדדי בית הכסא.

He overheard them saying that these[60] men are [our] husbands just as the Nehardeans [were] our husbands. Let us tell our captors to remove us to a distance from here, so that our husbands may not come and hear and ransom us.

שמעינהי דקא אמרי עדי גברין נהרדעי גברין. לימ' ליה לשבויין דלירחקינהו מהכא דלא לישמעו אנשין וליתו ליפרוקינן.

He arose and fled, along with the other man. For him a miracle was performed, and he got across the river crossing.

קם ערק. אתא איהו וההוא גבריא.

לדידיה איתרחיש ליה ניסא עבר מעברא.

They found the other man and killed him.

וההוא גברא אשכחוה קטלוה.

When they came back,[61] they would stir the cauldron by witchcraft.

כי הדרן אתין הוה קא בחשן קדירה בכשפים.

Though there is much in this tale that is of great interest from assorted per-

---

59   Michael Sokoloff, *A Dictionary of Jewish Babylonian Aramaic of the Talmudic and Geonic Periods* (Ramat Gan and Baltimore: Bar Ilan University Press and Johns Hopkins University Press, 2003), 789.

60   J. N. Epstein, *A Grammar of Babylonian Aramaic*, ed. Ezra Zion Melamed (Jerusalem: Magnes Press, 1960), 20 [Hebrew]; Sokoloff, *Babylonian*, 845.

61   The printed versions alone insert here "He said" implying that Rav 'Ilish was the author of the concluding comment. See Joshua Levinson, "Enchanting Rabbis: Contest Narratives between Rabbis and Magicians in Late Antiquity," *The Jewish Quarterly Review* 100, no. 1 (2010): 76 n. 57.

spectives, particularly in the glimpses that it provides about attitudes toward witchcraft[62] and marital infidelity in a distinguished rabbinic family,[63] the main focus for purposes of the present study will be on the Talmud's portrayal of the raven and the dove as transmitters of a message to Rav 'Ilish.[64]

As regards the birds, the text makes some interesting statements and assumptions: Their message was not understandable by Rav 'Ilish, but

---

62   See, e.g., Meir Bar-Ilan, "Witches in the Bible and Talmud," in *Approaches to Ancient Judaism: Historical, Literary and Religious Studies*, ed. Herbert W Basser and Simcha Fishbane, vol. New Series 5, South Florida Studies in the History of Judaism 82 (Atlanta: Scholars Press, 1993), 7–32; Ludwig Blau, *Das altjüdische Zauberwesen*, Cambridge Library Collection - Spiritualism and Esoteric Knowledge (Cambridge: Cambridge University Press, 2011), 25; Jonathan Seidel, "Charming Criminals: Classification of Magic in the Babylonian Talmud," in *Ancient Magic and Ritual Power*, ed. Paul Allan Mirecki and Marvin W. Meyer, Religions in the Graeco-Roman World 129 (Leiden: E J Brill, 1995), 151; Simcha Fishbane, "Most Women Engage in Sorcery: An Analysis of Female Sorceresses in the Babylonian Talmud," in *Approaches to Ancient Judaism: Historical, Literary, and Religious Studies*, ed. Simcha Fishbane and Herbert W Basser, vol. New Series 5, South Florida Studies in the History of Judaism 82 (Atlanta: Scholars Press, 1993), 143–165; [="'Most Women Engage in Sorcery': An Analysis of Sorceresses in the Babylonian Talmud," *Jewish History* 7, no. 1 (1993): 30–31]; Rebecca Lesses, "Exe(o)Rcising Power: Women as Sorceresses, Exorcists, and Demonesses in Babylonian Jewish Society of Late Antiquity," *Journal of the American Academy of Religion* 69, no. 2 (2001): (which does not cite this passage).

63   Yaakov Elman has called attention to the crucial role played by Rav Naḥman as a conveyor of Iranian cultural norms in Babylonian Jewish society, norms that extend to a relaxed attitude toward monogamy. In this connection he notes how "his daughters were accused of not attempting to escape the danger of rape under conditions of captivity" ["Middle Persian Culture and Babylonian Sages: Accommodation and Resistance in the Shaping of Rabbinic Legal Tradition," in *The Cambridge Companion to the Talmud and Rabbinic Literature*, ed. Charlotte Elisheva Fonrobert and Martin S. Jaffee, Cambridge Companions to Religion (Cambridge UK and New York NY: Cambridge University Press, 2007), 172]. See also Yaakov Elman, "'He in His Cloak and She in Her Cloak': Conflicting Images of Sexuality in Sasanian Mesopotamia," in *Discussing Cultural Influences: Text, Context and Non-Text in Rabbinic Judaism*, ed. Rivka Ulmer, Studies in Judaism (Lanham, MD: University Press of America, 2007), 129–163; Shai Secunda, *The Iranian Talmud: Reading the Bavli in*

only by the "certain man" who was trained to understand their language.[65] The content of that message was nonetheless quite personal and specific; not only was it addressed to the rabbi by name—and the implication of the narrative seems to be that the interpreter had no previous acquaintance with Rav 'Ilish—but it was also based on accurate foreknowledge that apparently derived from a supernatural source.[66] To be sure, the predictions were filtered by the Jewish sage in accordance with his own religious val-

---

Its Sasanian Context, 1st ed., Divinations: Rereading Late Ancient Religion (Philadelphia: University of Pennsylvania Press, 2014), 4, 147–8; Kimberly B. Stratton, *Naming the Witch: Magic, Ideology, and Stereotype in the Ancient World* (New York: Columbia University Press, 2013), 166–168; Eliezer Segal, *The Babylonian Esther Midrash: A Critical Commentary*, Brown Judaic studies no. 291-293 (Atlanta, Ga: Scholars Press, 1994), 2:216-217; 3:266; Jacob Neusner, *A History of the Jews in Babylonia* (Brill, 1966), 3:61-75. On Rav Naḥman's treatment of women in judicial settings see Shulamit Valler, "Women in Rav Nahman's Court," *Nashim: A Journal of Jewish Women's Studies & Gender Issues* 4 (2001): 35–55. The most sophisticated attempt to integrate the role of the birds into the broader narrative about Rav Naḥman's daughters' sorcery (and a more general competition between holy rabbis and profane magic) is likely that of Joshua Levinson, "Enchanting Rabbis: Contest Narratives between Rabbis and Magicians in Late Antiquity," *The Jewish Quarterly Review* 100, no. 1 (2010): especially 75-83. Notably: "The dilemma concerning the nature of the daughters is mirrored in the cawing of the birds. Both represent a problem of interpretation for Ilish, and his lack of ability to distinguish between the raven and the dove parallels his inability to differentiate between the righteousness or the sorcery of the daughters...The question is, are the women ravens or doves?"

64 On this fourth-generation Babylonian sage see Albeck, *Intro. to Talmuds*, 373; Margalioth and Aizenberg, *Encyclopedia*, 288.

65 Rabbi Akiva Eger, in his *Gilyon ha-Sha"S* glosses to the passage, notes that Rabbi Nathan ben Jehiel wrote in his *'Arukh* that Rav 'Ilish himself understood the language of birds [Kohut and Krauss, *Aruch Completum*, 4:142-143]. He was however refuted by Rabbi Jehiel Heilprin [*Seder ha-Dorot* (Warsaw: I. Goldman, 1882), 2:303].

66 The talmudic story shares some intriguing motifs with Josephus's account of Agrippa's release from imprisonment as related in the *Jewish Antiquities* 18:7 (195-204) and 19:2 (346-352) [Louis H. Feldman, trans., *Josephus in Nine Volumes*, Loeb Classical Library 433 (London and Cambridge MA: William Heinemann and Harvard University Press, 1969), 9:122-127; 9:378-383]. While the king was in chains, a horned owl landed on the tree on which he was leaning, and a German prisoner inter-

ues,[67] so that he refrained from accepting them from the suspect raven;[68] but in the end they turned out to be reliable. At any rate, if we continue to restrict our focus to the observable phenomena, it appears evident that the birds were not speaking in any language that could be understood by normal humans, but presumably in a distinctive avian idiom that could only be deciphered by appropriately trained specialists who would then convey it to its lay recipients.[69] When viewed in this manner, there is good reason

---

preted this as an assurance from the gods that he would be freed and restored to great power and prosperity, but that the next time he saw the owl it would signify his imminent death. Although Agrippa dismissed these predictions as ridiculous, they both came to pass. Cf. G. Bohak's claim that during the Second Temple era augury by birds was among the divinatory practices that were "entirely forbidden" [*Ancient Jewish Magic*, 77]. Philostratus writes admiringly of the cleverness of Apollonius of Tyana who succeeded in learning in his sojourn with the Arab tribes how to understand the language of the animals; "for it is quite common for the Arabs to listen to the birds prophesying like any oracles, but they acquire this faculty of understanding them by feeding themselves, so they say, either on the heart or liver of serpents" [(1:20) Frederick Cornwallis Conybeare, trans., *Philostratus. Life of Apollonius of Tyana, Epistles of Apollonius and Treatise of Eusebius.*, Loeb Classical Library (London and New York: William Heinemann and the MacMillan Co., 1912), 1:56-57]; see Lynn Thorndike, *A History of Magic and Experimental Science.* (New York: Macmillan, 1929), 1:261-262; Levinson, "Enchanting Rabbis," 78 n. 60. The imaginative traveler Iambulus claimed to have visited an exotic island paradise whose inhabitants (among other remarkable virtues), "are very versatile as to the sounds they can utter, since they imitate not only every articulate language used by man but also the varied chatterings of the birds, and, in general, they reproduce any peculiarity of sounds" [cited in Charles Henry Oldfather, trans., *Diodorus of Sicily*, Loeb Classical Library 303 (Cambridge, Mass: Harvard University Press, 1933), (2:56:6) 70-71]. Gera infers that this included the ability to conduct meaningful conversations with the respective creatures, but that does not seem to be the plain sense of the passage [*Greek Ideas on Speech*, 34]. Porphyry as well writes of peoples who understand the sounds made by animals with whom they are very close. "Thus, the Arabians understand the language of crows, and the Tyrrhenians of eagles." The animal sounds are sufficiently nuanced to be regarded as legitimate languages, and can be deciphered (though not completely) by "diviners...who predict from ravens and crows." [*De Abstinentia* 3:4]; Gilhus, *Animals, Gods and Humans*, 26.

67 On the role of Babylonian rabbis as mediators between traditional Jewish values and the widespread popular acceptance of local folk beliefs and Iranian religious ideas

to characterize the story not so much as an instance of animal language as of augury or ornithomancy.[70]

The art or science of augury was developed in elaborate detail by the Romans who resorted to it for major political and strategic policy,[71] and for which responsibility was assigned to magistrates. The augurs who were originally consulted for technical interpretation of the signs belonged to a prestigious *collegium* and were held in great esteem.[72] Prominent among the omens to be consulted by the augurs were those derived *"ex*

---

see Isaiah Gafni, *The Jews of Babylonia in the Talmudic Era: A Social and Cultural History*, Monographs in Jewish History (Jerusalem: Zalman Shazar Center for Jewish History, 1990), 161–176 [Hebrew].

68   The choice of raven and dove for these purposes was likely intended to evoke their roles in the story of Noah's ark, where they were sent to reconnoitre whether "the coast is clear," and only the dove was able to return with a positive report. See Bos, "Divination with Birds," 2. Though the Romans often consulted ravens or crows in connection with augury, doves and pigeons were not used for that purpose (on Greek sources, particularly those associated with the oracle at Dodona, see discussion elsewhere). In rejecting the raven in favor of the dove, Rav 'Ilish's intention might have been to formulate a distinctively Jewish variation on the pagan practice. Cf. The commentary of R' Samuel Edels ["Maharsha"] who argues that the Noah story teaches that ravens are liars—a claim that incurred criticism from subsequent commentators, such as R' Isaiah Berlin [Pick] in his *Oṣar Balum*.

In Ovid's *Fasti* 451-452 (discussed above), the dove is adduced as a particularly pathetic and heart-rending instance of a virtuous creature that is doomed by the religious conventions to the altar flames, often in situations where a wife is torn cruelly away from her husband ["ergo saepe suo coniunx abducta marito uritur in calidis alba columba focis"]; see Steven J. Green, "Malevolent Gods and Promethean Birds: Contesting Augury in Augustus's Rome," *Transactions of the American Philological Association (1974-)* 139, no. 1 (2009): 160.

69   See the discussion below in connection with Greek and Roman sources. In Greek such a specialist was known as an ὀρνῑθοσκόπος, an observer of birds. This in fact is how the term תעוננו ("seek omens") is rendered in the Septuagint to Leviticus 19:26 [e.g., Alan England Brooke, Norman McLean, and H. St J. Thackeray, eds., *The Old Testament in Greek According to the Text of Codex Vaticanus* (Cambridge: The University Press, 1906), 372.]. In Latin this official was an *augur* or *auspex*. See Johnston, *Ancient Greek Divination*, 128–129. In general, the Greek traditions refer more to spontaneous appearances of the birds, whereas the Romans institutionalized the practice and maintained special chickens or other fowl for purposes of augury. For surveys of pertinent Jewish material see Blau, *Zauberwesen*, 65; Joshua Trachten-

avibus," from birds;[73] and the birds in question were subdivided into two main kinds, with only a limited number of species considered suitable for augury, principally: ravens (*corvus*,[74]κόραξ),[75] crows (*cornix*),[76] eagles, vultures, owls and chickens.

Cicero De Divinatione 1:53 (120):[77]

Eademque efficit in avibus divina mens, ut tum huc, tum illuc	The Divine Will accomplishes like results in the case of birds,

---

berg, *Jewish Magic and Superstition: A Study in Folk Religion*, Temple Books (New York: Atheneum, 1982), 211.

70   See, e.g., Levinson, "Enchanting Rabbis," 78; Bos, "Divination with Birds," 5. For a cross-cultural anthropological study of the (very widespread) use of ravens in augury see Mortensen, "Raven Augury."

71   The sages of the midrash appear to have projected the role of augury in military planning upon the war of the biblical Israelites against the Midianites as related in Numbers 31. Among the justifications that were supplied for that campaign of vengeance, *Sifre* to Numbers (157) suggests that the Midianites were "מטירין regarding Israel" [The expression is missing in the printed versions, but is found in the reliable MS Vatican 32; Menahem I. Kahana, *Sifre on Numbers: An Annotated Edition* (Jerusalem: Press, 2011), C:83; S. Horovitz, ed., *Siphre d'be Rab; Fasciculus primus: Siphre ad Numeros adjecto Siphre zutta*, Corpus Tannaiticum 3:3 (Jerusalem: Wahrmann Books, 1966), 209.]. Horovitz interprets the word as "They would practice divination against Israel by means of birds; and it is possible that it expounded in this manner because of the verse (Numbers 22:7): "And the elders of Moab and the elders of Midian departed with divinations in their hand.'" M. Moreshet speculates that the midrashic exposition in the Sifre might have been inspired by a word-play on a passage that appears later in the section, in which Numbers 31:10, "And they burnt...all their goodly castles [טירותם]," is expounded as "a place where they were בטריון" which he interprets as divination [*A Lexicon of the New Verbs in Tannaitic Hebrew* (Ramat-Gan: Bar-Ilan University Press, 1980), 179 n. 7*; Kohut and Krauss, *Aruch Completum*, 4:86; Arthur B. Hyman and Yitsḥak Shiloni, eds., *Yalḳuṭ Shim'oni le-Rabbenu Shim'on ha-Darshan: Sefer Bemidbar* (Jerusalem: Mossad Harav Kook, 1986), 626 l.12 and n.; but cf. Kahana, *Sifre Numbers*, C:84 ll.45, 46; David ben Amram Adani, *Midrash Ha-Gadol 'al Ḥamishah Ḥumshe Torah: Sefer Bemidbar*, ed. Zvi Meir Rabinowitz (Jerusalem: Mossad Harav Kook, 1973), 540.] Kohut derives טיריון from θεωρία in the sense of a place for viewing idolatrous spectacles.

72   Cf. Cicero, *De Divinatione* 2:34: "In our forefathers' time the magistrates on such occasions used to call in some expert person [*peritus*] to take the auspices–but in these days anyone will do" [William Armistead Falconer, trans., *Cicero. De Senectute, De*

Cicero De Divinatione 1:53 (120):

volent alites, tum in hac, tum in illa parte se occultent, tum a dextra, tum a sinistra parte canant oscines.

and causes those known as *alites*, which give omens by their flight, to fly hither and thither and disappear now here and now there, and causes those known as *oscines*, which give omens by their cries, to sing now on the left and now

---

Amicitia, De Divinatione, The Loeb Classical Library 154 (London and Cambridge MA: W. Heinemann Ltd. and Harvard University Press, 1971), 450–453]. For a general description of the pertinent institutional structures see Georg Wissowa, "Augures," ed. August Friedrich Pauly and Georg Wissowa, *Paulys Realencyclopädie der classischen Altertumswissenschaft* (Stuttgart: Metzler, 1896); Auguste Bouché-Leclercq, *Histoire de la divination dans l'antiquité* (Paris E. Leroux, 1879); D. Wardle, *Cicero on Divination: De Divinatione, Book 1*, Clarendon Ancient History Series (Oxford and New York: Clarendon Press and Oxford University Press, 2006), 2–3; Peter Struck, "Animals and Divination," in *The Oxford Handbook of Animals in Classical Thought and Life*, ed. Gordon Lindsay Campbell, First Edition. (Oxford: Oxford University Press, 2014), 313; Green, "Malevolent Gods," 147; Gilhus, *Animals, Gods and Humans*, 26–28.

73 It has been plausibly suggested that the attention paid to birds should be seen as a natural consequence of the perception that they are capable of traveling between the lower domain of mortals and the heavenly abodes of the gods. Peter Struck quips that this hypothesis "is often remarked by scholars, but less often by ancient testimony" ["Animals and Divination," 312]. See Johnston, *Ancient Greek Divination*, 129. Cicero, arguing that belief in divination is shared and esteemed by all human societies (with perhaps the unique exception of the followers of Epicurus!), the precise form that the divination will take will vary with the environmental conditions of the respective societies. In this connection he surmises that cattle-herding societies, like those of the Arabs, Phrygians and Cilicians, "are constantly wandering over the plains and mountains in winter and summer and, on that account, have found it quite easy to study the songs and flights of birds [*cantus avium et volatus*]" [*De Divinatione* 1:39-41 (84-92)1:42 (94); Falconer, *Senectute Amicitia Divinatione*, 316–325]. Pliny, *Natural History* 8:63 (165) mentions a talking dog ("canem lucutum") as one of the portents foreshadowing Tarquin's overthrow [Pliny the Elder, *Natural History*, ed. H. (Harris) Rackham, Loeb Classical Library (Cambridge, MA: William Heinemann and Harvard University Press, 1972), 106–109]; Thorsten Fögen, "Animal Communication," in *The Oxford Handbook of Animals in Classical Thought and Life*, ed. Gordon Lindsay Campbell, First Edition. (Oxford: Oxford University Press,

Cicero De Divinatione 1:53 (120):

on the right.

The most widely used form of bird augury paid attention to auspicious or inauspicious flight paths of the *Alites* as well as other subtle nuances of their movements, direction, directional placement, timing, seasons and more (*spectio*). A small group of birds, however, were classified as *Os-*

2014), 224. In his *De Sollertia Animalium* 22 (975a-975b), Plutarch discourses at some length on the characteristics that make birds especially amenable to serving as the principal conduits for auguries:

> It is, in fact, no small or ignoble division of divination, but a great and very an-cient one, which takes its name from birds; for their quickness of apprehension and their habit of responding to any manifestation, so easily are they diverted, serves as an instrument for the god, who directs their movements, their calls or cries, and their formations which are sometimes contrary, sometimes favouring, as winds are; so that he uses some birds to cut short, others to speed enterprises and inceptions to the destined end. [Harold Cherniss and William Helmbold, trans., "Whether Land or Sea Animals Are Cleverer. (De Sollertia Animalium)," in *Plutarch's Moralia in Sixteen Volumes*, vol. 12, The Loeb Classical Library 406 (Cambridge, MA and London: Harvard University Press and William Heinemann Ltd., 1962), 12:412-413].

74 See Claus Haebler, "Corvus 4," ed. August Friedrich Pauly and Georg Wissowa, *Paulys Realencyclopädie der classischen Altertumswissenschaft* (Stuttgart: Metzler, 1897). In Leviticus Rabbah 32:2 Rabbi Jeremiah bar Eleazar interpreted Ecclesiastes 10:20, "a bird of the air shall carry the voice," in connection with ravens and the craft of ornithomancy (וחכמת טיארין) Mordecai Margulies, ed., *Midrash Vayyikra Rabbah* (New York and Jerusalem: The Jewish Theological Seminary of America, 1993), 737 and notes; Bos, "Divination with Birds," 5–6. For lexicographic discus-sions of the word טיר and useful lists of occurrences see Kohut and Krauss, *Aruch Completum*, 4:29-30; Moreshet, *A Lexicon of the New Verbs in Tannaitic Hebrew*, 179; Michael Sokoloff, *A Dictionary of Jewish Palestinian Aramaic of the Byzantine Period*, Dictionaries of Talmud, Midrash, and Targum (Ramat-Gan, Israel: Bar Ilan University Press, 1990), 223. Of all the Jewish Aramaic versions, the Targum Pseudo-Jonathan has a special propensity for employing that root for the root נח"ש, as noted by A. Shinan [*The Embroidered Targum: The Aggadah in Targum Pseudo-Jonathan of the Pentateuch*, Publications of the Perry Foundation for Biblical Re-search in the Hebrew University of Jerusalem (Jerusalem: Magnes Press, the Hebrew University, 1992), 145-146 and n. 235.]

cines whose calls and songs were analyzed as portents of future events.[78] Evidently, the Oscines qualified for that purpose principally by virtue of the fact they were capable of uttering complex sounds that lent themselves to diverse and meaningful interpretations.[79] Ravens and crows were treated as Oscines[80] (though other aspects of their behavior were also considered significant).[81] I am not aware of examples from Greek or Latin authors where the birds' sounds were interpreted as making up coherent sen-

---

75 Horace refers in *Odes* 3:27 (perhaps with a measure of irony) to the "prophetic raven" (oscinem corvum); see Niall Rudd, trans., *Horace: Odes and Epodes*, Loeb Classical Library 33 (Cambridge, MA: Harvard University Press, 2004), 204–205; David West, *Odes III: Dulce Periculum* (Oxford and New York: Oxford University Press, 2002), 227–228; see also Edmund Lammert, "Korax 3," ed. August Friedrich Pauly and Georg Wissowa, *Paulys Realencyclopädie der classischen Altertumswissenschaft* (Stuttgart: Metzler, 1922).

76 There has in fact been some scholarly dispute over which words designate the crow and which the raven; see A. J. Macleane, Reginald Heber Chase, and Charles Beck, *The Works of Horace, with English Notes* (Boston and Cambridge: Sever, Francis, & Co, 1869), 381.

77 William Armistead Falconer, trans., *Cicero. De Senectute, De Amicitia, De Divinatione*, The Loeb Classical Library 154 (London and Cambridge MA: W. Heinemann Ltd. and Harvard University Press, 1971), 354–355.

78 Thus, Cicero suggests as proof of God's providential concern for the welfare of humans the fact that "we think there are some birds, the Alites and Oscines, as our augurs call them, which were made merely to foretell events" [*De Natura Deorum* 44].

79 See Pliny the Elder, *Natural History*, 10:58-59 (117-120) pp. 366-371; See Fögen, "Animal Communication," 224; Francis D. Lazenby, "Greek and Roman Household Pets (2)," *The Classical Journal* 44, no. 5 (1949): 300.

80 The third-century B.C.E. Stoic thinker Chrysippus of Soloi, according to Varro, insisted that ravens and crows (as well as young children) are not uttering real speech: "as a man's sculptured bust is not the real man, so in the case of ravens, crows, and boys making their first attempts to speak, their words are not real words, because they are not talking" [Marcus Terentius Varro, *On the Latin Language*, trans. Roland G. Kent, Loeb Classical Library (Cambridge, MA and London: Harvard University Press and W. Heinemann, 1938), 5:56 (1:222-223)]. On Chrysippus see Hans von Arnim, "Chrysippos 14," ed. August Friedrich Pauly and Georg Wissowa, *Paulys Realencyclopädie der classischen Altertumswissenschaft* (Stuttgart: Metzler, 1931).

81 See William Smith, ed., "Augur, Augurium," *Dictionary of Greek and Roman Antiquities* (Boston: Milford House, 1973), 174–179. In ancient mythology the raven

tences.[82]

The "certain man" consulted by Rav 'Ilish was accordingly acting in a capacity equivalent to that of an augur interpreting the sounds that issued from Oscines, as outlined previously. At any rate, the Talmud's story does not really question the fundamental validity of the auguries; at the most it implies that one should not automatically give credence to predictions issuing from certain kinds of fowl—that, at least, was the attitude taken by Rav 'Ilish, and the author of the story might well have intended to imply

---

possessed a distinctly prophetic place as the vehicle through which Phoebus Apollo, the messenger god, conveyed his messages to the mortal world. Indeed, a venerable tradition had it that the raven had originally been white and that its black color was imposed upon it as a punishment by the god for revealing to him the indiscretion of his beloved Coronis; as preserved in Callimachus' poem *Helaces*:

> when the raven, which now might vie in color even with swans, or with milk, or with the finest cream of the wave, shall put on a sad plumage, black as pitch, the reward that Phoebus will one day give him for his message, when he learns terrible tidings of Coronis, daughter Phlegyas, that she has gone with Ischys, the driver of horses.

The story is better known from Ovid's adaptation in *Metamorphoses* 2:536-539 [G. P. Goold, ed., *Ovid: Metamorphosis*, trans. Frank Justus Miller, vol. 3, Loeb Classical Library 43 (Cambridge, MA and London: Harvard University Press and W. Heinemann, 1977), 98–99]. See West, *Odes III*, 69–72; A. M. Keith, *The Play of Fictions: Studies in Ovid's Metamorphoses Book 2*, Michigan Monographs in Classical Antiquity (Ann Arbor: University of Michigan Press, 1992), 19–62; Gudrun Schmidt, *Rabe Und Krähe In Der Antike: Studien Zur Archäologischen Und Literarischen Überlieferung* (Wiesbaden: Reichert, 2002), 11–28; Gianpiero Rosati, "Narrative Techniques and Narrative Structures in the Metamorphoses," in *Brill's Companion to Ovid*, ed. Barbara Weiden Boyd (Leiden: Brill Academic Publishers, 2002), 287–288; Ioannis Ziogas, *Ovid and Hesiod: The Metamorphosis of the Catalogue of Women* (Cambridge and New York: Cambridge University Press, 2013), 111–129; Green, "Malevolent Gods," 163 n. 40; James J. Clauss, "An Attic-Speaking Crow on the Capitoline: A Literary Émigré from the 'Hecale,'" *Zeitschrift für Papyrologie und Epigraphik* 96 (1993): 167–173. Clauss theorizes how the (metric) quote from Callimachus—originally spoken by an elderly crow to a fellow bird (possibly an owl)—eventually evolved into Suetonius' account of the crow who foretold the demise of Domitian (8:3): "A few months before he was killed, a crow perched on the Capitolium and cried "All will be well [Ante paucos quam occideretur menses cornix in Capitolio elocuta est: ἔσται πάντα καλῶς]" [John Carew Rolfe, trans., *Suetonius*, Loeb Classical Library 38 (Cambridge, Mass: Harvard University Press,

that his distrust of the raven (or its interpreter) was ultimately misguided.[83] P. Struck has noted that "The Romans understood divine signs as rendering judgment on the timing, not the content, of the action proposed... Roman auspices did not indicate the future, only divine approval or disapproval for the proposed action."[84]

The merging of the functions of understanding animal languages and of foretelling the future is reminiscent of figures from Greek myth and legend. For example, Pseudo-Apollodorus[85] recounted the legend about the

---

1997), 368–369]; see F. R. D. Goodyear, "History and Biography," in *The Cambridge History of Classical Literature*, ed. E. J. Kenney and W. V. Clausen, vol. 2. Latin Literature (Cambridge: Cambridge University Press, 1982), 663.

82 On the other hand, the natural sounds emitted by crows or ravens could occasionally be interpreted as Greek or Latin words, including single-word clauses. Thus, according to the *Apophthegmata Patrum*, Epiphanius reported how crows circled over the temple of Serapis stubbornly crying "Κρᾶς, Κρᾶς," which Athanasius interpreted as a Latin word for "tomorrow," an intimation of the imminent death of the emperor Julian. Benedicta Ward, ed., *The Desert Christian: Sayings of the Desert Fathers: The Alphabetical Collection*, 1st American ed. (New York: Macmillan, 1980), 56–57; See Andrew S. Jacobs, *Epiphanius of Cyprus: A Cultural Biography of Late Antiquity* (Oakland, California: University of California Press, 2016), 48; Levinson, "Enchanting Rabbis," 78.

83 See Neusner, *A History of the Jews in Babylonia*, 3:108. The birds' predictions are linked to the "miracle" of the rabbi's successful escape. Although there is a temptation to minimize the significance of such descriptions, it seems clear that the Talmud is using the term "miracle" in its literal sense of a supernatural feat that would otherwise be impossible for a normal human; e.g., flying across the river. The narrative is thereby ascribing the augury to an authentically divine source, even though the interpreter might not have been a Jew. Christian authors characterized divination from birds' cries as a typically Jewish superstition unworthy of Christians; see Matthew W. Dickie, "The Fathers of the Church and the Evil Eye," in *Byzantine Magic*, ed. Henry Maguire (Washington, DC: Dumbarton Oaks Research Library and Collection distributed by Harvard University Press, 1995), 28; cited by Bos, "Divination with Birds," 4 and n. 19.

84 "Animals and Divination," 314.

85 On the "Bibliotheca' [or: "Library"] and its immense assemblage of mythological traditions see James George Frazer, ed., *Apollodorus: The Library*, LCL 121–122 (London and New York: W. Heinemann and G. P. Putnam's Sons, 1921), Introduction; Robin Hard, ed., *Apollodorus: The Library of Greek Mythology*, 1 edition., Oxford World's Classics (Oxford and New York: Oxford University Press, 2008), Intro-

seer Melampus who was vouchsafed a reward from a pair of orphaned snakes whom he had tended to compassionately:

Pseudo-Apollodorus, The Library 1:9:11:[86]

οἱ δὲ γενόμενοι τέλειοι παραστάντες αὐτῷ κοιμωμένῳ τῶν ὤμων ἐξ ἑκατέρου τὰς ἀκοὰς ταῖς γλώσσαις ἐξεκάθαιρον. ὁ δὲ ἀναστὰς καὶ γενόμενος περιδεὴς	And when the young were full grown, they stood beside him at each of his shoulders as he slept, and they purged his ears with their tongues. He started up in a

duction (vii-xxxi); Aubrey Diller, "The Text History of the Bibliotheca of Pseudo-Apollodorus," *Transactions and Proceedings of the American Philological Association* 66 (1935): 296–313; M. Van der Valk, "On Apollodori Bibliotheca," *Revue des Etudes Grecques* 71 (n.d.): 100–168. For some interesting observations about Pseudo-Apollodorus's conceptions of prophecy (relating principally to the figure of Teireisias), see Armin Lange, "Greek Seers and Israelite-Jewish Prophets," *Vetus Testamentum* 57, no. 4 (2007): 461–482.

86 James George Frazer, ed., *Apollodorus: The Library*, LCL 121–122 (London and New York: W. Heinemann and G. P. Putnam's Sons, 1921), 1:86-87.. In his notes and especially in his detailed Appendix [2:350-358] on "Melampus and the Kine of Phylacus," Frazer copies and discusses the passage from the Scholiast on Homer based on Pherecydes and Eusthathius, according to which Melampus assists his brother Bias to win the hand of the lovely Pero. Towards that end, Melampus allowed himself to be imprisoned and was able to foretell the collapse of the ceiling thanks to his eavesdropping on the conversation of the worms or termites. He subsequently was able to cure the infertility of Iphiclus with the help of advice from consulting with all the birds, and finally with a vulture who had the solution. As is to be expected, Frazer enriches his discussion with ample illustrations from classical authors and world folklore. Pliny (Nat. Hist. 10:49) writes mockingly about credulous types who "would also assuredly not deny that snakes by licking the ears of the augur Melampus gave him the power to understand the language of birds, or the story handed down by Democritus, who mentions birds from a mixture of whose blood a snake is born, whoever eats which will understand the conversations of birds... as even without these stories life is involved in enormous uncertainty with respect to auguries." [Pliny the Elder, *Natural History*, ed. H. (Harris) Rackham, Loeb Classical Library (Cambridge, MA: William Heinemann and Harvard University Press, 1972), 3:380-381]. See Mary Beagon, *The Elder Pliny on the Human Animal: Natural History, Book 7*, Clarendon Ancient History Series (Oxford and: New York: Clarendon Press and Oxford University Press, 2005), 312; Arthur Bernard Cook, "Descriptive Animal Names in Greece," *The Classical Review* 8, no. 9 (1894): 385; Jan N. Bremmer, "Balaam, Mopsus and Melampous: Tales of Travelling Seers," in *Prestige of the Pagan*

Pseudo-Apollodorus, The Library 1:9:11:

τῶν ὑπερπετομένων ὀρνέων τὰς φωνὰς συνίει, καὶ παρ' ἐκείνων μανθάνων προύλεγε τοῖς ἀνθρώποις τὰ μέλλοντα. προσέλαβε δὲ καὶ τὴν διὰ τῶν ἱερῶν μαντικήν, περὶ δὲ τὸν Ἀλφειὸν συντυχὼν Ἀπόλλωνι τὸ λοιπὸν ἄριστος ἦν μάντις.

great fright, but understood the voices of the birds flying overhead, and from what he learned from them he foretold to men what should come to pass. He acquired besides the art of taking the auspices, and having fallen in with Apollo at the Alpheus he was ever after an excellent soothsayer.[87]

A similar ability was ascribed by Pseudo-Apollodorus (3:6:7)[88] to the seer Tiresias who, after being stricken blind my the gods, was partially compensated by Athena by being granted the power to prophesy by means of his understanding of the language of the birds.[89]

Prophet Balaam in Judaism, Early Christianity and Islam, ed. George H. Van Kooten and Jacques Van Ruiten, Themes in Biblical Narrative 11 (Leiden: Brill, 2008), 60–66; Sarah Iles Johnston, *Ancient Greek Divination*, Blackwell Ancient Religions (Malden, MA and Oxford: Wiley-Blackwell, 2008), 64.

87 Herodotus (*Persian Wars* 2:49 (2)) suggests that it was Melampus who first introduced the arts of prophecy and divination to the Greeks, having learned them from the Egyptians [ἐγὼ μέν νυν φημὶ Μελάμποδα γενόμενον ἄνδρα σοφὸν μαντικήν τε ἑωυτῷ συστῆσαι καὶ πυθόμενον ἀπ' Αἰγύπτου]; [*Herodotus, with an English Translation*, Loeb Classical Library 117–120 (London: W. Heinemann, 1921), 1:336-337]. See Vivienne J. Gray, "Herodotus on Melampus," in *Myth, Truth, and Narrative in Herodotus*, ed. Emily Baragwanath and Mathieu de Bakker (Oxford University Press, 2012), 167–192; Gerrit Bos, "Jewish Traditions on Divination with Birds (Ornithomancy)," 2015, 3, https://www.researchgate.net/ publication/ 280976904_ Jewish_Traditions_ on_ Divination_ with_ Birds_ Ornithomancy. Gray has particularly insightful observations to offer regarding Herodotus' motives and methods in describing Melampus' combination of importation and alteration of the foreign elements, details regarding which Herodotus confesses to possessing imperfect knowledge.

88 Transl. Frazer, 360-363. In the accompanying note Frazer discourses on the evolution of these motifs. See Charilaos N. Michalopoulos, "Tiresias Between Texts and Sex," *Eugesta: Journal of Gender Studies in Antiquity* 2 (2012): 223.

As we found in several Greek and Latin writers, the ancients were much impressed by the ability of some birds to imitate human speech;[90] and especially when the proper sounds could be produced in appropriate situations, this was considered a powerful argument in favor of ascribing a human-like moral standing to birds and other creatures.[91] Nevertheless, in the relatively small proportion of Greek and Latin texts about divination that deal with the augury of Oscine birds I have not found many that ex-

89 This is a widely accepted inference from "τὰς ἀκοὰς διακαθάρασαν πᾶσαν ὀρνίθων φωνὴν ποιῆσαι συνεῖναι;" though of course φωνή, as noted elsewhere, does not designate coherent syntactic language, a sense that Aristotle, the Stoics and others assigned to λόγος. In Callimachus' hymn "On the Bath of Pallas" Athena declares that Tiresias "shall know the birds (γνωσεῖται δ᾽ ὄρνιχας)—which is of good omen among all the countless birds that fly and what birds are of ill-omened flight"; and this would seem to refer to observations of their flights etc., but does not contain any explicit allusion to his understanding their language [G. R. Mair, *Callimachus and Lycophron*, trans. A. W. Mair, The Loeb Classical Library (London, New York: W. Heinemann and G.P. Putnam's Sons, 1921), (l. 5:123); 120-121]. For extensive comparative analyses of Callimachus' portrayal of the Tiresias legend see Richard Hunter, "Writing the God: Form and Meaning in Callimachus, Hymn to Athena," *Materiali e discussioni per l'analisi dei testi classici*, no. 29 (1992): 2–22; Heather van Tress, *Poetic Memory: Allusion in the Poetry of Callimachus and the Metamorphoses of Ovid*, Mnemosyne, bibliotheca classica Batava, Supplementum 258 (Leiden: Brill, 2004), 72–110; (see also Michalopoulos, "Tiresias Between Texts and Sex," 230). Sophocles' Oedipus ("Oedipus Tyrannus" ll. 310-311) greets Tiresias with the words: "So do not begrudge us the voice of the birds or any other path of prophecy" [σύ νυν φθονήσας μήτ᾽ ἀπ᾽ οἰωνῶν φάτιν \ μήτ᾽ εἴ τιν᾽ ἄλλην μαντικῆς ἔχεις ὁδόν]. (According to *LSJ*, οἰωνός has the senses of "a large bird, bird of prey" as well as "omen.") [Hugh Lloyd-Jones, *Sophocles: Ajax. Electra. Oedipus Tyrannus*, vol. 1, The Loeb Classical Library 20 (Cambridge, MA: Harvard University Press, 1994), 1:352-353]; see also Hanna M. Roisman, "Teiresias, the Seer of Oedipus the King: Sophocles' and Seneca's Versions," *Leeds International Classical Studies* 2, no. 5 (2003): 3.

90 See, e.g., Pliny, *Natural History* 10:58 (117) on parrots (psittaci): "Above all, birds imitate the human voice, parrots indeed actually talking. .... It greets its masters, and repeats words given to it, being particularly sportive over the wine [super omnia humanas voces reddunt, psittaci quidem etiam sermocinantes... imperatores salutat et quae accipit verba pronuntiat]" [Pliny the Elder, *Natural History*, 3:66-67]. Additional examples are assembled by Lazenby, "Greek and Roman Household Pets (2),"

plicitly discuss actual verbal messages. Thus, in *De Divinatione* 1:34,[92] Quintus Cicero relates how at the battle of Leuctra in 371 B.C.E. "at Lebadia, in Boeotia, while divine honors were being paid to Trophonius, the cocks in the neighborhood began to crow vigorously and did not leave off. Thereupon the Boeotian augurs declared that the victory belonged to the Thebans, because it was the habit of cocks to keep silence when conquered and to crow when victorious."[93] That is to say, it was the fact or the intensity of the crowing that was relevant to the augury—not any specific content addressed to a particular person, as was the case in the story about Rav 'Ilish.

Some Latin authors involved themselves in extensive theoretical discussions about the "theology" of augury; and specifically, to defining the roles of the birds (or other natural creatures) in the process.[94] In general, the Stoics were known for their defense of divination whereas Epicurus

---

299–300; see also Bigwood, "Ctesias' Parrot," 326–327.

91   Cf. Fögen, "Pliny the Elder's Animals," 190:

However, although humans and birds share what Aristotle calls διάλεκτος, it is only humans who have "real" language... For this view, Aristotle gives an ethical reason: human beings are distinguished from animals by their λόγος, which enables them to develop and discuss principles of justice and therefore establish an ethical awareness that guarantees the possibility of living together in complex social communities.

92   Falconer, *Senectute Amicitia Divinatione*, 304–305.

93   Marcus Cicero has his turn at analyzing the story and its implications in 2:56 (ed. Falconer, 434-437). He argues, among other things: "Do you really believe that Jupiter would have employed chickens to convey such a message to so great a state? And is it true that these fowls are not accustomed to crow except when they are victorious? But at that time they did crow and they had not yet been victorious..." After ridiculing the notion that the birds would react differently to human victories than to their own barnyard triumphs, he proceeds to enumerate several naturalistic explanations for the vocal habits of cocks. See Malcolm Schofield, "Cicero for and against Divination," *The Journal of Roman Studies* 76 (1986): 54–55.

94   In the excursus about augury in n. 1 note to the P. Holland translation of Pliny's Natural History, the editor states (without citing a source) that : "The birds themselves that afforded these prognostications were supposed to be moved *ab anima sua*, by an inward action proceeding from the influence of Deity" [Wernerian Club, ed., *Pliny's Natural History in Thirty-Seven Books / a Translation ... with Critical and Explanatory Notes*, trans. Philemon Holland (London: Barclay, 1847), 200].

and his school led the opposition.[95] The most influential treatise to be devoted to the question[96] was Cicero's *De Divinatione*, which was constructed as a debate between Quintus Cicero who defends the institution[97] and his brother Marcus Cicero himself, speaking as a skeptic who dismisses divination as a concept rooted in superstition. Scholars are divided as to whether the author's personal opinion is reflected in that of his literary persona who gets the last word in the discussion, or whether he considers the matter unresolved, in keeping with the treatise's closing words.[98]

---

95 See Green, "Malevolent Gods," 148; A. A. Long, "Post-Aristotelian Philosophy," in *The Cambridge History of Classical Literature*, ed. P. E. Easterling and Bernard Knox, vol. 1. Greek Literature (Cambridge: Cambridge University Press, 1982), 625–628.

96 "No area of religion was more written about in late Republican Rome than divination. We know of the existence of (but few details about their contents) numerous books on augury, mostly by men who—like Cicero—were themselves augurs" [Schofield, "Cicero for and against Divination," 49]. Most of the material about Roman divination relates to its official, public manifestations. For a study of accounts related to private individuals see Pauline Ripat, "Roman Omens, Roman Audiences, and Roman History," *Greece & Rome* 53, no. 2 (2006): 155–174.

97 This approach was most prominently associated with the Stoic school. For an attempt to give a serious hearing to that position according to the science of the time, see R. J. Hankinson, "Stoicism, Science and Divination," *Apeiron* 21, no. 2 (1988): 123–160. Quintus (1:53 (120)) asserts that the source of the messages vouchsafed to the birds lies in the divine will ("Eademque efficit in avibus divina mens") [Falconer, *Senectute Amicitia Divinatione*, 354–355].

98 On the book's purpose and Cicero's personal position *vis à vis* divination, see Lily Ross Taylor, *Party Politics in the Age of Caesar*, Sather Classical Lectures 22 (Berkeley: University of California Press, 1949), 76–97; Robert J. Goar, "The Purpose of De Divinatione," *Transactions and Proceedings of the American Philological Association* 99 (1968): 241–248; Mary Beard, "Cicero and Divination: The Formation of a Latin Discourse," *The Journal of Roman Studies* 76 (1986): 33–46; Schofield, "Cicero for and against Divination"; Wardle, *Cicero on Divination*, 1–28; L. P. Wilkinson, "Cicero and the Relationship of Oratory to Literature," in *The Cambridge History of Classical Literature*, ed. E. J. Kenney and W. V. Clausen, vol. 2. Latin Literature (Cambridge: Cambridge University Press, 1982), 264–265. These scholars also compare Cicero's skeptical treatment of the philosophical issue with his defense of the civil practice of augury as one that promotes the consolidation of consensus among the (unsophisticated) masses. In proper talmudic spirit, his critique sometimes appears to be leveled more at the cogency of the arguments than at the ac-

Cicero notes that the type of divination practiced in his days in Rome was substantially different from the older type that had been cultivated by the Greeks, in that the Romans did not generally turn to auguries with a view to producing detailed predictions of future events, but merely to determine the advisability of particular enterprises or courses of action.[99] In the context of *auspicium*,[100] he also makes a distinction between "artificial," ritualized methods and the interpretation of unexpected "natural" meteorological and other phenomena that might be sent by the gods in order to advise mortals about taking or turning away from a course of action.

An important question that is dealt with by Greek and Latin thinkers who uphold the validity of augury is how to understand the role that the birds are playing in the divinatory process: if we accept the validity of the portents, must it follow from this premise that the birds are actually privy to supernatural insights into the future developments?

Peter Struck has outlined a useful schematic of three principal ancient theories to explain the channels by means of which animals are able to communicate advice about their enterprises to humans.[101] To be sure, the focus of these approaches is principally on dreams and other types of divination, and they have to be adapted considerably to extend their relevance to verbal messages. All three reflect a quasi-pantheistic world-view that regards the totality of physical being as a unified organism; and they are founded on the premise of a strong shared destiny of animals and humans in the universe. In fact, for our purposes the Platonic and Aristotelian theories can be treated as virtually identical, in that they are both founded on an "evolutionary" theory[102] according to which nature compensates those

---

tual positions that are being argued.

99 See Wardle, *Cicero on Divination*, 6.

100 See Georg Wissowa, "Auspicium," ed. August Friedrich Pauly and Georg Wissowa, *Paulys Realencyclopädie der classischen Altertumswissenschaft* (Stuttgart: Metzler, 1896); Jørgen Christian Meyer, "Omens, Prophecies and Oracles in Ancient Decision-Making," in *Ancient History Matters. Studies Presented to Jens Erik Skydsgaard on His 70th Birthday*, ed. Karen Ascani et al., Analecta Romana Instituti Danici Suppl. 30 (Rome: L'Erma di Bretschneider, 2002), 173–83.

101 "Animals and Divination," 318–322.

102 For Plato the situation harkens back to a perception of the universe as an interconnected organism, where all animals developed out of the primordial man.

persons who are not utilizing their distinctively human rational faculty by endowing them with animal-like instincts or intuitions that allow the gods to communicate positive advice or to alert them to danger. Though humans maintain all three original components of the soul—the intellectual / rational, animal / perceptive, and vegetative / nutritive— their actions and decisions should be governed by the highest of them, the intellect; yet a vestige of the animal instincts was left in the human anatomy (for Plato: primarily in the form of the liver) which operates as a divinatory [μαντική] conduit for dreams sent by the gods (and which is the final station for auditory information).[103] In Stoic thought all creatures are defined by their particular types of spirit, πνεῦμα; with humans being being moved by a rational soul: λογικὴ ψυχή.[104] The generic πνεῦμα, however, binds humans with all the other types of creatures, creating a shared affinity with the cosmic whole, which allows individual beings to sense knowledge generated by their fellow beings and by the universe as a whole.[105]

---

103 The biological theory is set out mostly in the *Timaeus* 70c-72c [Robert Gregg Bury, trans., *Plato: Timaeus, Critias, Cleitophon, Menexenus, Epistles*, vol. 9, 12 vols., Loeb Classical Library 234 (Cambridge MA: Harvard University Press, 1960)]., though features of it appear in other places in Plato's writings. See Hendrik Lorenz, "The Cognition of Appetite in Plato's Timaeus," in *Plato and the Divided Self*, ed. Rachel Barney, Tad Brennan, and Charles Brittain (Cambridge: Cambridge University Press, 2012), 244–247. Aristotle's theories are located in: W. S. Hett, trans., "On Prophecy in Sleep," in *Aristotle: On the Soul. Parva Naturalia. On Breath*, vol. 8, Loeb Classical Library 288 (Cambridge MA and London: Harvard University Press, 2000), 374–387.

104 A variation on this cosmological theory is argued by the Neoplatonist Plotinus; e.g., in Ennead 2:3:7-8; A. H. Armstrong, trans., *Plotinus*, Loeb Classical Library 441 (Cambridge MA and London: Harvard University Press, 2001), 2:68-73; see Thorndike, *Magic and Experimental Science*, 302–305.

105 See P. A. Meijer, *Stoic Theology: Proofs for the Existence of the Cosmic God and of the Traditional Gods: Including a Commentary on Cleanthes' Hymn on Zeus* (Delft: Eburon, 2007), 91; Anna Eunyoung Ju, "Chrysippus on Nature and Soul in Animals," *The Classical Quarterly* 57, no. 1, New Series (2007): 97–108; Hankinson, "Stoicism, Science and Divination"; Marcia L. Colish, *The Stoic Tradition from Antiquity to the Early Middle Ages: Stoicism in Christian Latin Thought Through the Sixth Century*, Studies in the History of Christian Thought 34–35 (Leiden, New York, Copenhagen and Köln: E. J. Brill, 1985), 31–33; Stephen Thomas Newmyer, "Being

An intriguing study by Steven J. Green[106] suggests that during the Augustan[107] era it was the poets (Virgil and Ovid) who played a major role in subtly raising questions about the validity or morality of the mythological underpinnings of the augural process, challenging the supposed premise that "there exists a positive interaction between gods and birds, whereby beneficent gods send reliable signs to expert mortals by means of certain birds, which act as the gods' messengers." In this connection, he analyzes the scene from the *Aeneid* (12:244-265)[108] where, prior to a battle between Aeneas's Trojans and the Latins in which a swarm of birds unite to drive away an eagle that had captured a swan, the Latin augur Tolumnius mistakenly took this as a sign of his sides' imminent victory.[109] Green[110] sides with the exegetical tradition that sees this phenomenon not as a misinterpretation of the sign, but as an inherently false—or even malevolent—

the One and Becoming the Other: Animals in Ancient Philosophical Schools," in *The Oxford Handbook of Animals in Classical Thought and Life*, ed. George Lindsay Campbell (Oxford: Oxford University Press, 2014), 512; Christoph Jedan, *Stoic Virtues: Chrysippus and the Theological Foundations of Stoic Ethics* (London and New York: Continuum, 2009), 26–29.

106 Green, "Malevolent Gods." He claims to be dealing with examples of observations of the birds "in flight," not with speaking or other audible communications; though this is not strictly true regarding the passage from Ovid below.

107 Ovid, *Fasti* 1:611-612 (18), points out the etymological link between the title "Augustus" and "augury" as expressions of gifts bestowed by Jupiter: "huius et augurium dependet origine verbi \ et quodcumque sua Iuppiter auget ope"; Ibid., 164–166.

108 H. Rushton Fairclough, trans., *Virgil with an English Translation*, Revised ed., with new introduction., Loeb Classical Library 63–64 (Cambridge MA: Harvard University Press, 1999), 2:318-319.

109 See William S. Anderson, "Two Passages from Book Twelve of the 'Aeneid,'" *California Studies in Classical Antiquity* 4 (1971): 49–65; W. Warde Fowler, *The Death of Turnus: Observations on the Twelfth Book of the Aeneid* (Oxford: B.H. Blackwell, 1919), 73; James J. O'Hara, *Death and the Optimistic Prophecy in Vergil's Aeneid* (Princeton: Princeton University Press, 1990), 85–87; Netta Berlin, "War and Remembrance: 'Aeneid' 12.554-60 and Aeneas' Memory of Troy," *The American Journal of Philology* 119, no. 1 (1998): 11–41.

110 P. 156.

message. Of especial interest is his example[111] from Ovid's *Fasti*[112] lines 441-456[113] in which the poet sympathizes ironically with the bitter fate of the peaceful and harmless birds that, in spite of all their virtues, were singled out by the gods to serve as sacrificial victims:

sed nihil ista iuvant, quia linguae crimen habetis,	But all that avails not, because ye are accused of chattering,
dique putant mentes vos aperire suas.	and the gods opine that ye reveal their thoughts.

---

111 Pp. 158-162. The passage invites comparison with the story in 1 Kings 22:1-28 and 2 Chronicles 18-19:1-27 in which God puts a "lying spirit" into the mouths of Micaiah ben Imlah and four hundred other prophets, foretelling victory to kings Ahab of Israel and Jehoshaphat of Judah ("Go, and prosper: for the Lord shall deliver it into the hand of the king"), in order to lure them to a defeat at Ramoth Gilead that will result in Ahab's death. See Simon J. De Vries, *Prophet Against Prophet: The Role of the Micaiah Narrative (i Kings 22) in the Development of Early Prophetic Tradition* (Grand Rapids: Eerdmans, 1978); R. W. L. Moberly, "Does God Lie to His Prophets? The Story of Micaiah Ben Imlah as a Test Case," *Harvard Theological Review* 96, no. 1 (2003): 1–23; "To Speak for God: The Story of Micaiah Ben Imlah," *Anvil* 14, no. 4 (1997): 243–253; David J. Zucker, "The Prophet Micaiah in Kings and Chronicles," *Jewish Bible Quarterly* 41, no. 3 (2013): 156–162; Jeffries M. Hamilton, "Caught in the Nets of Prophecy? The Death of King Ahab and the Character of God," *The Catholic Biblical Quarterly* 56, no. 4 (1994): 649–663; Ehud Ben Zvi, "A Contribution to the Intellectual History of Yehud: The Story of Micaiah and Its Function Within the Discourse of Persian-Period Literati," in *Historian and the Bible: Essays in Honour of Lester L. Grabbe*, ed. Philip R. Davies and Diana Vikander Edelman, Library of Biblical Studies (New York: T & T Clark, 2010), 89–102; Robert B. Jr. Chisholm, "Does God Deceive," *Bibliotheca Sacra* 155, no. 617 (1998): 11–28; Geoffrey David Miller, "The Wiles of the Lord: Divine Deception, Subtlety, and Mercy in I Reg 22," *Zeitschrift für die alttestamentliche Wissenschaft* 126, no. 1 (2014): 45–58; David A Robertson, "Micaiah Ben Imiah: A Literary View," in *Biblical Mosaic: Changing Perspectives*, ed. Robert M. Polzin and Eugene Rothman, Society of Biblical Literature Semeia Studies (Philadelphia: Fortress Press, 1982), 139–146; Wolfgang M. W. Roth, "The Story of the Prophet Micaiah (1 Kings 22) in Historical-Critical Interpretation: 1876-1976," in *Biblical Mosaic: Changing Perspectives*, ed. Robert M. Polzin and Eugene Rothman, Society of Biblical Literature Semeia Studies (Philadelphia: Fortress Press, 1982), 105–137; Peter J. Williams, "Lying Spirits Sent by God?: The Case of Micaiah's Prophecy," in *Trustworthiness of God: Perspectives on the Nature of Scripture*, ed. Paul Heim and Carl R. Trueman (Grand Rapids: Eerdmans and Apollos, 2002), 58–66; Kurt Lesher Noll, "The De-

nec tamen hoc falsum: nam, dis ut proxima quaeque,	Nor is the charge untrue; for the nearer ye are to the gods,
nunc pinna veras, nunc datis ore notas.	the truer are the signs ye give, whether by wing or voice.

In spite of a widespread scholarly reluctance to accept the simplest reading of the passage,[114] it seems to be assuming that in communicating divine intentions to mortals, the birds are not serving as messengers, but on the

construction of Deuteronomism in the Former Prophets: Micaiah Ben Imlah as Example," in *Far from Minimal: Celebrating the Work and Influence of Philip R. Davies*, ed. Duncan Burns and J. W. Rogerson, Library of Hebrew Bible / Old Testament Studies 484 (New York: T & T Clark, 2012), 325–334; Jonathan Grossman, "Micaiah's Narrative and the Death of Ahab (1 Kings 22) — Proactive Editing," *Studies in Bible and Exegesis* 10: Presented to Shmuel Vargon (2011): 157–158 [Hebrew]. Similar (albeit not so explicit) theological and ethical difficulties are provoked by passages like the hardening of Pharaoh's heart in Exodus or the "fattening" of the Israelites' in Isaiah 6:9-10; [see, e.g., Craig A. Evans, *To See and Not Perceive: Isaiah 6.9-10 in Early Jewish and Christian Interpretation*, Journal for the Study of the Old Testament 64 (Sheffield: Sheffield Academic Press, 1989); Robert P. Carroll, "Blindsight and the Vision Thing," in *Writing and Reading the Scroll of Isaiah: Studies of an Interpretive Tradition*, ed. Craig C. Broyles and Craig A. Evans (Leiden and New York: Brill, 1997), especially 82-83; Francis Landy, "Prophecy as Trap," *Studia Theologica: Nordic Journal of Theology* 69, no. 1 (2015): 74–91]. To the best of my knowledge none of these attracted much attention from the talmudic and midrashic interpreters. On the rabbinic treatment of such issues see Robert Goldenberg, "The Problem of False Prophecy: Talmudic Interpretations of Jeremiah 28 and 1 Kings 22," in *Biblical Mosaic: Changing Perspectives*, ed. Robert M. Polzin and Eugene Rothman, Society of Biblical Literature Semeia Studies (Philadelphia, PA: Fortress Press, 1982), 87–103; Evans, *To See and Not Perceive*, 139–143; Benno Jacob, "Gott und Pharao," *Monatsschrift für Geschichte und Wissenschaft des Judentums* 68, no. 2–4 (1923): 2:118-126; Claire Mathews McGinnis, "The Hardening of Pharaoh's Heart in Christian and Jewish Interpretation," *Journal of Theological Interpretation* 6, no. 1 (2012): 50–52.

112 On the work see E. J. Kenney, "Ovid," in *The Cambridge History of Classical Literature*, ed. E. J. Kenney and W. V. Clausen, vol. 2. Latin Literature (Cambridge: Cambridge University Press, 1982), 428–430.

113 James George Frazer, trans., *Ovid's Fasti*, The Loeb Classical Library 253 (London and New York: W. Heinemann Ltd. and G.P. Putnam's Sons, 1996), 32–33.

contrary—they are (at least in some cases) violating confidences and acting against the gods' wills, a transgression that makes them deserving of punishment, at least from the gods' point of view.[115]

Prompted by the accounts of Julian the Apostate and his willful (and apparently inconsistent) dismissal of divination and augury, the historian Ammianus Marcellinus inserted a digression on the general subject of divination.[116] For the most part, he provides a lucid restatement of the Platonic thesis that the signs are of authentically divine origin, and that they derive entirely from their celestial source,[117] so that we should not impute any profound prophetic abilities to the birds or animals who serve as the mediators for communicating them to humans.[118]

---

114 Green: "This is an extraordinary and unparalleled statement for Ovid to make, and its implications have so far not been explored." He invokes the analogy of Prometheus.

115 See Green, 166.

116 See John Matthews, *The Roman Empire of Ammianus* (Baltimore: Johns Hopkins University Press, 1989), 179–182; J. H. W. G. Liebeschuetz, "Ammianus, Julian, and Divination," in *Roma Renascens: Beiträge Zur Spätantike Und Rezeptionsgeschichte*, ed. Michael Wisseman (Frankfurt a/M: Peter Lang, 1988), 198–213; Jan Willem Drijvers and David Hunt, *The Late Roman World and Its Historian: Interpreting Ammianus Marcellinus* (London and New York: Routledge, 1999); Timothy David Barnes, *Ammianus Marcellinus and the Representation of Historical Reality* (Cornell University Press, 1998), 170–171; R. L. Rike, *Apex Omnium: Religion in the Res Gestae of Ammianus*, The Transformation of the Classical Heritage 15 (Berkeley, Los Angeles, London: University of California Press, 1987), 13–14, 44–45, etc.; Daniël den Hengst, *Emperors and Historiography: Collected Essays on the Literature of the Roman Empire by Daniël Den Hengst*, ed. Diederik W. P. Burgersdijk and Joop A. van Waarden, Mnemosyne supplements. Monographs on Greek and Roman language and literature v. 319 (Leiden and Boston: Brill, 2010), 314–315; Menahem Stern, *Greek and Latin Authors on Jews and Judaism*, Fontes ad Res Judaicas Spectantes (Jerusalem: Israel Academy of Sciences and Humanities, 1974), 2:600-603.

117 The Neoplatonist Plotinus argues for a similar version of this theory in the *Enneads* 2:3.3-8 Armstrong, *Plotinus*, 2:60-71; see Thorndike, *Magic and Experimental Science*, 1:302-305.

118 I. Gilhus discusses how Christian thinkers strove to deal with the embarrassing fact that birds appear to be endowed with a sublime physical feature that is lacking in supposedly superior humans, namely the wings that allow them to fly. [*Animals, Gods and Humans*, 248–250].

Ammianus Marcellinus, *Rerum Gestarum* 21:1:7-14:[119]

Auguria et auspicia non volucrum arbitrio futura nescientium colliguntur (nec enim hoc vel insipiens quisquam dicet) sed volatus avium dirigit deus, ut rostrum sonans aut praetervolans pinna, turbido meatu vel leni, futura praemonstret. Amat enim benignitas numinis, seu quod merentur homines, seu quod tangitur eorum affectione, his quoque artibus prodere quae impendent.	Auguries and auspices are not gained from the will of the fowls of the air which have no knowledge of future events (for that not even a fool will maintain), but a god so directs the flight of birds that the sound of their bills or the passing flight of their wings in disturbed or in gentle passage foretells future events. For the goodness of the deity, either because men deserve it, or moved by his affection for them, loves by these arts also to reveal impending events.

Indeed, according to Xenophon's *Memorabilia* (1.1.2-3),[120] an accusation of disbelief in divination figured prominently in the prosecution of Socrates on charges of "atheism," and Xenophon was moved to defend his teacher by explaining actions that were misconstrued by his critics:

> First then, that he rejected the gods acknowledged by the state — what evidence did they produce of that?... He made use of divination with as little secrecy [as with sacrifices] [καὶ μαντικῇ χρώμενος οὐκ ἀφανὴς ἦν].[121] Indeed it had become notorious that Socrates claimed to be guided by 'the deity:' it was out of this claim, I think, that the charge of bringing in strange deities

---

119 John Carew Rolfe, trans., *Ammianus Marcellinus History*, Loeb Classical Library (Cambridge, Mass., London, 1935), 3:94-95.

120 E. C. Marchant and O. J. Todd, trans., *Xenophon: Memorabilia, Oeconomicus, Symposium, Apology*, Revised., Xenophon 168 (Cambridge, MA and London: Harvard University Press, 2013), 2–3.

121 See A. A. Long, "15. Socrates in Later Greek Philosophy," in *The Cambridge Companion to Socrates*, ed. Donald R. Morrison, Cambridge Companions to Philosophy, Religion and Culture (Cambridge: Cambridge University Press, 2010), 374–375; Mary P. Nichols, *Socrates on Friendship and Community: Reflections on Plato's Symposium, Phaedrus, and Lysis* (Cambridge and New York: Cambridge University Press, 2009), 106.

arose. He was no more bringing in anything strange than are other believers in divination, who rely on augury, oracles, coincidences and sacrifices.

οὗτοί τε γὰρ ὑπολαμβάνουσιν οὐ τοὺς ὄρνιθας οὐδὲ τοὺς ἀπαντῶντας εἰδέναι τὰ συμφέροντα τοῖς μαντευομένοις, ἀλλὰ τοὺς θεοὺς διὰ τούτων αὐτὰ σημαίνειν, κἀκεῖνος δὲ οὕτως ἐνόμιζεν.

For these men's belief is not that the birds or the folk met by accident know what profits the inquirer, but that they are the instruments by which the gods make this known; and that was Socrates' belief too.

ἀλλ᾽ οἱ μὲν πλεῖστοί φασιν ὑπό τε τῶν ὀρνίθων καὶ τῶν ἀπαντώντων ἀποτρέπεσθαί τε καὶ προτρέπεσθαι: Σωκράτης δ᾽ ὥσπερ ἐγίγνωσκεν, οὕτως ἔλεγε: τὸ δαιμόνιον γὰρ ἔφη σημαίνειν.

Only, whereas most men say that the birds or the folk they meet dissuade or encourage them, Socrates said what he meant: for he said that the deity gave him a sign

Whereas Socrates' prosecutors were accusing him of unacceptable religious innovation by virtue of his reluctance to credit the birds or other sources of supernatural guidance, Xenophon argues that there are "other men" (though presumably not all, and perhaps not even most of them) who subscribe to a similar conviction that the source of the divinatory information is not the bird or other physical thing, but rather the god who is employing it as a vehicle of revelation; and Socrates preferred to refer to the original source rather than to a mere agent.[122]

Origen cites an argument from Celsus that our reliance on fowl and other creatures with prophetic gifts for knowledge of future events implies

---

122 Of course this passage is referring to diverse omens and not to verbal messages. Nonetheless, in other allusions to the revelations that Socrates claimed to receive through his daemon (and which are equated here with divination), he suggests more explicitly that the communications contained specific content that likely was conveyed in some sort of speech. Of particular interest to scholars is the passage in Plato's *Phaedrus* (242b-c) in which Socrates says:

> when I was about to cross the stream, the spirit and the sign that usually comes to me came—it always holds me back from something I am about to do—and I thought I heard a voice from it which forbade my going away before clearing my conscience, as if I had committed some sin against deity. Now I am a seer, not a very good one...; so now I understand my error. How prophetic the soul is, my friend! [Plato, *Euthyphro. Apology. Crito. Phaedo. Phaedrus*, trans. Harold North Fowler, Loeb Classical Library 36 (Harvard University Press, 1914), 458–459].

that those creatures are wiser and have a more elevated and beloved status than humans in the divine hierarchy. "The more intelligent of men, moreover, say that the animals hold meetings which are more sacred than our assemblies, and that they know what is said at these meetings, and show that in reality they possess this knowledge." Although Origen challenges the veracity of this last statement, it is unlikely that Celsus would have ventured it unless he was convinced that a sizable portion of the populace were convinced of its accuracy. Origen can at best claim that the matter is "the subject of dispute among those philosophers, not only among the Greeks, but also among the Barbarians, who have either discovered or learned from certain demons some things about birds of augury and other animals, by which certain prophetic intimations are said to be made to men."[123]

Origen also argued that the inspired wisdom that the augurs ascribed to the birds and beasts that they consulted should also guide their behavior in other ways to protect them against dangers and predators. There are however numerous instances in the canonical poets where this clearly did not occur:

Origen, *Contra Celsum* 4:91:[124]

Ἀλλὰ καὶ εἴπερ οἰωνοὶ οἰωνοῖς μάχονται [καί], ὥς φησιν ὁ Κέλσος, θείαν φύσιν ἔχοντες οἱ μαντικοὶ ὄρνεις καὶ τὰ ἄλλα ἄλογα ζῷα καὶ ἐννοίας τοῦ θείου καὶ πρόγνωσιν περὶ μελλόντων τὰ τοιαῦτα ἑτέροις προεδήλουν· οὔτ' ἂν ἡ καθ' Ὅμηρον στρουθὸς ἐνόσσευσεν ὅπου δράκων

But besides, if birds of augury converse with one another, as Celsus maintains they do, the prophetic birds having a divine nature, and the other rational animals also possess ideas of the divinity and foreknowledge of future events; and if they had communicated this knowledge to oth-

---

123 The Neoplatonist Iamblichus, while denying that animals possess true prophetic powers, did believe that they enjoy a quasi-prophetic "natural prescience," rooted in part by their closeness to nature, that enables them to sense developments before humans become aware of them. See Thorndike, *Magic and Experimental Science*, 1:315; Gilhus, *Animals, Gods and Humans*, 26.

124 Migne *PG* 11: 1167-1170; Alexander Roberts et al., eds., *The Ante-Nicene Fathers. Translations of the Writings of the Fathers down to a. D. 325* (New York: C. Scribner's sons, 1899), 538.

Origen, *Contra Celsum* 4:91:

ἔμελλεν αὐτὴν καὶ τὰ τέκνα
ἀφανίσειν, οὔτ' ἂν ὁ κατὰ τὸν
αὐτὸν ποιητὴν δράκων οὐκ
ἐφυλάξατο ὑπὸ τοῦ ἀετοῦ
ληφθῆναι. Φησὶ γὰρ ὁ ἐν ποιήσει
θαυμαστὸς Ὅμηρος περὶ μὲν τοῦ
προτέρου τοιαῦτα...

ers, the sparrow mentioned in Homer would not have built her nest in the spot where a serpent was to devour her and her young ones,[125] nor would the serpent in the writings of the same poet have failed to take precautions against being captured by the eagle. For this wonderful poet says, in his poem regarding the former...[126]

Ἆρ' οὖν ὁ μὲν ἀετὸς ἦν
μαντικός, ὁ δὲ δράκων, ἐπεὶ καὶ
τούτῳ χρῶνται τῷ ζῴῳ οἱ
οἰωνοσκόποι, οὐκ ἦν μαντικός; Τί
δέ, ἐπεὶ τὸ ἀποκληρωτικὸν
εὐέλεγκτόν ἐστιν, οὐχὶ καὶ τὸ
ἀμφοτέρους εἶναι μαντικοὺς
ἐλεγχθείη ἄν; Οὐκ ἂν γὰρ ὁ
δράκων ὢν μαντικὸς οὐκ
ἐφυλάξατο τάδε τινὰ ἀπὸ τοῦ
ἀετοῦ παθεῖν; Καὶ ἄλλα δ' ἂν
μυρία τοιαῦτα εὕροι τις
παραδείγματα, παριστάντα ὅτι οὐ
τὰ ζῷα μέν ἐστιν ἐν ἑαυτοῖς
ἔχοντα μαντικὴν ψυχήν· ἀλλὰ
κατὰ μὲν τὸν ποιητὴν καὶ τοὺς
πολλοὺς τῶν ἀνθρώπων αὐτὸς
Ὀλύμπιος ἧκε φόωσδε, κατὰ δέ τι
σημεῖον καὶ Ἀπόλλων ἀγγέλῳ
χρῆται ἱέρακι· "κίρκος" γὰρ
"Ἀπόλλωνος»" εἶναι λέγεται
"ταχὺς ἄγγελος".

Did the eagle, then, possess the power of divination, and the serpent (since this animal also is made use of by the augurs) not? But as this distinction can be easily refuted, cannot the assertion that both were capable of divination be refuted also? For if the serpent had possessed this knowledge, would not he have been on his guard against suffering what he did from the eagle? And innumerable other instances of a similar character may be found, to show that animals do not possess a prophetic soul, but that, according to the poet and the majority of mankind, it is the "Olympian himself who sent him to the light." And it is with a symbolical meaning that Apollo employs the hawk as his messenger, for the hawk is called the "swift messenger of Apollo."

---

125 Homer, *Iliad*, 2:308 ll. 308-330.
126 Here he cites in full the text of the *Iliad*, 12:200 ll. 220-229.

The validity of augury is not accepted universally; but even among those who do accept the basic premises of divination, they "are not agreed about the manner of the divination; since some maintain that it is from certain demons or gods of divination that the animals receive their impulses to action—the birds to flights and sounds of different kinds... Others, again, believe that their souls are more divine in their nature, and fitted to operations of that kind, which is a most incredible supposition." That is to say: while some would accept the Socratic notion that augury is entirely under the control of the god who is sending us his messages, there are those who do ascribe special spiritual insight and wisdom to the birds who are prophesying future developments.[127]

The Ways of Amorite Ravens

Two chapters in Tosefta *Shabbat*[128] are devoted to enumerating various

127 Origen devotes the remainder of Book 4 to a caustic refutation of Celsus' arguments for the prophetic superiority of birds and animals. Interestingly, he observes that the animals normally associated with augury are vicious predators and therefore unworthy to receive revelations from the Christian God. This leads him to theorize that the source of those pagan omens is in fact of demonic origin, whereas true prophecy is confined to humans. See Thorndike, *Magic and Experimental Science*, 1:256, 459–461.

128 Chs. 6 and most of 7 in the Vienna manuscript that served as the basis for Lieberman's edition; 7-8 in MS London and the printed versions. According to Rabbi Meir in Sifra Aḥare Mot pereḳ 13, the category was apparently already a well-known defined grouping "that the sages enumerated" and to which the Mishnah (*Shabbat* 6:6) alluded. The passage actually belongs to the "*Mekhilta de-'Arayot*," the fragmentary tannaitic exposition to Leviticus 18 from the school of Rabbi Ishmael that was cited by the *Yalḳuṭ Shim'oni* and other medieval authorities; see Arthur B. Hyman, Isaac N. Lerer, and Yitsḥaḳ Shiloni, eds., *Yalḳuṭ Shim'oni le-Rabbenu Shim'on ha-Darshan: Sefer Vayyiḳra* (Jerusalem, Israel: Mossad Harav Kook, 1984), 2:556-559; J. N. Epstein, *Introduction to Tannaitic Literature: Mishna, Tosephta and Halakhic Midrashim*, ed. E. Z. Melamed (Jerusalem and Tel-Aviv: The Magnes Press and Dvir, 1957), 634–643; Stemberger, *Introduction to the Talmud and Midrash*, 265–266; Giuseppe Veltri, *A Mirror of Rabbinic Hermeneutics: Studies in Religion, Magic and Language Theory in Ancient Judaism*, Studia Judaica 82 (Berlin: De Gruyter, 2015), 4, 58, 108. It is not clear why the foreign nations here were identifed as "Amorites" as distinct from "Canaanites" or any of the other (traditionally: seven) nations who inhabited the holy land before the conquest.

practices that it classifies as "the ways of the Amorite"; that is to say, they are prohibited to Jews because of their associations with the primordial heathen inhabitants of the land of Israel. It appears that the category, which parallels and overlaps the prohibition "after the doings of the land of Canaan, whither I bring you, shall ye not do: neither shall ye walk in their ordinance" (Leviticus 18:3) was used principally as a catch-all term to designate identifiably foreign practices that were not included in the Torah's condemnations of idolatrous cults and were not necessarily objectionable for any reason other than their very foreignness or their un-Jewishness;[129] however the usage was not entirely consistent, and the listing does include some items that were forbidden as idolatrous, divinatory or superstitious.[130] Indeed, scholars have found numerous parallels to these customs in Greek and Roman literature.[131]

---

129 The prohibited "ordinances" include such things as styles of haircuts, attendance at theaters and circuses whose religious or cultic implications are not evident (or stressed in the early sources).

130 For charactarizations of the concept of "ways of the Amorite" see Saul Lieberman, *Tosefta Ki-Feshutah* (New York and Jerusalem: Jewish Theological Seminary of America, 1995), 3:79-80; Blau, *Zauberwesen*, 64; Shelomoh Josef Zevin, ed., "Darkhei Ha-Emori," *Talmudic Encyclopedia* (Jerusalem, 1981), 7:706-712; Veltri, *Mirror of Rabbinic Hermeneutics*, ibid.; Efraim Elimelech Urbach, *The Sages: Their Concepts and Beliefs* (Cambridge, MA: Harvard University Press, 1987), 108 and 725 n. 8; Sacha Stern, "Jewish Identity in Early Rabbinic Writings," Arbeiten zur Geschichte des antiken Judentums und des Urchristentums [Bd.] 23 (Leiden: E.J. Brill, 1994), 181–191; Giuseppe Veltri, "The Rabbis and Pliny the Elder: Jewish and Greco-Roman Attitudes toward Magic and Empirical Knowledge," *Poetics Today* 19, no. 1 (April 1, 1998): 63–89; Yuval Harari, *Jewish Magic before the Rise of Kabbalah*, 1st edition., Raphael Patai Series in Jewish Folklore and Anthropology (Detroit: Wayne State University Press, 2017), 82–90. Veltri astutely observes (p. 108) that it "is a conglomeration of different magical genres, superstitions, and medical-magical recipes, which can be compared to Graeco-Roman magic literature... The customs which were forbidden or allowed by the rabbis under this label 'ways of the Amorite' encompass all aspects of everyday life and point up the broad variety of procedures ane beliefs taken into consideration by the rabbis."

131 Note as well the fascinating parallel that Veltri (p. 156) draws with Eligius' very similar list of pagan customs that are to be avoided by Christians.

The text in the Tosefta includes the following (ed. Lieberman, p. 23).
It is transmitted in two slightly differing versions:

MS Vienna[132]	MS London

קרא עורב ואמ' לו צרח קרא עורב ואמ' לו חזור לאחוריך הרי זה מדרכי האמורי	קרא עורב ואמר צרה קרא עורב ואמר חזור לאחוריך הרי זה מדרכי האמורי
If a raven called and he said to it: Croak!	If a raven called and he said: "Distress!";
If a raven called and he said "Turn back!"	if a raven called and he said "Turn back!"
—this is an instance of the ways of the Amorite.	—this is an instance of the ways of the Amorite.[133]

As understood by S. Lieberman,[134] in the MS Vienna version the human is
addressing the raven instructing it to produce the favorable omen; whereas
in the MS London version, the humans are merely responding to the
raven's (non-verbal) sounds and acting accordingly.[135] The MS Vienna version would thus seem to imply that ravens are able to at least understand
human language.[136] Nevertheless, given that the passage is describing for-

---

132 Generally similar to MS Ehrfurt and printings.

133 To be precise, Lieberman writes, "According to this, the meaning is that the person
said that it is a time of trouble now, and if (he or a companion) sets out on a journey
he says: Turn back because you will not succeed."

134 *Tosefta Ki-Feshutah*, 3:86; See also Levinson, "Enchanting Rabbis," 78.

135 Lieberman points out that the premise of this version is similar to that of *b.Shabbat*
67b: האומר לעורב צרח ולעורבתא שריקי והחזירי לי זנביך לטובה יש בו משום דרכי האמורי [One
who says to a (male) raven: Scream, and one who says to a female raven: Whistle—
this is an instance of the ways of the Amorite]. See also Blau, *Zauberwesen*, 65; Bos,
"Divination with Birds," 5.

136 Also implying that the ravens can be influenced by human speech, Horace writes:
"oscinem corvum *prece suscitabo* \ solis ab ortu" (I shall *rouse with my prayer* the
prophetic raven from the rising sun) [Charles E. (Charles Edwin) Bennett, trans.,
Horace: The Odes and Epodes, with an English Translation, vol. 33, Loeb Classical

bidden superstitious behavior, it appears unreasonable to infer anything
from here about the rabbis' beliefs regarding the speaking abilities of
ravens or other creatures.

From *Pirḳe deRabbi Eliezer* to *Sefer Ḥasidim*

Several traditions preserved in late midrashic or medieval collections tell
about how the earliest humans learned to bury the first corpse, Abel who
was murdered by his brother Cain. It is likely that the earliest documented
instance of the traditions is the one preserved in the Qur'an 5:31:[137]

Then Allah sent a raven,[138] who scratched the ground, to show him [Cain] how to hide the shame of his brother. "Woe is me!" said he; "Was I not even able to be as this raven, and to hide the shame of my brother?" Then he became full of regrets.	فَبَعَثَ اللَّهُ غُرَابًـا يَبْحَثُ فِي الْأَرْضِ لِيُرِيَـهُ كَيْفَ يُوَارِي سَوْءَةَ أَخِيهِقَالَ يَا وَيْلْتَـا أَعَجَزْتُ أَنْ أَكُونَ مِثْلَ هَـٰذَا الْغُرَابِ فَأُوَارِيَ سَوْءَةَ أَخِيفَأَصْبَحَ مِنَ النَّادِمِينَ

In its narrative setting, the burial is depicted as a symptom of Cain's
shame at his terrible crime; though it could also serve as a general precedent for the practice of burying the dead. There is no hint in the wording
that the birds were capable of speech; and at any rate, their actions were
presumably orchestrated by the divine hand that sent them.

Library (Cambridge MA: Harvard University Press, 1968), 3:27 (pp. 204-205)].

137 See also Ṭabarī, *General Introduction, and, From the Creation to the Flood*, trans.
Franz Rosenthal, The History of al-Ṭabarī 1 (Albany: State University of New York
Press, 1988), 311.

138 The Arabic word used here (غُرَابًا) is a cognate of the Hebrew עורב.

A very similar exposition[139] is found in *Pirḳé deRabbi Eliezer* 21:[140]

...The same dog that used to guard Abel's sheep during his lifetime now guarded his corpse in death. Adam and his help-mate[141] were sitting and weeping, and they did not know what to do., since burial was not yet customary.[142] A raven died. Its com-

כלב שהיה משמר את צאנו שלהבל בחייו הוא היה משמר נבלתו במותו. והיה אדם ועזרו יושבין ובוכיןולא היו יודעין מה לעשות. שלא היו נוהגין בקבורה. עורב אחד מת רעהו אמר אין אני מודיע לאדמה יעשה. מיד לקח את חבירו וחפר בארץ בפניהן וקברו, אמר אדם כהעורב הזה אני עושה להבל. ולקח את נבלתו

---

139 The presence of allusions to Islam and the Qur'an has long stood as the principal complication for dating *Pirḳei deRabbi Eliezer* whose framework narrative—but obviously not its content—would otherwise ascribe it to the Yavnean sage who gives it its name.; and scholars have debated whether those allusions are part of the original body of the work (which seems at any rate to be a composite text, though not necessarily a complete one) or extraneous additions. Leopold Zunz, *Die gottesdienstlichen Vorträge der Juden, historisch en wickelt. Ein beitrag zur alterthumskunde und Biblischen Kritik, zur Literatur-und Religionsgeschichte* (Berlin: A. Asher, 1832), 283–290; = *ha-Derashot be-Yisrael*, ed. Chanoch Albeck (Jerusalem: Bialik Institute, 1954), 136–140; Bernhard Heller, "Muhammedanisches und Antimuhammedanisches in den Pirke Rabbi Eliezer," *Monatsschrift für Geschichte und Wissenschaft des Judentums* 69 (n. F. 33), no. 1/2 (1925): 47–54; *Pirke de Rabbi Eliezer (The Chapters of Rabbi Eliezer the Great)*, 2d American ed. (New York: Hermon Press, 1965), liii–lv; Joseph Heinemann, *Aggadah and Its Development*, Sifriyat Keter--'Am Yisra'el ve-Tarbuto: 4. Hagut vva-Halakhah (Jerusalem: Keter, 1974), 181–199 [Hebrew]; Lewis M. Barth, "Lection for the Second Day of Rosh Hashanah: A Homily Containing the Legend of the Ten Trials of Abraham," *Hebrew Union College Annual* 58 (1987): 4 n. 16 [Hebrew]; Stemberger, *Introduction to the Talmud and Midrash*, 356–358; Reuven Firestone, *Journeys in Holy Lands: The Evolution of the Abraham-Ishmael Legends in Islamic Exegesis* (Albany: State University of New York Press, 1990); Aviva Schussman, "Abraham's Visits to Ishmael—The Jewish Origin and Orientation," *Tarbiz* 49, no. 3–4 (1980): 325–345 [Hebrew]; Carol Bakhos, "Abraham Visits Ishmael: A Revisit," *Journal for the Study of Judaism in the Persian, Hellenistic and Roman Period* 38, no. 4 (2007): 553–580; Steven Daniel Sacks, *Midrash and Multiplicity: Pirke De-Rabbi Eliezer and the Renewal of Rabbinic Interpretive Culture*, Studia Judaica, Forschungen zur Wissenschaft des Judentums 48 (Berlin and New York: Walter de Gruyter, 2009), 160–164; Avigdor Shinan, "The Late Midrashic, Paytanic, and Targumic Literature," in *The Cambridge History of Judaism*, ed. Steven T. Katz, vol. 4. The Late Roman-Rabbinic Period (Cambridge: Cambridge University Press, 2006), 690 and n. 27; Rachel Adelman, "The Return of the Repressed: Pirḳe De-Rabbi Eliezer and the Pseudepigrapha,"

panion said: Shall I not inform Adam what he should do? At once he took his companion, dug into the earth before them, and buried him. Adam said: I shall do for Abel just as the raven did; so he took his corpse, dug into the earth and buried it.

What reward did the ravens receive for this? —That he feeds his offspring out of nothing. This is what is written (Job 38:41): "He giveth to the beast his food, and to the young ravens which cry." And it also says (Psalms 147:9): "Who provideth for the raven his food? When his young ones cry unto God, they wander for lack of meat."[143]

 וחפר בארץ וקברה.

ומה שכר נטלו העורבים על כך,
שהוא זן את בניהן מאין. הדא היא דכתיב
נותן לבהמה לחמה לבני עורב אשר
יקראו. ואומר מי יכין לעורב צידו, כי
ילדיו אל אל ישועו.

אמרו: העורב הזה אכזריוכששהוא
מוליד את ביניו ורואה אותן שהן לבנים
והוא שחור הוא מניחן והולך, והקב"ה
מזמן להן מזונותינן.

Supplements to the Journal for the study of Judaism ; v. 140 (Leiden: Brill, 2009), 6, 16, 35–42; Bos, "Divination with Birds," 7. A. Mirsky has argued that *Pirḳei deRabbi Eliezer* was used extensively by the liturgical poet Yosé ben Yosé who flourished (in his authoritative view) in the fifth century; see his *Yosse ben Yosse: Poems. Edited with an Introduction, Commentary and Notes* (Jerusalem, 1977), 32–37 [Hebrew]. This position was opposed by Joseph Yahalom, *Priestly Palestinian Poetry* (Jerusalem: Magnes Press, 1996), 46–54 [Hebrew]; and Adelman, "The Return of the Repressed," 6, n. 16.

140 *PRE Friedlander*, 156–157. I am citing the text from the medieval anthology *Midrash HaGadol* to Genesis 4:16 where this passage is introduced as "R' Eliezer says" [*Midrash Ha-Gadol 'al Ḥamishah Ḥumshe Torah: Sefer Bereshit* (Jerusalem: Mossad Harav Kook, 1975), 125].

141 This peculiar euphemism for Eve (based on Genesis 2:18) is found elsewhere in *Pirḳé deRabbi Eliezer*. See Louis Ginzberg, *The Legends of the Jews*, trans. Henrietta Szold (Philadelphia, PA: The Jewish Publication Society of America, 1909), 5:146 n. 42.

142 As noted by Friedlander and others, this contradicts the statement a few lines previously according to which Cain had buried Abel's body in order to hide the evidence. At any rate, this would not have provided a precedent for interment of dead bodies as a normative procedure. See also ibid., 5:140 n. 23.

They have said:[144] The raven is cruel, and when it sires offspring and observes that they are white while he is black, it abandons them.[145] However the Holy One provides sustenance for them.

Unlike the tale in the Qur'an, there is a suggestion here that the raven ver-

---

143 A similar supposition regarding divine provision for the ravens underlies Jesus's reassurances in Luke 12:24: "Consider the ravens [κατανοήσατε τοὺς κόρακας]: for they neither sow nor reap; which neither have storehouse nor barn; and God feedeth them: how much more are ye better than the fowls?" This version of the passage from the Q source is generally deemed more authentic than the more generic formulation in Matthew 6:26: "Behold the fowls of the air... [ἐμβλέψατε εἰς τὰ πετεινὰ τοῦ οὐρανοῦ]. Scholars have found support for the primacy of the Luke tradition in the remnants of the Gospel of Thomas, especially the fragmentary papyrus P.Oxyrhynchus 655. See Richard J. Dillon, "Ravens, Lilies, and the Kingdom of God (Matthew 6:25-33/Luke 12:22-31)," *The Catholic Biblical Quarterly* 53, no. 4 (1991): 605–627; Robert H. Gundry, "Spinning the Lilies and Unravelling the Ravens: An Alternative Reading of Q 12.22b-31 and P.Oxy. 655," *New Testament Studies* 48, no. 2 (April 2002): 159–180; James M. Robinson, "The Pre-Q Text of the (ravens and) Lilies: Q 12:22-31 and P Oxy 655 (gos Thom 36)," in *Text und Geschichte: Facetten theologischen Arbeitens aus dem Freundes- und Schülerkreis: Dieter Lührmann zum 60 Geburtstag* (Marburg: N G Elwert, 1999), 143–180; James M. Robinson and Christoph Heil, "Noch einmal: der Schreibfehler in Q 12,27," *Zeitschrift für die neutestamentliche Wissenschaft und die Kunde der älteren Kirche* 92, no. 1–2 (2001): 113–122; James M. Robinson, "A Written Greek Sayings Cluster Older than Q: A Vestige," *Harvard Theological Review* 92, no. 1 (1999): 61–77; John S. Kloppenborg, *The Formation of Q: Trajectories in Ancient Wisdom Collections*, Studies in Antiquity and Christianity (Philadelphia: Fortress Press, 1987), 218.

144 The following paragraph is found in *Tanḥuma 'Ekev* 2 as party of a contrast between the cruelty of the raven and the compassion of the eagle; which is linked in turn to a homily about the rewards for commandments that do or do not involve financial loss.

145 Talmudic traditions generally hold that ravens lack compassion toward their young. A passage in the Palestinian Talmud (*y.Pe'ah* 1:1 (15d); *y.Ḳiddushin* 1:7 (61b-61c)) expounds Proverbs 30:17, "The eye that mocketh at his father, and despiseth to obey his mother, the ravens of the valley shall pick it out, and the young eagles shall eat it" as an instance of poetic justice for one who has violated the precepts of honoring parents or of sending away the mother bird before taking her eggs or young: "Let the

balized its plan to teach Adam and Eve (not Cain, as in the Qur'an) about burying corpses; insofar as it was not communicating with another being, however, it appears far more plausible that the reference is, as is common in Hebrew usage, to thought and internal conversation rather than to audible speech. After all, if the raven was capable of talking, then it would have made better sense for it to speak to the humans directly.[146]

Tanḥuma Bereshit 10:[147]

At the moment when Cain killed Abel, he was thrown down and Cain did not know what do do. The Holy One brought before him two clean birds and one of them killed the other, and then it dug with its hand and buried it.	כיון שהרגו קין להבל היה מושלך ולא היה יודעמה לעשות לו. זימן לו הקב"ה שני עופות טהורות והרג מהן את חבירו וחפר ברגלו וקברו ומהן למד קין וחפר וקבר את הבל. לפי כך זכו העופות לכסות את דמן.

raven come, which is cruel, and pick it out, so it will not benefit; and let the eagle come, which is compassionate, and derive benefit from it." In the Babylonian Talmud (*b. ʿEruvin* 22a) Raba applied the imagery of Song of Songs 5:11 in which the lover's tresses are described as "black as a raven," to a Torah scholar "who can bring himself to be cruel to his children and household like a raven," abandoning them to pursue his studies. Elsewhere (*b.Ketubbot* 49b,) it relates that Rav Ḥisda would publicly chastise fathers who refused to support their minor children by declaring "the raven desires its children but this man does not desire his children." The Talmud there, which is alluded to here in *Pirḳé deRabbi Eliezer,* was impelled to resolve a contradiction between this tradition and the contrary implication of Psalms 147:9 by introducing the distinction between white and black offspring. For variants, cross-references and extensive references to traditional commentators see Moshe Hershler, ed., *Masekhet Ketubot*, Talmud Bavli (Jerusalem: Institute for the Complete Israeli Talmud, 1972), 1:364. As it happens, scientific research does strongly indicate that ravens express empathy or consolation to their fellows in situations of crisis; see Or-laith N. Fraser and Thomas Bugnyar, "Do Ravens Show Consolation? Responses to Distressed Others," *PLOS ONE* 5, no. 5 (May 12, 2010): e10605.

146 See Viktor Aptowitzer, "The Rewarding and Punishing of Animals and Inanimate Objects On the Aggadic View of the World," *Hebrew Union College Annual* (n.d.): 133.

147 Text according to *Midrash Ha-Gadol ʿal Ḥamishah Ḥumshe Torah: Sefer Bereshit* (Jerusalem: Mossad Harav Kook, 1975), 124–12. The passage is not found in the Buber edition of the *Tanḥuma* [Salomon Buber, ed., *Midrash Tanḥuma Ha-Ḳadum Veha-Yashan* (Vilna: Romm, 1885), 1:19 (par. 25)].

Tanḥuma Bereshit 10:

> Cain learned from this, and he
> dug a grave and buried Abel. For
> this reason, birds merited that the
> blood must be covered.

The choice of "clean birds" to serve as Cain's teachers in this version of the legend was rooted in its function as an etiological explanation of precept in Leviticus 17: 13: "any beast or fowl that may be eaten; he shall even pour out the blood thereof, and cover it with dust."[148]

---

148 To be sure, that objective would have been better served if the role had been assigned to a "beast" (according to rabbinic law: a kosher quadruped other than sheep, goats or cattle).

Sefer Ḥasidim #1873:[149]

Why did the Holy One arrange for Elijah that ravens would come to provide for him? In the Chapters of Rabbi Eliezer:[150] Because the raven taught Adam and Eve to bury Abel, because a raven came and buried its dead in order to inform him that Cain had killed his brother. And they buried Abel. And since he had already departed from the garden of Eden he did not understand his language, but only his gestures [רמיזותיו]. It was for this reason that he issued a decree that the raven should pray for mercy for rainfall, as it says (Psalms

---

149 Judah ben Samuel, *Das Buch Der Frommen [Sepher Chassidim]*, ed. Jehuda Wistinetzki, Mekize Nirdamim (Frankfurt a. M.: M. A. Wahrmann, 1924), 454. *Sefer Ḥasidim*, the "Book of the Pious," is an eclectic compendium produced by the Jewish German pietistic school known in Hebrew as *Ḥasidei Ashkenaz*. The work is generally attributed to Rabbi Judah ben Samuel of Regensburg (1150-1217), though there is some disagreement about how much of it may have been contributed by other members of his circle. The work consists of a diverse scrapbook of teachings related to the school's ideals, interpretations, mystical doctrines and many other kinds of teachings. On the book, its author and questions surrounding its author's identity see Gershom G. Scholem, *Major Trends in Jewish Mysticism* (New York: Schocken, 1961), 80–91; Joseph Dan, *History of Jewish Mysticism and Esotericism: The Middle Ages*, vol. 5 (Jerusalem: The Zalman Shazar Center, 2011), 64–74 [Hebrew]; *R. Judah he-Hasid*, Gedole ha-ruaḥ yeha-yetsirah ba-'am ha-Yehudi (Jerusalem: The Zalman Shazar Center for Jewish History, 766), 25–31; Fritz Isaac Baer, "The Religious-Social Tendency of 'Sefer Hassidim,'" *Zion* 3, no. 2 (n.d.): 6–7 [Hebrew]; Ivan G. Marcus, "The Recensions and Structure of Sefer Hasidim.," *Proceedings of the American Academy for Jewish Research* 45 (1978): 131–153; "Piety and Society: The Jewish Pietists of Medieval Germany," Études sur le judaisme médiéval ; t. 10 (Leiden: Brill, 1981), 136–143; "The Politics and Ethics of Pietism in Judaism: The Hasidim of Medieval Germany," *Journal of Religious Ethics* 8, no. 2 (1980): 252–253, n. 6; Haym Soloveitchik, "Piety, Pietism and German Pietism: Sefer Ḥasidim and the Influence of Ḥasidei Ashkenaz," *Jewish Quarterly Review* 92, no. 3–4 (2002): 455–493. Note that the passage presently under discussion does not belong to segment of *Sefer Ḥasidim* that Soloveitchik (following J. Reifmann) ascribes to different authorship.

150 This legend is found there in Chapter 21; *PRE Friedlander*, 156–157; Ginzberg, *Legends*, 1:113; see Aptowitzer, "Rewarding and Punishing," 133. The parallel to the Qur'an was also noted by Louis Ginzberg, *Jewish Folklore: East and West: A Paper Delivered at the Harvard Tercentenary Conference of Arts and Sciences*, Harvard Tercentenary Publications (Cambridge, MA: Harvard University Press, 1937). (He did not, however, cite the Qur'anic tradition in *Legends* 5:142-143, n. 31.)

147:8), "who prepareth rain for the earth"; and it juxtaposes this to (9) "and to the young ravens which cry".

"And the ravens brought him bread and flesh" (1 Kings 17:6)—in order to inform him that he should not provide rainfall because they did not yet re-pent from their error. And just as ravens pray for mercy for rainfall, and now they brought him bread and meat, in order to inform that "he that withholdeth corn, the people shall curse him" (Proverbs 11:26); and one who is be-grudging, even the fowl of the heavens curse him. But they bless Elijah be-cause he acted justly, and the sin was Ahab's and his household.

And Elijah implored the ravens (Job 38:41), "Who provideth for the raven his food."

One who sees ravens while he is eating should cast them some bread, as they did for Elijah.

In proper midrashic manner, *Sefer Ḥasidim* draws links between mentions of ravens scattered through the Bible.[151] The legend about how ravens taught Adam and Eve the procedures for burial is indeed found in *Pirkei deRabbi Eliezer*, but other important aspects of the retelling here seem to have originated with the author of *Sefer Ḥasidim*.[152] Most pertinent to our purposes, of course, is the premise that Adam was deprived of his ability to understand the ravens' language following the expulsion from Paradise, and he therefore had to rely on signs and gestures. This implies that as long as he was still residing in the garden of Eden, Adam was able to com-municate with all creatures—not just the snake—and that the creatures spoke their own language (or languages), not the language of humans.[153]

---

151 Thus, in *Genesis Rabbah* 33:5 Noah's raven is promised a starring role in the Elijah episode as a reassurance or reward for accepting his mission from the ark. See Mar-cus, "The Mission of the Raven (Gen. 8," 77.

152 Perhaps the exegesis here can be adduced as an illustration of Haym Soloveitchik's suggestion that *Sefer Ḥasidim*, in advocating an internal spiritual instinct not based on formal texts, was absorbing the medieval Christian concept of the "book of crea-tures," according to which the wonders and commonplaces nature should be studied by the religiously sensitive soul as sources of religious guidance; see his "Three Themes in the Sefer Ḥasidim," *AJS Review* 1 (1976): 315–316.

153 It is interesting to compare this historical outlook with the thesis argued by Fritz Isaac Baer, "Theory of Natural Equality of Early Man according to Ashkenazi Hasid-ism," *Zion* 32, no. 1 (1967): 117–152 [Hebrew]. Baer refers to works by exponents of the Ḥasidut Ashkenaz movement that speak of a primordial golden age in which

The premise that humans had once understood animal languages, but lost the ability except for the interpretation of non-verbal gestures evokes one of Ibn Ezra's explanations, and might very well be adapted from it..[154] No such systematic treatment is found in the Talmud or Midrash, so we may assume that it is original to the *Sefer Ḥasidim* or that it is rooted in a theological or exegetical discourse that has not come down to us.

Concluding Observations

In the present chapter we had the opportunity to note the special place occupied by birds —ravens and doves—in the rabbinic discourse related to animal language. When expounding the biblical episode where Noah dispatched a raven to check whether the floodwaters had receded, third-century rabbis introduced dialogues between Noah and the raven that served (among other things) to elicit the audiences' sympathies for the bird's situation. Notwithstanding the rabbis' employment of standard hermeneutical

---

all of humanity lived in complete equality and no person was subservient to another. He traces this motif from the Stoa to Christian writers through whom the ideas would have become known to Jews in medieval Germany. I find it remarkable, though not surprising (given what we have seen of the Stoic insistence on denying animal language or intelligence), that in all the glowing words about harmony and universal egalitarianism there is no suggestion that this ideal also encompassed non-human species. Quite the contrary, the situation is perceived as one that allows humans to defend themselves against threats from the hostile animal kingdom. See *Sefer Ḥasidim*, ed. Wistinetzki, #1171, p. 295 [cited by Baer, 134-135], where Adam's curse is understood to mean that from now on he would have to fence off his fields and orchards to defend them from the animals who had previously submitted to their human masters.

154 For the most part, the circles that comprised the Ḥasidei Ashkenaz movement had an intense antipathy toward rationalist philosophy, especially of the Maimonidean type. They did however make exceptions of Saadiah, (whose doctrine of a logos-like "created glory" occupied an important place in their mystical theories) and neoplatonists like Ibn Gabirol and Ibn Ezra. Joseph Dan observes that they did not regard Ibn Ezra as a philosopher, but as a mystical visionary (*Avraham ha-ḥozeh*), and Rabbi Judah ben Samuel composed a commentary to Ibn Ezra's *Yesod Mora* on the reasons for the commandments; *Ashkenazi Hasidism in the History of Jewish Thought*, vol. 1 (Ramat-Aviv: The Open University, 1990), 31–34; Howard Theodore Kreisel, *Prophecy: The History of an Idea in Medieval Jewish Philosophy*, Amsterdam Studies in Jewish Thought 8 (Kluwer Academic Publishers, 2001), 56.

devices to justify the insertion of these dialogues into the scriptural text, it was probable that they originated in the preachers' desire to enhance the story's emotional impact. As with the texts studied in previous chapters, we could not be sure whether the authors of these discourses expected their listeners to accept their expansions as literal facts—or even whether they were conscious of a meaningful distinction between factual and narrative truth. At any rate, the authors might well have been influenced by a tacit cultural assumption that ravens enjoy a special closeness to communication through language. This assumption is indeed borne out by many Greek and Roman sources.

Other texts adduced instances involving talking birds that supposedly occurred to rabbis during the talmudic era. The Babylonian Talmud's tale about Rav Kahana 's experience with the "Herodian doves" contained suggestions of an underlying disagreement among the rabbis about the factuality of the birds' speech, one that might have carried over into the Talmud's redactional strata. Rabbi Ḥanina denied the story's credibility, and the Talmud's conclusion appeared to be that doves can be made to speak with the help of appropriate magic spells. A similar disagreement was noted in Herodotus's tale about the oracles allegedly spoken by doves in Dodona and Libya, for which Herodotus offered a naturalistic explanation.

In the tale about Rav 'Ilish, a raven and a dove were able to convey an accurate oracle to the rabbi with the assistance of an expert interpreter of their language—evidently in a language that was inaccessible to outsiders. The procedures described in that story were quite consistent with those of augury as it was widely practiced among the Greeks and Romans. Classical sources most often attached significance to the behavior of the birds rather than to the contents of their utterances; though this was not invariably the case. Cicero and other writers speculated as to the relationships between the birds and their messages: were they just mechanical vehicles that were manipulated by the gods, or were they active agents who were privy to the divine counsels and secret plans? Other than some vague allusions, there is nothing in rabbinic literature that compares with these intense discussions by the Greek and Roman thinkers.[155]

---

155 It should be noted that talking birds held an important place in Zoroastrian myth and eschatology. The Middle-Persian cosmogenic compendium Bun-dahišnīh, for ex-

The last group of examples told the legend of how the raven taught the first humans to bury their dead. It was clear that in the earliest version —whether it was the Qur'an or a prior tradition from which it drew—the ravens conveyed their lesson by means of action and not through verbal instruction; and this remained the case in the early medieval Jewish "midrashic"compendia. It was interesting to observe how the paraphrase of the *Pirkei deRabbi Eliezer* in the thirteenth-century German *Sefer Ḥasidim* was impelled to insert a discussion of how it had come about that the ravens could no longer speak in intelligible language as they had been able prior to the expulsion from Eden—the kind of theoretical concern that is so glaringly absent from the talmudic and midrashic sources.

---

ample, describes the Karšift or Karsiptar who "can speak with words knows how to speak, and it was it who carried the Avesta / Religion to the Yima-built protective Vara-, and propagated it; and there they recite the Avesta in the language of birds." See Reuven Kiperwasser and Dan D. Y. Shapira, "Irano-Talmudica Ii: Leviathan, Behemoth and the 'Domestication' of Iranian Mythological Creatures in Eschatological Narratives of the Babylonian Talmud.," in *Shoshannat Yaakov: Jewish and Iranian Studies in Honor of Yaakov Elman*, ed. Shai Secunda and Steven Fine, Brill Reference Library of Judaism 35 (Leiden and Boston: Brill, 2012), 209–213; "Irano-Talmudica Iii: Giant Mythological Creatures in Transition from the Avesta to the Babylonian Talmud," in *Orality and Textuality in the Iranian World; Patterns of Interaction Across the Centuries*, ed. Julia Rubanovich, Jerusalem Studies in Religion and Culture 19 (Leiden and Boston: Brill, 2015), 90–91.

Phoenixes, Frogs and Some Cows—Oh My!

"THAT'S WHAT YOU CALL METAPHOR," SAID
RINCEWIND.

"LYING," THE SERGEANT EXPLAINED, KINDLY.[1]

In the present chapter I have collected additional texts from talmudic and midrashic literature that have some bearing on the issue of animal language. The texts do not fit into the categories—cries of distress, ravens, doves or the snake in the garden of Eden—that were examined in previous chapters.

The Nazirite Cow:

In order to illustrate a formulation of a vow that is inherently nonsensical, the Mishnahemployed the following case:

m.Nazir 2:2:[2]

If one said: This cow said: "I am a nazirite if I stand"... The house of Shammai said: he is a nazirite. The house of Hillel said: he is not a Nazirite.	אמר, אמרה פרה זו הריני נזירה אם עומדת אני... בית שמי אמ' נזיר; בית והילל א', אינו נזיר.
Rabbi Judah said: even when the house of Shammai said this, they were referring only to one who says, "This cow is a sac-	אמ' ר' יהודה אף כשאמרו בית שמי לא אמרו אלא באומר הרי פרה זו קרבן אם עומדת היא.

---

1   Terry Pratchett, *Eric* (London: V. Gollancz, 1990).
2   Cited according to Ms. Kaufmann A 50, Library of the Hungarian Academy of Sciences, Budapest.

m. Nazir 2:2:

> rifice if it stands up."'

The point of the discussion is not that anyone takes seriously the person's claim about the talking cow, but rather whether that particular absurd detail can be legally bracketed off from the rest of the person's statement, so as to leave us with a valid and binding vow; or whether the entire statement is thereby invalidated and hence no vow needs to be observed.[3] Underlying all the positions is the uncontested premise that cows obviously are not capable of speech.

Like the Ministering Angels

A somewhat more explicit example of rabbinic views regarding the status of human and animal speech might be the following statement about the creation of man:

---

3   The choice of a cow for the illustration was presumably influenced by the fact that vows in rabbinic law were rooted in the prohibition of items devoted to the Temple. Thus Rabbi Judah argues that the statement qualifies as a generic "*neder*" vow rather than the specific nazirite vow as delineated in Numbers 6:1–21. The Babylonian Talmud passage (10a) explained that the owner was figuratively ascribing such thinking to the animal who was stubbornly refusing to stand. Maimonides in his Mishnah Commentary, after citing the Talmud's interpretation, notes that the statement should be undestood "in a metaphoric sense, even as people in our own time [עלי טריק אל מג׳אז כמא יקול אלנאס פי זמאננא] often express themselves with respect to inanimate objects that require strenuous effort, 'this thing has sworn not to be cooperative.' In the same way, no doubt, people were accustomed to expressing themselves in their days." [citation based on MS National Library of Israel, Jerusalem,Heb. 4°5703]

Genesis Rabbah 8:11[4]

R' Joshua be-R' Nehemiah in the name of R' Ḥinena bar Isaac,[5] and the Rabbis in the name of Rabbi Leazar:[6] He created in him four features of those above and four of those below.

רבי יהושע בר נחמיה בשם רבי חנינא בר יצחק ורבנן בשם ר"א אמרי ברא בו ארבע בריות מלמעלה וארבעה מלמטן,

Four like those above: [1] he stands upright like the ministering angels, and [2] speaks like the ministering angels,[7] and [3] he

ארבע מלמעלה: עומד כמלאכי השרת, מדבר כמלאכי השרת, יש בו דעת כמלאכי השרת, ורואה כמלאכי השרת, ובהמה אינו רואה, אתמהא.

---

4   Julius Theodor and Chanoch Albeck, eds., *Midrash Bereshit Rabba* (Jerusalem, Israel: Wahrman, 1965), 64–65; cited by Deborah Levine Gera, *Ancient Greek Ideas on Speech, Language, and Civilization* (Oxford and New York: Oxford University Press, 2003), 58 n. 132; Louis Ginzberg, *The Legends of the Jews*, trans. Henrietta Szold (Philadelphia, PA: The Jewish Publication Society of America, 1909), 1:50; 5:65-66; Solomon Schechter, *Some Aspects of Rabbinic Theology* (New York, NY: Macmillan, 1909), 81–82; Efraim Elimelech Urbach, *The Sages: Their Concepts and Beliefs* (Cambridge, MA: Harvard University Press, 1987), 221–222, 786. Parallel versions are listed and discussed in the Theodor-Albeck commentary.

5   Ch. Albeck, *Introduction to the Talmud. Babli and Yerushalmi* (Tel-Aviv: Dvir, 1969), 237.

6   Ibid., 224–227; Günter Stemberger, *Introduction to the Talmud and Midrash*, 2nd ed. (Edinburgh: T. & T. Clark, 1996), 98; Wilhelm Bacher, *Die Agada der palästinensischen Amoräer* (Strassburg i. E: K. J. Trübner, 1892), 2:1-87; = *Agadat Amora'e Erets-Yiśra'el*, trans. Alexander Siskind Rabinovitz (Tel-Aviv: Dvir, 1928), 2:1:3-83; Mordecai Margalioth and Yehudah Aizenberg, eds., *Entsiḵlopedyah le-Ḥakhme ha-Talmud yeha-Ge'onim*, Revised edition. (Tel-Aviv: Yavneh and Chemed, 1995), 1:47-49.

7   Note that in *Avot deRabbi Natan A* 37: "and they converse in the holy tongue like the ministering angels"; Solomon Schechter, ed., *Aboth De-Rabbi Nathan* (Vienna: Ch. D. Lippe, 1887), 109 and n. 2; Judah Goldin, ed., *The Fathers According to Rabbi Nathan* (New York: Schocken Books, 1974), 153 and n. 4. John Heath observes that Homer depicts the gods as speaking in a different and more elevated language than mortals [*The Talking Greeks: Speech, Animals, and the Other in Homer, Aeschylus, and Plato* (Cambridge: Cambridge University Press, 2005), 51–57]. G. S. Kirk characterized Homer's Cyclopes as "an extraordinary mixture of the divine and the brutish" [*Myth: Its Meaning and Functions in Ancient and Other Cultures*, Sather Clas-

Genesis Rabbah 8:11

understands like the ministering angels, and [4] he sees like the ministering angels. [And a beast does not see?!	אלא זה מצדד.
—Rather, that one sees from the sides.]	
Four like those below: [1] He eats and drinks like a beast, [2] he reproduces like a beast, [3] he defecates like a beast, and [4] he dies like a beast...	וארבעה מלמטן, אוכל ושותה כבהמה, פרה ורבה כבהמה, ומטיל גללים כבהמה, ומת כבהמה...

The implicit assumption of this text is that among created beings, the ability to speak is shared uniquely by humans with the angels. Like similar pronouncements by Greek philosophers who defined humans as "speaking animals" and the like, speech serves to differentiate humans from the lower animals[8] with whom they nonetheless share basic biological functions.[9] Notwithstanding those significant implications, this can hardly be

---

sical Lectures 40 (Cambridge [UK] and Berkeley: Cambridge University Press; University of California Press, 1970), 175; quoted by Deborah Levine Gera, *Ancient Greek Ideas on Speech, Language, and Civilization* (Oxford and New York: Oxford University Press, 2003), 13].

8   It is intriguing to note that the Church Father Lactantius, determined to situate humans above other animals in the natural hierarchy, must single out the human capacity for religious understanding as the operational differentiator from the lower creatures (notably in Chapter 7 of his *De Ira Dei*) [Alexander Roberts and James Donaldson, eds., *The Works of Lactantius*, trans. William Fletcher, vol. 2, Ante-Nicene Christian Library 22 (Edinburgh: T. & T. Clark, 1871), 9–11].. Although verbal speech might technically be a uniquely human ability, there is sufficient evidence of speech-like behavior (as well as emotional expressions like laughter) to mitigate its usefulness as the distinguishing criterion between the species. See Ingvild Sælid Gilhus, *Animals, Gods and Humans: Changing Attitudes to Animals in Greek, Roman and Early Christian Ideas* (London: Routledge, 2006), 247–248.

9   The "Onkelos" Aramaic Targum to Genesis 2:7 translates נפש חיה ["living soul"] as לרוח ממללא: "a speaking spirit," though the same expression describing the creation of animals in 1:20, 24 is rendered simply as נפשא חיתא. Similar translations appear in

seen as a systematic discourse on the linguistic abilities or the general intelligence of animals.[10]

Singing Bovines

Genesis Rabbah 54:4:[11]

"Then the cows went straight up [	וישרנה הפרות בדרך
וישרנה] [toward Beth Shemesh,	

the other Jewish Targums: Pseudo-Jonathan and MS Neofiti. See Alexander Sperber, ed., *The Bible in Aramaic: Based on Old Manuscripts and Printed Texts*, 3rd ed. (Leiden and Boston: Brill, 2013), 2–3; Bernard Grossfeld, *Targum Onkelos to Genesis: A Critical Analysis Together with an English Translation of the Text: (Based on a. Sperber's Edition)*, ed. Moses Aberbach (New York and Denver: Ktav for Center for Judaic Studies, University of Denver, 1982), 44-45 and n. 4; Michael Maher, ed., *Targum Pseudo-Jonathan, Genesis*, The Aramaic Bible 1B (Collegeville, MN: Liturgical Press, 1992), 22 and n. 19; Moses Ginsburger, ed., *Targum Yonatan ben 'Uzi'el 'al ha-Torah* (Berlin: S. Calvary, 1903), 4; Bernard Grossfeld and Lawrence H. Schiffman, *Targum Neofiti 1: An Exegetical Commentary to Genesis: Including Full Rabbinic Parallels* (New York: Sepher-Hermon Press, 2000), 57 and n. 14; Basil Herring, "Speaking of Man and Beast," *Judaism* 28, no. 2 (1979): 170.

10 This exposition presupposes a hierarchical perception of the universe in which humans stand at the mid-point between the upper and lower realms. It is unclear to what extent these sages—or rabbinic thought in general—would have subscribed to a systematic doctrine of the "great chain of being"; but the basic pattern seems unmistakably similar. See Arthur O. Lovejoy, *The Great Chain of Being: A Study of the History of an Idea* (Cambridge, MA: Harvard University Press, 1950). Lovejoy traced this concept from Plato's conviction (found principally in the *Timaeus*) that the "plenitude" of all Ideas must be implemented in the physical universe; through to Aristotle's graded classification of natural species; and culminating in the Neoplatonic doctrine formulated by Plotinus that "Reason did not make gods only, but first gods, then spirits, the second nature, and then men, and then animals, in a continuous series—not through envy, but because its rational nature contains an intellectual variety." (*Enniads* 3:2.11; cited by Lovejoy, 65). A more precise rendering of the Plotinian hierarchy, in which the central criterion is "priority or posteriority by nature," may be found in: Dominic J. O'Meara, "The Hierarchical Ordering of Reality in Plotinus," in *The Cambridge Companion to Plotinus*, ed. Lloyd P. Gerson (Cambridge UK and New York: Cambridge University Press, 1996), 66–81. As noted elsewhere, this outlook would come to influence the interpretations of Saadiah Gaon and other rationalist commentators in the medieval era. See David R. Blumenthal,

Genesis Rabbah 54:4:

keeping on the road and lowing all the way; they did not turn to the right or to the left]" (1 Samuel 6:12)—	מהלכות בישרות.
They were walking in straightness.	

"Lovejoy's Great Chain of Being and the Medieval Jewish Tradition," in *Jacob's Ladder and the Tree of Life: Concepts of Hierarchy and the Great Chain of Being*, ed. Marion Leathers Kuntz and Paul Grimley Kuntz, American University Studies, Series 5, Philosophy 14 (New York: Peter Lang, 1987), 179–190; Ann Cline Kelly, "Talking Animals in the Bible: Paratexts as Symptoms of Cultural Anxiety in Restoration and Early Eighteenth-Century England," *Journal for Eighteenth-Century Studies* 33, no. 4 (2010): 441; Mira Wasserman, *Jews, Gentiles, and Other Animals: The Talmud After the Humanities*, Divinations: Rereading Late Ancient Religion (Philadelphia: University of Pennsylvania Press, 2017), 33, 166,234-235, 248–249 n. 55; George Lakoff and Mark Turner, *More than Cool Reason: A Field Guide to Poetic Metaphor* (Chicago and London: University of Chicago Press, 2009), 160–212; Gilhus, *Animals, Gods and Humans*, 264. Wasserman's analyses are rooted in post-modern theories expounded by the likes of Jacques Derrida and Mel Y. Chen for which there are correlations between the hierarchical perception of humans and animals and socially discriminatory attitudes toward other races, genders, etc. In any case, none of the texts that she discusses (which are confined to a particular tractate in the Babylonian Talmud) deal with the phenomena of animal intelligence or verbal communication. See Wasserman's bibliographical listing on 258-259; with particular reference to: Jacques Derrida, *The Animal That Therefore I Am*, trans. Marie-Louise Mallet (New York: Fordham University Press, 2008); Mel Y. Chen, *Animacies: Biopolitics, Racial Mattering, and Queer Affect*, Perverse Modernities (Durham, NC: Duke University Press, 2012); Aaron S. Gross, "Animals, Empathy, and 'Rahamim' in the Study of Religion: A Case Study of Jewish Opposition to Hunting.," *Studies in Religion / Sciences Religieuses* 46, no. 4 (2017): 514. On rabbinic views of a universal natural order see Max Kadushin, *The Rabbinic Mind*, 3d ed. (New York: Bloch, 1972), 143–152; discussed by Reuven Kiperwasser, "Sidro shel ʿOlam: ʿAl Yaḥasei Adam va-Ṭevaʿ be-Maḥsheet HaZa"L," *Akdamot: A Journal of Jewish Thought* 5 (1998): 35–49 [Hebrew].

11   Julius Theodor and Chanoch Albeck, eds., *Midrash Bereshit Rabba* (Jerusalem, Israel: Wahrman, 1965), 581; Louis Ginzberg, *The Legends of the Jews*, trans. Henrietta Szold (Philadelphia, PA: The Jewish Publication Society of America, 1909), 4:3;

Genesis Rabbah 54:4:

They turned their faces toward the ark and recited song.

הפכו פניהם כלפי ארון ואמרו שירה.

And this is what is written: וישרנה.

והיינו דכתיב וישרנה.אמרו שירה בפה.

Which song did they recite?

אי זו שירה אמרו.

Rabbi Meir says: They recited the song of the sea (Exodus 15)...

רבי מאיר אומר שירת הים אמרו...

Rabbi Yoḥanan said: "Sing to the Lord a new song" (Psalm 98:1).

רבי יוחנן אמר שירו לה' שיר חדש.

Rabbi Leazar said: "Give thanks unto the Lord, call upon his name" (1 Chronicles 16:8).

רבי לעזר אמר הודו לה' קראו בשמו.

The rabbis say: "The Lord reigns, let the earth be glad" (Psalms 97:1).

רבנן אמרי ה' מלך תגל הארץ.

Rabbi Jeremiah said three: "Sing to the Lord a new song"; "sing to the Lord, all the earth"; "the Lord reigns, let the nations tremble" (Psalms 99:1).

רבי ירמיה בשם רבי שמואל בר יצחק אמר תלת:

שירו לה' שיר חדש,

שירו לה' כל הארץ,

ה' מלך ירגזו עמים

Elijah taught: Exalt, exalt, acacia! Stretch forth in the fulness of thy majesty, girdled in golden embroidery, praised in the recesses of the palace, resplendent in the finest of ornaments.[12]

תני אליהו: רומי השיטה, התנופפי ברוב הדרך, המחושקת ברקמי זהב, המהוללה בדביר ארמון, המעולפת מבין שני כרובים.

6:225 n. 36.

12 In keeping with the conventions of Hebrew liturgical poetry, fundamental concepts and persons are not identified directly, but through the use of indirect expressions

Genesis Rabbah 54:4:

Said Rabbi Samuel bar Nahman: How much toil did the son
of Amram have to expend before
he taught the Levites to sing—
and you recite the song by your-
selves! More power to you!

אמר רבי שמואל בר נחמן כמה
יגיעות יגע בו בן עמרם עד שלימד שירה
ללוים ואתם אומרות שירה מאליכם יישר
חילכם.

This midrashic interpretation relates to the story about the return of the ark
of the covenant after it had been captured by the Philistines. When they
found themselves cursed with a plague of tumors and rats, they sent the
ark back to the Israelites. They placed it on a cart pulled by two milk-
cows; and in order to test whether the process was truly being guided by
the Hebrew God, they watched to see whether the cows would steer a
straight, direct course—and this was indeed what occurred.[13]

Not content with the miracle that was related explicitly in the biblical
tale, the rabbis, as was their custom, found allusions to additional layers of

---

taken from biblical usage. Thus, "acacia" refers to the ark which was fashioned from
acacia wood (Exodus 25:10), plated with pure gold (32:2) and cherubs (25:18-21),
etc. See Ezra Fleischer, *Hebrew Liturgical Poetry in the Middle Ages*, 2nd expanded
edition. (Jerusalem: Magnes Press, 2007), 105–107 [Hebrew]; Joseph Yahalom, *Po-
etry and Society in Jewish Galilee of Late Antiquity*, Sifriyat "Helal ben Hayim"
(Tel-Aviv: Hakibbutz Hameuchad and Yad Izhak Ben-Zvi, 1999), 116–122
[Hebrew]; Aaron Mirsky, *Reshit ha-Piyyut*, 'Iyyunim 34 (Jerusalem: The Jewish
Agency for Israel of Youth Aliyah Department: Training Section, 725), 72–73
[Hebrew]; *Yosse ben Yosse: Poems. Edited with an Introduction, Commentary and
Notes* (Jerusalem, 1977), 61–65 [Hebrew].

13 According to Josephus *(Antiquities* 6.2-3[8-11]*),* the cows were placed at the inter-
section of three roads so that the Philistines could observe whether it was divine
guidance that made them choose the way to Judea [H. St J. Thackeray and Ralph
Marcus, trans., *Josephus in Nine Volumes*, vol. 5, Loeb Classical Library 433 (London and Cambridge MA: William Heinemann and Harvard University Press, 1950),
5:70-71]. A similar tradition is preserved in Pseudo-Philo, *Biblical Antiquities*
[Pseudo-Philo, *The Biblical Antiquities of Philo*, trans. M. R. James, Translations of
Early Documents. Series I: Palestinian Jewish Texts (Pre-Rabbinic) (New York: Ktav
Pub. House, 1971), 226-227 and n. 7].

supernatural intervention.[14] The Hebrew verb וישרנה, "they went straight," was read as if it were from the similar root meaning "sing," conjuring up a picture of cows singing the praises of the Lord as they bear the holiest of objects on its way to its proper home.[15] A diverse list of sages spanning several generations of the tanna'itic and amoraic eras propose appropriate passages from Psalms and other texts that the cows (albeit *Philistine* cows) might have been chanting.

A very similar passage appears in the Babylonian Talmud *'Avodah Zarah* 24b, based on the same Hebrew word-play between the words for walking straight and for singing.[16] An almost identical list of biblical songs is proposed, though ascribed to different rabbis (including a larger proportion of Babylonian teachers). The last proposal, the one that does not consist of a scriptural text, appears there as follows:

R' Isaac Nappaḥa[17] says: "Re-   ר' יצחק נפחא או' רני רני השטה התנופפי

14 On the tendency of the rabbis of the *aggadah*—in contrast to ancient philosophical interpreters of the Bible—to multiply the instances of miraculous divine intervention, see Isaak Heinemann, *Darkhe Ha-Agadah* (Jerusalem: Magnes Press, 1970), 80–82; Eliezer Segal, *The Babylonian Esther Midrash: A Critical Commentary (Volume 3: Esther Chapter 5 to End)*, Brown Judaic studies no. 291-293 (Atlanta: Scholars Press, 1994), 254–256.

15 Compare Efraim Elimelech Urbach, "The Traditions Concerning Mystical Doctrine in the Period of the Tannaim," in *Studies in Mysticism and Religion, Presented to Gershom G. Scholem on his Seventieth Birthday by Pupils, Colleagues and Friends*, ed. Efraim Elimelech Urbach, R. J. Zwi Werblowsky, and Chaim Wirszubski (Jerusalem: Magnes Press, 1967), 10–11 [Hebrew]. For possible influence of the passage on some later Jewish liturgical practices see Daniel Sperber, *Minhage Yisra'el: Meḳorot Ve-Toladot*, vol. 1 (Jerusalem: Mosad Harav Kook, 1989), 8:141-142 [Hebrew].

16 According to Mira Beth Wasserman, the inclusion of this passage alongside several others involving animals is impelled by a deliberate policy of the redactors of this chapter in the Babylonian Talmud and "reflects a deep and thoroughgoing engagement with the questions of what it means to be a person and what it means to be a Jew"; see *Jews, Gentiles, and Other Animals*, 103–104.

17 Rabbi Isaac was a disciple of Rabbi Yohanan in third-century Tiberias who later migrated to Babylonia; see Wilhelm Bacher, *Die Agada der palästinensischen Amoräer* (Strassburg i. E: K. J. Trübner, 1892), 2:205-295; *Agadat Amora'e Erets-Yiśra'el*, trans. Alexander Siskind Rabinovitz (Tel-Aviv: Dvir, 1928), 2:1:187-269; Ch. Albeck, *Introduction to the Talmud. Babli and Yerushalmi* (Tel-Aviv: Dvir, 1969), 252–

<table>
<tr><td>

joice, rejoice acacia! Stretch forth in the fulness of thy majesty, girdled in golden embroidery, praised in the recesses of the palace."[18]

</td><td dir="rtl">

ברוב הדריך המחושקה ברקמי זהב
המהוללה בדביר [ו]ארמון

</td></tr>
</table>

Of particular interest is the last proposal, the one ascribed in *Genesis Rabbah* to Elijah in his capacity of a mystical figure who divided his time between the heavenly realm and his occasional interactions with worthy rabbis on earth.[19] The current passage evidently belongs to the body of "*Tanna deve Eliyahu*" traditions, a few or which are cited in midrashic and talmudic literature, and are the focus of a remarkable and enigmatic aggadic compendium whose present form scholars generally ascribe to the tenth century.[20] The passage played a significant part in determining Ger-

---

253; Günter Stemberger, *Introduction to the Talmud and Midrash*, 2nd ed. (Edinburgh: T. & T. Clark, 1996), 89; Mordecai Margalioth and Yehudah Aizenberg, eds., *Entsiklopedyah le-Ḥakhme ha-Talmud yeha-Ge'onim*, Revised edition. (Tel-Aviv: Yavneh and Chemed, 1995), 2:230-231.

18 Cited here according to MS New York - JTS Rab. 15; Shraga Abramson, *Masekhet 'Avodah Zarah* (New York: The Jewish Theological Seminary of America, 1957) [Hebrew]. The hymn is translated according to Gershom G. Scholem, *Jewish Gnosticism, Merkabah Mysticism, and Talmudic Tradition* (New York: Jewish Theological Seminary of America, 1960), 25.

19 Kristen H Lindbeck, *Elijah and the Rabbis: Story and Theology* (New York: Columbia University Press, 2010), 4–5, 101–102.

20 Cf. Meïr Friedmann, ed., *Seder Eliyahu Rabah* (Jerusalem: Wahrman, 1969), Introduction [Hebrew]; Jacob Mann, "Date and Place of Redaction of Seder Eliyahu Rabba and Zuṭṭa," *Hebrew Union College Annual* 4 (1927): 302–310; Günter Stemberger, *Introduction to the Talmud and Midrash*, 2nd ed. (Edinburgh: T. & T. Clark, 1996), 340; Jacob Elbaum, "The Midrash Tana Devei Eliyahu and Ancient Esoteric Literature," *Jerusalem Studies in Jewish Thought* 6, no. 1–2 (1987): 139–150 [Hebrew]. A version of Elijah's hymn does in fact appear in *Seder Eliyahu* 11 (12), Friedmann, *Seder Eliyahu Rabah*, 58; William G. Braude and Israel J. Kapstein, eds., *Tanna Děbé Eliyyahu = The Lore of the School of Elijah* (Philadelphia: Jewish Publication Society of America, 1981), 32. The midrashic interpretation is not preceded by an attribution other than what is implied by its being found in a work ascribed to Elijah:

וכשהן מהלכין בדרך נשאו (פרות) [הפרות] (השירה) [שירה] בקולן, וכך אמרו, רוני רוני השיטה,
התנופפי ברוב הדרייך, המחושקה ברקמי זהב, המהוללה בדביר ארמון, המאופדת בין שני הכרובים,

shom Scholem's position regarding the age of the "Heikhaloth" genre of Jewish mysticism. Our knowledge of this school (characterized by texts describing mystical ascents through a hierarchy of "palaces" and culminating in a vision of the throne of God borne upon an angelic chariot) comes from texts emanating from the medieval era, albeit the texts consist of teachings that are ascribed pseudepigraphically to ancient rabbis. Exercising scholarly caution, Scholem was initially unready to date the phenomenon earlier than the documents in which it was recorded. Later, however, he collected a number of pieces of evidence attesting to the existence of Heikhaloth motifs in texts from the classical rabbinic era. This is one of those texts. Scholem points to the extraordinary resemblance between the song placed in the mouths of the cows[21] and the hymns sung by angelic beings in the Heikhaloth literature. As he observes:[22]

> Now this seems to me a most significant hymn. The choice of words, the majesty of phrase, and the lyrical rhythm are strongly reminiscent of the Hekhaloth hymns I have been describing. Why did R. Isaac Nappaḥa put such a hymn into the mouths of the kine? The answer is as clear as it has been over-looked up to date: this is an imitation of the setting in the Hekhaloth hymns. Just as the Holy Living Creatures, bearing the throne, sing hymns to the throne, so do these kine, bearing the Ark, sing hymns to the Ark.

Precisely because of its unusual mystical character, it is clear that the authors of this tradition did not regard the singing of the cows in that uniquely miraculous episode as an indication that bovines, or any other

---

שנאמר וישרנה הפרות בדרך על דרך בית שמש וגו'

And as they were walking along the way, the cows raised up a song saying: Rejoice, rejoice acacia! Stretch forth in the fulness of thy majesty, girdled in golden embroidery, praised in the recesses of the palace. Vested in two cherubs. As it says: "Then the cows went straight up toward Beth Shemesh, etc."

21   The song clearly qualifies as a *piyyuṭ* and conforms to the tropes of that genre. It is listed in Israel Davidson, *Otsar Ha-Shirah Veha-Piyyuṭ* (New York: Ktav Publishing House, 1970), 3:389 (#755) [Hebrew].

22   Gershom G. Scholem, *Jewish Gnosticism, Merkabah Mysticism, and Talmudic Tradition* (New York: Jewish Theological Seminary of America, 1960), 25. He is actually citing the version that appears in b.'*Avodah Zarah* 24b where the hymn is ascribed to Rabbi Isaac Nappaḥa. I suspect that he chose to focus on the Babyonian version of the midrash because he was able to identify Rabbi Isaac as one who was involved in mystical pursuits.

non-human creatures, are ordinarily capable of speech or other forms of vocal communication.[23] This attitude is strongly suggested by Rabbi Samuel bar Nahman's quip in *Genesis Rabbah* about how much easier it was to get the cows to sing than the human Levites. Perhaps we should sense some underlying discomfort in the following addendum that is attached to the Babylonian pericope:

Rav Ashi[24] applies Rabbi Isaac's statement to this: "And it came to pass, when the ark set forward, that Moses said..." (Numbers 10:35).	רב אשי מתני [לה] לדר' יצחק נפחא אהא ויהי בנסוע הארון ויאמר משה ...

We may speculate that Rav Ashi was uncomfortable with a tradition (albeit one that by his time was well established among rabbinic preachers and expositors) that accepted the existence of talking animals and that he therefore chose instead to attach the whole discussion to a different (but comparable) context, the traveling of the ark of the covenant in the wilderness during the time of Moses.[25]

---

23 Note the passage from *Yalkuṭ Shim'oni* to Exodus 22:30 [Arthur B. Hyman, Isaac N. Lerer, and Yitsḥak Shiloni, eds., *Yalkuṭ Shim'oni le-Rabbenu Shim'on ha-Darshan: Sefer Shemot* (Jerusalem, Israel: Mossad Harav Kook, 1977), 1:111]; cited by Viktor Aptowitzer, "The Rewarding and Punishing of Animals and Inanimate Objects: On the Aggadic View of the World," *Hebrew Union College Annual* 3 (1926): 131; see also James Davila, *Descenders to the Chariot: The People Behind the Hekhalot Literature* (Leiden and Boston: Brill, 2001), 118–119; David J. Halperin, *The Faces of the Chariot: Early Jewish Responses to Ezekiel's Vision*, Texte und Studien zum antiken Judentum 16 (Tübingen: J.C.B. Mohr, 1988), 361.

24 Wilhelm Bacher, *Die Agada der babylonischen Amoräer: Ein Beitrag zur Geschichte der Agada und zur Einleitung in den babylonischen Talmud* (Frankfurt a. M., 1913), 144–145; Stemberger, *Introduction to the Talmud and Midrash*, 98; Albeck, *Intro. to Talmuds*, 427–430; Margalioth and Aizenberg, *Encyclopedia*, 1:166–168.

25 Similar considerations would appear to warrant the exclusion of some other texts in which animals were imagined as mystically inspired to burst out in spiritual or prophetic song. Viktor Aptowitzer attached significance to a passage in *Avot deRabbi Natan B Ch. 43* which contains an exposition of Joel 2:28-29, "and it shall come to pass afterward, that I will pour out my spirit upon all flesh... Even on the male and female servants," as inclusive of "humans, animals and fowl"; see "Rewarding and

Conversing with the Avarshana

"YES, MISTER OATS. AND WHEN DOES THE PHOENIX
SOMETIMES LAY TWO EGGS? WHEN IT NEEDS TO.
HODGESAARGH WAS RIGHT. A PHOENIX IS OF THE NA-
TURE OF BIRDS. BIRD FIRST, MYTH SECOND."[26]

The Babylonian Talmud contains the following whimsical tale,[27] related as
it were by Noah's son Shem to Abraham's servant Eliezer.[28] The passage
includes several episodes whose combined effect is to produce a vivid picture of the physical and emotional difficulties that beset Noah and his family in providing care for the numerous and diverse creatures who had to

---

Punishing," 120. In fact, Schechter (n. 26 to his edition of *Avot deRabbi Nathan*) was
of the opinion that the interpretation regarding animals should be read as a scribal insertion based on similar kinds of exegesis that are found elsewhere in rabbinic literature. Aptowitzer also regarded *Pereḳ Shirah*, a remarkable work in which numerous
biblical verses are identified as the songs of divine praise uttered by natural creatures
of fauna and flora, as relevant to the belief in the religious stature and moral judgment of animals. He attributed *Pereḳ Shirah* to mystical circles during the Ge'onic
era, a claim that was based largely on its being cited by the "minor tractate" *Kallah
Rabbati* which he associated with the school of the eighth-century Rav Yehudai
Gaon. See Malachi Beit-Arié, "Pereḳ Shirah: Introductions and Critical Edition"
(Ph.D., The Hebrew University of Jerusalem, 1966) [Hebrew]; Eric Lawee, "The
Sins of the Fauna in Midrash, Rashi, and Their Medieval Interlocutors," *Jewish
Studies Quarterly* 17, no. 1 (2010): 57; Nosson Slifkin, *Nature's Song: An Elucida-
tion of Pereḳ Shirah*, Torah Universe (Southfield, MI and Nanuet, NY: Targum dis-
tributed by Feldheim, 2001). On the penitent animals of Nineveh who go so far as to
fast and don sackcloth (Jonah 3:7-8; see also 4:11) in response to Jonah's preaching
(in what might be intended as a parody), see John A. Miles, "Laughing at the Bible:
Jonah as Parody," *The Jewish Quarterly Review* 65, no. 3 (1975): 176–177, 180.

26 Terry Pratchett, *Carpe Jugulum: A Novel of Discworld*, 1st U.S. ed. (New York:
HarperPrism, 1999), 374.

27 See Louis Ginzberg, *The Legends of the Jews*, trans. Henrietta Szold (Philadelphia,
PA: The Jewish Publication Society of America, 1909), 1:161; 5:181-182 n. 37. The
story is discussed briefly by Maren R. Niehoff, "The Phoenix in Rabbinic Literature," *Harvard Theological Review* 89, no. 3 (1996): 259.

28 For other incidents of the incorporation of Eliezer into whimsical or satirical contexts
in the Babylonian Talmud, see Eliezer Segal, "A Funny Thing Happened on My Way
to Sodom," *Journal for the Study of Judaism in the Persian, Hellenistic, and Roman
Period* 46, no. 1 (2015): 103–129.

coexist in the cramped quarters of the ark. As they appear in the completed pericope (and with a general stylistic consistency), it would appear that they all belong to a single quote by the same rabbi; though it is not inconceivable that they derive from separate contexts and were afterwards assembled together skilfully by an editor.

b. Sanhedrin 108b:[29]

Said Rav Ḥana bar Bizna:[30] Eliezer said to Shem the great[31]...	א' רב חנא בר ביזנא א' ליה אליעזר לשם רבא...

---

29 According to Editio Princeps.

30 The name varies in the textual witnesses: Rav Ḥana bar Bizna; Rav Huna bar Livai/ Levi, Rabbi Jeremiah ben Eleazar, etc. On the former, a third-century Babylonian sage specializing principally in aggadah, see Albeck, *Intro. to Talmuds*, 288; Margalioth and Aizenberg, *Encyclopedia*, 1:131. Huna bar Livai is not listed in the standard lexicons of talmudic rabbis.

31 The addition "the great" is found in several witnesses, but not all.

b. *Sanhedrin 108b:*

The "*avarshana*"[32]— Father found him sleeping in a side-room[33] of the ark.

He said to him: Do you not want food?

He said: I observed that you were busy,[34] so I decided that I

אורשינה אשכחיניה אבא דגני
בסיפנא דתיבותא

אמ' ליה לא בעית מזוני

אמ' ליה חזיתיך דהות טרידת
אמינא לא אצערך

אמ' ליה יהא רעוא דלא תמות שנ'
ואומ' עם קני אגיע וכחול ארבה ימים

---

32 The Genizah fragment Oxford c. 17/63-64 (cited by the Friedberg Project) inserts "did not come for three days to take food. Father went and found him..."

33 See Michael Sokoloff, *A Dictionary of Jewish Babylonian Aramaic of the Talmudic and Geonic Periods* (Ramat Gan and Baltimore: Bar Ilan University Press and Johns Hopkins University Press, 2003), 823.

34 Meir Abulafia and *Yalḳuṭ* Job: "You have troubles greater than my troubles." See Raphael Nathan Rabinowitz, *Diḳduḳe Sofrim: Variae Lectiones in Mischnam in Talmud Babylonicum* (Munich, 1883), 9:346 n. ט.

b. Sanhedrin 108b:

> would not trouble you.
>
> He said to him: May it be his will that you should not die,[35] as it says (Job 29:18): "Then I said, I shall die in my nest, and I shall multiply my days as the *ḥol.*"

The *hapax legomenon* "avarshana," which is susceptible to numerous possible vocalizations, has inspired many attempts at identifying the humble and virtuous creature in Noah's ark. For purposes of the present study, it does indeed make some difference whether we are dealing with an ordinary animal or bird, or with a fabulous and mythic being for whom speech might be considered just another legendary characteristic.[36]

Modern lexicographers, following in the steps of Ge'onic scholarship,[37] generally prefer to derive the word from a Semitic term for dove or pigeon.[38] Nevertheless, much of the scholarly discourse on these questions

---

35 The reading in the *'Arukh* (as in the Oxford Genizah text) has: יהא רעוה דתיקוש ותינוק "ולא תמות": May it be his will that you grow old, be rejuvenated [lit. Suck], and not die. [Alexander Kohut and Samuel Krauss, eds., *Aruch Completum ['Arukh Ha-Shalem]* (Jerusalem: Makor, 1969), 3:386; as translated by Sokoloff, *Babylonian*, 1051].

36 For purposes of this study, I have not dealt with other texts that were adduced by scholars as evidence for rabbinic ideas about the phoenix, particularly those that make reference to the "*ziz.*"

37 E.g., Max Weisz, *Geniza Fragmente der Bibliothek David Kaufmann S. A. im Besitze der ungarischen Akademie der Wissenschaften* (Budapest: Katz Katzburg, 1922), 82; Albert Harkavy, *Zikhron Kamah Ge'onim*, vol. 1:4, Zikkaron la-Rishonim ve-gam la-Aḥaronim (Berlin: Matzkowski, 1887), 145 (350); Louis Ginzberg, ed., *Genizah Studies in Memory of Doctor Solomon Schechter*, vol. 2, Jewish Studies Classics (Piscataway, NJ: Gorgias Press, 2003), 400; Zwi Taubes, *Otsar ha-Ge'onim le-Masekhet Sanhedrin* (Jerusalem: Mosad Harav Kook, 1966), 541.

38 Jacob Levy, *Wörterbuch über die Talmudim und Midraschim*, 2nd ed. (Berlin and Vienna: B. Harz, 1924), 1:47-48; See B. Geiger's note in Samuel Krauss, *Additamenta ad Librum Aruch Completum* (Jerusalem: Makor, 1970), 14; Michael Sokoloff, *A Dictionary of Jewish Babylonian Aramaic of the Talmudic and Geonic Periods*

pivots on the proof-text from Job.[39] In *Genesis Rabbah* and elsewhere,[40] the same verse is expounded in connection with its tradition that Eve had offered the forbidden fruit to all the creatures in the garden and only the bird named *ḥol* had remained obedient to the divine command,[41] for which it was rewarded with wondrous longevity or immortality.[42] Regarding this virtuous creature, rabbis from the early third century explain that immortality in terms that dovetail incontestably with the Greek traditions about the lifespan of the mythic phoenix:

(Ramat Gan and Baltimore: Bar Ilan University Press and Johns Hopkins University Press, 2003), 1051. They cite cognates in Akkadian, Syriac, Arabic and other languages. For a (rather farfetched, in my opinion) attempt at a Greek etymology; see L. Lewysohn, *Die Zoologie des Talmuds* (Frankfurt am Main: Author and Joseph Baer, 1858), 352–353; cf. Niehoff, "Phoenix," 256; Nosson Slifkin, "Sacred Monsters: Mysterious and Mythical Creatures of Scripture, Talmud and Midrash" (Brooklyn, N.Y: Zoo Torah, 2007), 233–234. Niehoff effectively (256) dismisses a Greek etymology for the name on the grounds that "the Babylonian Talmud, where this name occurs, generally lacks close familiarity with Greek culture and language. It is therefore rather unlikely that a Greek name for the phoenix should first appear precisely in this document." Of course, more recent scholarship (by Boyarin and others) has made a compelling case for extensive hellenization in talmudic Babylonia. Ginzberg, *ibid.*, speaks of "the animal urshana" and insists that "The word is most likely of Persian origin, but it must not be identified with the phoenix, though both of them are considered among the immortals."

39   Several modern scholars have offered detailed philological arguments as to why this should be the preferred interpretation of the biblical text. See Roelof van den Broek, *The Myth of the Phoenix: According to Classical and Early Christian Traditions*, Études préliminaires aux religions orientales dans l'Empire Romain 24 (Leiden: E. J. Brill, 1971), 58–59; Mitchell Joseph Dahood, "Hol 'Phoenix' in Job 29:18 and in Ugaritic," *The Catholic Biblical Quarterly* 36, no. 1 (1974): 85–88; "Nest and Phoenix in Job 29:18," *Biblica* 48, no. 4 (1967): 542–544; Niehoff, "Phoenix," 255. The Greek Job rendered *ḥol* as στέλεχος φοίνικος [=like the trunk of a palm tree], employing the homonym for "phoenix." Some have contended that the insertion of the trunk (to make it clear that the reference is to a tree) reflects a second-order emendation designed to correct an original translation as "phoenix." See Joseph Nigg, *The Phoenix: An Unnatural Biography of a Mythical Beast* (University of Chicago Press, 2016), 86; Niehoff, "Phoenix," 256; Slifkin, "Sacred Monsters," 229–231. Slifkin cites several traditional Jewish exegetes who discuss the interpretation of the verse. Rashi was the authority responsible for applying the phoenix tradition to the avarshana.

Genesis Rabbah 19:5:[43]

The school of R' Yannai and R' Judan be"R' Simeon: The academy of R' Yannai[44] say: It lives for a thousand years, and at the conclusion of the thousand years a flame emerges from its nest and burns it up and there remains an egg from which it regenerates limbs and it lives[45]	דבית ר' ייני ור' יודן בר' שמעון: דבית ר' ייני אמ': אלף שנים הוא חי, בסוף אלף שנים אש יוצאה מתוך קנו ושורפתו, ומשתייר בו כביצה וחוזר ומגדל אברים וחי.

---

40 Notably, *Midrash Samuel* 12:2 [Berachyahu Lifshitz, *Midrash Shmuel*, The Midrash Project of the Schechter Institute of Jewish Studies (Jerusalem: Schechter Institute of Jewish Studies, 2009), 44 (commentary on 263)].

41 See Ginzberg, *Legends*, 1:32-33; 5:51 n. 151. No verbal conversation is related or implied between Eve and the animals, though they are assumed to have the judgment to be making moral decisions.

42 See Aptowitzer, "Rewarding and Punishing," 135 and n. 39.

43 19:5; Hebrew text cited according to MS Vatican 30 [from Hebrew Language Academy resource]; see Julius Theodor and Chanoch Albeck, eds., *Midrash Bereshit Rabba* (Jerusalem, Israel: Wahrman, 1965), 174–175; discussed in Roelof van den Broek, *The Myth of the Phoenix: According to Classical and Early Christian Traditions*, Études préliminaires aux religions orientales dans l'Empire Romain 24 (Leiden: E. J. Brill, 1971), 70 and n. 1; Maren R. Niehoff, "The Phoenix in Rabbinic Literature," *Harvard Theological Review* 89, no. 3 (1996): 257–259; Nosson Slifkin, "Sacred Monsters: Mysterious and Mythical Creatures of Scripture, Talmud and Midrash" (Brooklyn, N.Y: Zoo Torah, 2007), 231–232.

44 Ch. Albeck, *Introduction to the Talmud. Babli and Yerushalmi* (Tel-Aviv: Dvir, 1969), 161–162; Mordecai Margalioth and Yehudah Aizenberg, eds., *Entsiklopedyah le-Ḥakhme ha-Talmud yeha-Ge'onim*, Revised edition. (Tel-Aviv: Yavneh and Chemed, 1995), 2:225. On this school see Aharon Oppenheimer, "Those of the School of Rabbi Yannai," in *Between Rome and Babylon: Studies in Jewish Leadership and Society*, ed. Nili Oppenheimer, Texts and Studies in Ancient Judaism 108 (Tübingen: Mohr Siebeck, 2005), 156–165. Oppenheimer argue that they were not a generic rabbinical academy devoted to religious scholarship, but a fellowship or commune spanning several generations who were deeply involved in the social and economic lives of the residents of Akhbarah.

45 See the critical apparatus in the Theodor-Albeck edition.

Genesis Rabbah 19:5:

Rabbi Judan be"R' Simeon[46] said: It lives a thousand years. At the conclusion of the thousand years[47] its body is destroyed and its wings are plucked and there remains the size of an egg which regenerates limbs and lives.

ר' יודן בר' שמעון: אלף שנים הוא
חי. בסוף אלף שנים גופו כלה וכנפיו
מתמרטים, משתייר בו כביצה והוא חוזר
ומגדל אברים וחי:

Legends about the long-lived and resurrecting phoenix (φοῖνιξ) likely originated in Egypt.[48] The myth was mentioned by Hesiod[49] and reappears among a diverse collection of authors including Herodotus, Ovid, Martial, Pliny the Elder, Tacitus, Lucian, Aelian and others.[50] Greek traditions were confused by the fact that the same word could be used to designate a date-

---

46   Ch. Albeck, *Introduction to the Talmud. Babli and Yerushalmi* (Tel-Aviv: Dvir, 1969), 183–184; Mordecai Margalioth and Yehudah Aizenberg, eds., *Entsiklopedyah le-Ḥakhme ha-Talmud yeha-Ge'onim*, Revised edition. (Tel-Aviv: Yavneh and Chemed, 1995), 1:174.

47   On the time-spans separating the phoenix's momentous reappearances see the thorough discussion in van den Broek, *The Myth of the Phoenix*, 66–131.

48   See Mary Francis McDonald, "Phoenix Redivivus," *Phoenix* 14, no. 4 (1960): 196–204; van den Broek, *The Myth of the Phoenix*, 14–48, 51–52; Nigg, *The Phoenix*, xvii.

49   Fragment 304; Glenn W. Most, *Hesiod*, Loeb Classical Library 57, 503 (Cambridge, MA: Harvard University Press, 2006), 324–325.

50   There are numerous studies that trace and analyze the evolution of the Phoenix legend in Greco-Roman and other cultures. Among the works that I consulted were: Jean Hubaux and Maxime Leroy, *Le Mythe du Phénix dans les Littératures Grecque et Latine*, Bibliothèque de la Faculté de philosophie et lettres de l'Université de Liège. Fasc. LXXXII (Liège, Paris: Faculté de philosophie et lettres et E. Droz, 1939); McDonald, "Phoenix Redivivus"; van den Broek, *The Myth of the Phoenix*; John Spencer Hill, "The Phoenix," *Religion & Literature* 16, no. 2 (1984): 61–66; Niehoff, "Phoenix"; Slifkin, "Sacred Monsters," 223–238; Nigg, *The Phoenix*.

palm,[51] Phoenicia[52] or Phoenician purple.[53] The image of the phoenix also made its way into Jewish writings that were composed or preserved in Greek, such as the Apocalypse of Baruch (3 Baruch),[54] 2 Enoch[55] and the Exagogé, a dramatic rendition of the biblical Exodus story, by Ezekiel the Tragedian.[56]

As scholars have remarked, the divergence between Rabbi Yudan and the school of Rabbi Yannai in the Midrash parallels the principal options

---

51 Thus, the Greek version of Psalms 91:13 ("The righteous shall flourish like *the palm tree* [כתמר])" could be read as "like the phoenix"—an option that was preferred by Tertullian, but which has no parallel in Jewish exegesis. See Niehoff, "Phoenix," 254; Nigg, *The Phoenix*, 84; Slifkin, "Sacred Monsters," 229.

52 See van den Broek, *The Myth of the Phoenix*, 52–57.

53 See ibid., 61–62. Various shades of red were so designated by Homer; see Nigg, *The Phoenix*, 36.

54 Chapters 6-8. For an extensive discussion and literature review see Daniel C. Harlow, *The Greek Apocalypse of Baruch (3 Baruch) in Hellenistic Judaism and Early Christianity*, Studia in Veteris Testamenti pseudepigrapha 12 (Leiden and New York: E.J. Brill, 1996), 131–140. In Baruch's version of Ezekiel's "chariot" vision at the Third Heaven, the great bird that he observes is the "guardian of the earth" sheltering humanity from exposure to the direct light of the sun, eating mannah and dew, and excreting a worm that produces exquisite cinnamon. See also Niehoff, "Phoenix," 260–263.

55 12:1. The phoenix appears at the Fourth Heaven in Enoch's ascent, "their size is nine hundred measures, their wings are like those of angels, each has twelve, and they attend and accompany the sun, bearing heat and dew, as it is ordered them from God." Nevill Forbes and R. H. Charles, "2 Enoch, or the Book of the Secrets of Enoch," in *The Apocrypha and Pseudepigrapha of the Old Testament*, ed. R. H. Charles, vol. Volume Two: Pseudepigrapha (Oxford: Clarendon Press, 1913), 436 (and notes).

56 McDonald, "Phoenix Redivivus," 188–189. Though the name "phoenix" is not employed by Ezekiel, the rare appearance of this exotic, multi-hewed giant bird fits its standard role and description as a supernatural sign accompanying a major historical event. The detail is inserted into the brief episode (Exodus 15:27) of the Israelites' encampment at Elim shortly after the parting of the Red Sea. Given the fragmentary nature of Ezekiel's play, at which point the scout reports, among other signs that this is a favorable place, the appearance of the immense, rare and multi-hued bird; whether it relates specifically to the Elim incident, to the presence of date-palms there; or to the more momentous importance of the Exodus itself (widely identified with the reign of Amasis when a phoenix-sighting was reported), or even to the per-

among classical authors[57] as to whether the phoenix ended its life in a con-flagration[58] or through a process of more gradual decomposition.[59]

The imagery of the phoenix became a fixture of Christian symbol-ism[60] from as early as the First Epistle of Clement[61]; it was adduced as proof (if true) or symbol (albeit legendary) of the future resurrection[62]—a theme that would have been very congenial to Jewish teachings, though the rabbis never use it for that purpose.[63]

M. Niehoff has observed that the midrashic story, in ascribing the phoenix's longevity to its unique resistance to the offer of forbidden fruit

---

ceived momentousness of the author's own time. Howard Jacobson, *The Exagoge of Ezekiel* (Cambridge, [Cambridgeshire]; New York: Cambridge University Press, 1983); See discussions in: Howard Jacobson, "Phoenix Resurrected," *Harvard Theological Review* 80, no. 2 (1987): 229–233; Thomas D. Kohn, "The Tragedies of Ezekiel," *Greek, Roman, and Byzantine Studies* 43, no. 1 (2011): 10–12; Jane Heath, "Ezekiel Tragicus and Hellenistic Visuality: The Phoenix at Elim," *The Journal of Theological Studies* 57, no. 1 (2006): 23–41; Rachel Bryant Davies, "Reading Ezekiel's Exagoge: Tragedy, Sacrificial Ritual, and the Midrashic Tradition," *Greek, Roman, and Byzantine Studies* 48, no. 4 (2010): 402.

57 van den Broek, *The Myth of the Phoenix*, 146–197, 220; Niehoff, "Phoenix," 258.

58 As claimed by the *Physiologus*. See Nigg, *The Phoenix*, xviii–xix.

59 This position is associated principally with Lucius Manilius (as cited by Pliny). See van den Broek, *The Myth of the Phoenix*, 68–69; Niehoff, "Phoenix," 258; Nigg, *The Phoenix*, xviii; Slifkin, "Sacred Monsters," 231–232.

60 See van den Broek, *The Myth of the Phoenix*, e.g.: 9, 42, 47, 130-131, 152, 160, 211, 224, 231, 234, 419; Anders Klostergaard Petersen, "Between Old and New: The Problem of Acculturation Illustrated by the Early Christian Use of the Phoenix Mo-tif," in *Jerusalem, Alexandria, Rome: Studies in Ancient Cultural Interaction in Honour of A. Hilhorst*, ed. Florentino García Martinez and Gerald P. Luttikhuizen (Leiden and Boston: BRILL, 2003), 148–164; Niehoff, "Phoenix," 251–255.

61 25:1. See van den Broek, *The Myth of the Phoenix*, 4; Nigg, *The Phoenix*, xix–xx. The description of its regeneration is close to that of Judan be"R' Simeon in the midrash; i.e., the death occurs naturally, without a conflagration. The motif was util-ized by Tertullian, Origen, Lactantius, the *Physiologus* and others.

62 The belief that the regeneration occurs at long intervals (of a thousand years, accord-ing to the prevailing theory) made it a convenient instrument for eschatological preaching (another theme that was not exploited in Jewish homilies). See Niehoff, "Phoenix," 258 and n. 62.

63 Ibid., 246, 251–255, 265; (contra Ginzberg, *Legends*, 51 n. 151).

in the garden of Eden, was implicitly providing an explanation to the difficult question: "if mortality came into the world as the result of Adam and Eve's first sin, why do the animals also have to die?"[64] Perhaps we would not be stretching that line of thinking too far if we were to relate it to the questions raised by Second-Temple and medieval thinkers about why and when the animals lost their primordial ability to converse with humans.

But then again—aside from the citation of the verse from Job (which might well be a later editorial addition and not integral to the original talmudic passage), there is no compelling reason to assume that the passage in the Babylonian Talmud is referring to the phoenix or to a comparable mythic creature.[65] The word "avarshana" does not appear in any of the other rabbinic texts that have been linked to the phoenix. It does nevertheless provide an instance of a non-human creature that is conducting a conversation with a human (though it is also unclear whether we are meant to understand that it was speaking Noah's language or Noah was communicating in the tongue of the avarshana).

Talking to the Walls

Exodus Rabbah 10:3:[66]

"[And the frogs shall come up] both in thee, and in thy people, and in all thy servants]"	"וּבְכָה וּבְעַמֶּ֖ךָ... [וּבְכָל עֲבָדֶ֑יךָ]."...
Said Rabbi Aḥa:[67] "in thee"- — precisely! For he would be drinking water and one drop	אמר רבי אחא ובכה ודאי.[68] שהיה שותה מים וטיפה אחת יורד על לבו

---

64 Niehoff, "Phoenix," 259.

65 The association with the "nest" in Job might at least have proved that the avarshana is a kind of bird; however, the same word is used in Genesis 6:14 to denote the compartments in the ark, a verbal similarity that is sufficient to create a midrashic association between Genesis and Job.

66 Avigdor Shinan, ed., *Midrash Shemot Rabbah, Chapters I-XIV* (Jerusalem: Dvir, 1984), 229–230; see Louis Ginzberg, *The Legends of the Jews*, trans. Henrietta Szold (Philadelphia, PA: The Jewish Publication Society of America, 1909), 2:349-350; 5:428-429 n. 179. Shinan's primary text is MS Jerusalem NLI 24° 5977.

Exodus Rabbah 10:3:

would trickle down his chest, and it would turn into a frog and split there.

ונעשה צפרדע ונבקעת שם.

Rabbi Yoḥanan said: In any place where there was earth and a drop of water descended, it would produce a frog.

ר' יוחנן אמר כל מקום שהיה שם
עפר והיה טפה של מים יורדתעושה
צפרדע.

Hezekiah beR'[69] said: If it were according to this approach, then the houses of the nobility would not have been afflicted, because they were made of marble and mosaics.

חזקיה בר' אמר אם כשיטה זו לא
לקו בתיהם של גדולים שהיו עשויין
בשיש ובסיפס.

Rather, this teaches that the frog would rise from the depths[70] and say to the marble: make room for me to come up and I shall perform my mission properly. Then the marble would split, and she would go up and grab their private parts and unsex them;[71]

אלא מלמד שהיה הצפרדע עולה מן
התהום ואומ' לשיש עשה לי מקום
שאעלה ואעשה שליחותי כראוי והיה
נבקע השיש ועולה ונוטלת בית הסתרים
שלהם ומחרסן

---

67   Ch. Albeck, *Introduction to the Talmud. Babli and Yerushalmi* (Tel-Aviv: Dvir, 1969), 316–318; Mordecai Margalioth and Yehudah Aizenberg, eds., *Entsiḳlopedyah le-Ḥakhme ha-Talmud yeha-Ge'onim*, Revised edition. (Tel-Aviv: Yavneh and Chemed, 1995), 1:28.

68   See Shinan's discussion on the textual variants and their significance.

69   Likely the 4th-5th generation Palestinian teacher described in Albeck, *Intro. to Talmuds*, 391–392.

70   On ancient perceptions of the "depths" (primordial waters) see Daniel Sperber, "On Sealing the Abysses," *Journal of Semitic Studies* 11, no. 2 (1966): 515–518.

71   The situation is reminiscent of the scene in Aristophanes in which the exasperating chorus of croaking frogs provokes Dionysius to complain "But I've got blisters, and my arsehole's been seeping, etc." (ἐγὼ δὲ φλυκταίνας γ' ἔχω, χὠ πρωκτὸς ἰδίει πάλαι); [Aristophanes, *Frogs. Assemblywomen. Wealth*, trans. Jeffrey Henderson, Loeb Classical Library 180 (Cambridge, MA: Harvard University Press, 1998), 56–

Exodus Rabbah 10:3:

<table>
<tr>
<td>

as it says (Psalms 78:45): "[He sent divers sorts of flies among them, which devoured them,] and frogs, which destroyed them; as you say (Leviticus 22:25): "[Neither from a stranger's hand shall ye offer the bread of your God of any of these,] because their corruption is in them, and blemishes be in them."

</td>
<td dir="rtl">

שנאמר וצפרדע ותשחיתם.

כמה דתימאכי משחתם בהם מום

בם:

</td>
</tr>
</table>

The rabbinic preachers vied with each other to magnify the miraculous dimensions of the Egyptian plagues and the humiliating suffering that was thereby inflicted on its targets, especially the wicked Pharaoh. The plague of frogs has always provided a particularly attractive subject for such narrative embellishments which must have given satisfaction and amusement to the congregations who heard them. The text in question appears in a midrashic compendium whose redaction is generally dated to the tenth century.[72]

The interpretations in this passage are based largely on a narrowly literal reading of various Hebrew words in thescriptural phraseology. Thus, they expounded that the frogs were to come up *inside* the bodies of Pharaoh and his subjects—in expressions that are rendered standardly in English in the sense of "on" or "upon." Similarly, according to Shinan, it was the wording of Exodus 8:3—"And the river shall bring forth frogs abundantly"— and Psalms 105:30—"Their land brought forth frogs in abun-

---

57].

72   The passage belongs to *"Exodus Rabbah* A" which is a separate and earlier work from the later section of the midrash on Exodus. For a discussion of the considerations leading to the dating, and a survey of previous scholarly discussions, see Avigdor Shinan, ed., *Midrash Shemot Rabbah, Chapters I-XIV* (Jerusalem: Dvir, 1984), 23–24; Stemberger, *Introduction to the Talmud and Midrash*, 308–309. Probably the single most important factor in this determination is the certainty that *Exodus Rabbah* made use of the *Tanḥuma* literature (Shinan 18-19). The lateness of the redaction does not necessarily preclude the accuracy of the attributions to the named sages.

dance, in the chambers of their kings"—that inspired Rabbis Aḥa and Yoḥanan to assert that frogs were actually generated directly and miraculously out of the elements of water and earth.

The detail about the removal of the Egyptians' private parts is given "lexicographical" support by showing how the same root (שחת) that is employed in Psalms to designate the destruction wreaked by the frogs is also found in a passage in Leviticus that enumerates physical injuries and blemishes that disqualify an animal from sacrificial use.

The feature of the passage that has relevance to the present study is, of course, the segment in which the frog asks permission of the marble floors or walls to pass through and complete its task. It is hard to imagine that the author of this exposition expected his listeners to accept this cartoon-like episode at face value.[73] After all, it is not just a matter of talking frogs,[74] but also of slabs of stone that seem able to hear, understand and obey the frogs' requests. It is far more plausible to suppose that the imagery was intended to convey a vivid symbolic picture of how all of nature was recruited to carry out the will of the Almighty—a message that is fully consistent with the role of the plagues in the original biblical narrative.[75]

Muzzling King Solomon

Largely owing to their inclusion in collections or paraphrases of rabbinic biblical legends, there is a widespread assumption that the midrash con-

---

73 This exposition resembles another well-known rabbinic tradition involving a far-fetched interpretation of the frog plague. In Exodus 8:6 the words "and the frogs came up" employ a grammatically singular (collective) form. This prompted Rabbi Akiva to expound:

> There was one frog that spawned and filled up the entire land of Egypt.
> R' Eleazar ben Azariah said to him: Akiva what business do you have with haggadah? Give it up and go to [the technical laws of] leprous plagues and [transfer of impurity by] "tents." [*Exodus Rabbah* 10:4 (ed. Shinan 231; *b.Sanhedrin* 67b, etc.]

Clearly there were differing tastes as to how fanciful a homiletical embellishment ought to be.

74 Though not necessarily in a conventional human-like language.

75 E.g., Exodus 9:14.

tains a body of tales about King Solomon's ability to talk to animals.[76] These have their scriptural basis in 1 Kings 5:13 [or 4:33]: "he spake also of beasts, and of fowl, and of creeping things, and of fishes" [וַיְדַבֵּר עַל-הַבְּהֵמָה וְעַל-הָעוֹף וְעַל-הָרֶמֶשׂ וְעַל-הַדָּגִים] The Hebrew lends itself, though somewhat awkwardly, to the sense of "spake *to*."

However, closer investigation reveals that the stories involving talking animals cited in Ginzberg 4:134-140 are not from real talmudic or midrashic sources, and that the authentic material may illustrate the wise monarch's dominion over the animals and his understanding of their ways, but not his understanding or speaking their languages. Thus, in a paean to King Solomon in Targum Sheni[77] to Esther 1:2, it states, "He understood

---

76 Ginzberg, *Legends*, 6:278-288 n.34; Howard Schwartz, *Gabriel's Palace: Jewish Mystical Tales* (OUP USA, 1994), 42; Gerrit Bos, "Jewish Traditions on Divination with Birds (Ornithomancy)," 2015, 8, https://www.researchgate.net/ publication/ 280976904_ Jewish_Traditions_ on_ Divination_ with_ Birds_ Ornithomancy. In recent discourse, the legend achieved some currency when Austrian zoologist Konrad Lorenz used it in the English title of his popular book about animal-human communications: King Solomon's Ring; New Light on Animal Ways, trans. Marjorie Kerr Wilson (New York: Crowell, 1952). *King Solomon's Ring; New Light on Animal Ways*, trans. Marjorie Kerr Wilson (New York: Crowell, 1952). The view that Solomon understood the languages of all animals is based on 1 Kings 5:13 (which was in fact the original German title of Lorenz's book). To the contrary, in Y. Shavit's thorough survey of the evolution of ancient interpretative traditions about the nature of Solomon's wisdom (including the legends of his enchanted ring), ranging from religious wisdom to magic, demonology and scientific knowledge, there does not appear to be a single instance of speaking with animals; see Yaacov Shavit, "'He Was Thoth in Everything": Why and When King Solomon Became Both Magister Omnium Physicorum and Master of Magic," in *Envisioning Judaism: Studies in Honor of Peter Schäfer on the Occasion of His Seventieth Birthday*, ed. Raanan Shaul Boustan et al., vol. 1, 2 vols. (Tübingen: Mohr Siebeck, 2013), 587–606. See also Raʿanan Boustan and Michael Beshay, "Sealing the Demons, Once and For All: The Ring of Solomon, the Cross of Christ, and the Power of Biblical Kingship," *Archiv für Religionsgeschichte* 16, no. 1 (2015). This article deals with the later traditions about Solomon's control over the demons, and concludes decisively that they did not originate within any Jewish setting.

77 For the dating of Targum Sheni see Bernard Grossfeld, *The Two Targums of Esther*, The Aramaic Bible v. 18 (Collegeville, Minn: Liturgical Press, 1991), 20–24. Grossfeld favors a late Byzantine—seventh century— Palestinian provenance.

upon hearing, the expressions of birds, together with those of cattle, (and) wild beasts, stags and rams. Lions and tigers ran before him. This one understood their expressions better than all nations together."[78] In the elaborate legend related in *b.Giṭṭin* 68a-68b in which Solomon ingeniously captures the stone-cutting *shamir*, the closest we come to a talking creature is the *tarnegola bara* ('wild rooster") who had an oath imposed on it by the "prince of the sea" and who committed suicide when informed that he had been tricked into violating that oath and betraying his trust.[79] On the other hand, the Qur'an (e.g., 27:16-29) speaks of Solomon mastering the language of the birds, marshaling them into his army and participating in conversations with ants and hoopoes.[80] While a case might be made (as Ginzberg frequently does) for the thesis that the Qur'an was drawing upon lost Jewish sources, the fact remains that the motif is not documented in classic rabbinic literature.[81]

---

78 Dov Noy, "The Jewish Versions of the 'Animal Languages' Folktale (AT 670): A Typological-Structural Study," in *Studies in Aggadah and Folk-Literature*, vol. 22, Scripta Hierosolymitana (Jerusalem: Magnes Press, 1971), 177; Sheldon Oberman, "Solomon and the Ant: And Other Jewish Folktales," 1st ed. (Honesdale, PA: Boyds Mills Press, 2006).

79 Leo Jung, "Fallen Angels in Jewish, Christian and Mohammedan Literature: A Study in Comparative Folk-Lore," *The Jewish Quarterly Review* 16, no. 2 (1925): 176–177.

80 See A. S. Rappoport and Raphael Patai, *Myth and Legend of Ancient Israel*, vol. 3 (New York: Ktav, 1966), 185–187.

81 Ultimately, Ginzberg himself concedes (6:289, n. 38) that "Solomon's knowledge of the languages of the animals is hardly referred to in the older literature"; and with respect to a certain legend he concludes "This legend seems to be of Arabic origin, since in genuinely Jewish legends animals do not talk" (5:332, n. 66). Ginzberg discusses his methodologies and criteria for using Muslim legends in *Jewish Folklore: East and West: A Paper Delivered at the Harvard Tercentenary Conference of Arts and Sciences*, Harvard Tercentenary Publications (Cambridge, MA: Harvard University Press, 1937), 13–15; see also Elbaum, "The Midrash Tana Devei Eliyahu and Ancient Esoteric Literature," 162; Marc G. Hirshman, *Midrash Ḳohelet Rabah 1-6: Critical Edition Based on Manuscripts and Geniza Fragments*, The Midrash Project of the Schechter Institute of Jewish Studies (Jerusalem: Schechter Institute of Jewish Studies, 2016), 5–7 [Hebrew]. On the scope and eclecticism of Ginzberg's use of non-rabbinic sources see David Stern, "Introduction to the 2003 Edition," in *Legends of the Jews*, 2nd ed., vol. 1 (Philadelphia: Jewish Publication Society, 2003), xvii–

Giving Names

Rabbinic literature contains some discussions of exegetical topics that, while not entirely identical with that of animal languages, were closely linked to them by other authors. One such topic involves the significance of Genesis 2:20: "And Adam gave names to all cattle, and to the fowl of the air, and to every beast of the field."[82] Several interpreters discerned in this detail important insights respecting the relationship between humans

---

xix; Jacob Elbaum, "Yalqut Shim'oni and the Medieval Midrashic Anthology," in *The Anthology in Jewish Literature*, ed. David Stern (Oxford: Oxford University Press, 2004), 162..

An instructive example of this phenomenon is the legend about Solomon and the ant, which was included in a collection of "midrash" though the editor (A. Jellineck) acknowledged that it was a medieval tale probably based on an Arabic original. (Cf. Alwyn Faber Scholfield, ed., *Aelian: On the Characteristics of Animals*, The Loeb Classical Library (London: W. Heinemann, 1958), 6:50 (pp. 68-71); Stephen Thomas Newmyer, *Animals in Greek and Roman Thought: A Sourcebook*, Routledge source-books for the ancient World (London and New York: Routledge, 2011), 19.) Nevertheless Ginzberg included it in his collection (4:163-164) and it has come to be viewed as a midrashic text; see Adolph Jellinek, ed., "Ma'aseh ha-Nemalah [= Salomo und die Ameise]," *Bet Ha-Midrasch* 5 (1938): 22-26 xi-xiii [Hebrew]; Gustav Weil, *Biblische Legenden der Muselmänner / aus arabischen Quellen zusammengetragen und mit jüdischen Sagen* (Frankfurt am Main: Litararische Anstalt, 1845), 237–239; = *The Bible, the Koran, and the Talmud: Or, Biblical Legends of the Mussulmans, Compiled from Arabic Sources, and Compared with Jewish Traditions* (London: Longman, Brown, Green, and Longmans, 1846), 211–212; David Sidersky, *Les Origines des Légendes Musulmanes dans le Coran et dans les Vies des Prophètes* (Paris: P. Geuthner, 1933), 121–122; Malachi Beit-Arié, "Pereḳ Shirah: Mevo'ot u-Mahadurah Biḳortit" (PhD, The Hebrew University, 1966), 2:25-26 n. 9; Haim Schwarzbaum, *Studies in Jewish and World Folklore*, Fabula. Supplement Serie. Reihe B: Untersuchungen 3 (Berlin: de Gruyter, 1968), 251–252; Bernard H. Mehlman and Seth M. Limmer, "The Episode of the Ant," in *Medieval Midrash: The House for Inspired Innovation*, Brill Reference Library of Judaism 52 (Brill, 2016), 96–106.

82   My discussion of this subject derives largely from that of Elimelech Epstein-Halevi, Parashiyot Ba-Agadah Le-or Meḳorot Yevaniyyim (Haifa: Haifa University Press, 1973), 42–44. Elimelech Epstein-Halevi, *Parashiyot Ba-Agadah Le-or Meḳorot Yevaniyyim* (Haifa: Haifa University Press, 1973), 42–44.

and animals, as well as clues to the identity of the primal natural language.[83]

Genesis Rabbah 17:4[84] tells that when God decided to create the first man he consulted with the ministering angels, and he sought to persuade them that the new creature was wiser than they were. It was this point that he was trying to prove when he asked Adam to choose appropriate names for all the living creatures—and even for himself[85] and for the Lord.[86]

---

83   Gerhard von Rad, *Genesis: A Commentary*, trans. John H. Marks, The Old Testament Library (Philadelphia: Westminster Press, 1972), 82–83. The assigning of names was discussed in Plato's influential *Cratylus* and came to be associated in ancient Stoic thought with the invention of written language, among important stages in the evolution of civilization that require supreme wisdom, and hence serve as irrefutable proof that the human soul that is capable of such discoveries must be of divine origin and not from a material source. This argument is made by Cicero in his *Tusculan Disputations* 1:25:62 [J. E. King, trans., *Cicero Tusculan Disputations with an English Translation*, The Loeb Classical Library (London and Cambridge, MA: William Heinemann and Harvard University Press, 1966), 72–73.] See Henry A. Fischel, *Rabbinic Literature and Greco-Roman Philosophy. a Study of Epicurea and Rhetorica in Early Midrashic Writings*, Studia Post-Biblica 21 (Leiden: E. J. Brill, 1973), 61, 143–144, nn. 56, 64; Ginzberg, *Legends*, 5:83, nn. 29–30; 5:113, n. 104; R. M. van den Berg, *Proclus' Commentary on the Cratylus in Context: Ancient Theories of Language and Naming*, Philosophia Antiqua 112 (Leiden ; Boston: Brill, 2008), 53–54; Roy Harris and Talbot Taylor, "The Bible on the Origin and Diversification of Language," in *Landmarks In Linguistic Thought Volume I: The Western Tradition From Socrates To Saussure*, second edition., Routledge History of Linguistic Thought (London and New York: Routledge, 2005), 35–44; Harry Austryn Wolfson, "The Veracity of Scripture in Philo, Halevi, Maimonides, and Spinoza," in *Alexander Marx; Jubilee Volume on the Occasion of His Seventieth Birthday*, ed. Saul Lieberman, vol. English Section (New York: The Jewish Theological Seminary of America, 1950), 610–612. It is notable that most of the sources that Wolfson (613-614) adduces as "rabbinic" are in fact medieval compilations (of the sort that figure prominently in Ginzberg's Legends *of the Jews*). Some interesting observations and speculations regarding the attitudes of rustic Greek culture toward the assigning of names to animals (including beliefs that at least some primordial figures were capable of conversing with the creatures) may be found in Arthur Bernard Cook, "Descriptive Animal Names in Greece," *The Classical Review* 8, no. 9 (1894): 381–385; Deborah Levine Gera, *Ancient Greek Ideas on Speech, Language, and Civilization* (Oxford and New York: Oxford University Press, 2003), 7, 8, 28, 116–117, 176, 180.

Adam performed his task brilliantly, whereas that ability was entirely lacking in the angels.[87]

This biblical text and its respective interpretations would be adduced by several medieval exegetes and theologians in connection with their views about human and animal languages.

   Variations on this theme in the European literary and intellectual tradition were assembled by Umberto Eco, *The Search for the Perfect Language*, trans. James Fentress, Making of Europe (Oxford, UK and Cambridge, MA: Blackwell, 1995), 8, 40, 184, 3tc.

84   Julius Theodor and Chanoch Albeck, eds., *Midrash Bereshit Rabba* (Jerusalem, Israel: Wahrman, 1965), 155–156. See also *Pesiḳta Rabbati* 14:10 [William G Braude, trans., *Pesikta Rabbati; Discourses for Feasts, Fasts, and Special Sabbaths*, Yale Judaica Series (New Haven: Yale University Press, 1968), 1:280] where Adam's choosing names is cited as an answer to Ecclesiastes 8:1 "Who is as the wise?"

85   But compare Philo, *Legum Allegoria* 1:29 (91) [Loeb, 1:206-207]; cited by Epstein-Halevi.

86   As noted by Epstein-Halevi, Philo gives an almost identical reading of the verse, as a test and demonstration of Adam's aptitude for sensing the essential qualities of beings and expressing them in suitable names, in *De Opificio Mundi* 52 (149-150) [Loeb, 1:118-119]; David T. Runia, *Philo of Alexandria: On the Creation of the Cosmos According to Moses*, Philo of Alexandria Commentary Series 1 (Atlanta: Society of Biblical Literature, 2005), 86, 348–353. In *Questions and Answers on Genesis*, trans. Ralph Marcus, vol. Supplement I, Loeb Classical Library (London and Cambridge, MA: William Heinemann and Harvard University Press, 1953), 13] Philo explains that Adam also assigned names to all inanimate and animate things, but that the Bible only mentioned the most challenging (i.e., complex and changeable) of the species. According to *Avot deRabbi Nathan* B 8 [ed. Schechter, 12a; transl. Saldarini, 78 and nn.19, 20] he named general categories as well as particular species, and he also named angels.

87   Plato's *Cratylus* was devoted to the question of whether the names employed for various things are reflect their essential natures or are merely conventional. See Umberto Eco, Roberto Lambertini, and Costantino Marmo, "On Animal Language in the Medieval Classification of Signs," in *On the Medieval Theory of Signs*, ed. Umberto Eco and Costantino Marmo, Foundations of Semiotics 21 (Amsterdam and Philadelphia: John Benjamins, 1989), 12; Wolfson, "Veracity of Scripture," 609–621. Wolfson traces the various philosophic conceptions regarding the natural and con-

Concluding Observations

To the extent that the passages enumerated in the previous pages had any substantial bearing on the question of animal speech, most of them implied a negative position regarding the phenomenon. The Mishnah on oaths treated the prospect of talking cows as an example of an obvious absurdity. The *Genesis Rabbah* traditions that place humans at an intermediary point between angels and lowly beasts was asserting that speech is a feature that defines our elevated status and separates us decisively from the dumb inferior species.

As for the legend of the cows who burst out in mystic song, the whole point of that tale was to present it as an extraordinary, miraculous event that was made possible by the presence of the holy ark of the covenant. The legend's power would have been neutralized if it were presumed that song or speech are accessible to animals under routine circumstances.

The tale of the phoenix-like "avarshana" and its touching conversation with Noah does indeed present an example of a talking animal, but it is hard to decide how it impacts on the broader question. On the one hand, it was a rare mythical bird whose speaking ability would accordingly be comparable to its other wondrous features. On the other hand, the manner in which the story is related appears to assume that verbal communication between Noah and the animals in his charge (like those with the raven and dove) was a customary occurrence during their sojourn on the ark, and might reflect the belief that such communications were normal in primordial times.

With regard to the legends about the wise king Solomon and his alleged mastery of the language of the beasts—we observed that these were

---

ventional models of language and names through Greek philosophy, Philo, rabbinic texts and medieval Jewish, Christian and Islamic discussions. Lucretius (presumably conveying the theory of Epicurus) was perhaps the most prominent of those who insisted that names evolved naturally and diversely out of the need to point at and identify things; Titus Lucretius Carus, *De Rerum Natura*, trans. W. H. D. Rouse, Loeb Classical Library 181 (Cambridge, MA: Harvard University Press, 1992), 5:1028-1055 (pp.458–461); Tobias Reinhardt, "Epicurus and Lucretius on the Origins of Language," *The Classical Quarterly* 58, no. 1 (2008): 127–140; Gera, *Greek Ideas on Speech*, 37–39, 170–177.

not authentic parts of ancient rabbinic lore, but rather made their appearance in medieval pseudo-midrashic collections, likely under the influence of Arabic sources (although those might well have originated in undocumented Jewish traditions).

Conclusions

HUMANS NEED FANTASY TO BE HUMAN. TO BE
THE PLACE WHERE THE FALLING ANGEL MEETS
THE RISING APE.[1]

When compared with what we have encountered in non-rabbinic Jewish texts from the Second Commonwealth and rabbinic eras, the vast body of rabbinic literatures contains little that would suggest that the Jewish sages were devoting very much thought to the issue of animal languages, whether as a general phenomenon or in connection with specific texts.[2] Of

---

1 Terry Pratchett, *Hogfather: A Novel of Discworld*, The Discworld series (New York: HarperPrism, 1999), 408. Upper-case in the original (i.e., it is spoken by Death).

2 It is very instructive to observe how in V. Aptowitzer's very thorough listing of rabbinic texts that treat animals as morally accountable beings there are virtually no citations from classical rabbinic texts. Similarly, in a recent volume by a traditional rabbi who was determined to include an appendix on "Conversations of Birds," the appendix in question did not amount to more than one page which contains a handful of examples from talmudic, medieval and modern sources; see Naftali Jehiel Weinberger, *Sefer Shaleaḥ Teshallaḥ: 'al Mitsvat Shilluaḥ ha-Ḵen*, 5th ed. (Jerusalem, 2001), 126. Rabbi Ḥayyim Joseph David Azulai, *Midbar Kedemot*, ed. Abraham Joseph Wertheimer (Jerusalem: Ma'yan Hachochmah, 1957), 57–59. It is hard to decide whether there is any significance to the fact that "the conversation of the animals and fowl" is not included among the lengthy enumeration illustrating the erudition of Rabban Yoḥanan ben Zakkai in *b.Sukkah* 28a and *b.Bava Batera* 134a which do mention such exotic topics as "the speech of the ministering angels, the speech of spirits, and the speech of palm-trees, fullers' parables and fox fables"; Jacob Neusner, *Development of a Legend; Studies on the Traditions Concerning Yoḥanan Ben Zakkai*, Studia Post-Biblica 16 (Leiden: Brill, 1970), 90, 152; Anthony J Saldarini, "End of the Rabbinic Chain of Tradition," *Journal of Biblical Literature* 93, no. 1 (1974): 100-101 and n. 14; cf. Eliezer Segal, *A Time for Every Purpose*, Alberta Judaic Library (Quid Pro Books, 2015), 190–195. Different versions of the passage

course, the relatively limited number of literary genres in which rabbinic teachings were preserved—principally: halakhah, midrash and talmudic debate—do not lend themselves naturally to explicit philosophical, theological, scientific or historical discourse. In some cases we might be able to draw indirect inferences about the rabbis' opinions concerning animal language from the ways they formulate statements about human speech or other phenomena.[3]

By way of attempting to explain the scarcity of theoretical discussions about the animal speech, it seems worthwhile to mention the thesis that was argued cogently by Maren R. Niehoff[4] that the rabbinic texts contain a new type of mythopoesis in which supernatural qualities are ascribed to

are found in *Avot deRabbi Natan A* Ch. 14; *Avot deRabbi Natan B* Ch. 28 (and compare what it says in Ch. 12 there about Rabbi Akiva [Solomon Schechter, ed., *Aboth De-Rabbi Nathan* (Vienna: Ch. D. Lippe, 1887), 57, 58 (and 29); Judah Goldin, ed., *The Fathers According to Rabbi Nathan* (New York: Schocken Books, 1974), 74; Anthony J. Saldarini, ed., *The Fathers According to Rabbi Nathan (Abot De Rabbi Nathan) Version B: A Translation and Commentary*, Studies in Judaism in Late Antiquity v. 11 (Leiden: Brill, 1975), 166 and n. 5 (and 94–95)].

The strange legend about the conception of the Amora Samuel, as found in the *Halakhot Gedolot*, end of the section on *Giṭṭin*, begins with an attempted seduction of his father in the land of Israel with a Median woman who "understood the language of the birds" [דהוה ידעא בלישנא דציפרי], though that detail does not seem to be relevant to the story—other, perhaps, than as a way of identifying her as a witch [Venice editions folio 420b; J. Hildesheimer, ed., *Die Vaticanische Handschrift Der Halachoth Gedoloth* (Berlin: H. Itzkowski, 1886), 337–338; Ezriel Hildesheimer, ed., *Sefer Halakhot Gedolot* (Jerusalem: Mekitse Nirdamim, 1971), 2:184]. The *Tosafot* to *Ḳiddushin* 73a and Asheri bring it in the name of the Yerushalmi, but it is not found there. On the phenomenon of stories that are "missing" from the Talmud see Eliezer Segal, *Case Citation in the Babylonian Talmud: The Evidence of Tractate Neziqin*, Brown Judaic Studies 210 (Atlanta: Scholars Press, 1990), 155–156; Yaakov Sussman, "The Ashkenazi Yerushalmi MS: 'Sefer Yerushalmi,'" *Tarbiz* 65, no. 1 (1995): 39–41.

3   In her quest to situate a body of talmudic material within the frameworks of Western humanist tradition and critical animal studies, M. Wasserman similarly concludes that the Bavli "shows little interest in either protecting the boundary between humans and other animals or in protesting it. That is, the editors of the Bavli are not humanists, and they are not posthumanists" [*Jews, Gentiles, and Other Animals: The Talmud After the Humanities*, Divinations: Rereading Late Ancient Religion (Philadelphia: University of Pennsylvania Press, 2017), 94].

animals (especially to legendary creatures like the leviathan or phoenix, personified earth and waters, etc.) as a straightforward fact of contemporary experience, rather than (as is the case in the mythic allusions in the Bible) as relics of the cosmic dynamics of the distant past. I suspect that Niehoff is attaching too much weight to a small number of examples (particularly the phoenix passages),[5] but that in general the quantity of evidence is not sufficient to support her thesis. For the most part, those instances can be subsumed under other explanations, such as a general receptiveness to Greco-Roman popular culture, or even the rhetorical palette of an effective preacher.

It is possible that assumptions about a primordial universal language were widespread in the cultural landscape, without necessarily being attached to any formal philosophical or theoretical systems.[6] According to

---

4   Maren R. Niehoff, "The Phoenix in Rabbinic Literature," *Harvard Theological Review* 89, no. 3 (1996): 245–265. Her ideas owe much to the approaches of Michael Fishbane and Yehuda Liebes both of who were concerned to trace trajectories leading from the Hebrew Bible to the medieval Kabbalah; see her p. 248 n. 11.

5   The thesis might nevertheless be more applicable to medieval pseudo-midrashic collections like *Pirkei deRabbi Eliezer* that abound in mythic and mystical elements.

6   Perhaps it is possible to discern an allusion to this tradition in the wording of the parable attributed to Rabbi Akiva on *b.Berakhot* 61b to illustrate the futility of abandoning Torah during the Hadrianic persecutions. The fox (=paganism) invites the fish (=Jews) to emerge from the sea (=Torah) and join him on dry land "and I and you will dwell together in the way that my ancestors and your ancestors dwelled together"[ונדור אני ואתם כדרך שדרו אבותי ואבותיכם]. See David Stern, *Parables in Midrash: Narrative and Exegesis in Rabbinic Literature* (Cambridge, MA: Harvard University Press, 1991), 46; Aharon M. Singer, "The Rabbinic Fable," *Jerusalem Studies in Jewish Folklore* 4 (1983): 79–91; Haim Schwarzbaum, *The Mishle Shu'alim (Fox Fables) of Rabbi Berechiah Ha-Nakdan: A Study in Comparative Folklore and Fable Lore* (Kiron: Institute for Jewish and Arab Folklore Research, 1979), 25–47; "Talmudic-Midrashic Affinities of Some Aesopic Fables," in *Proceedings of the Fourth International Congress for Folk-Narrative Research*, ed. G. Megas (Athens, 1965), 466–483; Eli Yassif, "Jewish Folk Literature in Late Antiquity," in *The Cambridge History of Judaism*, ed. Steven Katz, vol. 4. The Late Roman-Rabbinic Period (Cambridge: Cambridge University Press, 2006), 739–741. Rabbi Samuel Edels (Maharsha) interprets the reference as an allusion to the dialogue between Caesar and Rabbi Tanḥum on *b.Sanhedrin* 39a in which Caesar invites the Jews to join in a single universal nation [תא ליהוו כולן לעמא חד]. The clause in question

the arguments of D. Gera, a prevalent stream of ancient Greek thought, traceable to Hesiod,[7] Homer, and Babrius, characterized their idyllic "age of Cronos (or, for the Romans: Saturn)" as a golden age in which a shared language united the gods, humans and animals:[8]

> When animals are able to communicate with men in the idyllic age of Kronos, apparently using the same language, this not only points to the harmony prevailing between the two groups, but also indicates that beasts and men are perceived as being essentially alike... Time and again, Greek thinkers stress man's unique possession of speech as a quality which distinguishes him from other creatures, so that when writers on the golden age bestow language upon animals they are assimilating these creatures to men.. (p. 58)

This view of a degeneration of the inter-species relationship since the Golden Age coexisted with an antithetical approach that regarded history as an evolution of increasing intellectual sophistication that progressed

---

is missing from the version of the story in both editions of the *Tanḥuma*: Ki Tavo (regular: #2; ed. Buber #4), as well as in Asheri's Torah commentary and Baḥya's *Kad Ha-Ḳemaḥ*.

7   Hesiod does not say this explicitly; Gera (60-61) infers it indirectly—and not quite convincingly; though the claim has since been widely presented as an actual description of Hesiod's position. Cf. Daniel Ullucci, "Before Animal Sacrifice, a Myth of Innocence," *Religion & Theology* 15 (2008): 363–366. Cf. the discussion of Hesiod's *Works and Days* elsewhere in this book.

8   Deborah Levine Gera, *Ancient Greek Ideas on Speech, Language, and Civilization* (Oxford and New York: Oxford University Press, 2003), especially Chapter 2; see also Robert M. Grant, *Early Christians and Animals* (London and New York: Routledge, 1999), 3; Liliane Bodson, "Attitudes Toward Animals in Greco-Roman Antiquity," *Societal Attitudes Toward Animals* 4, no. 4 (1983): 315; Stephen R. L. Clark, "Animals in Classical and Late Antique Philosophy," in *The Oxford Handbook of Animal Ethics*, ed. Tom Beauchamp and R. G. Frey, vol. 1, Oxford Handbooks (Oxford: Oxford University Press, 2011), 49; John Heath, *The Talking Greeks: Speech, Animals, and the Other in Homer, Aeschylus, and Plato* (Cambridge: Cambridge University Press, 2005), 13–14; Charles Taylor, *Human Agency and Language*, Philosophical Papers 1 (Cambridge UK and New York NY: Cambridge University Press, 1985), 74; Umberto Eco, *The Search for the Perfect Language*, trans. James Fentress, Making of Europe (Oxford, UK and Cambridge, MA: Blackwell, 1995); Tom Hawkins, "Eloquent Alogia: Animal Narrators in Ancient Greek Literature," *Humanites* 6, no. 37 (2017): 3; cf. Ian Stewart and Jack Cohen, *Darwin's Watch: The Science of Discworld III*, First Anchor Books Edition. (New York: Anchor Books, 2015), 164–165.

from a primitive state of beast-like inarticulacy.[9]

While the attitudes to human-animal communication in Jewish sources, including the Book of Jubilees, Josephus Flavius[10] and some rabbinic texts, can indeed be explained according to considerations emerging from the biblical narrative itself, it is not out of the question to propose that the Greek cultural environment might have influenced the evolution of the traditions about a primeval stage when all species could speak a common tongue. This would be consistent with the fact that among the small number of instances of talking birds and animals in the rabbinic corpus, a large proportion of them occurred in expansions of the early chapters of Genesis, even though the rest of the Hebrew Bible is not lacking in creatures who could have joined in the conversation.

The rabbinic and classical works that were cited so far were characterized for the most part by their cautious formulations when it came to ascribing actual verbal communication to the various animals who were expressing their distress or similar feelings. A very different attitude finds expression in the following passage from the "Acts of Philip," an apocryphal Christian work from the fourth century C.E. that records the adventures of a fellowship of apostles charged with bringing the good news to the world. The current passage describes how the company of human apostles, consisting of Philip, Bartholomew and Mariamne (perhaps referring to Mary Magdalene), had their first encounter with a leopard and kid who would join their company through their subsequent exploits.

Acta Philippi 8:17:[11]

Καὶ ὁ Φίλιππος· Εν τῳ ὀνόματι Ἰησοῦ Χριστοῦ, λάλει. Καὶ ὁ λεόπαρδος ἀναλαβὼν τελείαν ἀνθρωπινην φωνὴν ἤρξατο	Philip said: "In the name of Jesus Christ, speak!" And the leopard assumed a perfect human voice and began to speak: "Listen to

---

9   Gera, *Greek Ideas on Speech*, 18–19.

10 Gera (20 and n. 8) notes the similarity between the Jewish and Greek traditions, citing Milka Rubin, "The Language of Creation or the Primordial Language: A Case of Cultural Polemics in Antiquity," *Journal of Jewish Studies* 49, no. 2 (1998): 309.

11 Max Bonnet, ed., *Acta Philippi et Acta Thomae accedunt Acta Barnabae* (Leipzig: Herman Mendelssohn, 1903), 37–38.

Acta Philippi 8:17:

λέγειν· Ἄκουέ μου Φίλιππε νυμφαγωγὲ τοῦ θείου λόγου·

ἐγένετο ἐν τῇ πρώτῃ νυκτί, παρῆλθον διὰ τῆς ἀγέλης τῶν αἰγῶν τῶν ἐξ ἐναντίας τοῦ ὄρους τῆς δρακαίνης μητρὸς τῶν ὄφεων, καὶ ἥρπασα ἔριφον· ὡς δὲ εἰσῆλθον εἰς τὸν δρυμὸν φαγεῖν αὐτόν, μετὰ τὸ πλῆξαί με αὐτόν, ἔλαβεν φωνὴν ἀνθρωπίνην καὶ ἔκλαυσεν ὡς παιδίον μικρόν, λέγων μοι· Ὦ λεόπαρδεᾶρον ἀπὸ σοῦ τὴν ἀγρίαν καρδίαν καὶ τὸ θηριῶδες τῆς γνιώμης, καὶ περιποίησον αὐτῷ ἡμερότητα· ὅτι οἱ ἀπόστολοι τοῦ θείου μεγέθους παρέρχεσθαι μέλλουσι διὰ τῆς ἐρήμου ταύτης, τελέσαι τελείως τὴν ἐπαγγελίαν τῆς δόξης τοῦ μονογενοῦς υἱοῦ τοῦ θεοῦ. Ἐν τούτοις οὖν τοῖς λόγοις τοῦ ἐρίφου νουθετοῦντός με ἠπόρουν ἐν ἐαυτῷ, καὶ κατὰ μικρὸν ἠλλάγη μου ἡ καρδία, καὶ ἥ· ἀγριότης μου ἐστράφη εἰς ἡμερότητα, καὶ ἐφεισάμην τοῦ φαγεῖν αὐτόν...

me, Philip, you who conduct us to the divine word as one who leads the bride to the bridegroom.

It happened in the first part of the night that I passed by a herd of goats opposite the mountain of the she-dragon, the mother of the serpents, and I seized a kid. But when I entered into the woods to eat it, after I struck it, it took on a human voice and cried like a small child, saying to me: 'Leopard, put off your fierce heart and savage intent and put on tameness. For the apostles of the divine greatness are about to pass through this wilderness to fulfill perfectly the promise of the glory of the only-begotten Son of God.' While the kid was admonishing me with these words, I was at a loss with myself, and little by little my heart was changed, and my fierceness was turned into tameness and I refrained from eating it...[12]

---

12 François Bovon and Christopher R. Matthews, eds., *The Acts of Philip: A New Translation* (Waco, Tex: Baylor University Press, 2012), 79; see also François Bovon, "Canonical and Apocryphal Acts of Apostles," *Journal of Early Christian Studies* 11, no. 2 (2003): 186; Frédéric Amsler, "The Apostle Philip, the Viper, the Leopard and the Kid: The Masked Actors of a Religious Conflict in Hierapolis of Phrygia (Acts of Philip VIII-XV and Martyrdom)," *Society of Biblical Literature Seminar Papers* 35 (1996): 432–437; Ingvild Sælid Gilhus, *Animals, Gods and Humans: Changing Attitudes to Animals in Greek, Roman and Early Christian Ideas* (London: Routledge, 2006), 251–258.

To be sure, the animals' speaking abilities are depicted here not as a normal natural phenomenon that exists in the present world, but rather as a miracle that was divinely invoked as part of the heroes' mission. Nevertheless, it does seem to prefigure the author's remarkable visions of a redemption in Christ that will ultimately remove the differences between man and beast,[13] in fulfillment of Isaiah's assurance (11:6) that in the redeemed world "the wolf also shall dwell with the lamb, and the leopard shall lie down with the kid."[14] The response that the kid elicits from the leopard involves a total transformation of the cat's predatory character that has no parallel in the reactions of Rabbi Judah—or, for that matter, in the audiences in the Roman circuses, who might have been expected to become more humane or conscious-stricken in their subsequent treatment of dumb beasts, but were not impelled to do away entirely with meat-eating or with animal spectacles.

There is nothing in the rabbinic corpus to compare with these animated and loquacious beasts.[15] On reflection, this situation could be re-

---

13 See Christopher R. Matthews, "Articulate Animals: A Multivalent Motif in the Apocryphal Acts of the Apostles," in *The Apocryphal Acts of the Apostles: Harvard Divinity School Studies*, ed. François Bovon, Ann Graham Brock, and Christopher R. Matthews, Religions of the World (Cambridge, Mass: Harvard University Center for the Study of World Religions, 1999), 205–232; Judith Perkins, "Animal Voices," *Religion & Theology* 12, no. 3–4 (2005): 385–396; François Bovon, "The Child and the Beast: Fighting Violence in Ancient Christianity," *Harvard Theological Review* 92, no. 4 (1999): 369–392.

14 Verbal conversation—leading to Christian conversion—are also an ingredient in the apocryphal *Acts of Paul*; see Grant, *Early Christians and Animals*, 19–20. The author of the Acts of Philip also appears to expect the redemption to bring about full equality between the sexes; see François Bovon, "Women Priestesses in the Apocryphal Acts of Philip," in *Walk in the Ways of Wisdom: Essays in Honor of Elisabeth Schüssler Fiorenza*, ed. Shelly Matthews, Cynthia Briggs Kittredge, and Melanie Johnson-DeBaufre (Harrisburg, London and New York: Trinity Press International, 2003), 109–121; Ingvild Sælid Gilhus, *Animals, Gods and Humans: Changing Attitudes to Animals in Greek, Roman and Early Christian Ideas* (London: Routledge, 2006), 161–162, 262.

15 According to Eliezer Diamond, the harmony depicted in hagiographic tales between individual Jewish saints and animals is meant to express a similar idea of reverting to the primordial harmony between the species as it prevailed in the Golden Age of Eden. See his "Lions, Snakes and Asses: Palestinian Jewish Holy Men as Masters of

garded as logically inevitable. The Christian authors of the apocryphal versions of Acts were animated by the conviction that they lived in a redeemed world; and one of the ways in which the redemption could be understood was by a redefinition of the relationship between humans and other beings in the natural order. Whatever the status of beasts might have been between Genesis and the Gospels, this was subject to radical transformation and spiritualization in keeping with the new covenant that came into effect with Christ's advent.[16] Such a perspective would be particularly compelling if one subscribed to the belief that this transformation was in reality a restoration of an original state of universal harmony.

This option was not available to rabbinic Jews. True, the account in Genesis implied that Adam and Eve were created to be vegetarians and that that permission for humans to eat meat was only granted (apparently as a concession to their weakness) as part of the revised covenant following Noah's flood. Nevertheless, the biblical creation story mandated humans to "have dominion over the fish of the sea, and over the fowl of the air, and over every living thing that moveth upon the earth" (Genesis 1:28), establishing a clearly unequal boundary between the dominating and dominated species.[17] The laws of the Torah not only sanctioned and regulated the eating of meat, but actively commanded the slaughter of sheep, cattle and fowl as central components of the sacrificial cult.[18] It would appear morally inconsistent to inflict that kind of treatment on crea-

---

the Animal Kingdom," in *Jewish Culture and Society under the Christian Roman Empire*, Interdisciplinary Studies in Ancient Culture and Religion 3 (Leuven: Peeters, 2003), 251–283. Nonetheless he acknowledges (p. 279) that "whereas Christian holy men often speak to animals, Jewish holy men never do." He suggests reasons to account for this difference, none of which are quite convincing. I find it revealing that in the chapter that Malachi Beit Arié devoted to adducing thematic examples from rabbinic literature of non-human creatures praising God as in *Pereḳ Shirah*, he does not cite any cases from the relevant historical era (as distinct from medieval "midrashic" compilations) of animals uttering those praises in words. See "Pereḳ Shirah: Mevo'ot u-Mahadurah Biḳortit" (PhD, The Hebrew University, 1966), 1:46–54.

16 Gilhus, *Animals, Gods and Humans*, 266.

17 Ibid., 161–162, 262.

18 On Christian opposition to and redefinition of sacrifice see ibid., 147–160.

tures who were believed to possess the intellectual capacity that is the prerequisite for coherent speech.

It is not surprising that in this respect, as in others, Jews traveled in the same intellectual company as Stoic philosophers. Indeed, the remarkable affinity between rabbinic and Stoic positions about the unintelligence and non-spirituality of animals may be added to an extensive list of issues, values, theological doctrines and rhetorical modes regarding which the Jewish sages found themselves aligned with the school of Zeno.[19]

Seen in this way, the story of the Patriarch Rabbi Judah ha-Nasi and the calf sets a conceptual limit to the degree of respect that Jews are able to bestow on animals: while acknowledging that they are deserving of sympathy and humane consideration in recognition of their susceptibility to emotions or emotion-like behavior, the fundamental religious truth is

---

19 Scholarship has recognized this resemblance in a general way, as exemplified by the presence of an entry in the *Encyclopedia Judaica* [Henry Albert Fischel and Lawrence V. Berman, "Stoicism," ed. Michael Berenbaum and Fred Skolnik, *Encyclopaedia Judaica* (Detroit: Macmillan Reference USA, 2007)]. A long list of similarities (along with several reservations) was assembled by Louis H. Feldman, *Jew and Gentile in the Ancient World: Attitudes and Interactions from Alexander to Justinian* (Princeton: Princeton University Press, 1993), 32–33; see also David Flusser, *Judaism of the Second Temple Period*, trans. Azzan Yadin, vol. 2 (Grand Rapids and Jerusalem: William B. Eerdmans and Hebrew University Magnes Press, 2007), 222–230; Norbert Samuelson, "Integrating Science and Religion—A Jewish Perspective," in *Science, Religion and Society: An Encyclopedia of History, Culture, and Controversy*, ed. Arri Eisen and Gary Laderman (London and New York: Routledge, 2015), 20. The phenomenon is more readily discernible in non-rabbinic Jewish writers like Philo, Josephus and Apocryphal texts (see my notes to discussions of Philo and Josephus in previous chapters), whereas it is possible that the rabbis intentionally suppressed references to "Greek wisdom" from their compendia; see my discussion in "'The Few Contained the Many': Rabbinic Perspectives on the Miraculous and the Impossible," *Journal of Jewish Studies* 54, no. 2 (2003): 273–282. D. Boyarin has argued strongly that the positing of an intermediary heavenly power was widely held by ancient Jews, as reflected in the Aramaic Targums and elsewhere, but not in the standard works of Talmud and Midrash. He and others maintain, however, that the Jewish *memra* is not really identical to the Stoic Logos, and should be regarded as largely an internal development within Judaism. See his *Border Lines: The Partition of Judaeo-Christianity*, Divinations (Philadelphia: University of Pennsylvania Press, 2004), 112–115.

that the divinely created natural order determines that their lives must be subordinated to the nutritional and other needs of the human species.

For all their acumen in applying the intricacies of logic or logic-like reasoning to the analysis of legal issues, the rabbis—like most pre-modern people—were simultaneously practitioners of an "organic thinking"[20] that often expressed itself as the desire to fashion a reality that makes religious or moral sense, and therefore differs from the bleaker realities of the observable impersonal world. It is perhaps analogous to our stereotypical image of straitlaced mathematicians and computer programmers who also immerse themselves in fantasies about mythic dragons and heroic quests through Middle Earth. When we operate in this mode, wondering what a dog, cat, pigeon or snake would tell us if it were capable of verbalizing its feelings, it is but a natural psychological step for the imagination to compose an actual script of those thoughts.[21] This has always been a normal feature of human cultures, and there is nothing extraordinary about its appearance in ancient Jewish traditions. The upshot of the process is a tale about a talking animal. In contrast to the testimonies of Greco-Roman or Jewish Second Temple or post-Talmudic literatures, the use of talking animals in the Midrash and Talmuds was no more than a rhetorical trope employed to enhance the delivery of a message; and not a theological or historical phenomenon to be pondered in its own right.

Toward the beginning of the mystical tract *Pereḳ Shirah*[22] we read the following charming exchange between King David, the proud author of the biblical Psalms, and a lowly frog:

---

20 As per Isaak Heinemann, *Darkhe Ha-Agadah* (Jerusalem: Magnes Press, 1970), 1–20; Max Kadushin, *Organic Thinking: A Study in Rabbinic Thought* (New York: The Jewish Theological Seminary of America, 1938).

21 See Hawkins, "Eloquent Alogia," 2.

22 See Beit-Arié, "Perek Shira Dissertation," 2:11, 22–27; Yehuda Avida, "Hakkarat Ṭovah ve-Tashlum Gemul-Ṭov la-Meṭiv be-Sifrutenu ha-'Aṭiḳah," in *Shai l-Isha'yahu: Sefer Yovel LaR" Yesha'yahu Vulfsberg ben ha-Shishim,'* ed. Yosef Tirosh (Tel-Aviv: Ha-Merkaz le-Tarbut shel ha-Po'el ha-Mizraḥi, 1956), 114–137. Many of Beit Arié's references to Jewish and non-Jewish parallels and to various scholarly studies of the traditions were culled from Louis Ginzberg, *The Legends of the Jews*, trans. Henrietta Szold (Philadelphia, PA: The Jewish Publication Society of America, 1909), 4:101-102 ; 6:262-263 n. 84.

And even King David, when he proclaimed the book of Psalms, became boastful. He said: Is there any person in the world who has produced song comparable to mine!

He happened to encounter a frog. It said to him: King David, do not allow yourself to be so boastful. For I recite more song than you do; and for each and every song that I utter I append three thousand *mashal*s.

As it says (1 Kings 4:32): "And he spake three thousand *mashal*: and his songs were a thousand and five."[23]

It is at once ironic and appropriate that this dialogue between a prominent biblical personality and a non-human creature creates a link between sacred song and the *mashal*, that versatile Hebrew term that embraces parables and fables as well as proverbs, allegories and analogies.[24] When preachers take it upon themselves to adorn their teachings with effective literary garments with a view to rendering them attractive and accessible to a broader audience, it seems almost inevitable that a few talking birds, beasts or reptiles will join in the conversation.

---

23 The biblical text is actually describing the wisdom of Solomon. See *b.'Eruvin* 21b and other sources listed by Beit-Arié, "Perek Shira Dissertation," 2:26 n. 11.

24 Stern, *Parables in Midrash*, 9–16.

Bibliography

Primary Texts

Abramson, Shraga. *Masekhet 'Avodah Zarah*. New York: The Jewish Theological Seminary of America, 1957.

Adani, David ben Amram. *Midrash Ha-Gadol 'al Ḥamishah Ḥumshe Torah: Sefer Bemidbar*. Edited by Zvi Meir Rabinowitz. Jerusalem: Mossad Harav Kook, 1973.

Adler, William, and Paul Tuffin, trans. *The Chronography of George Synkellos: A Byzantine Chronicle of Universal History from the Creation*. New York and Oxford: Oxford University Press, 2002.

Aelian. *On the Characteristics of Animals*. Translated by Alwyn Faber Scholfield. The Loeb Classical Library 446. Cambridge MA: Harvard University Press, 1958.

Aristophanes. *Frogs. Assemblywomen. Wealth*. Translated by Jeffrey Henderson. Loeb Classical Library 180. Cambridge, MA: Harvard University Press, 1998.

Aristotle. *Posterior Analytics*. Edited by Hugh Tredennick. Loeb Classical Library 391. Cambridge MA and London: Harvard University Press and William Heinemann Ltd., 1966.

Armstrong, A. H., trans. *Plotinus*. 7 vols. Loeb Classical Library 441. Cambridge MA and London: Harvard University Press, 2001.

Arnim, Hans Friedrich August von. *Stoicorum Veterum Fragmenta*. Editio stereotypa editionis primae. Sammlung wissenschaftlicher Commentare. München: K.G. Saur, 2004.

Augustine. *The Catholic and Manichaean Ways of Life*. Translated by Donald A Gallagher and Idella J. Gallagher. The Fathers of the Church: A New Translation 56. Catholic University of America Press, 1966.

———. *The City of God*. Translated by George E. McCracken. Vol. 1. The Loeb Classical Library 411. Cambridge: Harvard University Press, 1957.

Bailey, D. R. Shackleton, ed. *Cicero: Letters to Friends*. 3 vols. Loeb Classical Library 205. Cambridge MA and London: Harvard University Press, 2001.

Barron, J. P., and P. E. Easterling. "Hesiod." In *The Cambridge History of Classical Literature*, edited by P. E. Easterling and Bernard Knox, 1. Greek Literature:92–105. Cambridge: Cambridge University Press, 1982.

Beagon, Mary. *The Elder Pliny on the Human Animal: Natural History, Book 7*. Clarendon Ancient History Series. Oxford and: New York: Clarendon Press and Oxford University Press, 2005.

Becker, Hans-Jürgen, ed. *Avot De-Rabbi Natan: Synoptische Edition Beider Versionen.* Texts and Studies in Ancient Judaism 116. Tubingen: Mohr Siebeck, 2006.

———, ed. *Geniza-Fragmente zu Avot de-Rabbi Natan.* Texte und Studien zum antiken Judentum 103. Tübingen: Mohr Siebeck, 2004.

Beit-Arié, Malachi. "Perek Shirah: Introductions and Critical Edition." Ph.D., The Hebrew University of Jerusalem, 1966.

———. "Perek Shirah: Mevo'ot u-Mahadurah Bikortit." PhD, The Hebrew University, 1966.

Bennett, Charles E. (Charles Edwin), trans. *Horace: The Odes and Epodes, with an English Translation.* Vol. 33. Loeb Classical Library. Cambridge MA: Harvard University Press, 1968.

Berechiah ben Natronai. *Fables of a Jewish Aesop.* Translated by Moses Hadas. A Nonpareil Book. Boston: David R. Godine, 2001.

Bonnet, Max, ed. *Acta Philippi et Acta Thomae accedunt Acta Barnabae.* Leipzig: Herman Mendelssohn, 1903.

Bovon, François. "Canonical and Apocryphal Acts of Apostles." *Journal of Early Christian Studies* 11, no. 2 (2003): 165–94.

Bovon, François, Bertrand Bouvier, and Frédéric Amsler, eds. *Acta Philippi.* Corpus Christianorum 11. Turnhout: Brepols, 1999.

Bovon, François, and Christopher R. Matthews, eds. *The Acts of Philip: A New Translation.* Waco, Tex: Baylor University Press, 2012.

Braude, William G, trans. *Pesikta Rabbati; Discourses for Feasts, Fasts, and Special Sabbaths.* Yale Judaica Series. New Haven: Yale University Press, 1968.

Braude, William G., and Israel J. Kapstein. *Pesikta De-Rab Kahana: R. Kahana's Compilation of Discourses for Sabbaths and Festal Days.* 2nd ed. Philadephia, Pa.: Jewish Publication Society, 2002.

———, eds. *Tanna Débé Eliyyahu = The Lore of the School of Elijah.* Philadelphia: Jewish Publication Society of America, 1981.

Brooke, Alan England, Norman McLean, and H. St J. Thackeray, eds. *The Old Testament in Greek According to the Text of Codex Vaticanus.* Cambridge: The University Press, 1906.

Buber, Salomon, ed. *Midrash Tanhuma Ha-Kadum Yeha-Yashan.* Vilna: Romm, 1885.

Bury, Robert Gregg, trans. *Plato: Timaeus, Critias, Cleitophon, Menexenus, Epistles.* Vol. 9. 12 vols. Loeb Classical Library 234. Cambridge MA: Harvard University Press, 1960.

Bury, Robert Gregg, ed. *Sextus Empiricus.* Vol. 1. 4 vols. The Loeb classical Library. London and Cambridge, MA: William Heinemann and Harvard University Press, 1961.

Cary, Earnest, ed. *Dio's Roman History.* Vol. 1. 9 vols. Loeb Classical Library. London and Cambridge, MA: William Heinemann and Harvard University Press, 1961.

Charles, R. H., ed. "The Book of Jubilees." In *The Apocrypha and Pseudepigrapha of the Old Testament,* 2: Pseudepigrapha:1–82. Oxford: Clarendon Press, 1913, 1913.

Charlesworth, James H., ed. "3 (Greek Apocalypse of) Baruch." In *The Old Testament Pseudepigrapha*, 1st ed., 650–80. Garden City, NY: Doubleday, 1983.

Cherniss, Harold, and William Helmbold, trans. "Whether Land or Sea Animals Are Cleverer. (De Sollertia Animalium)." In *Plutarch's Moralia in Sixteen Volumes*, 12:318–479. The Loeb Classical Library 406. Cambridge, MA and London: Harvard University Press and William Heinemann Ltd., 1962.

Clarke, G., trans. *Porphyry: On Abstinence from Killing Animals*. Ancient Commentaries on Aristotle. London, New Delhi, New York and Sydney: Bloomsbury, 2014.

Cohen, Menachem, ed. *Mikra'ot Gedolot "Haketer."* Vol. 1: Genesis Part 1. Ramat-Gan, Israel: Bar-Ilan University Press, 1997.

Colson, F. H., and G. H Whitaker, eds. *Philo*. 11 vols. Loeb Classical Library. London and Cambridge, MA: William Heinemann and Harvard University Press, 1949.

Conybeare, Frederick Cornwallis, trans. *Philostratus. Life of Apollonius of Tyana, Epistles of Apollonius and Treatise of Eusebius*. 2 vols. Loeb Classical Library. London and New York: William Heinemann and the MacMillan Co., 1912.

Diogenes Laertius. *Lives of Eminent Philosophers*. Edited by Robert Drew Hicks. The Loeb Classical Library. London, Cambridge, MA: W. Heinemann and Harvard University Press, 1931.

Epstein, J. N. *Der Gaonäische Kommentar Zur Ordnung Tohoroth: Eine Kritische Einleitung Zu Dem R. Hai Gaon Zugeschriebenen Kommentar*. Berlin: Mayer & Müller, 1915.

Euripides. *Trojan Women, Iphigenia Among the Taurians, Ion*. Translated by David Kovacs. Loeb Classical Library 10. Cambridge, MA: Harvard University Press, 1999.

Evelyn-White, Hugh G., ed. *Hesiod. The Homeric hymns. And Homerica*. The Loeb Classical Library 57. Cambridge MA and London: Harvard University Press and Heinemann, 1982.

Fairclough, H. Rushton, trans. *Virgil with an English Translation*. Revised ed., with New introduction. Loeb Classical Library 63–64. Cambridge MA: Harvard University Press, 1999.

Falconer, William Armistead, trans. *Cicero. De Senectute, De Amicitia, De Divinatione*. 28 vols. The Loeb Classical Library 154. London and Cambridge MA: W. Heinemann Ltd. and Harvard University Press, 1971.

Feldblum, Meyer S., ed. *Dikduke Sopherim Tractate Gittin*. New York: Horeb, Yeshiva University, 1966.

Feldman, Louis H., ed. *Flavius Josephus: Judean Antiquities 1-4*. Boston: Brill Academic, 2004.

Feldman, Louis H., trans. *Josephus in Nine Volumes*. Loeb Classical Library 433. London and Cambridge MA: William Heinemann and Harvard University Press, 1969.

Frazer, James George, ed. *Apollodorus: The Library*. 2 vols. LCL 121–122. London and New York: W. Heinemann and G. P. Putnam's Sons, 1921.

Frazer, James George, trans. *Ovid's Fasti*. The Loeb Classical Library 253. London and New York: W. Heinemann Ltd. and G.P. Putnam's Sons, 1996.

Friedlander, Gerald, ed. *Pirke de Rabbi Eliezer (The Chapters of Rabbi Eliezer the Great)*. 2d American ed. New York: Hermon Press, 1965.

Ginsburger, Moses, ed. *Targum Yonatan ben 'Uzi'el 'al ha-Torah*. Berlin: S. Calvary, 1903.

Goldin, Judah, ed. *The Fathers According to Rabbi Nathan*. New York: Schocken Books, 1974.

Goldschmidt, Lazarus, ed. *The Babylonian Talmud Seder Nazikin*. Makor, 1969.

Greenbaum, Aaron, ed. *The Biblical Commentary of Rav Samuel ben Hofni Gaon*. Jerusalem: Mossad Harav Kook, 1978.

Grossfeld, Bernard. *Targum Onkelos to Genesis: A Critical Analysis Together with an English Translation of the Text: (Based on a. Sperber's Edition)*. Edited by Moses Aberbach. New York and Denver: Ktav for Center for Judaic Studies, University of Denver, 1982.

———. *The Two Targums of Esther*. The Aramaic Bible, v. 18. Collegeville, Minn: Liturgical Press, 1991.

Grossfeld, Bernard, and Lawrence H. Schiffman. *Targum Neofiti 1: An Exegetical Commentary to Genesis: Including Full Rabbinic Parallels*. New York: Sepher-Hermon Press, 2000.

Hard, Robin, ed. *Apollodorus: The Library of Greek Mythology*. 1 edition. Oxford World's Classics. Oxford and New York: Oxford University Press, 2008.

Harkavy, Albert. *Zikhron Kamah Ge'onim*. Vol. 1:4. Zikkaron la-Rishonim ve-gam la-Aharonim. Berlin: Matzkowski, 1887.

Henderson, Jeffrey, ed. *Plato: Statesman, Philebus, Ion*. Translated by Harold North Fowler. Vol. 8. The Loeb Classical Library 164. London and New York: William Heinemann ; G.P. Putnam's Sons, 1917.

Herodotus, with an English Translation. Loeb Classical Library 117–120. London: W. Heinemann, 1921.

Hett, W. S., trans. "On Prophecy in Sleep." In *Aristotle: On the Soul. Parva Naturalia. On Breath*, 8:374–87. Loeb Classical Library 288. Cambridge MA and London: Harvard University Press, 2000.

Hildesheimer, Ezriel, ed. *Sefer Halakhot Gedolot*. 3 vols. Jerusalem: Mekitse Nirdamim, 1971.

Hildesheimer, J., ed. *Die Vaticanische Handschrift Der Halachoth Gedoloth*. Berlin: H. Itzkowski, 1886.

Hirshman, Marc G. *Midrash Ḳohelet Rabah 1-6: Critical Edition Based on Manuscripts and Geniza Fragments*. The Midrash Project of the Schechter Institute of Jewish Studies. Jerusalem: Schechter Institute of Jewish Studies, 2016.

Homer. *Iliad*. Edited by William F. Wyatt. Translated by A. T. Murray. 2nd ed. Loeb Classical Library 170–171. Cambridge, Mass: Harvard University Press, 1999.

Horovitz, S., ed. *Siphre d'be Rab; Fasciculus primus: Siphre ad Numeros adjecto Siphre zutta.* Corpus Tannaiticum, 3:3. Jerusalem: Wahrmann Books, 1966.

Horovitz, S., and I. A Rabin, eds. *Mechilta D'Rabbi Ismael cum variis lectionibus et adnotationibus.* Jerusalem: Wahrmann, 1970.

House, D. K. "The Life of Sextus Empiricus." *The Classical Quarterly* 30, no. 1 (1980): 227–38.

Hyman, Arthur B., Isaac N. Lerer, and Yitshak Shiloni, eds. *Yalḳuṭ Shim'oni le-Rabbenu Shim'on ha-Darshan: Sefer Shemot.* 2 vols. Jerusalem, Israel: Mossad Harav Kook, 1977.

———, eds. *Yalḳuṭ Shim'oni le-Rabbenu Shim'on ha-Darshan: Sefer Vayyiḳra.* 2 vols. Jerusalem, Israel: Mossad Harav Kook, 1984.

Hyman, Arthur B., and Yitshak Shiloni, eds. *Yalḳuṭ Shim'oni le-Rabbenu Shim'on ha-Darshan: Sefer Bemidbar.* 1 vols. Jerusalem: Mossad Harav Kook, 1986.

Ilan, Tal. *Massekhet Hullin: Text, Translation, and Commentary.* A Feminist Commentary on the Babylonian Talmud, V/3. Tübingen: Mohr Siebeck, 2017.

Jellinek, Adolph, ed. "Ma'aseh ha-Nemalah [= Salomo und die Ameise]." *Bet Ha-Midrasch* 5 (1938): 22-26 xi-xiii.

Jones, Horace Leonard, ed. *The Geography of Strabo.* Vol. 6. 8 vols. Loeb Classical Library. Cambridge MA and London: Harvard University Press and William Heinemann Ltd., 1960.

Josephus, Flavius. *Flavius Josephus, Translation and Commentary.* Edited by Louis H. Feldman. Vol. 3: Judean Antiquities I-IV. Leiden, Boston, Koln: Brill, 2000.

Judah ben Samuel. *Das Buch Der Frommen [Sepher Chassidim].* Edited by Jehuda Wistinetzki. Mekize Nirdamim. Frankfurt a. M.: M. A. Wahrmann, 1924.

Kafaḥ, Yosef, ed. *Iyov 'im Targum u-Feirush Rabbenu Sa'adiyah ben Yosef al-Fayumi.* Jerusalem: American Academy for Jewish Research, 1973.

———, ed. *Peirushei Rabbeinu Sa'adiah Ga'on 'al ha-Torah.* New revised. Jerusalem: Mossad Harav Kook, 1984.

Kahana, Menahem I. *Sifre on Numbers: An Annotated Edition.* Jerusalem: Press, 2011.

Kamelhar, Moshe, ed. *Peirushei Rabbi David Ḳimḥi 'al ha-Torah.* Jerusalem: Mossad Harav Kook, 1970.

Kasher, Menahem M. *Torah Shelemah (The Complete Torah).* 12 vols. Jerusalem, Israel: The Torah Shelemah Institute, 1992.

King, J. E., trans. *Cicero Tusculan Disputations with an English Translation.* The Loeb Classical Library. London and Cambridge, MA: William Heinemann and Harvard University Press, 1966.

Kohn, Thomas D. "The Tragedies of Ezekiel." *Greek, Roman, and Byzantine Studies* 43, no. 1 (2011): 5–12.

Lamb, Walter Rangeley Maitland, trans. *Plato.* Vol. 2. 12 vols. Loeb Classical Library 165. London and Cambridge MA: Harvard University Press, 1924.

Lamberton, Robert. *Hesiod.* Hermes Books. New Haven: Yale University Press, 1988.

Layton, Bentley, ed. *Nag Hammadi codex II, 2-7: together with XIII, 2*, Brit. Lib. Or. 4926(1), and P. OXY. 1, 654, 655: with contributions by many scholars.* Nag Hammadi Studies 20–21. Leiden ; New York: E.J. Brill, 1989.

———, ed. *The Gnostic Scriptures: A New Translation with Annotations and Introductions.* 1st British ed. London: SCM Press, 1987.

———. "The Hypostasis of the Archons (Conclusion)." *The Harvard Theological Review* 69, no. 1/2 (1976): 31–101.

———. "The Hypostasis of the Archons, or 'The Reality of the Rulers.'" *Harvard Theological Review* 67, no. 4 (1974): 351–425.

Lieberman, Saul. *Midrash Debarim Rabbah.* Jerusalem: Wahrmann Books, 1974.

———, ed. *The Tosefta.* New York: The Jewish Theological Seminary of America, 1995.

Liss, Abraham, ed. *The Babylonian Talmud with Variant Readings: Tractate Sotah (1).* Jerusalem: Yad Harav Herzog—Rabbi Herzog World Academy Institute for the Complete Israeli Talmud, 1977.

Lloyd-Jones, Hugh. *Sophocles: Ajax. Electra. Oedipus Tyrannus.* Vol. 1. 3 vols. The Loeb Classical Library 20. Cambridge, MA: Harvard University Press, 1994.

Lucretius Carus, Titus. *De Rerum Natura.* Translated by W. H. D. Rouse. Loeb Classical Library 181. Cambridge, MA: Harvard University Press, 1992.

Macleane, A. J., Reginald Heber Chase, and Charles Beck. *The Works of Horace, with English Notes.* Boston and Cambridge: Sever, Francis, & Co, 1869.

Maher, Michael, ed. *Targum Pseudo-Jonathan, Genesis.* The Aramaic Bible 1B. Collegeville, MN: Liturgical Press, 1992.

Mandelbaum, Bernard, ed. *Pesikta de Rav Kahana.* 2 vols. New York: Jewish Theological Seminary of America, 1962.

Marchant, E. C. *Xenophon: Scripta Minora.* The Loeb Classical Library. London and New York: W. Heinemann and G.P. Putnam's Sons, 1918.

Marchant, E. C., and O. J. Todd, trans. *Xenophon: Memorabilia, Oeconomicus, Symposium, Apology.* Revised. Xenophon 168. Cambridge, MA and London: Harvard University Press, 2013.

Margulies, Mordecai, ed. *Midrash Vayyikra Rabbah.* New York and Jerusalem: The Jewish Theological Seminary of America, 1993.

Midrash Ha-Gadol 'al Ḥamishah Ḥumshe Torah: Sefer Bereshit. Jerusalem: Mossad Harav Kook, 1975.

Mirsky, Aaron. *Yosse ben Yosse: Poems. Edited with an Introduction, Commentary and Notes.* Jerusalem, 1977.

Most, Glenn W. *Hesiod.* Loeb Classical Library 57, 503. Cambridge, MA: Harvard University Press, 2006.

Neusner, Jacob, ed. *Ketubot.* Chicago Studies in the History of Judaism 22. Chicago: University of Chicago Press, 1985.

Norlin, George, trans. *Isocrates.* 3 vols. The Loeb Classical Library. London and New York: W. Heinemann ltd. and G. P. Putnam's sons, 1928.

Nussbaum, Martha Craven. *Aristotle's De Motu Animalium: Text with Translation, Commentary, and Interpretive Essays.* Princeton: Princeton University Press, 1978.

Oldfather, Charles Henry, trans. *Diodorus of Sicily.* Loeb Classical Library 303. Cambridge, Mass: Harvard University Press, 1933.

Pagels, Elaine H. *The Gnostic Gospels.* 1st Vintage Books ed. New York: Vintage Books, 1981.

Peck, A. L., trans. *Aristotle : History of Animals, Books IV-VI.* Loeb Classical Library. London; Cambridge (Mass.): Harvard University Press, 1993.

Perrin, Bernadotte, ed. *Plutarch's Lives.* Vol. 1. 11 vols. The Loeb Classical Library [Greek Authors]. London and New York: W. Heinemann and Macmillan, 1914.

Perry, B. E., ed. *Aesopica: A Series of Texts Relating to Aesop or Ascribed to Him or Closely Connected with the Literary Tradition That Bears His Name.* New edition. Urbana: University of Illinois Press, 2007.

———. *Babrius and Phaedrus.* The Loeb Classical Library 436. Cambridge, MA and London, UK: Harvard University Press and W. Heineman, 1984.

Philo. *Questions and Answers on Genesis.* Translated by Ralph Marcus. Vol. Supplement I. 2 vols. Loeb Classical Library. London and Cambridge, MA: William Heinemann and Harvard University Press, 1953.

Plato. *Euthyphro. Apology. Crito. Phaedo. Phaedrus.* Translated by Harold North Fowler. Loeb Classical Library 36. Harvard University Press, 1914.

———. *Plato's Theaetetus.* Translated by Francis MacDonald Cornford. New York: Prentice Hall, 1985.

Pliny the Elder. *Natural History.* Edited by H. (Harris) Rackham. Loeb Classical Library. Cambridge, MA: William Heinemann and Harvard University Press, 1972.

Pratchett, Terry. *Carpe Jugulum: A Novel of Discworld.* 1st U.S. ed. New York: HarperPrism, 1999.

———. *Eric.* London: V. Gollancz, 1990.

———. *Hogfather: A Novel of Discworld.* The Discworld Series. New York: HarperPrism, 1999.

———. *Lords and Ladies: A Novel of Discworld.* Discworld Series. New York: HarperPrism, 1994.

———. *Moving Pictures.* London: V. Gollancz, 1990.

———. *Small Gods: A Novel of Discworld.* 1st U.S. ed. New York: HarperCollins, 1992.

———. *Soul Music: A Novel of Discworld.* New York: HarperPrism, 1995.

———. *Thud!: A Novel of Discworld.* 1st ed. New York: HarperCollins, 2005.

———. *Where's My Cow?* 1st U.S. ed. New York: HarperCollins, 2005.

Pseudo-Philo. *The Biblical Antiquities of Philo.* Translated by M. R. James. Translations of Early Documents. Series I: Palestinian Jewish Texts (Pre-Rabbinic). New York: Ktav Pub. House, 1971.

Rackham, H., ed. *Politics.* Loeb Classical Library 264. Cambridge MA and London: William Heinemann and Harvard University Press, 1940.

Roberts, Alexander, and James Donaldson, eds. *The Works of Lactantius.* Translated by William Fletcher. Vol. 2. Ante-Nicene Christian Library 22. Edinburgh: T. & T. Clark, 1871.

Roberts, Alexander, James Donaldson, A. Cleveland Coxe, Allan Menzies, Ernest Cushing Richardson, and Bernhard Pick, eds. *The Ante-Nicene Fathers. Translations of the Writings of the Fathers down to a. D. 325.* New York: C. Scribner's sons, 1899.

Robinson, James M., and Richard Smith, eds. *The Nag Hammadi Library in English.* 4th rev. ed. Coptic Gnostic Library Project. Leiden and New York: E.J. Brill, 1996.

Rolfe, John Carew, trans. *Ammianus Marcellinus History.* Loeb Classical Library. Cambridge, Mass., London, 1935.

Rolfe, John Carew, trans. *Suetonius.* Loeb Classical Library 38. Cambridge, Mass: Harvard University Press, 1997.

Rosenthal, David. *Babylonian Talmud Codex Florence: Florence National Library II 1 7-9.* 4 vols. Jerusalem: Makor Publishing Ltd., 1972.

Rosenthal, E. S, ed. *Yerushalmi Neziqin.* Jerusalem: Publications of the Israel Academy of Sciences and Humanities. Seciton of Humanities, 1983.

Runia, David T. *Philo of Alexandria: On the Creation of the Cosmos According to Moses.* Philo of Alexandria Commentary Series 1. Atlanta: Society of Biblical Literature, 2005.

Saldarini, Anthony J., ed. *The Fathers According to Rabbi Nathan (Abot De Rabbi Nathan) Version B: A Translation and Commentary.* Studies in Judaism in Late Antiquity, v. 11. Leiden: Brill, 1975.

Schäfer, Peter, and Gottfried Reeg, eds. *Synopse zum Talmud Yerushalmi.* Texte und Studien zum Antiken Judentum 67. Tübingen: J.C.B. Mohr (Paul Siebeck), 1992.

Schechter, Solomon, ed. *Aboth De-Rabbi Nathan.* Vienna: Ch. D. Lippe, 1887.

Schodde, George H., trans. *The Book of Jubilees.* Oberlin, OH: E. J. Goodrich, 1888.

Scholfield, Alwyn Faber, ed. *Aelian: On the Characteristics of Animals.* 3 vols. The Loeb Classical Library. London: W. Heinemann, 1958.

Sherry, A. P., ed. *Midrash Bereshit Rabba Codex Vatican 60 (Ms. Vat. Ebr. 60).* Jerusalem, Israel: Makor, 1972.

Shinan, Avigdor, ed. *Midrash Shemot Rabbah, Chapters I-XIV.* Jerusalem: Dvir, 1984.

Smith, Richard, ed. *The Nag Hammadi Library in English.* 4th rev. ed. Leiden and New York: E.J. Brill, 1996.

Sokoloff, Michael, ed. *Midrash Bereshit Rabba-Ms. Vat. Ebr. 30.* Jerusalem: Makor, 1982.

———, ed. *The Geniza Fragments of Bereshit Rabba.* Publications of the Israel Academy of Sciences and Humanities: Section of Humanities. Jerusalem: The Israel Academy of Sciences and Humanities, 1982.

———. "The Hebrew of 'Bĕrēšit Rabba' According to Ms. Vat. Ebr. 30." *Lěšonénu: A Journal for the Study of the Hebrew Language and Cognate Subjects* 33, no. 1 (1968): 25–42.

Sperber, Alexander, ed. *The Bible in Aramaic: Based on Old Manuscripts and Printed Texts*. 3rd ed. Leiden and Boston: Brill, 2013.

Stern, Menahem. *Greek and Latin Authors on Jews and Judaism*. Fontes Ad Res Judaicas Spectantes. Jerusalem: Israel Academy of Sciences and Humanities, 1974.

Stone, Michael E., and Esther Eshel. "4QExposition on the Patriarchs." In *Qumran Cave 4*, edited by Magen Broshi, 14: Parabiblical Texts:215–30. Discoveries in the Judean Desert 19. Oxford: Clarendon Press, 1995.

Strickman, H. Norman, and Arthur M Silver. *Ibn Ezra's Commentary on the Pentateuch*. New York, N.Y: Menorah, 1988.

Tabarī. *General Introduction, and, From the Creation to the Flood*. Translated by Franz Rosenthal. The History of Al-Ṭabarī 1. Albany: State University of New York Press, 1988.

Taubes, Zwi. *Otsar ha-Ge'onim le-Masekhet Sanhedrin*. Jerusalem: Mosad Harav Kook, 1966.

Taylor, Charles, ed. *Sayings of the Jewish Fathers. Sefer Dibre Aboth Ha-Olam. Comprising Pirque Aboth in Hebrew and English with Critical Notes and Excursuses*. 2d ed. Amsterdam: Philo Press, 1970.

Taylor, Thomas, trans. *Porphyry: Selected Works*. Great Works of Philosophy Series 6. Lawrence, KN: Selene Books, 1988.

Terian, Abraham, ed. *Philonis Alexandrini De Animalibus*. Studies in Hellenistic Judaism, no. 1. Chico, Calif: Scholars Press, 1981.

Thackeray, H. St. John. *Josephus: With an English Translation*. Vol. 4. 9 vols. Loeb Classical Library. London and New York: William Heinemann Ltd. and G. P. Putnam's Sons, 1926.

Theodor, Julius, and Chanoch Albeck, eds. *Midrash Bereshit Rabba*. Jerusalem, Israel: Wahrman, 1965.

Tobiah ben Eliezer. *Midrash Lekaḥ Ṭov*. Edited by Salomon Buber. Jerusalem, 1959.

Trigg, Joseph Wilson. *Origen*. The Early Church Fathers. London and New York: Routledge, 1998.

Varro, Marcus Terentius. *On the Latin Language*. Translated by Roland G. Kent. 2 vols. Loeb Classical Library. Cambridge, MA and London: Harvard University Press and W. Heinemann, 1938.

Ward, Benedicta, ed. *The Desert Christian: Sayings of the Desert Fathers: The Alphabetical Collection*. 1st American ed. New York: Macmillan, 1980.

Wardle, D. *Cicero on Divination: De Divinatione, Book 1*. Clarendon Ancient History Series. Oxford and New York: Clarendon Press and Oxford University Press, 2006.

Weiser, Asher, ed. *Perushe Ha-Torah Le-Rabbenu Avraham Ibn Ezra*. 3 vols. Jerusalem: Mosad Harav Kook, 1976.

Weisz, Max. *Geniza Fragmente der Bibliothek David Kaufmann S. A. im Besitze der ungarischen Akademie der Wissenschaften*. Budapest: Katz Katzburg, 1922.

Werman, Cana. *The Book of Jubilees: Introduction, Translation, and Interpretation.* Between Bible and Mishnah: The David and Jemima Jeselsohn Library. Jerusalem: Yad Izhak Ben-Zvi, 2015.

Wernerian Club, ed. *Pliny's Natural History in Thirty-Seven Books / a Translation ... with Critical and Explanatory Notes.* Translated by Philemon Holland. London: Barclay, 1847.

Wertheimer, Solomon Aaron. *Ḳohelet Shelomoh.* Jerusalem: A. M. Luntz, 1899.

West, David. *Odes III: Dulce Periculum.* Oxford and New York: Oxford University Press, 2002.

Whiston, William, trans. *The Complete Works of Josephus Flavius.* Nashville: T. Nelson Publishers, 1998.

Zucker, Moshe, ed. *A Critique against the Writings of R. Saadya Gaon by R. Mubashshir Halevi.* New York: Feldheim, 1955.

———, ed. *Saadya's Commentary on Genesis.* New York: The Jewish Theological Seminary of America, 1984.

Zuckermandel, Moses Samuel, ed. *Tosefta: Based on the Erfurt and Vienna Codices.* Jerusalem, Israel: Wahrmann Books, 1963.

Secondary Works

Abelson, Joshua. *The Immanence of God in Rabbinical Literature.* New York: Hermon Press, 1969.

Abramson, Shraga. *Masekhet 'Avodah Zarah.* New York: The Jewish Theological Seminary of America, 1957.

Achard, Martin. "Philosophie Antique. Logos Endiathetos et Théorie Des Lekta Chez Les Stoïciens." *Laval Théologique et Philosophique* 57, no. 2 (2001): 225–33.

Acosta-Hughes, Benjamin. *Polyeideia: The Iambi of Callimachus and the Archaic Iambic Tradition.* Hellenistic Culture and Society 35. Berkeley: University of California Press, 2002.

Adelman, Rachel. "Jonah Through the Looking Glass: Pirqe De-Rabbi Eliezer's Portrait of an Apocalyptic Prophet." *ARC* 39 (2011): 79–92.

———. "The Return of the Repressed: Pirqe De-Rabbi Eliezer and the Pseudepigrapha." Supplements to the Journal for the Study of Judaism ; v. 140. Leiden: Brill, 2009.

Albeck, Ch. *Introduction to the Talmud. Babli and Yerushalmi.* Tel-Aviv: Dvir, 1969.

———. *Mavo U-Maftehot le-Midrash Bereshit Rabba.* Second edition. Vol. 1. Veröffentlichungen der Akademie für die Wissenschaft des Judentum. Jerusalem: Shalem Books, 1996.

Alexander, Caroline. *The War That Killed Achilles: The True Story of the Iliad.* London: Faber & Faber, 2010.

Alexandre Júnior, Manuel. *Rhetorical Argumentation in Philo of Alexandria.* Brown Judaic Studies Studia Philonica Monographs, 322. 2. Atlanta: Scholars Press, 1999.

Allan, George. *The Patterns of the Present: Interpreting the Authority of Form*. Albany: SUNY Press, 2001.

Alon, Gedalia. *The Jews in Their Land in the Talmudic Age, 70-640 C.E.* Translated by Gershon Levi. Jerusalem: Magnes Press, 1980.

Alter, Robert. *The Art of Biblical Narrative*. Rev. & Updated ed. New York: Basic Books, 2011.

Altmann, Alexander. "The Gnostic Background of the Rabbinic Adam Legends." In *Essays in Jewish Intellectual History*, 1–16. Hanover, NH: University Press of New England for Brandeis University Press, 1981.

Amir, Yehoshua. "The Transference of Greek Allegories to Biblical Motifs in Philo." In *Nourished with Peace: Studies in Hellenistic Judaism in Memory of Samuel Sandmel*, edited by Edward Greenspahn, Earl Hilgert, and Burton Lee Mack, 15–25. Chico, CA: Scholars Press, 1984.

Amsler, Frédéric. "The Apostle Philip, the Viper, the Leopard and the Kid: The Masked Actors of a Religious Conflict in Hierapolis of Phrygia (Acts of Philip VIII-XV and Martyrdom)." *Society of Biblical Literature Seminar Papers* 35 (1996): 432–37.

Anderson, William S. "Two Passages from Book Twelve of the 'Aeneid.'" *California Studies in Classical Antiquity* 4 (1971): 49–65.

Aptowitzer, Viktor. "The Rewarding and Punishing of Animals and Inanimate Objects: On the Aggadic View of the World." *Hebrew Union College Annual* 3 (1926): 117–55.

Armayor, O. Kimball. "Did Herodotus Ever Go to Egypt." *Journal of the American Research Center in Egypt* 15 (1978): 59–73.

Arnim, Hans von. "Chrysippos 14." In *Paulys Realencyclopädie der classischen Altertumswissenschaft*, edited by August Friedrich Pauly and Georg Wissowa, 3:2:2502–9. Stuttgart: Metzler, 1931.

Assaf, Simha. *Tekufat Ha-Ge'onim Ve-Sifrutah*. Jerusalem: Mossad Harav Kook, 1955.

Avida, Yehuda. "Hakkarat Ṭovah ve-Tashlum Gemul-Ṭov la-Meṭiv be-Sifrutenu ha-'Atiḳah." In *Shai l-Isha'yahu: Sefer Yovel LaR" Yesha'yahu Vulfsberg ben ha-Shishim,'* edited by Yosef Tirosh, 114–37. Tel-Aviv: Ha-Merkaz le-Tarbut shel ha-Po'el ha-Mizraḥi, 1956.

Ax, Wolfram. "Ψόφος, Φωνή Und Διάλεκτος Als Grundbegriffe Aristotelischer Sprachreflexion." *Glotta* 56, no. 3/4 (1978): 245–71.

Azulai, Ḥayyim Joseph David. *Midbar Kedemot*. Edited by Abraham Joseph Wertheimer. Jerusalem: Ma'yan Hachochmah, 1957.

Bacher, Wilhelm. *Agadat Amora'e Erets-Yiśra'el*. Translated by Alexander Siskind Rabinovitz. Tel-Aviv: Dvir, 1928.

———. *Agadot Ha-Tanna'im*. Translated by Alexander Siskind Rabinovitz. Jerusalem, Israel: Dvir, 1922.

———. *Die Agada der babylonischen Amoräer: Ein Beitrag zur Geschichte der Agada und zur Einleitung in den babylonischen Talmud*. Frankfurt a. M., 1913.

———. *Die Agada der palästinensischen Amoräer*. 3 vols. Strassburg i. E: K. J. Trübner, 1892.

———. *Die Agada der Tannaiten*. Strassburg: K.J. Truebner, 1890.

Baer, Fritz Isaac. "On the Problem of Eschatological Doctrine during the Period of the Second Temple." *Zion* 23–24, no. 1–2 (1959 1958): 3–34.

———. "The Religious-Social Tendency of 'Sefer Hassidim.'" *Zion* 3, no. 2 (n.d.): 1–50.

———. "Theory of Natural Equality of Early Man according to Ashkenazi Hasidism." *Zion* 32, no. 1 (1967): 117–52.

Bakhos, Carol. "Abraham Visits Ishmael: A Revisit." *Journal for the Study of Judaism in the Persian, Hellenistic and Roman Period* 38, no. 4 (2007): 553–80.

Bar-Ilan, Meir. "Witches in the Bible and Talmud." In *Approaches to Ancient Judaism: Historical, Literary and Religious Studies*, edited by Herbert W Basser and Simcha Fishbane, New Series 5:7–32. South Florida Studies in the History of Judaism 82. Atlanta: Scholars Press, 1993.

Barnes, Timothy David. *Ammianus Marcellinus and the Representation of Historical Reality*. Ithaca and London: Cornell University Press, 1998.

Baron, Salo Wittmayer. *A Social and Religious History of the Jews*. 2d ed., revised and enlarged. Vol. Vol. 2: Christian Era. The First Five Centuries. New York: Columbia University Press, 1952.

———. *A Social and Religious History of the Jews*. 2nd Revised edition. Vol. Vol. 6: Laws, Homilies, and the Bible: High Middle Ages. New York: Columbia University Press, 1958.

———. *A Social and Religious History of the Jews*. 2nd Revised edition. Vol. Vol. 8: Philosophy and Science: High Middle Ages. New York: Columbia University Press, 1958.

Barron, J. P., and P. E. Easterling. "Hesiod." In *The Cambridge History of Classical Literature*, edited by P. E. Easterling and Bernard Knox, 1. Greek Literature:92–105. Cambridge: Cambridge University Press, 1982.

Barth, Lewis M. *An Analysis of Vatican 30*. Monographs of the Hebrew Union College 1. Cincinnati: Hebrew Union College-Jewish Institute of Religion, 1973.

———. "Lection for the Second Day of Rosh Hashanah: A Homily Containing the Legend of the Ten Trials of Abraham." *Hebrew Union College Annual* 58 (1987).

Basser, H. W. "Josephus as Exegete." *Journal of the American Oriental Society* 107, no. 1 (1987): 21–30.

Baumgarten, Albert I. "Rabbi Judah I and His Opponents." *Journal for the Study of Judaism in the Persian, Hellenistic and Roman Period* 12, no. 2 (December 1981): 135–72.

Beagon, Mary. *The Elder Pliny on the Human Animal: Natural History, Book 7*. Clarendon Ancient History Series. Oxford and: New York: Clarendon Press and Oxford University Press, 2005.

Beard, Mary. "Cicero and Divination: The Formation of a Latin Discourse." *The Journal of Roman Studies* 76 (1986): 33–46.

Becker, Hans-Jürgen. *Die Grossen Rabbinischen Sammelwerke Palästinas: Zur Literarischen Genese von Talmud Yerushalmi Und Midrash Bereshit Rabba*. Texte Und Studien Zum Antiken Judentum 70. Tübingen: Mohr Siebeck, 1999.

Beit-Arié, Malachi, Jeremy Schonfield, and Emile G. L. Schrijver. *Perek Shirah: An Eighteenth-Century Illuminated Hebrew Book of Praise: Companion Volume to the Facsimile Edition*. London: Facsimile Editions Limited, 1996.

Belkin, Samuel. *The Midrash of Philo*. Edited by Elazar Hurvitz. New York: Yeshiva University Press, 1989.

Ben Zvi, Ehud. "A Contribution to the Intellectual History of Yehud: The Story of Micaiah and Its Function Within the Discourse of Persian-Period Literati." In *Historian and the Bible: Essays in Honour of Lester L. Grabbe*, edited by Philip R. Davies and Diana Vikander Edelman, 89–102. Library of Biblical Studies. New York: T & T Clark, 2010.

Benoit, William. "Isocrates and Aristotle on Rhetoric." *Rhetoric Society Quarterly* 20, no. 3 (1990): 251–59.

———. "Isocrates and Plato on Rhetoric and Rhetorical Education." *Rhetoric Society Quarterly* 21, no. 1 (1991): 60–71.

Ben-Yehuda, Eliezer. *A Complete Dictionary of Ancient and Modern Hebrew*. Vol. 2. 8 vols. New York: T. Yoseloff, 1960.

Berg, R. M. van den. *Proclus' Commentary on the Cratylus in Context: Ancient Theories of Language and Naming*. Philosophia Antiqua 112. Leiden ; Boston: Brill, 2008.

Berger, David. "Judaism and General Culture in Medieval and Early Modern Times." In *Judaism's Encounter with Other Cultures: Rejection or Integration?*, edited by Gerald J. Blidstein and Jacob J. Schacter, 57–142. Northvale, NJ: Jason Aronson, 1997.

Berlin, Netta. "War and Remembrance: 'Aeneid' 12.554-60 and Aeneas' Memory of Troy." *The American Journal of Philology* 119, no. 1 (1998): 11–41.

Berns, Laurence. "Rational Animal-Political Animal: Nature and Convention in Human Speech and Politics." *The Review of Politics* 38, no. 2 (1976): 177–89.

Bigg, Charles. *A Critical and Exegetical Commentary on the Epistles of St. Peter and St. Jude*. International Critical Commentary. Edinburgh: T. & T. Clark, 1987.

Bigwood, J. M. "Aristotle and the Elephant Again." *American Journal of Philology* 114, no. 4 (2013): 537–55.

———. "Ctesias' Parrot." *The Classical Quarterly* 43, no. 1 (1993): 321–27.

Blau, Ludwig. *Das altjüdische Zauberwesen*. Cambridge Library Collection - Spiritualism and Esoteric Knowledge. Cambridge: Cambridge University Press, 2011.

Blenkinsopp, Joseph. *Creation, Un-Creation, Re-Creation: A Discursive Commentary on Genesis 1-11*. London and New York: T & T Clark, 2011.

Blumenthal, David R. "Lovejoy's Great Chain of Being and the Medieval Jewish Tradition." In *Jacob's Ladder and the Tree of Life: Concepts of Hierarchy and the Great Chain of Being*, edited by Marion Leathers Kuntz and Paul Grimley Kuntz,

179–90. American University Studies, Series 5, Philosophy 14. New York: Peter Lang, 1987.

Bockmuehl, Markus N. A., Guy G. Stroumsa, and Yonatan Moss, eds. "The Language of Paradise: Hebrew or Syriac? Linguistic Speculations and Linguistic Realities in Late Antiquity." In *Paradise in Antiquity: Jewish and Christian Views*, 120–37. Cambridge and New York: Cambridge University Press, 2010.

Bodson, Liliane. "Attitudes toward Animals in Greco-Roman Antiquity." *International Journal for the Study of Animal Problems* 4, no. 4 (1983): 312–20.

Bohak, Gideon. *Ancient Jewish Magic: A History.* 1st pbk. ed. Cambridge, UK and New York: Cambridge University Press, 2011.

Bonfil, Robert. *History and Folklore in a Medieval Jewish Chronicle: The Family Chronicle of Aḥima'az Ben Paltiel.* Studies in Jewish History and Culture 22. Leiden and Boston: Brill, 2009.

Bonnet, Max, ed. *Acta Philippi et Acta Thomae accedunt Acta Barnabae.* Leipzig: Herman Mendelssohn, 1903.

Booth, A. Peter. "The Voice of the Serpent: Philo's Epicureanism." In *Hellenization Revisited: Shaping a Christian Response Within the Greco-Roman World*, edited by W. Helleman, 159–72. Lanham, MD: University Press of America, 1994.

Borgen, Peder. "Man's Sovereignty Over Animals and Nature According to Philo of Alexandria." In *Texts and Contexts: Biblical Texts in Their Textual and Situational Contexts: Essays in Honor of Lars Hartman*, edited by Tord Fornberg and David Hellholm, 369–89. Oslo: Scandinavian University Press, 1995.

Bos, Gerrit. "Jewish Traditions on Divination with Birds (Ornithomancy)," 2015. https://www.researchgate.net/publication/280976904_Jewish_Traditions_on_Divination_-with_Birds_Ornithomancy.

Bouché-Leclercq, Auguste. *Histoire de la divination dans l'antiquité.* Paris E. Leroux, 1879.

Boustan, Raʿanan, and Michael Beshay. "Sealing the Demons, Once and For All: The Ring of Solomon, the Cross of Christ, and the Power of Biblical Kingship." *Archiv Für Religionsgeschichte* 16, no. 1 (2015).

Bovon, François. "Canonical and Apocryphal Acts of Apostles." *Journal of Early Christian Studies* 11, no. 2 (2003): 165–94.

———. "The Child and the Beast: Fighting Violence in Ancient Christianity." *Harvard Theological Review* 92, no. 4 (1999): 369–92.

———. "Women Priestesses in the Apocryphal Acts of Philip." In *Walk in the Ways of Wisdom: Essays in Honor of Elisabeth Schüssler Fiorenza*, edited by Shelly Matthews, Cynthia Briggs Kittredge, and Melanie Johnson-DeBaufre, 109–21. Harrisburg, London and New York: Trinity Press International, 2003.

Bovon, François, and Glenn E. Snyder, eds. *New Testament and Christian Apocrypha: Collected Studies Ii.* Wissenschaftliche Untersuchungen Zum Neuen Testament 237. Tübingen: Mohr Siebeck, 2009.

Bowersock, Glen Warren. "The Literature of the Empire: Between Philosophy and Rhetoric: Cassius Dio and Herodian." In *The Cambridge History of Classical Literature*, edited by E. J. Kenney and W. V. Clausen, 2. Latin Literature:710–13. Cambridge: Cambridge University Press, 1982.

Bowie, E. L. "The Literature of the Empire: Between Philosophy and Rhetoric: Aelian." In *The Cambridge History of Classical Literature*, edited by E. J. Kenney and W. V. Clausen, 2. Latin Literature:680–82. Cambridge: Cambridge University Press, 1982.

Boyarin, Daniel. *Border Lines: The Partition of Judaeo-Christianity*. Divinations. Philadelphia: University of Pennsylvania Press, 2004.

———. *Carnal Israel: Reading Sex in Talmudic Culture*. The New Historicism 25. Berkeley: University of California Press, 1993.

Brakke, David. *The Gnostics: Myth, Ritual, and Diversity in Early Christianity*. Cambridge, MA: Harvard University Press, 2010.

Brand, Joshua. *Kele Zekhukhit Be-Sifrut Ha-Talmud*. Jerusalem: Mossad haRav Kook, 1978.

Bregman, Marc. *Tanhuma-Yelammedenu Literature: Studies in the Evolution of the Versions*. Piscataway, NJ: Gorgias Press, 2003.

Bremmer, Jan N. "Balaam, Mopsus and Melampous: Tales of Travelling Seers." In *Prestige of the Pagan Prophet Balaam in Judaism, Early Christianity and Islam*, edited by George H. Van Kooten and Jacques Van Ruiten, 49–67. Themes in Biblical Narrative 11. Leiden: Brill, 2008.

———. *The Rise and Fall of the Afterlife: The 1995 Read-Tuckwell Lectures at the University of Bristol*. London and New York: Routledge, 2002.

Brennan, Tad. "Stoic Moral Psychology." In *The Cambridge Companion to the Stoics*, edited by Brad Inwood, 257–94. Cambridge, UK: Cambridge University Press, 2003.

Brody, Robert. *Rav Se'adya Gaon*. Gedolei ha-Ruaḥ veha-Yetsirah ba-'Am ha-Yehudi. Jerusalem: Zalman Shazar Center for Jewish History, 2006.

———. *Sa'adyah Gaon*. Translated by Betsy Rosenberg. Oxford and Portland, OR: The Littman Library of Jewish Civilization, 2013.

———. *The Geonim of Babylonia and the Shaping of Medieval Jewish Culture*. New Haven: Yale University Press, 1998.

———. "The Geonim of Babylonia as Biblical Exegetes." In *Hebrew Bible / Old Testament. I: From the Beginnings to the Middle Ages (Until 1300)*, edited by Magne Saebo, Part 2: The Middle Ages:74–88. Vandenhoeck & Ruprecht, 2000.

Broek, Roelof van den. *The Myth of the Phoenix: According to Classical and Early Christian Traditions*. Études Préliminaires Aux Religions Orientales Dans l'Empire Romain 24. Leiden: E. J. Brill, 1971.

Brown, Francis. *The New Brown, Driver, and Briggs Hebrew and English Lexicon of the Old Testament*. Lafayette, IN: Associated Publishers and Authors, 1981.

Brunner, Fernand. *Métaphysique d'Ibn Gabirol et de La Tradition Platonicienne*. Edited by Daniel Schulthess. Variorum Collected Studies Series CS589. Aldershot and Brookfield, VT: Ashgate, 1997.

Büchler, Adolf. "The Reading of the Law and Prophets in a Triennial Cycle." *The Jewish Quarterly Review*, Old Series, 5–6, no. 3, 1 (1893): 420–68, 1–73.

————. *Types of Jewish-Palestinian Piety from 70 B.C.E. to 70 C.E.: The Ancient Pious Men*. Jews' College Publications 8. London: Jews' College, 1922.

Burkert, Walter. *Lore and Science in Ancient Pythagoreanism*. Translated by Edwin L. Minar Jr. Cambridge, Mass: Harvard University Press, 1972.

Carroll, Robert P. "Blindsight and the Vision Thing." In *Writing and Reading the Scroll of Isaiah: Studies of an Interpretive Tradition*, edited by Craig C. Broyles and Craig A. Evans, 79–94. Leiden and New York: Brill, 1997.

Casey, R. P. "Naassenes and Ophites." *The Journal of Theological Studies* 27, no. 108 (1926): 374–87.

Catchpole, David R. *The Quest for Q*. Edinburgh: T. & T. Clark, 1993.

Charlesworth, James H. "Serpent Symbolism in the Hebrew Bible (Old Testament)." In *Good and Evil Serpent*, 269–351. New Haven: Yale University Press, 2000.

Chen, Mel Y. *Animacies: Biopolitics, Racial Mattering, and Queer Affect*. Perverse Modernities. Durham, NC: Duke University Press, 2012.

Chisholm, Robert B. Jr. "Does God Deceive." *Bibliotheca Sacra* 155, no. 617 (1998): 11–28.

Clark, Stephen R. L. "Animals in Classical and Late Antique Philosophy." In *The Oxford Handbook of Animal Ethics*, edited by Tom Beauchamp and R. G. Frey, 1:35–60. Oxford Handbooks. Oxford: Oxford University Press, 2011.

————. *Aristotle's Man: Speculations Upon Aristotelian Anthropology*. Oxford: Clarendon Press, 1983.

————. *Understanding Faith: Religious Belief and Its Place in Society*. St. Andrews Studies in Philosophy and Public Affairs. Exeter, UK and Charlottesville, VA: Imprint Academic, 2009.

Clauss, James J. "An Attic-Speaking Crow on the Capitoline: A Literary Émigré from the 'Hecale.'" *Zeitschrift Für Papyrologie Und Epigraphik* 96 (1993): 167–73.

Clay, Jenny Strauss. "Demas and Aude: The Nature of Divine Transformation in Homer." *Hermes* 102 (1974): 129–136.

————. "The Generation of Monsters in Hesiod." *Classical Philology* 88, no. 2 (1993): 105–16.

Clayman, Dee L. *Callimachus' Iambi*. Mnemosyne, Bibliotheca Classica Batava 59. Leiden: Brill, 1980.

Cleve, Felix M. *The Giants of Pre-Sophistic Greek Philosophy: An Attempt to Reconstruct Their Thoughts*. 3d ed. 2 vols. The Hague: Martinus Nijhoff, 1973.

Cline Kelly, Ann. "Talking Animals in the Bible: Paratexts as Symptoms of Cultural Anxiety in Restoration and Early Eighteenth-Century England." *Journal for Eighteenth-Century Studies* 33, no. 4 (2010): 437–51.

Cohen, Boaz. *Mishnah and Tosefta: A Comparative Study*. New York: Jewish Theological Seminary of America, 1935.

Colish, Marcia L. *The Stoic Tradition from Antiquity to the Early Middle Ages: Stoicism in Christian Latin Thought Through the Sixth Century*. Studies in the History of Christian Thought 34–35. Leiden, New York, Copenhagen and Köln: E. J. Brill, 1985.

Conley, Thomas M. "Philo's Rhetoric: Studies in Style, Composition, and Exegesis." Monograph of the Center for Hermeneutical Studies in Hellenistic and Modern Culture 1. Berkeley: Center for Hermeneutical Studies in Hellenistic and Modern Culture, 1987.

Cook, Arthur Bernard. "Descriptive Animal Names in Greece." *The Classical Review* 8, no. 9 (1894): 381–85.

Dahood, Mitchell Joseph. "Hol 'Phoenix' in Job 29:18 and in Ugaritic." *The Catholic Biblical Quarterly* 36, no. 1 (1974): 85–88.

———. "Nest and Phoenix in Job 29:18." *Biblica* 48, no. 4 (1967): 542–44.

Daly, Lloyd W. "Hesiod's Fable." *Transactions and Proceedings of the American Philological Association* 92 (1961): 45–51.

Dan, Joseph. *Ashkenazi Hasidism in the History of Jewish Thought*. Vol. 1. 3 vols. Ramat-Aviv: The Open University, 1990.

———. *History of Jewish Mysticism and Esotericism: The Middle Ages*. Vol. 5. Jerusalem: The Zalman Shazar Center, 2011.

———. *R. Judah he-Hasid*. Gedole ha-ruaḥ yeha-yetsirah ba-'am ha-Yehudi. Jerusalem: The Zalman Shazar Center for Jewish History, 766.

———. "Samael and the Problem of Jewish Gnosticism." In *Perspectives on Jewish Thought and Mysticism*, edited by Alexander Altmann, Alfred L. Ivry, Elliot R. Wolfson, Allan Arkush, and Institute of Jewish Studies (London, England), 257–76. Amsterdam: Harwood Academic Publishers, 1998.

———. *The Hebrew Story in the Middle Ages*. Sifriyyat Keter: 'Am Yisra'el ve-Tarbuto. Jerusalem: Keter, 1974.

Daube, David. "Rabbinic Methods of Interpretation and Hellenistic Rhetoric." *Hebrew Union College Annual* 22 (1949): 239–64.

Davidson, Israel. *Otsar Ha-Shirah Veha-Piyyuṭ*. New York: Ktav Publishing House, 1970.

Davidson, John. *The Gospel of Jesus: In Search of His Original Teachings*. Rockport, MA: Element, 1995.

Davies, Rachel Bryant. "Reading Ezekiel's Exagoge: Tragedy, Sacrificial Ritual, and the Midrashic Tradition." *Greek, Roman, and Byzantine Studies* 48, no. 4 (2010): 393–415.

Davila, James. *Descenders to the Chariot: The People Behind the Hekhalot Literature*. Leiden and Boston: Brill, 2001.

De Vries, Simon J. *Prophet Against Prophet: The Role of the Micaiah Narrative (i Kings 22) in the Development of Early Prophetic Tradition*. Grand Rapids: Eerdmans, 1978.

Delcor, M. "The Selloi of the Oracle of Dodona and the Oracular Priests of the Semitic Religions." In *Wort, Lied, Und Gottesspruch: Beiträge Zur Septuaginta: Festschrift Für Joseph Ziegler*, edited by Josef Schreiner, 31–38. Forschung Zur Bibel 1–2. Würzburg: Echter Verlag, 1972.

Derrida, Jacques. *The Animal That Therefore I Am*. Translated by Marie-Louise Mallet. New York: Fordham University Press, 2008.

DeVries, Simon J. *Prophet Against Prophet*. Wm. B. Eerdmans Publishing, 1978.

Diamond, Eliezer. "Lions, Snakes and Asses: Palestinian Jewish Holy Men as Masters of the Animal Kingdom." In *Jewish Culture and Society under the Christian Roman Empire*, 251–83. Interdisciplinary Studies in Ancient Culture and Religion 3. Leuven: Peeters, 2003.

Dickie, Matthew W. "The Fathers of the Church and the Evil Eye." In *Byzantine Magic*, edited by Henry Maguire, 9–34. Washington, DC: Dumbarton Oaks Research Library and Collection distributed by Harvard University Press, 1995.

Dierauer, Urs. *Tier und Mensch im Denken der Antike: Studien zur Tierpsychologie, Anthropologie und Ethik*. Studien zur antiken Philosophie 6. Amsterdam: Grüner, 1977.

Diller, Aubrey. "The Text History of the Bibliotheca of Pseudo-Apollodorus." *Transactions and Proceedings of the American Philological Association* 66 (1935): 296–313.

Dillon, Richard J. "Ravens, Lilies, and the Kingdom of God (Matthew 6:25-33/Luke 12:22-31)." *The Catholic Biblical Quarterly* 53, no. 4 (1991): 605–27.

Dinur, Benzion. *Pirke Aboth*. Dorot. Jerusalem: Bialik Institute, 1972.

Drijvers, Jan Willem, and David Hunt. *The Late Roman World and Its Historian: Interpreting Ammianus Marcellinus*. London and New York: Routledge, 1999.

Dulkin, Ryan Scott. "The Devil Within: A Rabbinic Traditions-History of the Samael Story in Pirkei De-Rabbi Eliezer." *Jewish Studies Quarterly* 21, no. 2 (2014): 153–75.

Dvorjetski, Estée. "The Medical History of Rabbi Judah the Patriarch: A Linguistic Analysis." *Hebrew Studies* 43 (2002): 39–55.

Dyson, Henry. *Prolepsis and Ennoia in the Early Stoa*. Berlin: Walter de Gruyter, 2009.

Easterling, P. E. "The Literature of the Empire: Between Philosophy and Rhetoric: The Fable." In *The Cambridge History of Classical Literature*, edited by P. E. Easterling and Bernard Knox, 1. Greek Literature:699–703. Cambridge: Cambridge University Press, 1982.

Easterling, P. E., and B. M. W. Knox, eds. *The Cambridge History of Classical Literature*. 1st pbk. ed. Vol. 1: Greek Literature. The Cambridge History of Classical Literature 1. Cambridge and New York: Cambridge University Press, 1989.

Eco, Umberto. *The Search for the Perfect Language*. Translated by James Fentress. Making of Europe. Oxford, UK and Cambridge, MA: Blackwell, 1995.

Eco, Umberto, Roberto Lambertini, and Costantino Marmo. "On Animal Language in the Medieval Classification of Signs." In *On the Medieval Theory of Signs*, edited by Umberto Eco and Costantino Marmo, 3–41. Foundations of Semiotics 21. Amsterdam and Philadelphia: John Benjamins, 1989.

Elbaum, Jacob. "The Midrash Tana Devei Eliyahu and Ancient Esoteric Literature." *Jerusalem Studies in Jewish Thought* 6, no. 1–2 (1987): 139–50.

———. "The Silent Revolution: The Legends of the Jews by Louis Ginzberg and the Genre of Midrashic Anthology." *Jewish Studies* 47 (2010): 47–56.

———. "Yalqut Shim'oni and the Medieval Midrashic Anthology." In *The Anthology in Jewish Literature*, edited by David Stern, 159–75. Oxford: Oxford University Press, 2004.

Ellis, Peter F. *The Yahwist: The Bible's First Theologian*. London: G. Chapman, 1969.

Elman, Yaakov. "'He in His Cloak and She in Her Cloak': Conflicting Images of Sexuality in Sasanian Mesopotamia." In *Discussing Cultural Influences: Text, Context and Non-Text in Rabbinic Judaism*, edited by Rivka Ulmer, 129–63. Studies in Judaism. Lanham, MD: University Press of America, 2007.

———. "Middle Persian Culture and Babylonian Sages: Accommodation and Resistance in the Shaping of Rabbinic Legal Tradition." In *The Cambridge Companion to the Talmud and Rabbinic Literature*, edited by Charlotte Elisheva Fonrobert and Martin S. Jaffee, 165–97. Cambridge Companions to Religion. Cambridge UK and New York NY: Cambridge University Press, 2007.

Epstein, J. N. *A Grammar of Babylonian Aramaic*. Edited by Ezra Zion Melamed. Jerusalem: Magnes Press, 1960.

———. *Introduction to Tannaitic Literature: Mishna, Tosephta and Halakhic Midrashim*. Edited by E. Z. Melamed. Jerusalem and Tel-Aviv: The Magnes Press and Dvir, 1957.

———. *Mevo'ot Lesifrut Ha-'Amora'im*. Jerusalem and Tel-Aviv: Magnes and Dvir, 1962.

Epstein-Halevi, Elimelech. *Agadot Ha-Amora'im*. Tel-Aviv: Dvir, 1977.

———. *Ha-Agadah Ha-Historit-Biyografit*. Tel Aviv: by author, 1975.

———. *'Olamah shel ha-Agadah*. Tel-Aviv, Israel: Dvir, 1972.

———. *Parashiyot Ba-Agadah Le-or Meḳorot Yevaniyyim*. Haifa: Haifa University Press, 1973.

———. *Parashiyot ba-'agadah le-'or meḳorot Yevaniyim*. Haifa: Haifa University Press, 1973.

Eshel, Ben-Zion. *Jewish Settlements in Babylonia during Talmudic Times: Talmudic Onomasticon*. Jerusalem: The Magnes Press, the Hebrew University, 1979.

Evans, Craig A. *To See and Not Perceive: Isaiah 6.9-10 in Early Jewish and Christian Interpretation*. Journal for the Study of the Old Testament 64. Sheffield: Sheffield Academic Press, 1989.

Fehling, Detlev. *Herodotus and His "Sources": Citation, Invention, and Narrative Art.* ARCA Classical and Medieval Texts, Papers, and Monographs 21. Leeds: Francis Cairns, 1990.

Feldman, Louis H. *Jew and Gentile in the Ancient World: Attitudes and Interactions from Alexander to Justinian.* Princeton: Princeton University Press, 1993.

———. "Josephus as Rewriter of the Bible." In *Josephus's Interpretation of the Bible,* 14–73. Hellenistic Culture and Society 27. Berkeley, Los Angeles, London: University of California Press, 1998.

Feliks, Jehuda. *Plant World of the Bible.* Ramat Gan: Masadah, 1968.

Firestone, Reuven. *Journeys in Holy Lands: The Evolution of the Abraham-Ishmael Legends in Islamic Exegesis.* Albany: State University of New York Press, 1990.

Fischel, Henry A. *Rabbinic Literature and Greco-Roman Philosophy. a Study of Epicurea and Rhetorica in Early Midrashic Writings.* Studia Post-Biblica 21. Leiden: E. J. Brill, 1973.

Fischel, Henry Albert, and Lawrence V. Berman. "Stoicism." In *Encyclopaedia Judaica,* edited by Michael Berenbaum and Fred Skolnik, 19:232–33. Detroit: Macmillan Reference USA, 2007.

Fishbane, Simcha. "'Most Women Engage in Sorcery': An Analysis of Sorceresses in the Babylonian Talmud." *Jewish History* 7, no. 1 (1993): 27–42.

Fleischer, Ezra. *Hebrew Liturgical Poetry in the Middle Ages.* 2nd expanded edition. Jerusalem: Magnes Press, 2007.

Flusser, David. *Judaism of the Second Temple Period.* Translated by Azzan Yadin. Vol. 2. 2 vols. Grand Rapids and Jerusalem: William B. Eerdmans and Hebrew University Magnes Press, 2007.

Fögen, Thorsten. "Animal Communication." In *The Oxford Handbook of Animals in Classical Thought and Life,* edited by Gordon Lindsay Campbell, First Edition., 216–32. Oxford: Oxford University Press, 2014.

———. "Pliny the Elder's Animals: Some Remarks on the Narrative Structure of Nat. Hist. 8–11." *Hermes* 135, no. 2 (2007): 184–98.

Forbes, P. B. R. "Hesiod versus Perses." *The Classical Review* 64, no. 3/4 (1950): 82–87.

Formigari, Lia. *A History of Language Philosophies.* Translated by Gabriel Poole. Amsterdam Studies in the Theory and History of Linguistic Science 105. Amsterdam and Philadelphia: John Benjamins Pub, 2004.

Fowler, Harold North, ed. *Plato with and English Translation.* Vol. 2: Theaetetus, Sophist. Loeb Classical Library. London and Cambridge, MA: William Heinemann and Harvard University Press, 1952.

Fowler, W. Warde. *The Death of Turnus: Observations on the Twelfth Book of the Aeneid.* Oxford: B.H. Blackwell, 1919.

Fraade, Steven D. "Before and After Babel: Linguistic Exceptionalism and Pluralism in Early Rabbinic LIterature and Jewish Antiquity." *Diné Israel* 28 (2011): 31*-68*.

———. "Moses and Adam as Polyglots." In *Envisioning Judaism: Studies in Honor of Peter Schäfer on the Occasion of His Seventieth Birthday,* edited by Raanan Shaul

Boustan, Klaus Hermann, Reimund Leicht, Annette Yoshiko Reed, and Giuseppe Veltri, 1:186–94. Tübingen: Mohr Siebeck, 2013.

Fraenkel, Jonah. *'Iyyunim Be-'olamo Ha-Ruhani Shel Sippur Ha-Aggadah*. Sifriyat "Helal ben Hayim." Tel Aviv: Hakibbutz Hameuchad, 2001.

———. *The Aggadic Narrative: Harmony of Form and Content*. Edited by Me'ir Ayali. Sifriyat "Helal Ben-Hayim." Tel Aviv: Hakibbutz Hameuchad, 2001.

Fraser, Orlaith N., and Thomas Bugnyar. "Do Ravens Show Consolation? Responses to Distressed Others." *PLOS ONE* 5, no. 5 (May 12, 2010): e10605.

Frazer, James George. *The Golden Bough: A Study in Magic and Religion*. Edited by Robert Fraser. Reissued. Oxford World's Classics. Oxford: Oxford University Press, 2009.

Friedländer, Michael. *Essays on the Writings of Abraham Ibn Ezra*. Jewish Philosophy in the Middle Ages. London: Trübner and Co. for the Society of Hebrew Literature, 1877.

———. "Life and Works of Saadia." *Jewish Quarterly Review*, Old Series, 5, no. 2 (1893): 177–99.

Friedman, Shamma. "La-Aggadah Ha-Historit Ba-Talmud Ha-Bavli." In *Saul Lieberman Memorial Volume*, 119–64. New York and Jerusalem: Jewish Theological Seminary of America, 1993.

———. "The Talmudic Proverb in Its Cultural Setting." *Jewish Studies: An Internet Journal* 2 (2003): 25–82.

Fuchs, Salomon. *Studien Über Abu Zakaria Jachja (R. Jehuda) Ibn Bal'âm*. Berlin: H. Itzkowski, 1893.

Gafni, Isaiah. *The Jews of Babylonia in the Talmudic Era: A Social and Cultural History*. Monographs in Jewish History. Jerusalem: Zalman Shazar Center for Jewish History, 1990.

Gera, Deborah Levine. *Ancient Greek Ideas on Speech, Language, and Civilization*. Oxford and New York: Oxford University Press, 2003.

Gesenius, Wilhelm, E. Kautzsch, and A. E. Cowley. *Gesenius' Hebrew Grammar*. 13th English ed. Oxford: The Clarendon press, 1976.

Gilhus, Ingvild Sælid. *Animals, Gods and Humans: Changing Attitudes to Animals in Greek, Roman and Early Christian Ideas*. London: Routledge, 2006.

Ginzberg, Louis, ed. *Genizah Studies in Memory of Doctor Solomon Schechter*. Vol. 2. 3 vols. Jewish Studies Classics. Piscataway, NJ: Gorgias Press, 2003.

———. *Jewish Folklore: East and West: A Paper Delivered at the Harvard Tercentenary Conference of Arts and Sciences*. Harvard Tercentenary Publications. Cambridge, MA: Harvard University Press, 1937.

———. *The Legends of the Jews*. Translated by Henrietta Szold. Philadelphia, PA: The Jewish Publication Society of America, 1909.

Goar, Robert J. "The Purpose of De Divinatione." *Transactions and Proceedings of the American Philological Association* 99 (1968): 241–48.

Goldenberg, Robert. "The Problem of False Prophecy: Talmudic Interpretations of Jeremiah 28 and 1 Kings 22." In *Biblical Mosaic: Changing Perspectives*, edited by Robert M. Polzin and Eugene Rothman, 87–103. Society of Biblical Literature Semeia Studies. Philadelphia, PA: Fortress Press, 1982.

Gomme, A. W. "The Legend of Cadmus and the Logographi.-II." *The Journal of Hellenic Studies* 33 (1913): 223–45.

Goodyear, F. R. D. "History and Biography." In *The Cambridge History of Classical Literature*, edited by E. J. Kenney and W. V. Clausen, 2. Latin Literature:639–66. Cambridge: Cambridge University Press, 1982.

Goor, Asaph. "The Place of the Olive in the Holy Land and Its History through the Ages." *Economic Botany* 20, no. 3 (1966): 223–43.

Gowan, Donald E. *From Eden to Babel: A Commentary on the Book of Genesis 1-11*. International Theological Commentary. Grand Rapids: W.B. Eerdmans Pub. Co, 1988.

Gowers, William. "African Elephants and Ancient Authors." *African Affairs* 47, no. 188 (1948): 173–80.

Grant, Robert M. *Early Christians and Animals*. London and New York: Routledge, 1999.

———. "Theophilus of Antioch to Autolycus." *Harvard Theological Review* 40, no. 4 (1947): 227–56.

Gray, Vivienne J. "Herodotus on Melampus." In *Myth, Truth, and Narrative in Herodotus*, edited by Emily Baragwanath and Mathieu de Bakker, 167–92. Oxford University Press, 2012.

Green, Steven J. "Malevolent Gods and Promethean Birds: Contesting Augury in Augustus's Rome." *Transactions of the American Philological Association (1974-)* 139, no. 1 (2009): 147–67.

Gross, Aaron S. "Animals, Empathy, and 'Rahamim' in the Study of Religion: A Case Study of Jewish Opposition to Hunting." *Studies in Religion / Sciences Religieuses* 46, no. 4 (2017): 511–535.

Grossman, Jonathan. "Micaiah's Narrative and the Death of Ahab (1 Kings 22) — Proactive Editing." *Studies in Bible and Exegesis* 10: Presented to Shmuel Vargon (2011): 157–58.

Gruenwald, Itamar. "The Problem of the Anti-Gnostic Polemic in Rabbinic Literature." In *Studies in Gnosticism and Hellenistic Religions: Presented to Gilles Quispel on the Occasion of His 65th Birthday*, edited by Roelof van den Van den Broek and Maarten Jozef Vermaseren, 171–89. Etudes Preliminaires Aux Religions Orientales Dans l'Empire Romain ; t. 91. Leiden: EJBrill, 1981.

Gundry, Robert H. "Spinning the Lilies and Unravelling the Ravens: An Alternative Reading of Q 12.22b-31 and P.Oxy. 655." *New Testament Studies* 48, no. 2 (April 2002): 159–80.

Guttmann, Julius. *The Philosophy of Judaism: The History of Jewish Philosophy from Biblical Times to Franz Rosenzweig*. Northvale, NJ: J. Aronson, 1988.

Haebler, Claus. "Corvus 4." In *Paulys Realencyclopädie der classischen Altertumswissenschaft*, edited by August Friedrich Pauly and Georg Wissowa, 4:2:1665–66. Stuttgart: Metzler, 1897.

Halperin, David J. *The Faces of the Chariot: Early Jewish Responses to Ezekiel's Vision.* Texte Und Studien Zum Antiken Judentum 16. Tübingen: J.C.B. Mohr, 1988.

Hamilton, Jeffries M. "Caught in the Nets of Prophecy? The Death of King Ahab and the Character of God." *The Catholic Biblical Quarterly* 56, no. 4 (1994): 649–63.

Hankinson, R. J. "Stoicism, Science and Divination." *Apeiron* 21, no. 2 (1988): 123–160.

Harari, Yuval. *Jewish Magic before the Rise of Kabbalah.* 1st edition. Raphael Patai Series in Jewish Folklore and Anthropology. Detroit: Wayne State University Press, 2017.

———. "The Sages and the Occult." In *The Literature of the Sages: Section 2, Literature of the Jewish People in the Period of the Second Temple and the Talmud*, edited by Shemuel Safrai and Peter J. Tomson, 521–66. Compendia Rerum Iudaicarum Ad Novum Testamentum. Assen, Netherlands: Van Gorcum ; Philadelphia : Fortress Press, 1987.

Harlow, Daniel C. *The Greek Apocalypse of Baruch (3 Baruch) in Hellenistic Judaism and Early Christianity.* Studia in Veteris Testamenti Pseudepigrapha 12. Leiden and New York: E.J. Brill, 1996.

Harris, Roy, and Talbot Taylor. "The Bible on the Origin and Diversification of Language." In *Landmarks In Linguistic Thought Volume I: The Western Tradition From Socrates To Saussure*, Second edition., 35–44. Routledge History of Linguistic Thought. London and New York: Routledge, 2005.

Haskins, Ekaterina V. *Logos and Power in Isocrates and Aristotle.* University of South Carolina Press, 2004.

Hawkins, Tom. "Eloquent Alogia: Animal Narrators in Ancient Greek Literature." *Humanites* 6, no. 37 (2017): 1–15.

Hay, David M. "Philo's References to Other Allegorists." *Studia Philonica Annual* 6 (1980): 41–75.

Heath, Jane. "Ezekiel Tragicus and Hellenistic Visuality: The Phoenix at Elim." *The Journal of Theological Studies* 57, no. 1 (2006): 23–41.

Heath, John. *The Talking Greeks: Speech, Animals, and the Other in Homer, Aeschylus, and Plato.* Cambridge: Cambridge University Press, 2005.

Heidel, William Arthur. "Hecataeus and the Egyptian Priests in Herodotus, Book II." *Memoirs of the American Academy of Arts and Sciences* 18, no. 2 (1935): 49–134.

Heilprin, Jehiel. *Seder ha-Dorot.* Warsaw: I. Goldman, 1882.

Heinemann, Isaak. *Darkhe Ha-Agadah.* Jerusalem: Magnes Press, 1970.

Heinemann, Joseph. *Aggadah and Its Development.* Sifriyat Keter--'Am Yisra'el ve-Tarbuto: 4. Hagut vva-Halakhah. Jerusalem: Keter, 1974.

———. "The Proem in Aggadic Midrashim—A Form-Critical Study." In *Studies in Aggadah and Folk-Literature*, edited by Dov Noy and Joseph Heinemann, 100–122. Scripta Hierosolymitana 22. Jerusalem: Magnes Press, 1971.

———. "The Triennial Lectionary Cycle." *Journal of Jewish Studies*, no. 19 (1968): 41–48.

Heller, Bernhard. "Muhammedanisches und Antimuhammedanisches in den Pirke Rabbi Eliezer." *Monatsschrift für Geschichte und Wissenschaft des Judentums* 69 (n. F. 33), no. 1/2 (1925): 47–54.

Hengst, Daniël den. *Emperors and Historiography: Collected Essays on the Literature of the Roman Empire by Daniël Den Hengst*. Edited by Diederik W. P. Burgersdijk and Joop A. van Waarden. Mnemosyne Supplements. Monographs on Greek and Roman Language and Literature, v. 319. Leiden and Boston: Brill, 2010.

Herr, Moshe David. "Aggadah u-Midrash be-'Olamam shel ḤaZa"L be-Eretz Yisrae'el: Meḳomot Hithavut, Sibbot Tzemiḥah u-Zmanei 'Arikhah." In *Higayon le-Yonah: New Aspects in the Study of Midrash, Aggadah and Piyut in Honor of Professor Yona Fraenkel*, edited by Jacob Elbaum, Galit Hasan-Rokem, and Joshua Levinson, 131–45. Jerusalem: The Hebrew University Magnes Press, 2006.

Herring, Basil. "Speaking of Man and Beast." *Judaism* 28, no. 2 (1979): 169–76.

Hezser, Catherine. *Jewish Travel in Antiquity*. Mohr Siebeck, 2011.

———. *The Social Structure of the Rabbinic Movement in Roman Palestine*. Texte Und Studien Zum Antiken Judentum 66. Tübingen: Mohr Siebeck, 1997.

Hiebert, Theodore. *The Yahwist's Landscape: Nature and Religion in Early Israel*. New York: Oxford University Press, 1996.

Hill, John Spencer. "The Phoenix." *Religion & Literature* 16, no. 2 (1984): 61–66.

Hirshman, Marc G. *A Rivalry of Genius: Jewish and Christian Biblical Interpretation in Late Antiquity*. SUNY Series in Judaica. Albany: State University of New York Press, 1996.

House, D. K. "The Life of Sextus Empiricus." *The Classical Quarterly* 30, no. 1 (1980): 227–38.

IJsseling, Samuel. *Rhetoric and Philosophy in Conflict: An Historical Survey*. The Hague: M. Nijhoff, 1976.

Inwood, Brad. *Ethics and Human Action in Early Stoicism*. Oxford: Clarendon Press, 1985.

Jacob, Benno. "Gott und Pharao." *Monatsschrift für Geschichte und Wissenschaft des Judentums* 68, no. 2–4 (1923): 118–26, 202–11, 268–89.

Jacobs, Andrew S. *Epiphanius of Cyprus: A Cultural Biography of Late Antiquity*. Oakland, California: University of California Press, 2016.

Jacobs, Jonathan. "The Allegorical Exegesis of Song of Songs by R. Tuviah Ben 'Eli'ezer: Lekaḥ Tov, and Its Relation to Rashi's Commentary." *AJS Review* 39, no. 1 (April 2015): 75–92.

Jacobs, Louis. "The Story of R Phinehas Ben Yair and His Donkey in B Hullin 7a-B." In *A Tribute to Geza Vermes: Essays on Jewish and Christian Literature and History*, edited by Richard T. White and Philip R. Davies, 193–205. Sheffield: JSOT Press, 1990.

Jacobson, Howard. "Phoenix Resurrected." *Harvard Theological Review* 80, no. 2 (1987): 229–33.

Jastrow, Marcus. *Dictionary of the Targumim, the Talmud Babli and Yerushalmi, and the Midrashic Literature.* Peabody, MA: Hendrickson Publishers, 2005.

Jażdżewska, Katarzyna. "Dialogic Format of Philo of Alexandria's De Animalibus." *Eos* 102 (2015): 45–56.

Jedan, Christoph. *Stoic Virtues: Chrysippus and the Theological Foundations of Stoic Ethics.* London and New York: Continuum, 2009.

Jennison, George. *Animals for Show and Pleasure in Ancient Rome.* Philadelphia: University of Pennsylvania Press, 2005.

Johnston, Sarah Iles. "Xanthus, Hera and the Erinyes (Iliad 19.400-418)." *Transactions of the American Philological Association (1974-)* 122 (1992): 85–98.

Jospe, Raphael. "Biblical Exegesis as a Philosophic Literary Genre: Abraham Ibn Ezra and Moses Mendelssohn." In *Jewish Philosophy and the Academy*, edited by Emil L. Fackenheim and Raphael Jospe, 48–92. Madison, Teaneck and London: Fairleigh Dickinson University Press and Associated University Presses in association with the Minneapolis Institute of Arts, 1996.

———. *Jewish Philosophy in the Middle Ages.* EMUNOT: Jewish Philosophy and Kabbalah. Boston: Academic Studies Press, 2009.

Jung, Leo. "Fallen Angels in Jewish, Christian and Mohammedan Literature: A Study in Comparative Folk-Lore." *The Jewish Quarterly Review* 16, no. 2 (1925): 171–205.

———. "Fallen Angels in Jewish, Christian and Mohammedan Literature. A Study in Comparative Folk-Lore." *The Jewish Quarterly Review* 15, no. 4 (1925): 467–502.

———. "Fallen Angels in Jewish, Christian and Mohammedan Literature. A Study in Comparative Folk-Lore." *The Jewish Quarterly Review* 16, no. 1 (1925): 45–88.

———. "Fallen Angels in Jewish, Christian and Mohammedan Literature: A Study in Comparative Folk-Lore." *The Jewish Quarterly Review* 16, no. 3 (1926): 287–336.

Kadushin, Max. *Organic Thinking: A Study in Rabbinic Thought.* New York: The Jewish Theological Seminary of America, 1938.

———. *The Rabbinic Mind.* 3d ed. New York: Bloch, 1972.

Kaestli, Jean-Daniel. "L'interpretation du serpent de Genese 3 dans quelques textes gnostiques et la question de la gnose 'ophite.'" In *Gnosticisme et monde hellenistique: actes du colloque de Louvain-la-Neuve, 11-14 mars 1980 ils*, 116–30. Louvain-La-Neuve: Universite Catholique de Louvain, 1982.

Kamesar, Adam. "The Logos Endiathetos and the Logos Prophorikos in Allegorical Interpretation: Philo and the D-Scholia to the Iliad." *Greek, Roman and Byzantine Studies* 44, no. 2 (2004): 163–81.

Kaminka, Armand. "Les Rapports Entre Le Rabbinisme et La Philosophie Stoïcienne." In *Essays in Greco-Roman and Related Talmudic Literature*, edited by Henry Albert Fischel, 23–42. New York: Ktav, 1977.

Keith, A. Berriedale. "Pythagoras and the Doctrine of Transmigration." *Journal of the Royal Asiatic Society of Great Britain and Ireland*, 1909, 569–606.

Keith, A. M. *The Play of Fictions: Studies in Ovid's Metamorphoses Book 2*. Michigan Monographs in Classical Antiquity. Ann Arbor: University of Michigan Press, 1992.

Kemezis, Adam M. *Greek Narratives of the Roman Empire Under the Severans: Cassius Dio, Philostratus and Herodian*. Greek Culture in the Roman World. Cambridge UK and New York: Cambridge University Press, 2014.

Kennedy, George A. "Oratory." In *The Cambridge History of Classical Literature*, edited by P. E. Easterling and Bernard Knox, 1. Greek Literature:498–526. Cambridge: Cambridge University Press, 1982.

Kenney, E. J. "Ovid." In *The Cambridge History of Classical Literature*, edited by E. J. Kenney and W. V. Clausen, 2. Latin Literature:420–57. Cambridge: Cambridge University Press, 1982.

King, Karen L. *What Is Gnosticism?* Cambridge, MA: Belknap Press of Harvard University Press, 2003.

Kiperwasser, Reuven. "Sidro shel 'Olam: 'Al Yaḥasei Adam va-Ṭeva' be-Maḥsheet ḤaZa"L." *Akdamot: A Journal of Jewish Thought* 5 (1998): 35–49.

Kiperwasser, Reuven, and Dan D. Y. Shapira. "Irano-Talmudica Ii: Leviathan, Behemoth and the 'Domestication' of Iranian Mythological Creatures in Eschatological Narratives of the Babylonian Talmud." In *Shoshannat Yaakov: Jewish and Iranian Studies in Honor of Yaakov Elman*, edited by Shai Secunda and Steven Fine, 203–35. Brill Reference Library of Judaism 35. Leiden and Boston: Brill, 2012.

———. "Irano-Talmudica Iii: Giant Mythological Creatures in Transition from the Avesta to the Babylonian Talmud." In *Orality and Textuality in the Iranian World; Patterns of Interaction Across the Centuries*, edited by Julia Rubanovich, 65–92. Jerusalem Studies in Religion and Culture 19. Leiden and Boston: Brill, 2015.

Kirk, G. S. *Myth: Its Meaning and Functions in Ancient and Other Cultures*. Sather Classical Lectures 40. Cambridge [UK] and Berkeley: Cambridge University Press; University of California Press, 1970.

Klein-Braslavy, Sara. *Maimonides' Interpretation of the Adam Stories in Genesis: A Study in Maimonides' Anthropology*. Brill's Studies in Intellectual History. Jerusalem: Reuben Mass, 1986.

———. "The Philosophical Exegesis." In *Hebrew Bible / Old Testament. I: From the Beginnings to the Middle Ages (Until 1300)*, edited by Magne Saebo, Part 2: The Middle Ages:302–20. Vandenhoeck & Ruprecht, 2000.

Kloppenborg, John S. *The Formation of Q: Trajectories in Ancient Wisdom Collections*. Studies in Antiquity and Christianity. Philadelphia: Fortress Press, 1987.

Knohl, Israel. "Cain: Son of God or Son of Satan?" In *Jewish Biblical Interpretation and Cultural Exchange*, edited by Natalie B. Dohrmann and David Stern. Jewish Culture and Contexts. Philadelphia: University of Pennsylvania Press, 2008.

Kohn, Thomas D. "The Tragedies of Ezekiel." *Greek, Roman, and Byzantine Studies* 43, no. 1 (2011): 5–12.

Kohut, Alexander. *Ueber die jüdische Angelologie und Daemonologie in ihrer Abhängigkeit vom Parsismus*. Leipzig: Kraus Reprint, 1866.

Kohut, Alexander, and Samuel Krauss, eds. *Aruch Completum ['Arukh Ha-Shalem]*. Jerusalem: Makor, 1969.

Kostuch, Lucynda. "Do Animals Have a Homeland? Ancient Greeks on the Cultural Identity of Animals." *Humanimalia* 9, no. 1 (2017): 69–87.

Krauss, Samuel. *Additamenta ad Librum Aruch Completum*. Jerusalem: Makor, 1970.

———. *Griechische und lateinische Lehnwörter im Talmud, Midrasch und Targum*. Berlin: S. Calvary, 1898.

———. *Paras ve-Romi ba-Talmud uva-Midrashim*. Jerusalem: Mossad Harav Kook, 708.

Kreisel, Howard Theodore. "Philosophical Interpretations of the Bible." In *The Cambridge History of Jewish Philosophy*, edited by Steven Nadler and T. M. Rudavsky, 1. From Antiquity to the Seventeenth Century:88–120. Cambridge: Cambridge University Press, 2009.

———. *Prophecy: The History of an Idea in Medieval Jewish Philosophy*. Amsterdam Studies in Jewish Thought 8. Kluwer Academic Publishers, 2001.

Kugel, James L. *A Walk Through Jubilees: Studies in the Book of Jubilees and the World of Its Creation*. Supplements to the Journal for the Study of Judaism, v. 156. Leiden and Boston: Brill, 2012.

Labarrière, Jean-Louis. "Aristote et la question du langage animal." *Mètis. Anthropologie des mondes grecs anciens* 8, no. 1 (1993): 247–60.

Lakoff, George, and Mark Turner. *More than Cool Reason: A Field Guide to Poetic Metaphor*. Chicago and London: University of Chicago Press, 2009.

Layton, Richard. "Didymus the Blind and the Philistores: A Contest over Historia in Early Christian Exegetical Argument." In *Studies on the Texts of the Desert of Judah: New Approaches to the Study of Biblical Interpretation In Judaism of the Second Temple Period and in Early Christianity : Proceedings of the Eleventh International Symposium of the Orion Center for the Study of the Dead Sea Scrolls and Associated Literature, Jointly Sponsored by the Hebrew University Center for the Study of Christianity, 9–11 January, 2007*, edited by Gary A. Anderson, Ruth A. Clements, and David Satran, 243–68. 106. Leiden and Boston: Brill, 2013.

Lazenby, Francis D. "Greek and Roman Household Pets (1)." *The Classical Journal* 44, no. 4 (1949): 245–52.

———. "Greek and Roman Household Pets (2)." *The Classical Journal* 44, no. 5 (1949): 299–307.

Lefkowitz, Jeremy B. "Aesop and Animal Fable." In *The Oxford Handbook of Animals in Classical Thought and Life*, edited by Gordon Lindsay Campbell, First Edition., 1–23. Oxford: Oxford University Press, 2014.

Leibowitz, Nehama. "The Serpent—the Evil Impulse—(2, 15-17; 3, 1-9) Anatomy of Temptation." In *Studies in the Book of Genesis in the Context of Ancient and Modern Jewish Bible Commentary*, translated by Aryeh Newman, 28–37. Jerusalem: World Zionist Organization, Dept. for Torah Education and Culture, 1972.

Lesses, Rebecca. "Exe(o)Rcising Power: Women as Sorceresses, Exorcists, and Demonesses in Babylonian Jewish Society of Late Antiquity." *Journal of the American Academy of Religion* 69, no. 2 (2001): 343–75.

Levine, Lee I. "R. Abbahu of Caesarea." In *Christianity, Judaism and Other Greco-Roman Cults: Studies for Morton Smith at Sixty*, edited by Jacob Neusner. Studies in Judaism in Late Antiquity 12. Leiden: Brill, 1975.

Levinson, Joshua. "Enchanting Rabbis: Contest Narratives between Rabbis and Magicians in Late Antiquity." *The Jewish Quarterly Review* 100, no. 1 (2010): 54–94.

Levy, Jacob. *Wörterbuch über die Talmudim und Midraschim*. 2nd ed. Berlin and Vienna: B. Harz, 1924.

Lewysohn, L. *Die Zoologie des Talmuds*. Frankfurt am Main: Author and Joseph Baer, 1858.

Lieberman, Saul. *Greek in Jewish Palestine: Studies in the Life and Manners of Jewish Palestine in the II-IV Centuries C. E.* New York: The Jewish Theological Seminary of America, 1942.

———. "How Much Greek in Jewish Palestine?" In *Studies and Texts*, edited by Alexander Altmann, 1. Biblical and Other Studies:123–41. Cambridge MA: Harvard University Press, 1963.

Lindbeck, Kristen H. *Elijah and the Rabbis: Story and Theology*. New York: Columbia University Press, 2010.

Loader, William. *Philo, Josephus, and the Testaments on Sexuality: Attitudes Towards Sexuality in the Writings of Philo and Josephus and in the Testaments of the Twelve Patriachs*. Grand Rapids, MI: Eerdmans, 2011.

Loewe, Raphael. *Ibn Gabirol*. Jewish Thinkers. London: Peter Halban, 1989.

Long, A. A. "15. Socrates in Later Greek Philosophy." In *The Cambridge Companion to Socrates*, edited by Donald R. Morrison. Cambridge Companions to Philosophy, Religion and Culture. Cambridge: Cambridge University Press, 2010.

———. "Aristotle." In *The Cambridge History of Classical Literature*, edited by P. E. Easterling and Bernard Knox, 1. Greek Literature:527–40. Cambridge: Cambridge University Press, 1982.

———. "Post-Aristotelian Philosophy." In *The Cambridge History of Classical Literature*, edited by P. E. Easterling and Bernard Knox, 1. Greek Literature:622–41. Cambridge: Cambridge University Press, 1982.

Lonsdale, Steven H. "Attitudes towards Animals in Ancient Greece." *Greece & Rome* 26, no. 2 (1979): 146–59.

Lorenz, Hendrik. "The Cognition of Appetite in Plato's Timaeus." In *Plato and the Divided Self*, edited by Rachel Barney, Tad Brennan, and Charles Brittain, 238–58. Cambridge: Cambridge University Press, 2012.

Lorenz, Konrad. *King Solomon's Ring; New Light on Animal Ways*. Translated by Marjorie Kerr Wilson. New York: Crowell, 1952.

Lovejoy, Arthur O. *The Great Chain of Being: A Study of the History of an Idea*. Cambridge, MA: Harvard University Press, 1950.

Luchte, James. *Pythagoras and the Doctrine of Transmigration: Wandering Souls*. Continuum Studies in Ancient Philosophy. London ; New York: Continuum, 2009.

Maciá, Lorena Miralles. "The Fable of 'the Middle-Aged Man with Two Wives': From the Aesopian Motif to the Babylonian Talmud Version in b. B. Qam 60b." *Journal for the Study of Judaism in the Persian, Hellenistic and Roman Period* 39, no. 2 (2008): 267–81.

Mader, Gottfried. "Triumphal Elephants and Political Circus at Plutarch, 'Pomp.' 14.6." *The Classical World* 99, no. 4 (2006): 397–403.

Malter, Henry. *Saadia Gaon: His Life and Works*. New York: Hermon Press, 1969.

Mann, Jacob. "Date and Place of Redaction of Seder Eliyahu Rabba and Zuṭṭa." *Hebrew Union College Annual* 4 (1927): 302–10.

———. *The Bible as Read and Preached in the Old Synagogue: A Study in the Cycles of the Readings from Torah and Prophets, as Well as from Psalms, and in the Structure of the Midrashic Homilies*. Library of Biblical Studies. New York: KTAV, 1971.

———. "The Last Geonim of Sura." *The Jewish Quarterly Review* 11, no. 4 (1921): 409–22.

Marcus, David. "The Mission of the Raven (Gen. 8:7)." *The Journal of the Ancient Near Eastern Society* 29 (2002): 71–80.

Marcus, Ivan G. "Piety and Society: The Jewish Pietists of Medieval Germany." Études Sur Le Judaisme Médiéval ; t. 10. Leiden: Brill, 1981.

———. "The Politics and Ethics of Pietism in Judaism: The Hasidim of Medieval Germany." *Journal of Religious Ethics* 8, no. 2 (1980): 227–58.

———. "The Recensions and Structure of Sefer Hasidim." *Proceedings of the American Academy for Jewish Research* 45 (1978): 131–53.

Marcus, Ralph. "The Armenian Translation of Philo's 'Quaestiones in Genesim et Exodum.'" *Journal of Biblical Literature* 49, no. 1 (1930): 61–64.

Margalioth, Mordecai, and Yehudah Aizenberg, eds. *Entsiḳlopedyah le-Ḥakhme ha-Talmud yeha-Ge'onim*. Revised edition. 2 vols. Tel-Aviv: Yavneh and Chemed, 1995.

McDonald, Mary Francis. "Phoenix Redivivus." *Phoenix* 14, no. 4 (1960): 187–206.

McGinnis, Claire Mathews. "The Hardening of Pharaoh's Heart in Christian and Jewish Interpretation." *Journal of Theological Interpretation* 6, no. 1 (2012): 43–64.

Mehlman, Bernard H., and Seth M. Limmer. *Medieval Midrash: The House for Inspired Innovation*. Brill Reference Library of Judaism 52. Brill, 2016.

———. "The Episode of the Ant." In *Medieval Midrash: The House for Inspired Innovation*, 96–106. Brill Reference Library of Judaism 52. Brill, 2016.

Meijer, P. A. *Stoic Theology: Proofs for the Existence of the Cosmic God and of the Traditional Gods: Including a Commentary on Cleanthes' Hymn on Zeus*. Delft: Eburon, 2007.

Meir, Ofra. *Rabbi Judah the Patriarch: Palestinian and Babylonian Portrait of a Leader*. Sifriyat Helal Ben-Ḥayim. Tel-Aviv: Hakibbutz Hameuchad, 1999.

———. "The She-Ass of R. Pinhas ben Yair." *Folklore Research Center Studies* 7 (1983): 117–37.

Melammed, Ezra Zion. *Bible Commentators*. Publications of the Perry Foundation for Biblical Research in the Hebrew University of Jerusalem. Jerusalem: Magnes Press, 1975.

Meyer, Jørgen Christian. "Omens, Prophecies and Oracles in Ancient Decision-Making." In *Ancient History Matters. Studies Presented to Jens Erik Skydsgaard on His 70th Birthday*, edited by Karen Ascani, Vincent Gabrielsen, Kirsten Kvist, and Anders Holm Rasmussen, 173–83. Analecta Romana Instituti Danici Suppl. 30. Rome: L'Erma di Bretschneider, 2002.

Michalopoulos, Charilaos N. "Tiresias Between Texts and Sex." *Eugesta: Journal of Gender Studies in Antiquity* 2 (2012): 221–39.

Miles, John A. "Laughing at the Bible: Jonah as Parody." *The Jewish Quarterly Review* 65, no. 3 (1975): 168–81.

Milikowsky, Chaim. Review of *On the Formation and Transmission of Bereshit Rabba and the Yerushalmi: Questions of Redaction, Text-Criticism and Literary Relationships*, by Hans-Jürgen Becker. *The Jewish Quarterly Review* 92, no. 3/4 (2002): 521–67.

Millar, Fergus. *A Study of Cassius Dio*. Oxford: Clarendon Press, 1964.

Miller, Geoffrey David. "The Wiles of the Lord: Divine Deception, Subtlety, and Mercy in I Reg 22." *Zeitschrift Für Die Alttestamentliche Wissenschaft* 126, no. 1 (2014): 45–58.

Miller, Stuart S. "'Epigraphical' Rabbis, Helios, and Psalm 19: Were the Synagogues of Archaeology and the Synagogues of the Sages One and the Same?" *Jewish Quarterly Review* 94, no. 1 (2004): 27–76.

Mirsky, Aaron. *Reshit ha-Piyyuṭ*. 'Iyyunim 34. Jerusalem: The Jewish Agency for Israel of Youth Aliyah Department: Training Section, 725.

Morag, Sh. "On the Form and Etymology of Hai Gaon's Name." *Tarbiz* 31, no. 1 (1961): 188–90.

Moreshet, Menahem. *A Lexicon of the New Verbs in Tannaitic Hebrew*. Ramat-Gan: Bar-Ilan University Press, 1980.

Moritz, Joshua M. "Animal Suffering, Evolution, and the Origins of Evil: Toward a 'Free Creatures' Defense." *Zygon* 49, no. 2 (2014): 348–80.

Mortensen, Eric David. "Raven Augury from Tibet to Alaska." In *Communion of Subjects: Animals in Religion, Science, and Ethics*, edited by Paul Waldau and Kimberley Patton, 423–36. New York: Columbia Univ Press, 2006.

Müller, F. Max. *Chips from a German Workshop*. Vol. Volume 1, Essays on the Science of Religion. Scholars Press Reprints and Translations Series. Chico, CA: Scholars Press, 1985.

Munson, Rosaria Vignolo. *Black Doves Speak: Herodotus and the Languages of Barbarians*. Washington and Cambridge MA: Harvard University Press for the Center for Hellenic Studies, 2005.

Nelson, Stephanie. "The Justice of Zeus in Hesiod's Fable of the Hawk and the Nightingale." *The Classical Journal* 92, no. 3 (1997): 235–47.

Neuberger (Keller), Zahava. "The Printed Edition of Midrash Devarim Rabba: Its Character and Place in the Tanhuma-Yelamdenu Literature." PhD, The Hebrew University of Jerusalem, 1999.

Neusner, Jacob. *A History of the Jews in Babylonia*. Brill, 1966.

———. *A Life of Yohanan Ben Zakkai, ca.1-80 C.E.* 2nd ed., completely revised. Studia Post-Biblica 6. Leiden: Brill, 1970.

———. *Development of a Legend; Studies on the Traditions Concerning Yohanan Ben Zakkai*. Studia Post-Biblica 16. Leiden: Brill, 1970.

———. *First Century Judaism in Crisis: Yohanan Ben Zakkai and the Renaissance of Torah*. Eugene OR: Wipf and Stock Publishers, 2006.

———. *Praxis and Parable: The Divergent Discourses of Rabbinic Judaism: How Halakhic and Aggadic Documents Treat the Bestiary Common to Them Both*. Studies in Judaism. Lanham, MD: University Press of America, 2006.

Newmyer, Stephen Thomas. *Animals in Greek and Roman Thought: A Sourcebook*. Routledge Sourcebooks for the Ancient World. London and New York: Routledge, 2011.

———. *Animals, Rights, and Reason in Plutarch and Modern Ethics*. New York: Routledge, 2006.

———. *Animals, Rights and Reason in Plutarch and Modern Ethics*. Routledge, 2013.

———. "Antoninus and Rabbi on the Soul: Stoic Elements of a Puzzling Encounter." In *Koroth, Vol 9, Special Issue, 1988: Proc of Third Int'l Symposium on Medicine in Bible and Talmud, Jerusalem, Dec 1987*, 108–23. Jerusalem: Israel Inst of History and Medicine, 1988.

———. "Being the One and Becoming the Other: Animals in Ancient Philosophical Schools." In *The Oxford Handbook of Animals in Classical Thought and Life*, edited by George Lindsay Campbell, 507–34. Oxford: Oxford University Press, 2014.

———. "Plutarch on the Moral Grounds for Vegetarianism." *The Classical Outlook* 72 (1995): 41–43.

———. "Speaking of Beasts: The Stoics and Plutarch on Animal Reason and the Modern Case against Animals." *Quaderni Urbinati Di Cultura Classica*, New Series, 63, no. 3 (1999): 99–110.

Nichols, Mary P. *Socrates on Friendship and Community: Reflections on Plato's Symposium, Phaedrus, and Lysis*. Cambridge and New York: Cambridge University Press, 2009.

Niditch, Susan. "The Cosmic Adam: Man as Mediator in Rabbinic Literature." *Journal of Jewish Studies* [34], no. 2 (1983): 137–46.

Niehoff, Maren R. *Jewish Exegesis and Homeric Scholarship in Alexandria*. Cambridge and New York: Cambridge University Press, 2011.

———. "Philo and Plutarch as Biographers: Parallel Responses to Roman Stoicism." *Greek, Roman, and Byzantine Studies* 52, no. 3 (2012): 361–392.

———. "The Phoenix in Rabbinic Literature." *Harvard Theological Review* 89, no. 3 (1996): 245–65.

Nigg, Joseph. *The Phoenix: An Unnatural Biography of a Mythical Beast*. University of Chicago Press, 2016.

Nissim, Rachel. "'Demut He-Ḥasid': 'Immut Bein R' Ḥanina Ben-Dosa Le-R' Pinḥas ben Ya'ir Le-Or 'Emdat ḤaZa"L Bi-Va'ayat Ha-Gemul." *'Ale śiaḥ / Literary Conversations* 12 (1982): 135–154.

Noll, Kurt Lesher. "The Deconstruction of Deuteronomism in the Former Prophets: Micaiah Ben Imlah as Example." In *Far from Minimal: Celebrating the Work and Influence of Philip R. Davies*, edited by Duncan Burns and J. W. Rogerson, 325–34. Library of Hebrew Bible / Old Testament Studies 484. New York: T & T Clark, 2012.

Nousek, Debra L. "Turning Points in Roman History: The Case of Caesar's Elephant Denarius." *Phoenix* 62, no. 3/4 (2008): 290–307.

Noy, Dov. "The Jewish Versions of the 'Animal Languages' Folktale (AT 670): A Typological-Structural Study." In *Studies in Aggadah and Folk-Literature*, 22:171–208. Scripta Hierosolymitana. Jerusalem: Magnes Press, 1971.

Nussbaum, Martha Craven. *Aristotle's De Motu Animalium: Text with Translation, Commentary, and Interpretive Essays*. Princeton: Princeton University Press, 1978.

———. "Beyond 'Compassion and Humanity.'" In *Animal Rights: Current Debates and New Directions*, edited by Cass R. Sunstein and Martha Craven Nussbaum, 299–320. Oxford: Oxford University Press, 2004.

———. *Upheavals of Thought: The Intelligence of Emotions*. Cambridge and New York: Cambridge University Press, 2001.

Obbink, Dirk, and Paul A. Vander Waerdt. "Diogenes of Babylon: The Stoic Sage in the City of Fools." *Greek, Roman and Byzantine Studies* 32, no. 4 (1991): 355–396.

Oberman, Sheldon. "Solomon and the Ant: And Other Jewish Folktales," 1st ed. Honesdale, PA: Boyds Mills Press, 2006.

O'Bryhim, Shawn. "A New Interpretation of Hesiod, 'Theogony' 35." *Hermes* 124, no. 2 (1996): 131–39.

———. "An Oracular Scene from the Pozo Moro Funerary Monument." *Near Eastern Archaeology* 64, no. 1/2 (2001): 67–70.

O'Hara, James J. *Death and the Optimistic Prophecy in Vergil's Aeneid*. Princeton: Princeton University Press, 1990.

O'Meara, Dominic J. "The Hierarchical Ordering of Reality in Plotinus." In *The Cambridge Companion to Plotinus*, edited by Lloyd P. Gerson, 66–81. Cambridge UK and New York: Cambridge University Press, 1996.

Oppenheimer, Aharon. *Rabbi Judah ha-Nasi*. Jerusalem: Zalman Shazar Center, 2007.

———. "Those of the School of Rabbi Yannai." In *Between Rome and Babylon: Studies in Jewish Leadership and Society*, edited by Nili Oppenheimer, 156–65. Texts and Studies in Ancient Judaism 108. Tübingen: Mohr Siebeck, 2005.

Oren, E. "Herodian Doves in Talmudic Literature." *Tarbiz* 34, no. 4 (1965): 356–62.

Oren, Eliezer David. "The 'Herodian Doves' in the Light of Recent Archaeological Discoveries." *Palestine Exploration Quarterly* 100, no. 1 (1968): 56–61.

Østerud, Svein. "The Individuality of Hesiod." *Hermes* 104, no. 1 (1976): 13–29.

Pagels, Elaine H. *Adam, Eve, and the Serpent*. 1st Vintage Books ed. New York: Vintage Books, 1989.

Patrick, Mary Mills. *Sextus Empiricus and Greek Scepticism*. Cambridge: Deighton Bell & Co., 1899.

Pearson, Birger A. "Jewish Haggadic Traditions in The Testimony of Truth from Nag Hammadi (CG Ix.3)." In *Ex Orbe Religionum: Studia Geo Widengren*, edited by J. Bergman, K. Drynjeff, and H. Ringgren, 458–68. Studies in the History of Religions; Supplements to Numen 21–22. Leiden: Brill, 1972.

———. "'She Became a Tree': A Note to GC II 4:89, 25-26." *Harvard Theological Review* 69, no. 3–4 (1976): 413–15.

Perkins, Judith. "Animal Voices." *Religion & Theology* 12, no. 3–4 (2005): 385–96.

Piccinini, Jessica. "Renaissance or Decline? The Shrine of Dodona in the Hellenistic Period." In *Hellenistic Sanctuaries: Between Greece and Rome*, edited by Milena Melfi and Olympia Bobou, 152–69. Oxford: Oxford University Press, 2016.

Poirier, John C. *The Tongues of Angels: The Concept of Angelic Languages in Classical Jewish and Christian Texts*. Tübingen: Mohr Siebeck, 2010.

Porter, James I. "Philo's Confusion of Tongues: Some Methodological Observations." *Quaderni Urbinati Di Cultura Classica*, New Series, 24, no. 3 (1986): 55–74.

Porter, Stanley E. "P.Oxy. 655 and James Robinson's Proposals for Q: Brief Points of Clarification." *The Journal of Theological Studies* 52, no. 1 (April 2001): 84–92.

Presley, Stephen O. *The Intertextual Reception of Genesis 1-3 in Irenaeus of Lyons*. The Bible in Ancient Christianity 8. Leiden and Boston: Brill, 2015.

Rabinowitz, Raphael Nathan. *Diḳduḳe Sofrim: Variae Lectiones in Mischnam in Talmud Babylonicum*. Munich, 1883.

Rad, Gerhard von. *Genesis: A Commentary*. Translated by John H. Marks. The Old Testament Library. Philadelphia: Westminster Press, 1972.

Rappoport, A. S., and Raphael Patai. *Myth and Legend of Ancient Israel*. Vol. 3. New York: Ktav, 1966.

Rasimus, Tuomas. "Ophite Gnosticism, Sethianism and the Nag Hammadi Library." *Vigiliae Christianae* 59, no. 3 (2005): 235–63.

———. "The Serpent in Gnostic and Related Texts." In *Colloque International "L'évangile Selon Thomas et Les Textes de Nag Hammadi": (Québec, 29-31 Mai 2003)*, 417–71. Québec: Presses de l'Université Laval and Peeters, 2007.

Ratner, Baer. *Ahawath Zion we-Jeruscholaim; Varianten und Erggänzungen des Textes des Jerusalemitschen Talmuds*. Vol. 6: Kila'im. Vilna: S. P. Garber, 1901.

Reinhardt, Tobias. "Epicurus and Lucretius on the Origins of Language." *The Classical Quarterly* 58, no. 1 (2008): 127–40.

Riedweg, Christoph. *Pythagoras: His Life, Teaching, and Influence*. Translated by Steven Rendall. Ithaca: Cornell University Press, 2005.

Rike, R. L. *Apex Omnium: Religion in the Res Gestae of Ammianus*. The Transformation of the Classical Heritage 15. Berkeley, Los Angeles, London: University of California Press, 1987.

Ripat, Pauline. "Roman Omens, Roman Audiences, and Roman History." *Greece & Rome* 53, no. 2 (2006): 155–74.

Robertson, David A. "Micaiah Ben Imiah: A Literary View." In *Biblical Mosaic: Changing Perspectives*, edited by Robert M. Polzin and Eugene Rothman, 139–46. Society of Biblical Literature Semeia Studies. Philadelphia: Fortress Press, 1982.

Robinson, James M. "A Written Greek Sayings Cluster Older than Q: A Vestige." *Harvard Theological Review* 92, no. 1 (1999): 61–77.

———. "The Pre-Q Text of the (ravens and) Lilies: Q 12:22-31 and P Oxy 655 (gos Thom 36)." In *Text und Geschichte: Facetten theologischen Arbeitens aus dem Freundes- und Schülerkreis: Dieter Lührmann zum 60 Geburtstag*, 143–80. Marburg: N G Elwert, 1999.

Robinson, James M., and Christoph Heil. "Noch einmal: der Schreibfehler in Q 12,27." *Zeitschrift für die neutestamentliche Wissenschaft und die Kunde der älteren Kirche* 92, no. 1–2 (2001): 113–22.

———. "P.Oxy. 655 und Q: zum Diskussionsbeitrag von Stanley E. Porter." In *For the children, perfect instruction: studies in honor of Hans-Martin Schenke on the occasion of the Berliner Arbeitskreis für koptisch-gnostische Schriften's thirtieth year*, 411–23. Leiden: Brill, 2002.

———. "The Lilies of the Field: Saying 36 of the Gospel of Thomas and Secondary Accretions in Q 12.22b–31." *New Testament Studies* 47, no. 1 (2001): 1–25.

———. "Zeugnisse eines schriftlichen, griechischen vorkanonischen Textes: Mt 6,18b Aleph*, P Oxy 655 I,1-17 (EvTh 36) und Q 12,27." *Zeitschrift für die neutestamentliche Wissenschaft und die Kunde der älteren Kirche* 89, no. 1–2 (1998): 30–44.

Rodgers, V. A. "Some Thoughts on ΔIKH." *The Classical Quarterly* 21, no. 2 (1971): 289–301.

Roisman, Hanna M. "Teiresias, the Seer of Oedipus the King: Sophocles' and Seneca's Versions." *Leeds International Classical Studies* 2, no. 5 (2003): 1–20.

Ron, Zvi. "The Book of Jubilees and the Midrash on the Early Chapters of Genesis." *Jewish Bible Quarterly* 41, no. 3 (2013): 143–55.

Rosati, Gianpiero. "Narrative Techniques and Narrative Structures in the Metamorphoses." In *Brill's Companion to Ovid*, edited by Barbara Weiden Boyd. Leiden: Brill Academic Publishers, 2002.

Rosen-Zvi, Ishay. "Measure for Measure as a Hermeneutical Tool in Early Rabbinic Literature: The Case of Tosefta Sotah." *Journal of Jewish Studies* 57, no. 2 (2006): 269–86.

———. "Two Rabbinic Inclinations?: Rethinking a Scholarly Dogma." *Journal for the Study of Judaism in the Persian, Hellenistic and Roman Period* 39, no. 4–5 (2008): 513–39.

Roth, Wolfgang M. W. "The Story of the Prophet Micaiah (1 Kings 22) in Historical-Critical Interpretation: 1876-1976." In *Biblical Mosaic: Changing Perspectives*, edited by Robert M. Polzin and Eugene Rothman, 105–37. Society of Biblical Literature Semeia Studies. Philadelphia: Fortress Press, 1982.

Royse, James R. "The Original Structure of Philo's Quaestiones." In *Studia Philonica 1976-1977*, 4:41–78. Chicago: Philo Institute, 1978.

———. "The Works of Philo." In *The Cambridge Companion to Philo*, edited by Adam Kamesar, 32–64. Cambridge: Cambridge University Press, 2009.

Rubin, Milka. "The Language of Creation or the Primordial Language: A Case of Cultural Polemics in Antiquity." *Journal of Jewish Studies* 49, no. 2 (1998): 306–33.

Rudolph, Kurt. *Gnosis: The Nature and History of Gnosticism*. Translated by Robert McLachlan Wilson. San Francisco: Harper & Row, 1983.

Ruiten, J. T. A. G. M. van. *Primaeval History Interpreted: The Rewriting of Genesis 1-11 in the Book of Jubilees*. Boston: Brill, 2000.

Runia, David T. "Exegesis and Philosophy: Studies on Philo of Alexandria." Collected Studies CS332. Aldershot: Variorum, 1990.

Ruzer, Serge. "The Seat of Sin in Early Jewish and Christian Sources." In *Transformations of the Inner Self in Ancient Religions*, edited by Jan Assmann and Guy G. Stroumsa, 367–92. Studies in the History of Religions (Supplements to Numen) 83. Leiden, Boston, Köln: Brill, 1999.

Sacks, Steven Daniel. *Midrash and Multiplicity: Pirke De-Rabbi Eliezer and the Renewal of Rabbinic Interpretive Culture*. Studia Judaica, Forschungen Zur Wissenschaft Des Judentums 48. Berlin and New York: Walter de Gruyter, 2009.

Safrai, Ze'ev. *Mishnat Eretz Israel: Tractate Avot (Neziqin 7): With Historical and Sociological Commentary*. Mishnat Eretz Israel Project, 2013.

Safrai, Ze'ev, and Aren M. Maeir. "אתא אגרתא ממערבא ('An Epistle Came from the West'): Historical and Archaeological Evidence for the Ties between the Jewish Communities in the Land of Israel and Babylonia during the Talmudic Period." *The Jewish Quarterly Review* 93, no. 3/4 (2003): 497–531.

Safren, Jonathan D. "Balaam and Abraham." *Vetus Testamentum* 38, no. 1 (1988): 105–13.

Saldarini, Anthony J. "End of the Rabbinic Chain of Tradition." *Journal of Biblical Literature* 93, no. 1 (1974): 97–106.

Samuelson, Norbert. "Integrating Science and Religion—A Jewish Perspective." In *Science, Religion and Society: An Encyclopedia of History, Culture, and*

Controversy, edited by Arri Eisen and Gary Laderman, 18–25. London and New York: Routledge, 2015.

Sandbach, F. H. "Plato and the Socratic Work of Xenophon." In *The Cambridge History of Classical Literature*, edited by P. E. Easterling and Bernard Knox, 1. Greek Literature:478–97. Cambridge: Cambridge University Press, 1982.

Sandmel, Samuel. *Philo of Alexandria: An Introduction.* New York: Oxford University Press, 1979.

Sarna, Nahum M. "Abraham Ibn Ezra as an Exegete." In *Rabbi Abraham Ibn Ezra: Studies in the Writings of a Twelfth-Century Polymath*, edited by Isadore Twersky and Jay Harris, 1–27. Cambridge MA and London: Harvard University Press, 1993.

Savran, George W. "Beastly Speech: Intertextuality, Balaam's Ass and the Garden of Eden." *Journal for the Study of the Old Testament* 64 (December 1994): 33–55.

Schechter, Solomon. *Some Aspects of Rabbinic Theology.* New York, NY: Macmillan, 1909.

Schenkeveld, D. M. "Studies in the History of Ancient Linguistics: III. The Stoic Texnh ΠΕΡΙ ΦΩΝΗΣ." *Mnemosyne* 43, no. 1/2 (1990): 86–108.

Schlanger, Jacques. *La Philosophie de Salomon Ibn Gabirol. Étude d'un Néoplatonisme.* Études Sur Le Judaîsme Médiéval, t. 3. Leiden: E. J. Brill, 1968.

Schmidt, Gudrun. *Rabe Und Krähe in Der Antike: Studien Zur Archäologischen Und Literarischen Überlieferung.* Wiesbaden: Reichert, 2002.

Schofield, Malcolm. "Cicero for and against Divination." *The Journal of Roman Studies* 76 (1986): 47–65.

Scholem, Gershom G. *Jewish Gnosticism, Merkabah Mysticism, and Talmudic Tradition.* New York: Jewish Theological Seminary of America, 1960.

———. *Major Trends in Jewish Mysticism.* New York: Schocken, 1961.

———. *Origins of the Kabbalah.* Translated by R. J. Zwi Werblowsky. 1st English ed. Philadelphia and Princeton: Jewish Publication Society and Princeton University Press, 1987.

Schreiner, Josef. *Wort, Lied und Gottesspruch: Festschrift für Joseph Ziegler.* Echter Verlag: Katholisches Bibelwerk, 1972.

Schröter, Jens. "Verschrieben?: klärende Bemerkungen zu einem vermeintlichen Schreibfehler in Q und tatsächlichen Irrtümern." *Zeitschrift für die neutestamentliche Wissenschaft und die Kunde der älteren Kirche* 92, no. 3–4 (2001): 283–89.

Schurer, Emil. "8. The Martyrdom of Isaiah." In *A History of the Jewish People in the Time of Jesus*, edited by Géza Vermès, Fergus Millar, and Martin Goodman, 3:1:335–41. Edinburgh: T. & T. Clark, 1986.

Schurer, Emil. *The History of the Jewish People in the Age of Jesus Christ (175 B.C.-A.D. 135).* Edited by Géza Vermès and Fergus Millar. Edinburgh: T. & T. Clark, 1973.

Schussman, Aviva. "Abraham's Visits to Ishmael—The Jewish Origin and Orientation." *Tarbiz* 49, no. 3–4 (1980): 325–45.

Schwartz, Daniel R. "Hordos Ba-Meḳorot Ha-Yehudim: Meḳorot, Sikkumim, Parshiyyot Nivḥarot ve-Ḥomer 'Ezer." In *Ha-Melekh Hordos u-Teḳufato*, edited by Mordechay Naor, 38–42. Sidrat 'Idan 5. Jerusalem: Yad Izhak Ben-Zvi, 1984.

Schwartz, Howard. *Gabriel's Palace: Jewish Mystical Tales*. OUP USA, 1994.

———. *Tree of Souls: The Mythology of Judaism: The Mythology of Judaism*. St. Louis MO: Oxford University Press USA, 2004.

Schwartz, Joshua. "Babylonian Commoners in Amoraic Palestine." *Journal of the American Oriental Society* 101, no. 3 (1981): 317–22.

———. "Cats in Ancient Jewish Society." *Journal of Jewish Studies* 52, no. 2 (2001): 211–34.

———. "Dogs in Jewish Society in the Second Temple Period and in the Time of the Mishnah and Talmud." *Journal of Jewish Studies* 55, no. 2 (2004): 246–77.

Schwartz, Seth. "Language, Power and Identity in Ancient Palestine." *Past & Present*, no. 148 (1995): 3–47.

Schwarzbaum, Haim. *Studies in Jewish and World Folklore*. Fabula. Supplement Serie. Reihe B: Untersuchungen 3. Berlin: de Gruyter, 1968.

———. "Talmudic-Midrashic Affinities of Some Aesopic Fables." In *Proceedings of the Fourth International Congress for Folk-Narrative Research*, edited by G. Megas, 466–83. Athens, 1965.

———. *The Mishle Shu'alim (Fox Fables) of Rabbi Berechiah Ha-Nakdan: A Study in Comparative Folklore and Fable Lore*. Kiron: Institute for Jewish and Arab Folklore Research, 1979.

———. "The Vision of Eternal Peace in the Animal Kingdom. (Aa-Th 62)." *Fabula* 10, no. 1 (1969): 107–131.

Scullard, Howard Hayes. *The Elephant in the Greek and Roman World*. Aspects of Greek and Roman Life. London: Thames and Hudson, 1974.

Secunda, Shai. *The Iranian Talmud: Reading the Bavli in Its Sasanian Context*. 1st ed. Divinations: Rereading Late Ancient Religion. Philadelphia: University of Pennsylvania Press, 2014.

Segal, Alan F. *Two Powers in Heaven: Early Rabbinic Reports About Christianity and Gnosticism*. Waco, Tex: Baylor University Press, 2012.

Segal, Eliezer. "A Funny Thing Happened on My Way to Sodom." *Journal for the Study of Judaism in the Persian, Hellenistic, and Roman Period* 46, no. 1 (2015): 103–29.

———. *A Time for Every Purpose*. Alberta Judaic Library. Quid Pro Books, 2015.

———. *Case Citation in the Babylonian Talmud: The Evidence of Tractate Neziqin*. Brown Judaic Studies 210. Atlanta: Scholars Press, 1990.

———. "Justice, Mercy and a Bird's Nest." *Journal of Jewish Studies* 42, no. 2 (1991): 176–95.

———. "Midrash and Literature: Some Medieval Views." *Prooftexts* 11, no. 1 (1991): 57–65.

————. *The Babylonian Esther Midrash: A Critical Commentary (Volume 3: Esther Chapter 5 to End)*. Brown Judaic Studies, no. 291-293. Atlanta: Scholars Press, 1994.

————. "'The Few Contained the Many': Rabbinic Perspectives on the Miraculous and the Impossible." *Journal of Jewish Studies* 54, no. 2 (2003): 273–82.

————. "'The Same from Beginning to End': On the Development of a Midrashic Homily." *Journal of Jewish Studies* 32, no. 2 (1981): 158–65.

Segal, Michael. *The Book of Jubilees: Rewritten Bible, Redaction, Ideology, and Theology*. Supplements to the Journal for the Study of Judaism 117. Atlanta: Society of Biblical Literature, 2007.

Seidel, Jonathan. "Charming Criminals: Classification of Magic in the Babylonian Talmud." In *Ancient Magic and Ritual Power*, edited by Paul Allan Mirecki and Marvin W. Meyer, 145–66. Religions in the Graeco-Roman World 129. Leiden: E J Brill, 1995.

Sharvit, Shimon. *Tractate Avoth Through the Ages: A Critical Edition, Prolegomena and Appendices*. Jerusalem: The Bialik Institute and the Ben-Yehuda Center for the History of Hebrew, The Hebrew University of Jerusalem, 2004.

Shavit, Yaacov. "'He Was Thoth in Everything": Why and When King Solomon Became Both Magister Omnium Physicorum and Master of Magic." In *Envisioning Judaism: Studies in Honor of Peter Schäfer on the Occasion of His Seventieth Birthday*, edited by Raanan Shaul Boustan, Klaus Hermann, Reimund Leicht, Annette Yoshiko Reed, and Giuseppe Veltri, 1:587–606. Tübingen: Mohr Siebeck, 2013.

Shelton, Jo-Ann. "Contracts with Animals: Lucretius, De Rerum Natura." *Between the Species* 11 (1995): 115–21.

Sherman, Phillip Michael. *Babel's Tower Translated: Genesis 11 and Ancient Jewish Interpretation*. Biblical Interpretation Series 117. Leiden: Brill, 2013.

Shinan, Avigdor. *The Embroidered Targum: The Aggadah in Targum Pseudo-Jonathan of the Pentateuch*. Publications of the Perry Foundation for Biblical Research in the Hebrew University of Jerusalem. Jerusalem: Magnes Press, the Hebrew University, 1992.

————. "The Late Midrashic, Paytanic, and Targumic Literature." In *The Cambridge History of Judaism*, edited by Steven T. Katz, 4. The Late Roman-Rabbinic Period:678–98. Cambridge: Cambridge University Press, 2006.

Shoshan, Ari. "The Illness of Rabbi Judah the Patriarch." *Korot: The Israel Journal of the History of Medicine and Science* 7 (1977): 521–24.

Sidersky, David. *Les Origines des Légendes Musulmanes dans le Coran et dans les Vies des Prophètes*. Paris: P. Geuthner, 1933.

Siegal, Michal Bar-Asher. *Early Christian Monastic Literature and the Babylonian Talmud*. Cambridge UK and New York: Cambridge University Press, 2013.

Singer, Aharon M. "The Rabbinic Fable." *Jerusalem Studies in Jewish Folklore* 4 (1983): 79–91.

Sirat, Colette. *A History of Jewish Philosophy in the Middle Ages.* Cambridge, UK, New York and Paris: Cambridge University Press and Editions de la Maison des Sciences de l'Homme, 1985.

Ska, Jean-Louis. "The Study of the Book of Genesis: The Beginning of Critical Reading." In *The Book of Genesis: Composition, Reception, and Interpretation,* edited by Craig A. Evans, Joel N. Lohr, and David L. Petersen, 3–26. Supplements to Vetus Testamentum 152. Brill, 2012.

Sklare, David Eric. *Samuel Ben Ḥofni Gaon and His Cultural World: Texts and Studies.* Etudes Sur Le Judaïsme Médiéval, t. 18. Leiden and New York: E.J. Brill, 1996.

Slifkin, Nosson. *Nature's Song: An Elucidation of Perek Shirah.* Torah Universe. Southfield, MI and Nanuet, NY: Targum distributed by Feldheim, 2001.

———. "Sacred Monsters: Mysterious and Mythical Creatures of Scripture, Talmud and Midrash." Brooklyn, N.Y: Zoo Torah, 2007.

Sly, Dorothy. *Philo's Perception of Women.* Brown Judaic Studies 209. Atlanta: Scholars Press, 1990.

Soloveitchik, Haym. "Piety, Pietism and German Pietism: Sefer Ḥasidim and the Influence of Ḥasidei Ashkenaz." *Jewish Quarterly Review* 92, no. 3–4 (2002): 455–93.

———. "Three Themes in the Sefer Ḥasidim." *AJS Review* 1 (1976): 311–57.

Sorabji, Richard. *Animal Minds and Human Morals: The Origins of the Western Debate.* Cornell Studies in Classical Philology; The Townsend Lectures, v. 54. Ithaca, NY: Cornell University Press, 1993.

Speiser, E. A. *Genesis: Introduction, Translation, and Notes.* 1st ed. The Anchor Bible. Doubleday, 1964.

Sperber, Daniel. "Divrei Rav Hai Ga'on 'al Teḳi'at Shofar veha-Pulmus ha-Ḳara'i." In *Bi-Hyoto Ḳarov: Asuppat Ma'amarim la-Yamim ha-Nora'im le-Zikhro shel Yeḥi'el Shai Finfṭer,* edited by Elchanan Ganzel, 246–54. Merkaz Shapira: Yeshivat Or Etzion, 2000.

———. *Magic and Folklore in Rabbinic Literature.* Bar-Ilan Studies in Near Eastern Languages and Culture. Ramat-Gan: Bar-Ilan University Press, 1994.

———. *Minhage Yisra'el: Meḳorot Ve-Toladot.* Vol. 1. 8 vols. Jerusalem: Mosad Harav Kook, 1989.

———. "On a Meaning of the Word 'Milah.'" *Revue Des Etudes Juives* 125 (1966): 385–89.

———. "On Sealing the Abysses." *Journal of Semitic Studies* 11, no. 2 (1966): 515–18.

———. "Varia Midrashica." *Revue Des Etudes Juives* 129 (1970): 85–92.

Stamatopoulou, Zoe. "The Quarrel with Perses and Hesiod's Biographical Tradition." *Greek, Roman, and Byzantine Studies* 56, no. 1 (2015): 1–17.

Starr, Joshua. *The Jews in the Byzantine Empire, 641-1204.* Judaica Series 8. New York: B. Franklin, 1970.

Stein, Dina. "Noah, his Family, and Other Animals: Midrash, Folklore and the Interpretation of a Biblical Story (or: Homage to Structuralism)." Edited by Avigdor

Shinan and Salomon. *Jerusalem Studies in Hebrew Literature* 25: TEXTURES: Culture, Literature, Folklore, for Galit Hasan-Rokem, Volume 1 (2013): 87–105.

Steiner, Gary. *Anthropocentrism and Its Discontents: The Moral Status of Animals in the History of Western Philosophy.* Pittsburgh: University of Pittsburgh Press, 2005.

Stemberger, Günter. *Introduction to the Talmud and Midrash.* 2nd ed. Edinburgh: T. & T. Clark, 1996.

Stern, David. "Introduction to the 2003 Edition." In *Legends of the Jews*, 2nd ed., 1:xv–xxiv. Philadelphia: Jewish Publication Society, 2003.

———. *Parables in Midrash: Narrative and Exegesis in Rabbinic Literature.* Cambridge, MA: Harvard University Press, 1991.

Stern, Josef. "Meaning and Language." In *The Cambridge History of Jewish Philosophy*, edited by Steven Nadler and T. M. Rudavsky, 230–66. Cambridge UK and New York NY: Cambridge University Press, 2009.

Stern, Sacha. "Jewish Identity in Early Rabbinic Writings." Arbeiten Zur Geschichte Des Antiken Judentums Und Des Urchristentums [Bd.] 23. Leiden: E.J. Brill, 1994.

———. "Rabbi and the Origins of the Patriarchate." *Journal of Jewish Studies* 54, no. 2 (2003): 193–215.

Stewart, Ian, and Jack Cohen. *Darwin's Watch: The Science of Discworld III.* First Anchor Books Edition. New York: Anchor Books, 2015.

Strack, Hermann Leberecht, and Paul Billerbeck. *Kommentar zum Neuen Testament aus Talmud und Midrasch.* Munich: Beck, 1922.

Stratton, Howard Fremont. *Dodona.* Philadelphia: Privately printed, 1937.

Stratton, Kimberly B. *Naming the Witch: Magic, Ideology, and Stereotype in the Ancient World.* New York: Columbia University Press, 2013.

Struck, Peter. "Animals and Divination." In *The Oxford Handbook of Animals in Classical Thought and Life*, edited by Gordon Lindsay Campbell, First Edition., 310–23. Oxford: Oxford University Press, 2014.

Sullivan, Shirley Darcus. *Psychological and Ethical Ideas: What Early Greeks Say.* Mnemosyne, Bibliotheca Classica Batava 144. Leiden and New York: E.J. Brill, 1995.

Sussman, Yaakov. "The Ashkenazi Yerushalmi MS: 'Sefer Yerushalmi.'" *Tarbiz* 65, no. 1 (1995): 37–63.

Ta-Shma, Israel M. "Midrash 'Leḳaḥ Ṭov'—Riḳ'o ve-'Ofyo." In *Studies in Medieval Rabbinic Literature*, 3. Italy & Byzantium:259–94. Jerusalem: Bialik Institute, 2005.

Taylor, Charles. *Human Agency and Language.* Philosophical Papers 1. Cambridge UK and New York NY: Cambridge University Press, 1985.

Taylor, Lily Ross. *Party Politics in the Age of Caesar.* Sather Classical Lectures 22. Berkeley: University of California Press, 1949.

Terian, Abraham. "A Critical Introduction to Philo's Dialogues." *Aufstieg Und Niedergang Des Römischen Welt* 2, no. 21.1 (1984): 272–94.

Thompson, Stith. *Motif-Index of Folk-Literature*. Revised and enlarged edition. Bloomington, IN: Indiana University Press, 1955.

Thorndike, Lynn. *A History of Magic and Experimental Science*. 14 vols. New York: Macmillan, 1929.

———. "The Attitude of Origen and Augustine toward Magic." *The Monist* 18, no. 1 (1908): 46–66.

Thorpe, W. H. "Talking Birds and the Mode of Action of the Vocal Apparatus of Birds." *Proceedings of the Zoological Society of London* 132, no. 3 (May 1, 1959): 441–55.

Trachtenberg, Joshua. *Jewish Magic and Superstition: A Study in Folk Religion*. Temple Books. New York: Atheneum, 1982.

Tress, Heather van. *Poetic Memory: Allusion in the Poetry of Callimachus and the Metamorphoses of Ovid*. Mnemosyne, Bibliotheca Classica Batava, Supplementum 258. Leiden: Brill, 2004.

Trigg, Joseph Wilson. *Origen: The Bible and Philosophy in the Third-Century Church*. Atlanta, Ga.: J. Knox Press, 1983.

Tsekourakis, Damianos. "Pythagoreanism or Platonism and Ancient Medicine: The Reasons for Vegetarianism in Plutarch's 'Moralia.'" In *Aufstieg Und Niedergang Der Römischen Welt / Rise and Decline of the Roman World*, edited by Wolfgang Haase and Hildegard Temporini, Vol. 36.1:366–93. Part II: Principate. Berlin and New York: Walter de Gruyter, 1987.

Tuominen, Miira. *The Ancient Commentators on Plato and Aristotle*. Ancient Philosophies 6. Berkeley: University of California Press, 2009.

Ullucci, Daniel. "Before Animal Sacrifice, a Myth of Innocence." *Religion & Theology* 15 (2008): 357–74.

Urbach, Efraim Elimelech. "Li-Sh'elat Leshono u-Meḳorotav Shel 'Seder Eliyah.'" *Leshonenu* 21 (1957).

———. "The Repentance of the People of Nineveh and the Jewish-Christian Polemic." *Tarbiz* 20, no. 1 (1950): 118–22.

———. *The Sages: Their Concepts and Beliefs*. Cambridge, MA: Harvard University Press, 1987.

———. "The Traditions Concerning Mystical Doctrine in the Period of the Tannaim." In *Studies in Mysticism and Religion, Presented to Gershom G. Scholem on his Seventieth Birthday by Pupils, Colleagues and Friends*, edited by Efraim Elimelech Urbach, R. J. Zwi Werblowsky, and Chaim Wirszubski, 1–29. Jerusalem: Magnes Press, 1967.

Valler, Shulamit. "Women in Rav Nahman's Court." *Nashim: A Journal of Jewish Women's Studies & Gender Issues* 4 (2001): 35–55.

Van der Valk, M. "On Apollodori Bibliotheca." *Revue Des Etudes Grecques* 71 (n.d.): 100–168.

VanderKam, James C. *The Book of Jubilees*. Guides to Apocrypha and Pseudepigrapha. Sheffield: Sheffield Academic Press, 2001.

Veltri, Giuseppe. *A Mirror of Rabbinic Hermeneutics: Studies in Religion, Magic and Language Theory in Ancient Judaism.* Studia Judaica 82. Berlin: De Gruyter, 2015.

―――. *Magie Und Halakha: Ansätze Zu Einem Empirischen Wissenschaftsbegriff Im Spätantiken Und Frühmittelalterlichen Judentum.* Texte Und Studien Zum Antiken Judentum 62. Tübingen: Mohr, 1997.

―――. "The Rabbis and Pliny the Elder: Jewish and Greco-Roman Attitudes toward Magic and Empirical Knowledge." *Poetics Today* 19, no. 1 (April 1, 1998): 63–89.

Vermès, Géza. "Ḥanina Ben Dosa (1)." *Journal of Jewish Studies* 23, no. 1 (1972): 28–50.

Wade-Gery, Henry Theodore. *Essays in Greek History.* Oxford: Basil Blackwell, 1958.

―――. "Hesiod." *Phoenix* 3, no. 3 (1949): 81–93.

Wasserman, Mira. *Jews, Gentiles, and Other Animals: The Talmud After the Humanities.* Divinations: Rereading Late Ancient Religion. Philadelphia: University of Pennsylvania Press, 2017.

Waterfield, Robin. "On 'Fussy Authorial Nudges' in Herodotus." *The Classical World* 102, no. 4 (2009): 485–94.

Weil, Gustav. *Biblische Legenden der Muselmänner / aus arabischen Quellen zusammengetragen und mit jüdischen Sagen.* Frankfurt am Main: Litararische Anstalt, 1845.

―――. *The Bible, the Koran, and the Talmud: Or, Biblical Legends of the Mussulmans, Compiled from Arabic Sources, and Compared with Jewish Traditions.* London: Longman, Brown, Green, and Longmans, 1846.

Weinberger, Naftali Jehiel. *Sefer Shaleaḥ Teshallaḥ: 'al Mitsvat Shilluaḥ ha-Ḳen.* 5th ed. Jerusalem, 2001.

West, M. L. *The Hesiodic Catalogue of Women: Its Nature, Structure, and Origins.* Oxford and: New York: Clarendon Press and Oxford University Press, 1985.

Westermann, Claus. *Genesis 1-11: A Continental Commentary.* Translated by John J. Scullion. 1st Fortress Press edition. Minneapolis: Fortress Press, 1994.

Wiertel, Derek Joseph. "Classical Theism and the Problem of Animal Suffering." *Theological Studies* 78, no. 3 (2017): 659–95.

Wilkinson, L. P. "Cicero and the Relationship of Oratory to Literature." In *The Cambridge History of Classical Literature*, edited by E. J. Kenney and W. V. Clausen, 2. Latin Literature:230–67. Cambridge: Cambridge University Press, 1982.

Williams, Howard. "The Ethics of Diet: A Catena of Authorities Deprecatory of the Practice of Flesh-Eating." Urbana: University of Illinois Press, 2003.

Williams, Michael A. *Rethinking "Gnosticism": An Argument for Dismantling a Dubious Category.* Princeton, NJ: Princeton University Press, 1996.

Williams, Peter J. "Lying Spirits Sent by God?: The Case of Micaiah's Prophecy." In *Trustworthiness of God: Perspectives on the Nature of Scripture*, edited by Paul Heim and Carl R. Trueman, 58–66. Grand Rapids: Eerdmans and Apollos, 2002.

Wilson, Robert McLachlan. "Philo and Gnosticism." *The Studia Philonica Annual* 5 (1993): 84–92.

Winston, David. "Aspects of Philo's Linguistic Theory." *The Studia Philonica Annual* 3 (1991): 109–25.

Wissowa, Georg. "Augures." In *Paulys Realencyclopädie der classischen Altertumswissenschaft*, edited by August Friedrich Pauly and Georg Wissowa, 2:2:2313–1344. Stuttgart: Metzler, 1896.

———. "Auspicium." In *Paulys Realencyclopädie der classischen Altertumswissenschaft*, edited by August Friedrich Pauly and Georg Wissowa, 2:2:2580–87. Stuttgart: Metzler, 1896.

Wolfson, Harry Austryn. *Philo: Foundations of Religious Philosophy in Judaism, Christianity, and Islam*. Cambridge MA: Harvard University Press, 1948.

———. *The Philosophy of the Kalam*. Structure and Growth of Philosophic Systems from Plato to Spinoza 4. Cambridge MA: Harvard University Press, 1976.

———. "The Veracity of Scripture in Philo, Halevi, Maimonides, and Spinoza." In *Alexander Marx; Jubilee Volume on the Occasion of His Seventieth Birthday*, edited by Saul Lieberman, English Section:603–30. New York: The Jewish Theological Seminary of America, 1950.

Yahalom, Joseph. *Poetry and Society in Jewish Galilee of Late Antiquity*. Sifriyat "Helal ben Hayim." Tel-Aviv: Hakibbutz Hameuchad and Yad Izhak Ben-Zvi, 1999.

———. *Priestly Palestinian Poetry*. Jerusalem: Magnes Press, 1996.

Yalon, Hanoch. *Introduction to the Vocalization of the Mishnah*. Jerusalem: Bialik Institute, 1964.

Yassif, Eli. "Jewish Folk Literature in Late Antiquity." In *The Cambridge History of Judaism*, edited by Steven Katz, 4. The Late Roman-Rabbinic Period:721–48. Cambridge: Cambridge University Press, 2006.

———. *The Hebrew Folktale: History, Genre, Meaning*. Folklore Studies in Translation. Bloomington, IN: Indiana University Press, 1999.

Zevin, Shelomoh Josef, ed. "Darkhei Ha-Emori." In *Talmudic Encyclopedia*, 7:706–12. Jerusalem, 1981.

Zhmud, Leonid. *Pythagoras and the Early Pythagoreans*. Translated by Kevin Windle and Rosh Ireland. Oxford: Oxford University Press, 2012.

Ziogas, Ioannis. *Ovid and Hesiod: The Metamorphosis of the Catalogue of Women*. Cambridge and New York: Cambridge University Press, 2013.

Zucker, David J. "The Prophet Micaiah in Kings and Chronicles." *Jewish Bible Quarterly* 41, no. 3 (2013): 156–62.

Zunz, Leopold. *Die gottesdienstlichen Vorträge der Juden, historisch en wickelt. Ein beitrag zur alterthumskunde und Biblischen Kritik, zur Literatur-und Religionsgeschichte*. Berlin: A. Asher, 1832.

———. *ha-Derashot be-Yisrael*. Edited by Chanoch Albeck. Jerusalem: Bialik Institute, 1954.

Index

www.ingramcontent.com/pod-product-compliance
Lightning Source LLC
Chambersburg PA
CBHW070840100426
42813CB00003B/687

9 7 8 1 9 9 9 0 4 3 8 0 3